Women and the Church of England

Women and the Church
of England

From the Eighteenth Century to the Present

Sean Gill

For Richard and my mother, and in memory of my father

First published in Great Britain 1994

Society for Promoting Christian Knowledge
Holy Trinity Church
Marylebone Road
London NW1 4DU

British Library Cataloguing-in-Publication Data

A catalogue record for this book is available from the British Library

ISBN   0-281-04768-5

Typesetting by David Mackinder, using *Nota Bene* software

Printed in Great Britain

Contents

Acknowledgements

All of my colleagues, past and present, in the Department of Theology and Religious Studies in the University of Bristol have provided a congenial atmosphere in which to think and write. My greatest debt is to Professor John Kent. This book lacks the incisiveness of mind and breadth of scholarship that he could have brought to the subject, but without the friendship and intellectual stimulation that I have received from him over many years it would never have been written at all. I am indebted too for help from the Rev. Angela Berners-Wilson, Father Peter Cobb, Roger Cozens, Philip Law, Sue Morgan, the Rev. Gary Wilton, and Pam Williams. Also, to the staff of the Bodleian Library, Rhodes House, and Pusey House, Oxford, the United Society for the Propagation of the Gospel, and the Fawcett Library. Many of the subjects I have touched upon would repay a great deal of further research, for the whole area of women and religion in the English Church in the modern period has not been as fully explored as it has been in America; even so, I have drawn heavily on the work of others, and I hope that I have documented this debt in the notes – particularly since many scholars may not agree with the interpretations that I have placed upon their work. The dedication expresses debts of an extent and nature that cannot adequately be put into words.

Introduction

Sir, a woman's preaching is like a dog's walking on his hinder legs. It is not done well; but you are surprised to find it done at all.

Dr Johnson[1]

Dr Johnson's voice is the voice of patriarchal Anglicanism at its most oracular, but potential readers might be more inclined to apply the latter part of his dictum to a book that sets out to analyse in less than three hundred pages the history of women's involvement with the Church of England over three centuries. Even though this study is limited to the established Church, and only discusses the often very different place of women in other denominations in so far as this illuminates the Anglican situation, any attempt to describe not only the part that women played within the life of the Church, but also the impact of Anglican theology on the evolution of more widespread attitudes to gender, runs the risk of becoming a general social history of the period.[2] In seeking to offer a manageable and coherent interpretation of such a broad subject, I have had three main aims in mind – though in stating them I am aware that each raises acute problems of methodology that it is easier to delineate than to solve.

Retrieving the past

First, I have tried to explore the massive contribution that women have made to the life of the Church in this period, for this is often ignored in traditional accounts that concentrate on the piety and policy

1

of its male clerical leadership.[3] Thus to write the history of Victorian Anglicanism in terms of the growth of Evangelicalism, Anglo-Catholicism, and the theological uncertainties brought about by scientific and social change – the 'men and movements' approach in which Newman, Shaftesbury, Maurice, and Gladstone are the ecclesiastical luminaries of the age – is to ignore the fact that while the leadership of the Church was overwhelmingly male, the rank and file in the pews was mainly female, and the Church's Sisyphean efforts in the fields of philanthropy and overseas missions were increasingly sustained by the commitment and abilities of women.[4]

However, the task of writing a 'her-story' of the Church of England rather than a 'his-tory' is fraught with problems. The aim of making women visible in the life of the Church – what one historian has called writing with a compensatory purpose[5] – is complicated by questions of class as well as gender, and this has to be taken into account if one is to avoid treating women in an essentialist and ahistorical manner. In the case of the Church of England, its active female membership has been predominantly middle and upper class throughout much of this period. This means that the impact of Anglican teaching upon the lives of women can appear very different depending upon whether one looks at, say, the ideology of domesticity and philanthropy from the viewpoint of the Victorian middle-class churchwomen whom it inspired to work for the moral and social reform of society, or from that of working-class women who were its intended beneficiaries.

Attempts to write women back into Anglican history also run up against intractable problems over the nature of the sources. In the case of the impact of philanthropy, for instance, far more evidence survives of middle-class ideals than of working-class responses. In making use of the mass of surviving letters, diaries, and biographies, one still has to ask how representative they really are. As has been pointed out, the very existence of written material about a woman tells us that she was exceptional, that she had the leisure and ability to write, and that she lived in a family conscious enough of its heritage to preserve family records.[6] To take one well-known example, Florence Nightingale's surviving writings provide a fascinating insight into the ambiguous and often contradictory role of religion in the life of an exceptional Victorian woman. They reveal not only her frustrations at the limitations imposed upon her by social conventions that drew much of their force from religious teaching, but also her own radical critique of those values inspired by a distinctive and unorthodox religious faith. However, deciding how typical her experience was of that of other women is quite another matter.[7]

There are also fundamental problems of purpose and perspective involved in writing a history of this kind, and the reader should be aware of these difficulties from the outset. As Selma Leydesdorff points out, a great deal of feminist historiography arose from a need for a past with which the feminist movement and women individually could identify.[8] The recovery of the history of women who were not merely passive recipients of patriarchal religious authority, but creative participants in the development of Christian life and spirituality, has also been an important element in the agenda of feminist theology.[9] The application of a truly critical feminist methodology to the Christian past, though, involves not only the reinstatement into the historical record of much previously marginalized experience, but also an unmasking and rejection of much that was androcentric and oppressive. Unless this balance is maintained, the need to draw inspiration from the past can easily lead to distortion and anachronism, and a failure to grasp the historical complexities of the choices facing women in a given period. It can also result in a teleological reading of history, in which women are judged according to their contribution to the development of the feminist movement.[10] Those who fail this test are then seen merely as victims of false consciousness, as having internalized the oppressive values of patriarchal society.

Such one-sided interpretations made in the light of contemporary concerns are unlikely, for example, to make much sense of the life of a woman such as Mary Astell, a devout High Anglican whose *A Serious Proposal to the Ladies* of 1694 and *Some Reflections upon Marriage* of 1700 have led to her being hailed as the first systematic feminist in England on account of their scathing criticism of the early eighteenth-century marriage market, and their demand for better education for women. Yet the radical Mary Astell who finds a place in the pedigree of modern English feminism was also the Tory advocate of the divine right of kings, of the maintenance of civil disabilities against dissenters, and of the subordination of women in marriage.[11]

The dangers of an oversimplified reading of history that fails to contextualize the lives of women are particularly strong in a work of this sort. In suggesting that the eighteenth century is an appropriate starting point because it saw significant changes in English society and theology that help us to understand the later history of women in the Church, there is a constant temptation to over-emphasize those aspects of the story that seem to contribute to the development of modernity. Moreover, a book written by a supporter of the ordination of women to the priesthood, which takes its accomplishment as the culmination of his story, also runs the risk of failing to do justice to the many women in the past who would neither have understood nor supported the arguments advanced in favour of such a momentous change in the Church's life.

Ideology and reality

My second aim has been to explore the relationship between Anglican teaching about the place of women in society and the lives that churchwomen actually led. Here, too, there are problems of evidence. I have made considerable use of sermons, theological works, and literature in seeking to portray Anglican attitudes, but it would be unwise to suppose that prescriptive writing in any straightforward sense corresponded to reality. Victorian exhortations from the pulpit urging women to find fulfilment in the home as dutiful wives and mothers may have inspired many to do so, but the strident tone of much of this preaching may also be an indication that fewer women were in reality either able, or willing, to conduct their lives in this way.

This gap between what was and what ought to have been was largely a result of the ambiguities and contradictions inherent in Anglican theologies of womanhood. Far from being natural or God-given, as their proponents claimed, Christian ideas about appropriate masculine and feminine roles in the Church were both shaped by, and helped to contribute to, shifting and often contested notions of gender identity in society at large.[12] For example, the claim that women were endowed with particular moral and spiritual qualities that qualified them to be the educators of the young and the creators and sustainers of Christian family values in the home, led paradoxically to their involvement in a wide range of Victorian public campaigns for social reform where, it was argued, these self-same virtues could also be utilized. One well-known example of a Christian social activist was Josephine Butler, the wife of an Anglican clergyman, who successfully campaigned against the Contagious Diseases Acts of the 1860s that attempted to control venereal disease in garrison towns by subjecting suspected prostitutes to compulsory medical examination. To Josephine Butler, this legislation was a brutal example of the double standard of sexual morality for men and women prevalent in her society, but the contradiction between the ideal of the sexually innocent and protected middle-class 'angel in the house' and Butler, the tough-minded exposer of the seamier side of Victorian sexual mores, was too stark to avoid unfavourable contemporary comment, and her campaign was dismissed as the wholly inappropriate involvement of a refined woman in subjects deemed to be obscene.[13]

Awareness of the ideological nature of Anglican theologies of womanhood makes it possible for us to understand the ways in which a resourceful woman like Josephine Butler was able to make use of their inbuilt ambiguities and contradictions for her own creative ends. It also, I hope, helps us to see a number of aspects of the traditional account of the ecclesiastical history of the period in a new light. To take two examples, both the eighteenth-century hostility to Methodism, and the Victorian debate over the nature of Christ, reveal a great deal about the anxieties over the maintenance of gender identity that helped to fuel them.

Theology and society in interaction

My third concern has been to explore the vexed question of the sources of Anglican attitudes towards women in this period. To what extent has theology functioned as an independent variable? How far has it merely reflected prevailing secular dogma? This of course is to raise a much wider question about the social determinants of religion to which social scientists have given differing answers. Surveying the work of Marx, Freud, Durkheim, Weber, James, Niebuhr, and Malinowski, the sociologists Glock and Hammond have concluded that to varying degrees in the corpus of classical sociological theories of religion, 'Variations in the form and content of religion came to be understood as a result of observable natural, rather than unseen and unseeable supernatural forces, but religion also came to be recognized as an independent variable helping to shape personality and helping to create, reinforce, or challenge forms of social organisation.'[14]

A nuanced perspective such as this can help us to avoid an over-simplistic form of determinism, and to understand how Christian theology was both moulded by, and helped to create, the norms of the society in which it was practised, but even then highly problematical questions remain about the nature of the interaction at any given time. To take one example, the eighteenth century saw the development of an ideal of womanhood in which earlier emphases on female sinfulness were largely replaced by a new stress on women as the repositories of moral and religious values and the guardians of Christian home life. Such a transformation was partly brought about by the burgeoning evangelical piety of the age, but, as historians have noted, it was also the result of changes in the economy that saw the decline of paid work for women, and the growth of a middle class that sought to establish a lifestyle and value system over and against that of the ruling aristocracy. In this case, developments in theology were not simply the result of economic growth, for the new religious ideal of female middle-class gentility was itself a potent force for change.[15]

The difficulty of understanding the social determinants of theology is also evident from the debate within the feminist movement about the origins of patriarchy. Defining patriarchy as any form of social organization in which men are predominant to the detriment of women, feminist historians and theologians have seen the Christian Church as an institution that has played a large part in creating and sustaining patriarchal modes of thought and practice.[16] This is a critical perspective that cannot be ignored in studying the history of the Church of England in the last three hundred years, but it is also one that is based on no clear consensus about the origins and nature of patriarchy itself. While Marxist feminists have tended to see gender inequality as a by-product of capitalism, psychoanalytically grounded theorists have stressed the importance of the unconscious in early childhood in the development of gender identity.

For the historian, the trouble with such over-arching theories is that they often suffer from a lack of historical concreteness. More recent postmodern and poststructuralist accounts of patriarchy have usefully highlighted the role of language and discourse (understood in Foucault's sense as a set of institutionally based social practices in opposition to others) in the creation of ideas of difference and subordination.[17] This approach draws attention to the way in which gender differences are produced linguistically through the generation of oppositions and hierarchies that value one term above another (male/female, spirit/matter, intellect/emotion), and raises important questions about the way in which theological language and Christian symbols have functioned in the creation of gender. By focusing on the shifting and unstable means by which identity and experience are constructed, sustained, and challenged, it also, as Joan Scott has pointed out, 'insists on greater historical variability and contextual specificity for the terms of gender itself than does the work of those relying on social scientific conceptualizations'.[18]

The call for greater historical variability and specificity is one that is congenial to historians, particularly those who shy away from theory, and it will become apparent that I have resorted to widely differing explanations and emphases in seeking to understand the development of Anglican attitudes towards women and their roles in the Church over such a lengthy period. Whether such theoretical eclecticism makes for clarity or confusion is for the individual reader to decide.

Notes

1. G. B. Hill (ed.), *Boswell's Life of Johnson* (6 vols, Oxford, Clarendon Press, 1934), vol. 1, p. 463. The remark was in response to Boswell saying that he had heard a woman preach at a Quaker meeting in 1763.

2. Throughout I have used capital letters to refer to the Church of England and to distinguish Anglican Evangelicalism from the wider evangelical movement. This is for convenience only, and implies no form of ecclesiological precedence.

3. This is true, for example, of the standard account of nineteenth-century English Christianity: O. Chadwick, *The Victorian Church* (2 vols, London, A. & C. Black, 1971 and 1972). Two works that attempt to rectify this imbalance are B. Heeney, *The Women's Movement in the Church of England 1850-1930* (Oxford, Clarendon Press, 1988); and G. Malmgreen (ed.), *Religion in the Lives of English Women, 1760-1930* (London, Croom Helm, 1986).

4. For a brief but suggestive discussion of the differences in religious outlook and practice between men and women in this period, see H. McLeod, *Religion and the People of Western Europe 1789-1970* (Oxford, OUP, 1981), pp. 28-35. In the absence of detailed data on Anglican church membership and attendance broken down by gender, the oft-repeated claim of higher levels of piety and practice among Anglican women is hard to quantify, but see Chapter 3 for contemporary views on this subject and an assessment of their significance.

5. J. W. Scott, 'The Problem of Invisibility', in S. J. Kleinberg (ed.), *Retrieving Women's History: Changing Perceptions of the Role of Women in Politics and Society* (Oxford, Berg, 1988), p. 12. For Scott, the drawback of an approach that sets out to show 'that women were actors in the past and provides information to prove that' is that it fails to analyse the formation of different ideas about masculinity and femininity, and hence to explain the origins of the invisibility that it seeks to redress. For a similar earlier critique, see G. Lerner, 'Placing Women in History: A 1975 Perspective', in B. A. Carroll (ed.), *Liberating Women's History. Theoretical and Critical Essays* (Urbana, University of Illinois Press, 1976), pp. 357–367. While accepting that work that attempts to 'fit women's past into the empty spaces of historical scholarship' is valuable, she argues that its chief limitation is that 'it deals with women in male-defined society and tries to fit them into the categories and value systems which consider man the measure of significance' (p. 360). This is a problem that is particularly acute in attempting to understand and articulate the forms of women's spirituality in a male-dominated Church.

6. A. D. Gordon, M. J. Buhle, and N. S. Dye, 'The Problem of Women's History', in Carroll (ed.), *Liberating Women's History*, p. 79.

7. These tensions are discussed in E. Showalter, 'Florence Nightingale's Feminist Complaint: Women, Religion, and Suggestions for Thought', in *Signs*, vol. 6 (1981), pp. 395–412. She shows that in freeing herself from the constraints imposed upon women by Anglican teaching, 'Nightingale strenuously evolved her own religious code of self-fulfilment, concluding that God wishes us not to sacrifice ourselves to duty but to develop our own strengths and abilities for the sake of humanity' (p. 408).

8. In A. Angerman *et al.* (eds), *Current Issues in Women's History* (London, Routledge, 1989), p. 14. Gordon, Buhle, and Dye take a much bleaker view of the uses of the past for contemporary feminism, observing that 'repeatedly the realization hits us that the past does not contain our vision', in Carroll (ed.), *Liberating Women's History*, p. 85.

9. See, for example, U. King, *Women and Spirituality: Voices of Protest and Promise* (London, Macmillan, 1989), pp. 94–109.

10. For a detailed discussion of the difficulties involved in applying the epithet feminist to the aspirations of women in the past, see K. Offen, 'Defining Feminism: A Comparative Historical Approach', in *Signs*, vol. 14 (1988–1989), pp. 119–157. As Offen points out, the term only began to be widely used in Europe and America in the late nineteenth century.

11. For a helpful discussion of Astell, and of the wider issues of historical interpretation raised by the complexity and ambiguity of her attitudes, see B. Hill, 'The First Feminist', in R. Samuel (ed.), *Patriotism: The Making and Unmaking of British National Identity* (London, Routledge, 1989), pp. 123–139. The nature of Astell's feminism is also addressed in her definitive modern biography: R. Perry, *The Celebrated Mary Astell, An Early English*

8

Feminist (Chicago, University of Chicago Press, 1986), pp. 13–19. Perry concludes that while 'It is perhaps problematic to call Mary Astell a feminist, to read into the past an ideology that could only be located in the present world', she was a precursor of modern feminism because of her 'recognition of women as a separate class, quite distinct from any other social or economic grouping, and a woman-centred identification with that class' (pp. 17–18).

12. It will be apparent that throughout this study I have made use of a feminist methodology that distinguishes between sex as constituting basic biological differences between men and women, and gender as a form of cultural construction that creates and sustains ideas about appropriate roles for women and men. For a wide-ranging discussion of the issues raised by such an approach, see J. W. Scott, 'Gender: A Useful Category of Historical Analysis', *American Historical Review*, vol. 91 (1986), pp. 1053–1075.

13. Her husband, the Rev. George Butler, experienced the same stigma: when in 1872 he tried to read a paper to a gathering of Anglican clergymen with the apparently uncontroversial title of 'The duty of the Church of England in moral questions', he was howled down. This incident is recorded in J. Butler, *Recollections of George Butler* (Bristol, J. W. Arrowsmith, 1892), p. 240.

14. C. Glock and P. Hammond (eds), *Beyond the Classics? Essays in the Scientific Study of Religion* (New York, Harper & Row, 1973), p. xiii. This account is of course meant to highlight some important general methodological assumptions in the work of sociologists of religion rather than to discuss the important ways in which they differed in assessing the extent to which religious beliefs and practices are socially determined. The passage is quoted in R. Gill, *Theology and Social Structure* (London, Mowbray, 1977), p. 27. Gill himself opts for an interactionist perspective in which 'theology would appear as a thoroughly determined discipline, originating from and being maintained by social factors . . . theology once socially constructed and maintained, in turn determines society at any one of four levels – theologians, preachers, listeners and outsiders – in proportion to their contact with the discipline' (p. 134).

15. For a discussion of the nature of this change and the widely differing interpretations of its origins put forward by historians, see M. LeGates, 'The Cult of Womanhood in Eighteenth-Century England', *Eighteenth-Century Studies*, vol. 10 (1976–1977), pp. 21–39. Gates emphasizes the widening economic gap between the upper and lower classes, and argues that 'the idea of the morally superior woman contributed an ideological prop to the family seen as a means of social consolidation in an increasingly class-conscious age' (p. 26).

16. This is a modern usage that should be distinguished from earlier political theories of patriarchalism that held that the origins and legitimacy of the state derive from the power of fathers over their families, and – in the case of theologically minded theorists – in the initial God-given power of Adam. As

we shall see, this way of thinking was still part of Anglican theology in the eighteenth century. As a political theory, patriarchalism is, of course, a prime example of what modern feminism means by patriarchy.

17. I have drawn heavily here on S. Walby, *Theorizing Patriarchy* (Oxford, Basil Blackwell, 1990).

18. J. Scott, 'Women's History', in P. Burke (ed.), *New Perspectives on Historical Writing* (Cambridge, Polity Press, 1991), pp. 42–66. For a critique of the poststructuralist approach as potentially damaging to the feminist cause, see J. Hoff's introductory essay in G. V. Fischer and C. Farnham (eds), *Journal of Women's History Guide to Periodical Literature* (Bloomington, Indiana UP, 1992), pp. 9–37. In Hoff's view, poststructuralism 'has become a potentially politically paralyzing and intellectually irrelevant exercise for endlessly analyzing myriad forms of cultural forms and discourses'. What is important, Hoff maintains, is not to lose sight of the fact that although gender differences are historically and culturally specific because they are socially rather than biologically determined, they are nevertheless not benign, neutral, or noncategorical in their effects on women's lives (p. 26).

CHAPTER ONE

The Theology of Subordination

Throughout the eighteenth century, women were seen as being more dependent on the comforts and consolations of religion than men were – a need that the Church of England endeavoured to satisfy by means of a theology that began by expounding a woman's place in the social and political order, and then proceeded to define her role as wife and mother. However, this religiously defined femininity was not in all respects an uncontested nor an unchanging ideal, and as the century wore on there was an increasing emphasis on the unique, albeit carefully circumscribed, superior moral and religious qualities of women.

Theology and social subordination

In his recent attempt at a sweeping reassessment of the Georgian era, Jonathan Clark has drawn attention to the importance of Anglican theology in maintaining the conservative intellectual and social hegemony of the traditional landed ruling classes, and to the continued vitality of patriarchalism as a viable theory of government.[1] The most influential patriarchal text of the late seventeenth century had been Sir Robert Filmer's *Patriarcha*, which was published in 1680 as a defence of the claims of absolute monarchy.[2] Filmer based his political philosophy on Scripture, arguing that society had originated in one man, Adam, and that consequently governmental authority derived from the supreme fatherly power of Adam and his successors. Making use of Scripture in this way had several implications. One was the inferiority and subjection of women to men, as

11

Eve had been created a secondary being. Another was the repudiation of theories of government, such as that advanced by John Locke. This posited an original state of nature in which mankind had been free, and based political sovereignty on notions of contract. Since contract implied consent, it could have implications for the status of women that were very different from those of patriarchal theory. For example, in his *Two Treatises of Government*, Locke cautiously entertained the possibility of divorce on the basis of contractual rights.

Not surprisingly, such potentially subversive speculations did not find favour within Anglican circles, with one clergyman later claiming that to make the marriage vow terminable by consent was to 'introduce a promiscuous concubinage'.[3] However, even though patriarchal theory was more congenial to the conservative Anglican caste of mind than contractualism, it presented eighteenth-century churchmen with a number of problems. The Glorious Revolution of 1688 had clearly repudiated Filmer's theory of absolutist monarchy, a fact recognized by the Non-Jurors who refused to swear allegiance to William and Mary, and while it might be true that many of the ordinary clergy harboured Jacobite sympathies in the early part of the eighteenth century, the higher ranks of the Church were rapidly filled by men who found little difficulty in accepting the Revolution and the Hanoverian monarchy, and for whom the divine right of kings and passive obedience had become antiquated and obsolete dogma. Even the reign of Queen Anne, who as a devout churchwoman and the eldest daughter of James II was more congenial to Tory High Churchmen, was not without difficulties for proponents of patriarchalism. In his sermon preached at the coronation in 1702, the Archbishop of York, John Sharp, chose as his text Isaiah 49.23, 'Kings shall be thy Nursing Fathers, and their Queens thy Nursing Mothers', in justification of female rule – somewhat uneasily presenting the latter as an addendum to princely power.[4]

It was left, however, to the redoubtable controversialist Benjamin Hoadly to discomfort patriarchalists by drawing attention to the implications of a female supreme governor of both Church and state, arguing that 'If Paternal Right were by God's appointment, the foundation of Civil Authority; then, either God's appointment is of little obligation, or it is impossible that any Prescription, or any Humane Constitution, can give to a Woman a Right to Civil Government.'[5] Patriarchalism would, he concluded, render the title of any queen nothing better than usurpation.[6] By 1760, a patriarchal political philosophy of a kind that Filmer would have understood had become

12

less common, but had not altogether disappeared from Anglican thought.[7] It was still to be found, for example, among followers of the High Church philosopher and scientist John Hutchinson, and was predictably strong at Oxford. For instance, in 1769 the President of Magdalen College, George Horne, who was later to become Bishop of Norwich, preached a sermon on the origins of civil government in which he repudiated contractualism, arguing that 'the state of nature was a state of subordination; since from the beginning some were born subject to others; and the power of the father, by whatever name it be called, must have been supreme at the first, when there was none superior to it'.[8]

However, even if patriarchalism as a political philosophy commanded only minority Anglican assent as the century wore on, it remained influential in more general theories about the nature of society.[9] In fact, as Filmer had been well aware, no direct lines of political authority could in fact be traced from the original divinely sanctioned government of Adam, for throughout the course of human history usurpation and revolution had often meant that might made right. What gave his argument plausibility was not a far-fetched and convoluted defence of the genealogy of royal power, but the claim that kingly rule was comparable to that of fathers over their families.[10] Patriarchalists were thus able to appeal to an everyday experience of the family as the basic unit of society and of the father as its head. For this reason, the analogy between the state and the family was a powerful and frequently repeated one. In his *Commentary on the Church Catechism*, William Wake, the Bishop of Lincoln and future Archbishop of Canterbury, was at pains to stress that the fifth commandment, to 'honour thy father and thy mother', extended in its application to the duty of subjects towards those in government, as well as to servants towards their masters, and wives towards their husbands.[11]

The connection between the right ordering of power within society and within the family was reinforced for churchmen by the upheavals of the Civil War and Interregnum. These cast a long shadow over Anglican thinking and suggested that the breakdown of political authority in the state was accompanied by a parallel attack on patriarchal power within the family – both fuelled by an appeal to dangerous notions of radical religious equality and the power of the spirit to transcend mere human conventions.[12] At the end of the century, in the midst of the moral and political panic occasioned by the French Revolution, the analogy between family and governmental authority still made sense to the staunchly conservative Laetitia Hawkins, who had no doubt that women were 'born to submit to authority', and went on to warn that 'she who has early imbibed an aversion towards the kingly character, will easily be persuaded to consider her husband as an unauthorized tyrant'. Republicans, it seemed, made bad wives.[13]

In eighteenth-century Anglican thought, the family, and the place of women within it, formed only part of an overall ordering of society that was based on the principle of subordination. One of the texts most frequently cited throughout the century by Anglican clergymen in enjoining obedience to government was 1 Peter 2, which also prescribed the subjection of servants to masters and of wives to husbands.[14] In the view of proponents of this vision of a Christian social order, class distinctions were held to be largely God-given and beneficial in their operation. The relationship between rich and poor was one of reciprocity and inter-dependence.[15] As the Bishop of Lincoln, George Pretyman, explained to his clergy at the height of the panic occasioned by the French Revolution, 'God himself makes one man to differ from another; that the distinctions of high and low, rich and poor, are the appointments of Divine Providence, and are made the sources of various duties, the bonds of mutual affection.'[16]

The position of women in relation to men was thus part of a complex hierarchy, and to tamper with it was both sinful and pregnant with danger to the general good. In a society that limited political power to the few, and in which prescriptive right and social influence counted for as much as natural ability, the subordination of women seemed neither unjust nor undesirable. Thus in his influential *The Complete Duty of Man*, published in 1763, and regarded as 'a sort of manifesto of the evangelical views',[17] the Rev. Henry Venn, in upholding the scripturally based duty of wives to obey the will of their husbands, went on to consider the objection that a woman might be more intelligent and better informed than her spouse. In such a case the same law held good, Venn argued, for 'if more than the liberty to advise were allowed on account of greater talents, it must follow that authority is founded on the superiority of intellectual endowments; a notion big with confusion and ruin to society'. If levelling views like these were countenanced, Venn feared, a servant might not submit to his betters in situations where 'though allowed to be superior in understanding, he is inferior in station'. The conclusion that both married women and servants should draw was that 'to gain the place of authority, or contend for it on account of gifts and parts, is to abuse them to the subverting that order which the sovereign Giver of them has himself established'.[18]

Christian marriage

'The utmost of a Woman's Character', wrote Richard Steele in *The Spectator* in 1712, 'is contained in domestick Life. . . . All she has to do in this World, is contained within the duties of a Daughter, a Sister, a Wife, and a Mother.'[19] The Rev. John Bennett agreed, claiming that 'If men are expected to distinguish themselves by science, valour, eloquence or the arts, a woman's greatest praise consists in the order and good government of her family.'[20] Women were normally expected to exercise their Christian vocation in marriage, and the Church provided detailed instruction on the duties expected from them and on the relationship between husbands and wives. In *The Relative Duties of Parents and Children, Husbands and Wives, Masters and Servants*, published in 1705, the Bishop of Ely, William Fleetwood, made it clear that the latter was clearly one of subordination, for 'both the Laws of God and Man have subjected the Wife to the Husband: She is not presum'd to have a Will contrary to her Husband's.'[21] For the Bishop, there were three reasons why authority within the home lay with men, not women. One was the argument from Scripture, where Fleetwood took 1 Timothy 2.11-15, 'Wives be in Subjection to your own Husband', as his proof text, and went on to draw out the implications of Paul's use of the Genesis creation myth to argue for a double theory of female subordination:

> From whence it appears, that he makes the Creation or Formation of Eve after Adam to be one Reason of her Subjection: And this Reason would have held good, if both had continued innocent, for it was a Reason before they transgressed; and therefore St. Paul urges the Subjection of all Women to their Husbands' upon that account, because the first of Men was before the first of Women. But the second Reason of the Women's Subjection is fetch'd from Eve's being first in the Transgression: She was deceiv'd first, and then deceiv'd her Husband; she was undone by disobeying God, and he undone by following her; she must therefore rule no more.[22]

It is an indication of how central the notions of hierarchy, power, and authority were to Fleetwood that he goes out of his way to emphasize that subjection was not primarily an undesirable consequence of the Fall, but was built into God's pre-lapsarian ordering of the cosmos – though he claimed that obedience was then no hardship since unfallen man 'would have then had no Folly, Vanity, Pride, Self-conceit or Ill-Nature from whence proceed all idle, harsh, ungrateful, and imperious Orders'.[23] The other reasons advanced by the Bishop for wifely submission were the general 'use and custom' of mankind (which he felt had often dealt too harshly with women) and the laws of Nature, which seemed to have endowed men with superior capacities for the conduct of what he regarded as the most important areas of human life, namely 'the carrying on Business at home, and Trade abroad . . . the defending one's Country from foreign Foes, and to the administering Justice to one another'. Although education and experience might improve women's abilities in these areas to some extent, he concluded that 'whether Women have naturally Strength and Abilities of Body and Mind to go through these Things if Men should for a while neglect them, need not be question'd: It is demonstrably certain that they have not.'[24]

Fleetwood's appeal to nature might strike modern readers as begging important questions about nature and nurture in the development of human personality, but it was a powerful one in an age when the prestige of Newtonian science led theologians to emphasize the harmonious correspondence between the laws of nature and revealed religion, and it was this consideration that he put forward first rather than the appeal to scriptural authority.[25] The most influential Anglican thinker on social questions in the late eighteenth century, the Archdeacon of Carlisle, William Paley, was less sure than Fleetwood had been that an appeal to nature settled the question of female inferiority, but his argument also involved a characteristic appeal to a mixture of prudential and scriptural considerations – as befitted a thinker who claimed to ground his political and social philosophy on 'the Will of God as Collected from Expediency':

Nature may have made and left the sexes of the human species nearly equal in their faculties, and perfectly so in their rights; but to guard against those competitions which equality, or a contested superiority is almost sure to produce, the Christian scriptures enjoin upon the wife that obedience which she here promises, and in terms so peremptory and absolute that it seems to extend to every thing not criminal, or not entirely inconsistent with the woman's happiness. 'Let the wife,' says St Paul, 'be subject to her own husband in everything.' 'The ornament of a meek and quiet spirit (says the same Apostle speaking of the duty of wives) is in the sight of God of great price.' No words ever expressed the true merit of the female character so well as these.[26]

For eighteenth-century Anglican theologians, there was no doubt that marriage and its responsibilities were divinely ordained, but theirs was not simply a scripturally based defence of male supremacy and the subordination of women. It was also an appeal to the divine will expressed in nature and in what appeared to be a commonsense appreciation of the right ordering of human life. It was just such an intermingling of secular and religious concerns on the basis of an appeal to reason, to be found not only in Latitudinarian churchmanship but also in Anglican Evangelicalism, that gave the Church's theology much of its appeal and coherence to sections of the middle and upper classes.[27]

Taken to its extreme but logical conclusion, such a view of marriage implied for a woman a total loss of selfhood of a kind that corresponded to the legal position in which married women had no separate existence and property rights apart from those of their husbands.[28] Thus the Rev. John Bennett commended Milton's *Paradise Lost* as beneficial reading for young ladies because of the picture that it placed before them of Eve, who reveres her husband, and before whom she 'feels herself annihilated and absorbed'.[29] Laetitia Hawkins was, if possible, even more insistent on the total self-immolation of women, claiming that 'Our Maker never designed us for anything but what he created us, a subordinate class of beings; a sort of noun adjective of the human species, tending greatly to the perfection of that to which it is joined; but incapable of sole-subsistence.'[30]

Even by the standards of her age, Laetitia Hawkins was something of a conservative – she argued, for example, in favour of slavery on the grounds that the protruding jaws of Africans resulted in their having smaller brains than those of Europeans. In practice, though, the Anglican view of marriage was not generally as extreme as it might appear, for once the basic authority of husbands had been established, Anglican theologians went on to emphasize that the relationship was to be one of mutual love and reciprocity. Just as in society at large, where those in authority had duties as well as rights, so husbands were to love and care for their wives as St Paul urged.[31] Nor could a wife's obedience to her husband be unlimited, for as Bishop Fleetwood pointed out, 'a Wife owes no Subjection to her

Husband, against the Laws of either God, or Man'. There were also less serious cases where a husband's wishes might be 'safely pass'd by; omitted rather than neglected or despis'd': for example, when his commands were 'unbecoming their Age, their Credit, Quality and Condition'. Nevertheless, Fleetwood was aware that the prior claims of religion and conscience were a potentially subversive force in their effects on patriarchal family relationships, and in cases where their opinions differed, it was not enough for women to oppose 'Reasons to Reasons', but they should be sure that the views of 'wise and impartial People' supported their stand.[32]

In her *Reflections upon Marriage* first published anonymously in 1700, Mary Astell agreed with Fleetwood that 'The Christian Institution of Marriage provides the best that may be for Domestic Quiet and Content, and for the Education of Children', but the social reality of her day, she believed, was that there were very few happy marriages.[33] A staunch High Churchwoman, Astell believed as completely as the Bishop of Ely in the wife's subordinate role, arguing that 'She then who Marrys ought to lay it down for an indisputable Maxim, that her Husband must govern absolutely and intirely, and that she has nothing else to do but to Please and Obey.'[34] In this situation, religion was the best support, for it would teach a woman 'not only what she may justly expect, but what she must be Content with. . . . Indeed nothing can assure Obedience, and render it what it ought to be, but the Conscience of Duty, the paying it for GOD's sake.'[35] The same recourse to Christian fortitude was urged by a later Anglican writer, Mrs Chapone, whose *Letters on the Improvement of the Mind*, a work of spiritual guidance for young ladies, was published in 1773. Where a woman found herself trapped in an unhappy marriage no public appeal was possible, and Mrs Chapone admitted that she was left in a situation where 'The comforts and helps of religion, with a firm resolution not to be driven out of the path of duty, can alone support you under such sorrow.'[36] In a society where divorce was rare and only possible for those rich enough to secure a private Act of Parliament, and where Christian teaching refused to countenance it, there was little more to be said.

As Mary Astell was aware, one of the reasons why marriage was so often a severe test of Christian sanctity for women was the familial pressure exerted upon them to marry for economic and social reasons, a consideration that sat uneasily beside the Christian emphasis upon mutual love and understanding. The tension between the two was well exemplified by Bishop Fleetwood, who stressed that parents were 'not to let the Consideration of Fortune and Estate so preponderate and over-weigh all other Considerations of Form and Favour, Birth and Education, Virtue and Good Qualities, as to neglect them all'.[37] In assessing the extent of parental authority, Fleetwood admitted that it was nowhere expressly laid down in Scripture that children could not marry against the wishes of their families, but it was, he felt, implicit in the commandment that children should honour their father and mother. What this might mean in practice is evident from the case of Mary Granville, who in 1718 was pressured by her parents and her uncle Lord Landsdowne into marrying against her will:

I had nobody to advise with; every one of the family had persuaded themselves that this would be an advantageous match for me – no one considered the sentiments of my heart; to be settled in the world, and ease my friends of an expense and care, they urged that it was my duty to submit, and that I ought to sacrifice everything to that one point.[38]

The result was a marriage 'to a man I looked upon as my tyrant – my jailor; one that I was determined to obey and oblige, but found it impossible to love'.[39]

The extent of filial obedience continued to be a topic for debate throughout the century, and historians such as Lawrence Stone and Ralph Trumbach have suggested that traditional notions of deference to the demands of kinship gave way to a greater emphasis on freedom of choice and the companionate nature of marriage, though the difficulty with arguments of this kind is that evidence about the emotional quality of relationships within marriage at different periods is limited and difficult to interpret.[40] In 1747–1748, Samuel Richardson raised the issue in his much discussed novel *Clarissa*, whose heroine flees from an arranged marriage based on 'family aggrandizement, and this great motive *paternal authority*', only to be held against her will and raped by the predatory Lovelace. Refusing to be in thrall to Lovelace's power, Clarissa dies a true Christian martyr's death by self-starvation, calling on the name of Jesus with her dying breath. The novel provoked the then unknown Hester Mulso, later Mrs Chapone, to enter into a hard-hitting correspondence with Richardson on the nature of Christian marriage and the limits of filial obedience.[41] The gospel, she pointed out, enjoins 'a marriage of souls as well as persons', whereas 'marriages which are made up by the parents are *generally* (amongst people of quality or great fortune), mere Smithfield bargains, so much ready money for so much land,

and my daughter flung into the bargain'.[42] Yet the reality for most women was that lack of financial independence made it difficult to defy parental wishes. By the end of the century the Rev. Thomas Gisborne was no longer arguing for parental control of a woman's choice of a husband, but he was well aware of the economic constraints placed upon her. After imposing a lengthy period of prudent restraint upon his daughter's wishes, it might still, in his view, be a father's duty to withhold some or all of her dowry if she married someone of whom he disapproved, on the grounds that it might be in her own best interests.[43]

Although the road to married happiness for women in eighteenth-century society was strewn with many moral mantraps, there remained the possibility of celibacy as a Christian ideal. Since the Reformation, married life had been held up as the Christian vocation for Protestant women, and the spiritual and social autonomy that medieval monasticism had offered to some had ceased to be possible within the Church of England.[44] The idea of female religious orders did not, however, disappear completely from discussion, despite its overtones of popery.[45] In 1698, the Rev. George Wheler had advocated the creation of nunneries whose members would be valuable to the Church because of 'their exemplary Virtue and Piety'. Wheler was also at pains to stress that family obligations came before any vocation that a woman might have – a point that was to recur whenever the idea of female Anglican orders was mooted, since it raised fears of a religiously inspired female autonomy that was potentially subversive of parental authority. At the same time, he provided a sinister comment on the plight of those women who did not marry and were often left destitute on the deaths of their parents: 'Whereupon, it too often comes to pass, that they are forced to wander about from Lodging to Lodging, to betake themselves to servile Employments; or, which is worse, are tempted to prostitute their Virtue to gain their Bread.'[46]

Wheler acknowledged his debt to Mary Astell's *A Serious Proposal to the Ladies for the Advancement of their True and Greatest Interests*, which had appeared in 1694 and was in its fourth edition by 1701. Astell proposed the creation of a 'Religious Retirement' for women, where they would say the daily Cathedral Offices of the Church, receive the Eucharist every Sunday and holy day, and observe the Fasts of the Church during Lent and on Fridays.[47] She did not, however, see any contradiction between withdrawal from the world and its service, since the women living in this way would engage in works of charity and undertake a course of education that would 'fit us to propagate Religion when we return into the World'.[48] Astell's was a vision of monastic life for the well-to-do, since the proposed annual membership fee was £500 to £600, and she saw no danger of envy or uncharitableness in a community 'amongst persons whose Dispositions as well as their Births are to be Generous'.[49] She was also careful to stress the limited aims of her programme: 'We pretend not', she wrote, 'that Women shou'd teach in the Church, or usurp Authority where it is not allow'd them',[50] and yet here, as elsewhere, her arguments were a carefully judged mixture of conservatism and potentially subversive radicalism. Like Wheler, she saw her nunneries as a refuge where 'Heiresses and Persons of Fortune may be kept secure from the rude attempts of designing men', a haven where a woman 'will neither be bought nor sold, nor be forc'd to marry for her own quiet, when she has no inclination to it, but what the being tir'd out with a restless importunity occasions'.[51] Most significantly, Mary Astell held up an ideal of a religiously inspired celibacy as in itself offering fulfilment for women; this was sharply at variance with the compulsory heterosexual norm of her society.[52] Not only would nunneries provide a useful way of life for an unmarried woman 'quite terrified with the dreadful Name of Old Maid, which yet none but Fools will reproach her with', but they also offered an opportunity for the development of a community based exclusively on female friendship:

> Happy retreat! which will be the introducing of you into such a *Paradise* as your Mother Eve forfeited, where you shall feast on Pleasures that do not like those of the World, disappoint your expectations, pall your Appetites, and by the disgust they give you put on the search after new Delights, which when obtain'd are as empty as the former; but such as will make you truly happy now, and prepare you to be perfectly so hereafter.

While such a vision for Astell was 'a Type and Antepast of Heav'n', not all her contemporaries (not surprisingly) saw it in this way.[53] It was said that the Bishop of Salisbury, Gilbert Burnet, dissuaded a lady from donating £10,000 to implement the scheme on the grounds that it was too Catholic for the Church of England, while an article in *The Tatler* in June 1709 seized upon the more disturbing implications of the proposal. Ridiculing Mary Astell as '*Madonella*, a Lady who had writ a fine book concerning the Recluse Life', the male protagonist 'sincerely wish'd Men might rise out of the Earth like

Plants; and that our Minds were not of Necessity to be sullied with carnivorous Appetites for the Generation, as well as Support of our Species', but this was not in fact the case, and happily more normal human appetites soon reasserted themselves and most of the ladies were mothers within the year.[54]

As an ideal, the religious life for women within the Church of England did not altogether disappear from eighteenth-century purview. In 1737, Sir William Cunningham wrote from Edinburgh to the Archdeacon of Northumberland, Dr Thomas Sharp, proposing a scheme for the creation of 'a Nunnery of Protestant religious and virtuous persons, well born and of the female sex', who were to take no vows and to be under the superintendence of a prioress and the diocesan bishop; however, despite these safeguards, Sharp demurred and nothing came of the proposal.[55] In 1761, Sarah Scott, the sister of the well-known bluestocking Elizabeth Montagu, published her novel *Millennium Hall*, in which a community of spinsters and widows live together – leading a life of religious devotion and running a school, an almshouse for the poor, and a home for the chronically sick. Nor was Sarah Scott's work merely a pious longing: it closely resembled her own way of life with Lady Bab Montagu at Easton near Bath, where they ran a school for twelve poor girls.[56]

A similar community was that presided over by the Rev. William Law, whose *Serious Call to a Devout and Holy Life* was published in 1729 and rapidly became one of the spiritual classics of English Christianity. Law was a fellow of Emmanuel College Cambridge, but as a Non-Juror he was forced to resign his fellowship in 1716. From 1740 he lived at his birthplace Kings Cliffe, in the company of a wealthy widow, Mrs Hutcheson, and the historian Edward Gibbon's niece, Hester. Law acted as chaplain and spiritual director to the women who lived a life of piety and good works by founding charity schools for the poor and a home for aged widows and spinsters. Law was well read in the works of the Early Fathers, and shared their view that while marriage was necessary in a fallen world for the continuation of the human species, it was essentially a lower form of Christian life than celibacy.[57] This unfavourable view of marriage was, he believed, a correct application of the teaching of St Paul, who 'had done everything to hinder a Minister of Jesus Christ from entering into Marriage, except calling it a sinful State'.[58]

A rather different challenge to the prevailing Christian orthodoxy on marriage, and in some ways a bizarre one, was the Rev. Martin Madan's pamphlet published in 1780, in which he suggested that polygamy was allowed by Scripture; and if introduced into English law might solve the problem of prostitution that Madan had seen at first hand as chaplain to the Lock Asylum, an institution created to reclaim fallen women. According to Madan's highly individual exegesis of Scripture, although Christ had condemned divorce, he says nothing specifically about the practice of polygamy, a significant omission since 'there cannot be the least doubt that numbers of our Lord's multitude of hearer's were polygamists, all in principle – many in practice'.[59] The real point of Madan's argument was the suggestion that the law should regard any man and woman who had sexual intercourse as married, and hence, since polygamy was to be legal, place the burden of responsibility for the maintenance of women and children on men. Madan's proposal was much less modern and far more grounded in the class-ridden assumptions of his age than this might at first sight suggest. If adopted, it would, he believed, not merely mitigate the effects of the double standard of sexual morality on which prostitution was based, but totally destroy it, since it was 'hardly to be imagined that men of family and fortune would pay their addresses, or rather lay their snares, where the accomplishment of their desires must be attended with an union, unsuitable in all respects to their rank of life'.[60]

Orthodox response to Madan's far-reaching proposals was predictably far from favourable, and he was forced to resign his chaplaincy.[61] The rector of Nantwich in Cheshire, the Rev. John Smith, published two sermons in reply, which he had felt obliged to preach since Madan's work had been much discussed in his parish. While he approved of Madan's rejection of divorce, polygamy was contrary to the laws of both God and man, and met none of the three purposes for which God had instituted marriage – namely, the 'peopling of the world', as 'a remedy for sin', and for 'the mutual society' of the spouses. In conclusion he dealt briskly with the problems of married life and the suggestion that the institution was in a state of crisis in his day, observing that 'the reason why we have so many unhappy marriages in the world, is briefly this: the parties concerned do not invite the Lord Jesus Christ to the wedding'.[62]

Notwithstanding the Rev. Madan's grandiose claim that his treatise on marriage was 'one of the most important and interesting publications that have appeared since the Days of the Reformation', and the vision of a religiously inspired life of celibate freedom dreamed of by Mary Astell, it was the rector of Nantwich who represented the predominant Anglican view of marriage in the Georgian era. Churchmen believed that higher standards of Christian life were the answer to marital breakdown, and despite the fact that divorce and the right to remarry required an expensive private Act of Parliament which was obtained on only 132 occasions between 1670 and 1800, they attempted to tighten rather than relax existing legislation. Thus in 1779 the Bishop of Llandaff, Shute Barrington, introduced a Bill into the House of Lords with what Hansard described as 'a feeling and eloquent exordium', which attempted to prohibit those granted a divorce in cases of adultery from marrying the co-respondent. Like Lord Athol's Bill of 1771, the Bishop's Bill was partly occasioned by suspicions of collusion between the parties involved in divorce proceedings, which were in effect opening the door to divorce by mutual consent. Calculated collusion of this kind was evidence in the Bishop's mind of 'the total extinction of the internal monitor of shame', and though he favoured the imposition of 'a brand of infamy on an adulteress', he recognized that given the degenerate state of public morals, legislative action was needed to prevent a woman from benefiting from her sin. While the Earl of Carlisle objected to a measure in which he felt 'all was to fall on the unfortunate woman', the Lord Chancellor drew attention to a far more weighty consideration, reminding his fellow peers that they could not be indifferent about adultery committed by a woman, nor could they see it as 'a mere consideration of morality', since what was really at stake was the evil of 'contaminating the blood of illustrious families'.[63] The Bill was lost in the Commons after a stirring speech by Charles Fox, who argued that since women were totally unrepresented in Parliament they needed 'tender treatment'.

The same fate befell Lord Auckland's Bill of 1800, which was opposed by the Archbishop of Canterbury and nineteen bishops out of an episcopal bench of twenty-six on the grounds that it would make divorce easier. Samuel Horsley, the Bishop of Rochester, argued strongly that Christ's teaching in Matthew 19.3-9 implied the doctrine of the indissolubility of marriage, though the following year when the House considered a private divorce Bill by George Taylor – whose wife had been seduced by a clergyman – Horsley and Shute Barrington differed as to whether Christ's teaching did or did not sanction divorce. This was a doubt that was to divide ecclesiastical opinion again in 1857 over the Matrimonial Causes Act, which instituted a system of civil divorce.[64]

Eighteenth-century Anglican attitudes to marriage and marital breakdown were based upon Christian principles that may in many cases have helped couples to live together in mutually satisfying ways, though we should be wary of supposing that the ideal of love within a union based upon female submission always corresponded to reality – for individual human temperament was less easy to mould than moralists tended to suppose. For example, the Rev. Henry Venn, whose *The Whole Duty of Man* has already been quoted as a staunchly patriarchal text enjoining the greatest degree of wifely submission, was (according to his friend, the Rev. James Stillingfleet) unable in his own domestic affairs to practise what he preached, being directed (in Stillingfleet's opinion) entirely by his wife: 'he had fallen into the conduct he so severely condemns in his chapter in *The Duty of Man* respecting conjugal duties, of giving up his authority like an officer in the army to his soldiers'.[65]

In the case of the Rev. Henry Jones, the curate and then rector of Broxbourne in Hertfordshire from 1781 until 1821, no such *modus vivendi* was achieved, and his diary is a sorry catalogue of recriminations and laments at what he regarded as his wife's unreasonable and volatile temper and her 'disputing about the mastery'.[66] Moreover, as the Bishop of Ely had been uneasily aware, religious principle might itself give grounds for wifely disobedience rather than submission. This was the case, for example, with John Wesley's parents, who differed over the legitimacy of the Revolution of 1688. Susanna was a Non-Juror, and when, as she told Lady Yarborough, she refused to say amen to her husband's prayer for King William, 'He immediately kneeled down and imprecated the divine Vengeance upon himself and all his posterity if ever he touched me more or came into a bed with me before I had begged God's pardon and his'; this she was unwilling to concede, claiming that 'since I'm willing to let him quietly enjoy his opinions he ought not to deprive me of my little liberty of conscience'.[67]

Anglican teaching on marriage was not without its strengths: it refused to countenance a double standard of sexual morality for men and women, and held that chastity was a Christian ideal for both sexes; moreover, its emphasis on mutual love and care as the basis of marital relationships somewhat mitigated the harsher aspects of its doctrine of female subordination. On the other hand, the Church fully accepted one consequence of the prevailing double standard of sexual morality, namely, the absolute distinction between virtuous women and those who had lost their chastity: the penitent Magdalen might be the object of care and reform, but she could never fully return to respectable society. The economic and social pressures that sustained prostitution were rarely considered. Most striking of all was the Church's inheritance of the paradox of a Puritan doctrine of a 'duty to desire', which showed scant understanding of, or sympathy for, the complex causes of marital breakdown.[68] Nor did it recognize that women were in a weak and vulnerable position within marriage, often pressurized into acceptance of uncongenial partners and deprived of property rights once married. As F. C. Mather has suggested, the bishops supported legislation that, had it been enacted, 'would have set back the evolution of a sensitive code of divorce law, and would have intensified the oppression of married women'.[69]

The ideal of Christian femininity

The eighteenth century saw a significant change in the way in which women were portrayed in religious discourse. The traditional emphasis on woman as Eve the temptress, a threat rather than an aid to piety and morality, gave way to a new representation of women as the repositories and sustainers of religious values in a way that was not true of men. Typical of the older attitude was a sermon preached by Bishop Ken of Bath and Wells in 1682. Ken was delivering a funeral panegyric on the life of Lady Margaret Mainard, whom he regarded as the embodiment of all the Christian virtues, as an 'incomparable lady now in heaven', yet he could still see her qualities as all the more remarkable 'because Women are made of a temper, more soft and frail, are more endangered by snares, and temptations, less able to control their passions, and more inclinable to extremes of good, or bad, than Men, and generally speaking, Goodness is a tenderer thing, more hazardous, and brittle in the former, than in the latter, and consequently a firm, and steady Virtue, is more to be valued in the weaker sex, than in the Stronger'.[70] Women were, it seemed, the 'weaker sex' not only physically, but also in terms of moral self-control.

The Rev. Philip Doddridge, whose *Family Expositor* was one of the most popular eighteenth-century biblical commentaries read by both Anglicans and Nonconformists, shared the older view in so far as he pointed to Eve's part in the myth of the Fall as 'an humbling consideration to all her daughters', and one that he hoped would 'make them less forward in attempting to be guides to others after such a miscarriage'; but he also argued that men acted unfairly by doing what he in fact had just done, namely 'ungenerously upbraiding

the daughters for the mother's fault, at the distance of so many generations'; moreover, it was also important to remember that Mary's
virtue in bearing Christ had in a sense cancelled out Eve's iniquity, so
that men should 'rather rejoice that as by woman came transgression,
so by her came redemption too'.[71] By the end of the eighteenth
century, the Evangelical clergyman Thomas Gisborne's tone was different:

> Women appear to be, on the whole, more disposed to religious
> considerations than men. They have minds more susceptible of
> lively impressions, which religion is pre-eminent in producing.
> They are less exposed than the other sex to the temptations of gross
> and open vice. They have quicker feelings of native delicacy, no
> inconsiderable supports to virtue. They are more easily excited to
> tenderness, benevolence, and sympathy. And they are subjected, in
> a peculiar degree, to vicissitudes of health adapted to awaken
> serious thought, and to set before them the prospect and the con-
> sequences of dissolution.[72]

Women were now no longer the sexually voracious sources of moral
danger that they had often been portrayed as being in the Christian
tradition. Alexander Pope's charge that 'every woman is at heart a
rake' had given way to an ideology in which women were elevated to
a moral pedestal far beyond the attainment of most men.[73]

The sphere where these newly acclaimed feminine qualities were to
be exercised was in the home. The Bishop of Norwich, George Horne
– who was not normally given to lyrical outpourings – was at his
most eloquent on this theme:

> Her fidelity is inviolable as the covenant of the most High, and her
> purity unsullied as the light of Heaven. Absent, as well as present,
> her husband relies on her, for the preservation of his possessions,
> and such a steward at home, freed from care and anxiety, he goes
> forth to his own employment, wherever it may be.[74]

Horne was providing a commentary on the portrait of a virtuous wife
in Proverbs, which should remind us that the eighteenth-century concentration on female domesticity, and the allied commendation of
sexless feminine virtue, were not new within the Christian tradition,
but rather represent a change of emphasis, albeit a very pronounced
one.[75] It was one, too, that was particularly associated with the growing Evangelical wing of the Church. Its poet, the devout and
unbalanced William Cowper, could refer to 'Domestic happiness,

thou only bliss of paradise that has survived the Fall'; while the leading luminary of the Clapham Sect, William Wilberforce, wrote to his wife in the midst of arduous parliamentary battles over the abolition of the slave trade that it was a comfort to know that those at home were safe 'on the top of the mountain, withdrawn from and above the storm . . . interceding for me who am scuffling in the vale below'.[76]

Changes in the ideal of female Christian womanhood were complex in origin, however, and far less black and white than a juxtaposition of quotations from the seventeenth and eighteenth centuries might suggest. Within patriarchal Christianity, women as 'the other' have often functioned as an ambiguous and polyvalent symbol capable of expressing both the fears and wishes of the male psyche at one and the same time – as Doddridge's text suggests. The new emphasis on female virtue did not in fact obliterate the older image of the sexually rampant woman; instead, it was projected on to the fallen woman whose existence in the form of organized prostitution was in one sense the guarantor of bourgeois family values and property rights.

Historians have suggested other ways in which the new attitude towards women needs to be understood in its social context. Leonore Davidoff and Catherine Hall have argued that the emphasis on women's spirituality and domesticity was part of a new middle-class attempt at self-definition over and against the values of both aristocratic and plebeian culture.[77] Rising living standards were creating a middle class that could afford to keep its women out of the workplace and that valued the moral and commercial ideals of sobriety and thrift over against what were perceived to be, in their different ways, the reckless improvidence and loose moral standards of both the rich and the poor. However, applying such an argument to the Georgian Church is not without difficulties. The language of class was largely alien to eighteenth-century society, which preferred to speak of ranks and orders, usage that points to the importance of geographical and horizontal divisions in society rather than the stark vertical oppositions of an industrialized society, and highlights the danger of anachronism in reading nineteenth-century changes too readily into the previous century.[78]

The notion of a nascent urban middle class defining itself by its religious values in contrast to those of the traditional landed aristocracy is also more easy to apply to Nonconformity than to an Anglican Church, in which the clergy themselves were members of the squirearchy and in which much ecclesiastical patronage was in the hands of the aristocracy and gentry.[79] As has been pointed out,

Anglican Evangelicalism in the late eighteenth century did not straightforwardly espouse urban values: the domestic idyll of both Hannah More and Cowper was created in a traditional context of rural paternalism. Nor were the first generation of Evangelical leaders themselves representatives of the new manufacturing classes, but rather they spanned the worlds of landed property and commerce. It is important, too, not to exaggerate Evangelical influence within the eighteenth-century Church: by 1800 there were only between three hundred and five hundred Evangelical clergy within the Church of England.[80] However, Evangelicalism was not without appeal to sections of the aristocracy and gentry, since its message of the need to transform society through the spiritual regeneration of the individual was combined with a strongly conservative sense of the God-given nature of the social hierarchy – a view that acquired added significance during the panic generated by the French Revolution. Moreover, many of the economic and cultural changes that affected the middle ranks of society in the latter part of the eighteenth century were also at work among the clergy, who experienced rising incomes as a result of enclosure, and were keen to separate themselves from the rough rural culture of their neighbours.[81] The growing attack on traditional rural pastimes in the latter half of the century is an indication of changes in the outlook of some Anglican clergy, changes that implied a rejection of an older style of communal rural life in favour of standards of gentility, among which the ideal of virtuous female domesticity was one of the most important.

The classic exposition of the new elevated standard of Christian femininity is to be found in William Wilberforce's *A Practical View of the Prevailing System of Professed Christians, in the Higher and Middle Classes in this Country, Contrasted with Real Christianity*, a highly influential manifesto of evangelicalism published in 1797. Here Wilberforce discusses women's greater capacity for piety and its social implications:

> This is more especially affecting in the female sex, because that sex seems, by the very constitution of its nature, to be more favourably disposed than ours to the feelings and offices of Religion; being thus fitted by the bounty of Providence, the better to execute the important task which devolves on it, of the education of our earliest youth. Doubtless, this more favourable disposition to Religion in the female sex, was graciously designed also to make women doubly valuable in the wedded state: and it seems to

afford to the married man the means of rendering an active share in the business of life more compatible, than it would otherwise be, with the liveliest devotional feelings; that when the husband should return to his family, worn and harassed by worldly cares of professional labours, the wife, habitually preserving a warmer and more unimpaired spirit of devotion than is perhaps consistent with being immersed in the bustle of life, might revive his languid piety that the religious impressions of both might derive new force and tenderness from the animating sympathies of conjugal affection. . . . It is surely no mean or ignoble office which we would allot to the female sex, when we would thus commit to them the charge of maintaining in lively exercise whatever emotions most dignify and adorn human nature; when we would make them as it were the medium of our intercourse with the heavenly world, the faithful repositories of the religious principle, for the benefit both of the present and of the rising generation.[82]

Wilberforce's encomium on pious femininity is worth quoting and considering at some length because it contains a number of ideas that were to be of great significance in the development of Christian attitudes towards women in the Victorian period. One theme that is not new is the way in which a woman's being and social functions are defined in relation to male needs. Equally striking is the sharp distinction between the public sphere of work and political power, and the private sphere of family life, with the former appearing as an exclusively male preserve. This partly reflects economic changes that had already lessened the significance of the domestic economy, and also points to the sexual division of labour that became the norm among the middle class, but not of course the working class, in the nineteenth century.

In setting the home apart as a haven of true religion in an unholy world, Wilberforce not only reveals something of the early evangelical temper that was suspicious of both secular society and other parts of the Church as lacking in earnest saving piety, but he also expresses the uneasiness felt by devout Christians increasingly forced to reconcile the competing demands of Christian altruism and scarcely restrained competitive capitalism. Not only was it an attractive ideological obfuscation to suppose that Christian family life could be unaffected by its social context, but there was also a sense in which the responsibility for counteracting the evils produced by an economic and political system over which they had little control was

30

nevertheless to be laid at the door of the domesticated middle-class woman.[83] The nature of this paradox was to be seized upon, albeit in a limited way, by Victorian women who argued that if they were indeed the creators and upholders of Christian values to the unique degree that Wilberforce and others claimed ('the medium of our intercourse with the heavenly world'), then they could and should use their power in philanthropy and social reform outside the home. Here was the beginnings of a potent but paradoxical model of Christian femininity which empowered and shackled women at one and the same time.

Notes

1. J. C. D. Clark, *English Society 1688-1832: Ideology, Social Structure and Political Practice during the Ancien Regime* (Cambridge, CUP, 1985). Clark's emphasis on the need to take religious ideas seriously, though welcome, was also part of the polemical Conservative attack on socialist political and social theory that characterized the 1980s, and which greatly exaggerated the latter's influence on English intellectual life while caricaturing its achievements. For a wide-ranging critique of Clark's work, see J. Innes, 'Jonathan Clark, Social History and England's "Ancien Regime"', *Past and Present*, vol. 115 (1987), pp. 165-200.

2. The work had been written, though not published, in the 1630s as a defence of Charles I's use of the royal prerogative, and was still relevant to the unresolved clash between royal and parliamentary power that led to the Revolution of 1688. See P. Laslett's introduction to *Patriarcha and Other Political Works of Sir Robert Filmer* (Oxford, Basil Blackwell, 1949).

3. P. Laslett (ed.), *John Locke. Two Treatises of Government* (Cambridge, CUP, 2nd edn, 1967), p. 339. The limits of Locke's views on sexual equality are discussed in L. Clark, 'Women and John Locke: or, Who Owns the Apples in the Garden of Eden?', in V. Chappell (ed.), *John Locke's Political Philosophy* (New York, Garland Publishing, 1992), pp. 1-26; and in M. Selinger, *The Liberal Politics of John Locke* (London, George Allen & Unwin, 1968), who concludes that he 'did not intend to dispute the natural preponderance of the male over the female' (p. 212).

4. J. Sharp, *A Sermon Preach'd at the Coronation of Queen Anne in the Abbey Church of Westminster April 23rd 1702* (London, Walter Kettliby, 1702).

5. Quoted in G. J. Schochet, *Patriarchalism in Political Thought. The Authoritarian Family and Political Speculation and Attitudes Especially in Seventeenth-Century England* (Oxford, OUP, 1975), p. 219, where Schochet discusses the debate over female rule and patriarchal theory.

6. The reign of Elizabeth I had created similar tensions over the desirability of

female government. For these, see S. P. Cerasano and M. Wynne-Davies (eds), *Gloriana's Face: Women Public and Private in the English Renaissance* (Hemel Hempstead, Harvester Wheatsheaf, 1992). They conclude that 'a female ruler was accepted by her contemporaries because of her exceptional qualities; they condoned the individual, not the concept of female majesty' (p. 2).

7. R. Hole, *Pulpits, Politics and Public Order in England 1760–1832* (Cambridge, CUP, 1989).

8. W. Jones (ed.), *The Works of the Right Reverend George Horne D.D., The Late Bishop of Norwich; To Which Are Prefixed Memoirs Of His Life, Studies, And Writings* (4 vols, London, Rivingtons, 2nd edn, 1818), vol. 2, pp. 439–440.

9. Hole, in *Pulpits, Politics and Public Order*, pp. 60–63, argues that Jonathan Clark fails to make a sufficient distinction between patriarchalism as a political philosophy and as a wider social theory.

10. For this aspect of Filmer's thought, see Laslett, *Patriarcha*, pp. 26–29; and W. H. Greenleaf, *Order, Empiricism and Politics. Two Traditions of English Political Thought 1500–1700* (Oxford, OUP, 1964), pp. 80–87.

11. W. Wake, *The Principles of the Christian Religion Explained in a Brief Commentary upon the Church Catechism* (London, Richard Sare, 3rd edn, 1708), p. 108.

12. As Jeremy Gregory has observed, eighteenth-century churchmen 'were for ever on the look-out for attributes of disorder which might foreshadow the outbreak of another civil war', in J. Black and J. Gregory (eds), *Culture, Politics and Society in Britain, 1660–1800* (Manchester, Manchester UP, 1991), p. 102. For the role of women as preachers and prophets in the seventeenth-century sects, see K. Thomas, 'Women and the Civil War Sects', in T. Aston (ed.), *Crisis in Europe 1560–1660* (London, Routledge & Kegan Paul, 1965), pp. 317–340; R. Greaves, 'Foundation Builders: The Role of Women in Early English Nonconformity', and D. Ludlow, 'Shaking Patriarchy's Foundations: Sectarian Women in England, 1641–1700', in R. Greaves (ed.), *Triumph over Silence: Women in Protestant History* (Westport, Connecticut, Greenwood Press, 1985), pp. 75–92, and 93–123; P. Mack, 'Women as Prophets During the English Civil War', *Feminist Studies*, vol. 8 (1982), pp. 19–45; A. Lawrence, 'A Priesthood of She-Believers: Women and Congregations in Mid-Seventeenth-Century England', in W. J. Sheils and D. Wood (eds), *Women in the Church*, Studies in Church History 27 (Oxford, Basil Blackwell, 1990), pp. 345–363. Mack, Lawrence, and Thomas discuss the limitations on women's participation in church life even in the radical sects, and the reassertion of patriarchalism after 1660. This does not, however, invalidate the view that Anglican perceptions of what had occurred reinforced strongly conservative modes of thought, including fears about the dangers of uncontrolled female religiosity.

13. L. Hawkins, *Letters on the Female Mind, Its Powers and Pursuits* (London, Hookham and Carpenter, 1793), pp. 105–106. For a brief discussion of the

eighteenth century as a transitional period between an age in which the links between the family and the state were fundamental to social thinking and practice, and the more privatized concept of the family that developed in the nineteenth century, see S. Amussen, *An Ordered Society: Gender and Class in Early Modern England* (Oxford, Basil Blackwell, 1988), pp. 186–189.

14. Hole, *Pulpits, Politics and Public Order*, pp. 12–13.

15. For eighteenth-century Anglican social thought, see R. A. Soloway, *Prelates and People: Ecclesiastical Social Thought in England 1783–1852* (London, Routledge & Kegan Paul, 1969); and E. R. Norman, *Church and Society in England 1770–1970* (Oxford, Clarendon Press, 1976), pp. 15–40.

16. Soloway, *Prelates and People*, p. 62.

17. J. Venn, *Annals of a Clerical Family* (London, Macmillan, 1904), p. 86. Henry Venn was vicar of Huddersfield and the father of John Venn, one of the leaders of the Evangelical Clapham Sect.

18. H. Venn, *The Complete Duty of Man: Or, a System of Doctrinal and Practical Christianity* (London, Longmans Green, 1841), p. 222.

19. D. F. Bond (ed.), *The Spectator* (5 vols, Oxford, OUP, 1965), vol. 3, p. 272. In their religious history of the period, Abbey and Overton describe Addison and his fellow contributors as 'true sons of the Church', and emphasize their role in defending Christian moral standards in society (C. J. Abbey and J. H. Overton, *The English Church in the Eighteenth Century* (2 vols, London, Longmans Green, 1878), vol. 1, p. 31).

20. J. Bennett, *Letters to a Young Lady on a Variety of Useful and Interesting Subjects* (2 vols, Warrington, W. Eyres, 1789), vol. 2, p. 213.

21. W. Fleetwood, *The Relative Duties of Parents and Children, Husbands and Wives, Masters and Servants; Considered in Sixteen Practical Discourses* (London, John Hooke, 2nd edn, 1716), p. 47.

22. Fleetwood, *The Relative Duties* . . ., p. 136.

23. Fleetwood, *The Relative Duties* . . ., p. 137. The question of how far Eve, as well as Adam, was made equally in the image of God before the Fall had long vexed theologians. For this, see Kari Elizabeth Borrensen (ed.), *Image of God and Gender Models in Judaeo-Christian Tradition* (Oslo, Solum Forlag, 1991). In her discussion of Luther, for example, Jane Douglass finds in his commentary on Genesis an 'ambivalence between Eve as fully equal to Adam in Paradise before sin and Eve as inherently inferior to Adam because she is female' (p. 234).

24. Fleetwood, *The Relative Duties* . . ., p. 134.

25. For the importance of nature in eighteenth-century theological thought, see B. Willey, *The Eighteenth-Century Background: Studies on the Idea of Nature in the Thought of the Period* (Harmondsworth, Penguin Books, 1962). Willey quotes Leslie Stephen's cautionary observation that 'Nature is a word contrived in order to introduce as many equivocations as possible into all the theories, political, legal, artistic, or literary, into

which it enters' (p. 10).

26. W. Paley, *The Principles of Moral and Political Philosophy* (2 vols, London, R. Foulder, 12th edn, 1799), vol. 2, pp. 341-342.

27. For the connections between evangelicalism and the rationalist assumptions of the period, see D. Bebbington, *Evangelicalism in Modern Britain. A History from the 1730s to the 1980s* (London, Unwin Hyman, 1989), pp. 57-60.

28. See B. Hill (ed.), *Eighteenth-Century Women: An Anthology* (London, George Allen & Unwin, 1984), pp. 108-122, for a discussion of women's legal position.

29. Bennett, *Letters to a Young Lady*, p. 190.

30. Hawkins, *Letters on the Female Mind*, p. 197.

31. Fleetwood, *The Relative Duties . . .*, p. 234.

32. Fleetwood, *The Relative Duties . . .*, p. 141.

33. B. Hill (ed.), *The First English Feminist. Reflections Upon Marriage and Other Writings by Mary Astell* (Aldershot, Gower/Maurice Temple Smith, 1986), pp. 127-128. The text is that of the third edition of 1706.

34. Hill (ed.), *The First English Feminist*, p. 116.

35. Hill (ed.), *The First English Feminist*, p. 128.

36. *The Works of Mrs Chapone* (4 vols, London, John Murray, 1807), vol. 4, p. 142. The quotation is from her *Letter to a New-Married Lady*.

37. Fleetwood, *The Relative Duties . . .*, pp. 43-44.

38. Lady Llanover (ed.), *The Autobiography and Correspondence of Mary Granville Mrs. Delany* (London, Richard Bentley, 1861), pp. 28-29. This and other similar cases are cited in K. M. Rogers, *Feminism in Eighteenth-Century England* (Brighton, Harvester Press, 1982), pp. 11-14.

39. Lady Llanover (ed.), *The Autobiography and Correspondence of Mary Granville Mrs. Delany*, p. 31. Her husband turned out to be a heavy drinker, and she shed few tears at his premature death in 1724, which left her with the relative independence of widowhood and later a much happier second marriage.

40. This case is argued by L. Stone, *The Family, Sex and Marriage in England 1500-1800* (London, Weidenfeld & Nicolson, 1977); and by R. Trumbach in his *The Rise of the Egalitarian Family: Aristocratic Kinship and Domestic Relations in Eighteenth-Century England* (New York, Academic Press, 1978). Trumbach claims that among the upper classes, the generation between 1720 and 1750 was the first in which 'romantic marriage became truly prestigious', and that by 1784 three marriages in four were romantic rather than arranged (p. 291). On the other hand, J. A. Sharpe, in his *Early Modern England: A Social History 1550-1760* (London, Edward Arnold, 1987), pp. 58-65, takes issue with Stone and concludes that 'the notion that

romantic love was an invention of the eighteenth century . . . seems totally wrong-headed' (p. 63).

41. *The Works of Mrs Chapone*, vol. 1, p. 31. For a discussion of Richardson's attitude towards women, see T. C. Eaves and B. D. Kimpel, *Samuel Richardson* (Oxford, Clarendon Press, 1971), pp. 556–558. He appears to have believed that children should have a negative voice in refusing a suitor whom they disliked, but he 'never made it clear whether Clarissa's running away from her parents was to be regarded as a flaw in her character or a result of highly peculiar circumstances' (p. 558).

42. *The Works of Mrs Chapone*, vol. 2, pp. 56–57, 122. For a discussion of this correspondence and its significance in the development of 'feminist consciousness', see S. Myers, *The Bluestocking Circle: Women, Friendship, and the Life of the Mind in Eighteenth-Century England* (Oxford, Clarendon Press, 1990), pp. 141–146.

43. Myers, *The Bluestocking Circle*, pp. 448–449.

44. For a wide-ranging analysis of the impact of the Reformation upon the lives of women and an assessment of the losses and gains that these changes entailed, see S. Marshall (ed.), *Women in Reformation and Counter-Reformation Europe* (Bloomington, Indiana UP, 1989).

45. See B. Hill, 'A Refuge from Men: The Idea of a Protestant Nunnery', *Past and Present*, vol. 117 (1987), pp. 107–130.

46. G. Wheler, *The Protestant Monastery: Or, Christian Oeconomicks Containing Directions for the Religious Conduct of a Family* (London, 1698), p. 17.

47. Hill (ed.), *The First English Feminist*, p. 156.

48. Hill (ed.), *The First English Feminist*, p. 164.

49. Hill (ed.), *The First English Feminist*, p. 157.

50. Hill (ed.), *The First English Feminist*, p. 154.

51. Hill (ed.), *The First English Feminist*, p. 165.

52. Ruth Perry, in *The Celebrated Mary Astell, An Early English Feminist* (Chicago, University of Chicago Press, 1986), pp. 112–113, considers how far Astell's ideas and her close relationships with women may be indicative of a lesbian sexual orientation, and concludes, as such discussions usually do, that there is no conclusive evidence to support this view. Janet Todd has pointed out, however, that lesbianism is a quite overt theme in some of the Restoration period's writing about separatist female communities, most notably in Delariver Manley's *The New Atlantis*. For this theme, see J. Todd, *The Sign of Angelica: Women, Writing and Fiction, 1660–1800* (London, Virago Press, 1989), p. 30.

53. Perry, *The Celebrated Mary Astell*, p. 151.

54. D. F. Bond (ed.), *The Tatler* (3 vols, Oxford, Clarendon Press, 1987), vol. 1, pp. 238–241.

55. J. Wickham Legg, *English Church Life from the Restoration to the Tractarian Movement* (London, Longmans Green, 1914), p. 289.

56. M. Reynolds, *The Learned Lady in England 1650-1760* (Boston, Houghton Mifflin, 1920), pp. 270-271. Elizabeth Montagu described the ladies' home as 'their convent, for by its regularity it resembles one'.

57. *The Works of the Reverend William Law* (9 vols, London, G. Moreton, 1893), vol. 4, pp. 77-79.

58. *The Works of the Reverend William Law*, vol. 6, p. 176.

59. *Thelyphthora; Or A Treatise On Female Ruin, In Its Causes, Effects, Consequences, Prevention, And Remedy; Considered on the Basis Of The Divine Law* (2 vols, London, J. Dodsley, 1780), vol. 1, p. 374.

60. *Thelyphthora*, vol. 2, p. 317.

61. B. Rodgers, *Cloak of Charity: Studies in Eighteenth-Century Philanthropy* (London, Methuen, 1949), p. 55.

62. J. Smith, *Polygamy Indefensible* (London, Alexander Hogg, 1780).

63. Hansard, 20, 592-597.

64. F. Mather, *High Church Prophet: Bishop Samuel Horsley (1733-1806) and the Caroline Tradition in the Later Georgian Church* (Oxford, Clarendon Press, 1992), pp. 283-294.

65. Quoted in M. Hennell, *John Venn and the Clapham Sect* (London, Lutterworth Press, 1958), p. 24.

66. O. F. Christie (ed.), *The Diary of the Rev. William Jones 1777-1821* (London, Brentano's, 1929).

67. Quoted in E. G. Rupp, *Religion in England 1688-1791* (Oxford, Clarendon Press, 1986), p. 25. Samuel subsequently rescinded his threat.

68. For this theme, see E. Leites, 'The Duty to Desire: Love, Friendship, and Sexuality in Some Puritan Theories of Marriage', *Journal of Social History*, vol. 15 (1981-1982), pp. 383-408. His conclusion is that Puritan demands upon spouses were not matched by the means that they gave to married couples to meet these demands.

69. Mather, *High Church Prophet*, p. 294.

70. Quoted in C. H. Sissons (ed.), *The English Sermon, volume II: 1650-1750* (London, Carcanet Press, 1976), p. 175. For further examples, see K. M. Rogers, *The Troublesome Helpmate: A History of Misogyny in Literature* (Seattle, University of Washington Press, 1966); and D. M. Stenton, *The English Woman in History* (London, George Allen & Unwin, 1957).

71. P. Doddridge, *Works* (6 vols, London, Rivingtons, 11th edn, 1821), vol. 5, p. 379. For the popularity of *The Family Expositor* (1738-1755) among Anglicans, see T. R. Preston, 'Biblical Criticism, Literature and the Eighteenth Century', in I. Rivers (ed.), *Books and their Readers in Eighteenth-Century England* (Leicester, Leicester UP, 1982), pp. 97-126.

72. T. Gisborne, *An Enquiry into the Duties of the Female Sex* (London, T. Cadell & W. Davies, 3rd edn, 1798), pp. 263–264. For a Nonconformist exposition of the same theme, see the Rev. James Fordyce, *The Character and Conduct of the Female Sex and the Advantages to be Derived by Young Men from the Society of Virtuous Women* (London, T. Cadell, 1776). Fordyce went out of his way to reject the tradition that assigned all the blame for the Fall to Eve rather than to Adam, and he also objected to the unjust way in which women's characters had been portrayed in the past, pointing out that Jesus 'was pleased to honour with a particular share of his attention' what had become the 'sex , so much depreciated in these days'. Nevertheless, such revisionism had its limits, as he had no doubt that 'Providence designed women for a state of dependence'.

73. There is a good discussion of these changes in both the British and American context in N. F. Cott, 'Passionlessness: An Interpretation of Victorian Sexual Ideology, 1790–1850', *Signs*, vol. 4 (1978), pp. 219–252. Cott suggests that the new ideology had considerable appeal to women, since it enhanced their power and self-respect, both by repudiating the traditional derogatory images of women within Christianity, and by opening up the possibilities of an intellectual education for women that was not based purely on the need to appear attractive to men. On the other hand, Patricia Spacks has made use of eighteenth-century novels and autobiographies to suggest ways in which such attitudes helped to create patterns of repression and denial in women's lives. See P. M. Spacks, 'Evr'y Woman is at Heart a Rake', *Eighteenth-Century Studies*, vol. 8 (1974–1975), pp. 27–46.

74. G. Horne, *The Female Character as it Ought to Appear when Formed* (London, G. Nicholson, 1801), p. 3.

75. For earlier expositions of this theme within the Christian tradition, see I. Maclean, *The Renaissance Notion of Woman* (Cambridge, CUP, 1980), pp. 20–24.

76. Quoted in C. Hall, 'The Early Formation of Victorian Domestic Ideology', in S. Burman (ed.), *Fit Work for Women* (London, Croom Helm, 1979), pp. 24–25.

77. L. Davidoff and C. Hall, *Family Fortunes. Men and Women of the English Middle Class 1780–1850* (London, Hutchinson, 1987). See, too, Hall's 'The Early Formation of Victorian Domestic Ideology', pp. 15–32. The kernel of the argument is that 'The evangelical emphasis on the creation of a new life-style, a new ethic, provided the framework for the emergence of the Victorian bourgeoisie' (p. 15). For discussions of this theme in eighteenth-century literature, see J. Spencer, *The Rise of the Woman Novelist From Aphra Behn to Jane Austen* (Oxford, Basil Blackwell, 1986); N. Armstrong, *Desire and Domestic Fiction. A Political History of the Novel* (Oxford, OUP, 1987); and J. Todd, *The Sign of Angelica: Women, Writing and Fiction 1660–1800* (London, Virago Press, 1989).

78. Even allowing for cautions such as these, Paul Langford in his *A Polite and Commercial People. England 1727–1783* (Oxford, Clarendon Press, 1989) sees the period as one of profound changes that 'have to do with the enrich-

ment and influence of a broad middle class whose concerns became ever more central to Georgian society and whose priorities determined so much both of debate and action' (p. xi).

79. Thus H. Perkin in *The Origins of Modern English Society 1780–1880* (London, Routledge & Kegan Paul, 1969) sees Old Dissent, not Anglicanism, as 'the midwife of class' (p. 196). See also pp. 17–38 for a good discussion of the problems of applying the language of class to Georgian England. Davidoff and Hall are aware of these issues, arguing that many early adherents of evangelicalism came from the margins of the gentry, and encouraged forms of domesticity among members of landed society that were not dissimilar to those found in the urban middle class. The difference was that while this might be a matter of choice for the former, it was mandatory among 'the oppositional culture of the provincial middle classes' (Davidoff and Hall, *Family Fortunes*, p. 21).

80. J. D. Walsh, 'The Anglican Evangelicals in the Eighteenth Century', in *Aspects de L'Anglicanisme* (Paris, Presses Universitaires de France, 1974), p. 102.

81. For the rise in clerical incomes in the course of the eighteenth century, see P. Virgin, *The Church in an Age of Negligence: Ecclesiastical Structure and Problems of Church Reform 1700–1840* (Cambridge, James Clarke & Co., 1989).

82. W. Wilberforce, *A Practical View of the Prevailing Religious System of Professed Christians, in the Higher and Middle Classes in this Country, Contrasted with Real Christianity* (London, T. Cadell & W. Davies, 2nd edn, 1799), pp. 434–435.

83. This idea continues to be influential – witness the recent politically convenient attempts to suggest that the social evils of the early 1990s have been caused by a breakdown in family discipline and traditional morality on the part of parents who are the product of the permissiveness of the 1960s, rather than being the result of an ethos of competitive individualism and growing inequality and social deprivation in the 1980s.

CHAPTER TWO

Women, Church, and Society in Georgian England

The contribution that Anglican women made to the life of the Georgian Church was limited by the constraints of both class and gender. Some clergymen encouraged the scholarly and devotional writings of a few talented and exceptional women such as Mary Astell and Elizabeth Carter, while the new emphasis on the socially regenerative power of female religiosity led to calls for upper- and middle-class women to be given an education that went beyond a training in what Evangelicals such as Hannah More regarded as the frivolous accomplishments of polite society. Ideas such as these were part of a wider debate that centred upon two controverted questions: did women have the same inherent intellectual capacities as men, and what constituted an appropriate curriculum for female education?[1]

Anglican writers who discussed these subjects tended to steer an uneasy course between the Scylla of condoning vain and irreligious ignorance, and the Charybdis of creating learned viragos whose intellectual abilities challenged male expectations about appropriate feminine behaviour. Less controversial was the need to offer working-class girls a basic but strictly limited education in the interests of promoting political and social stability, and upper- and middle-class women played a large part in the creation and running of charity and Sunday schools for the poor.

What were perceived to be the very different educational needs of rich and poor was part of a much wider cultural gulf separating the life experiences and values of well-to-do Anglican women from those of the rural and urban poor. Even where religion can be shown to have played a significant part in the lives of the latter, it often involved beliefs and practices that were regarded as superstitious and sub-Christian by the often increasingly affluent ladies of the parsonage. Yet however much the material and social standing of many Anglican clerical wives may have risen in the course of the eighteenth century, the limits on their practical involvement in the day-to-day life of the Church were rigidly defined. Female preaching, much less any question of ordination, aroused memories of the social and political radicalism of the Interregnum, and its hesitant acceptance within Methodism was seen as one of the many instances of that movement's espousal of an enthusiasm inimical to both religious and social order.

The Church and education

In the view of conservative educationalists it was inappropriate for women to receive the same education as men for two reasons: first, because their intellectual capacities were regarded as more limited, and second, because of their different social duties. According to Fénélon's influential *Treatise on the Education of Daughters*, first published in English in 1707, men should be on their guard against making women 'ridiculously learned' for they possess 'a weaker but more inquisitive mind than men'; moreover, since 'They are not formed to govern the state, to make war, or to enter into the Church . . . they may well dispense with any profound knowledge relating to politics, military tactics, philosophy, and theology.'[2] However, Fénélon went on to stress that women's education could not for these reasons be neglected, since women were primarily responsible for the maintenance of family life and for the early education of children – and society's well-being depended upon these things.

Despite Fénélon's guarded support for women's education, writers in *The Gentleman's Magazine* in the 1730s were still prepared to argue about women's intellectual abilities and the desirability of their receiving anything beyond a basic education. One such writer saw women as capable of attaining 'Knowledge of the most difficult Arts and Sciences with, at least, an equal Facility', but another ridiculed learned women who attempted to 'talk Politicks and Metaphysics', and claimed that women who strayed beyond 'the narrow limits of Domestic Offices . . . move eccentrically, and consequently without Grace'.[3] However, it was the increasing emphasis on women's religious role as the guardians of the home and the educators of the young that led Anglican writers to put aside such doubts and to insist on the need to provide women with a serious education – but not one that in any way challenged the intellectual and social status of men, or led them away from their primary familial obligations. As the Rev. Thomas Gisborne argued, women needed an education, but only up to a certain point:

> It must also be admitted, that the more profound researches of philosophy and learning are not the pursuits most improving to the female mind, and most congenial to its natural occupations. But if we speak of intelligent and well-informed women in general, of women, who, without becoming absorbed in the depths of erudition, and losing all esteem and all relish for social duties, are distinguished by a cultivated understanding, a polished taste, and a memory stored with useful and elegant information; there appears to be no reason to dread from the possession of these endowments a neglect of the duties of the mistress of a family.[4]

The most interesting Anglican discussion of women's education was that provided by the leading female evangelical of her age, Hannah More. A prominent supporter of Sunday schools for the poor, and noted for her own learning and works of popular religious edification, More's attitude towards female education reveals a great deal about the ambiguities and contradictions inherent in religious attempts to advocate learning for women while at the same time limiting its potentially radical implications for traditional views of gender relations. On the vexed question of women's innate intellectual capacities, More steered a cautious course between conservative views of women's inferiority, and radical notions of equality such as those advanced by Mary Wollstonecraft, concluding that, 'till the female sex are more carefully instructed, this question will always remain as undecided as to the degree of difference between the masculine and feminine understandings, as the question between the understandings of blacks and whites'.

That there was such a distinction More did not doubt, since it was 'clearly marked by the defining finger of the creator', but its extent could never be ascertained 'till the understandings of women are made the most of'.[5] In strongly advocating a more rigorous intellectual training for women, More disowned any suggestion that this might lead to any change in the status quo with regard to the relationship between the sexes. In More's view, Mary Wollstonecraft's *Vindication of the Rights of Woman* led women to 'an impious discontent with the part which God has assigned them in this world', and it was the purpose of education properly conceived to make women realize that 'there can be no happiness in any society where there is a perpetual struggle for power'.[6] Ultimately such subordination was of little consequence, since viewed *sub specie aeternae* men and women were spiritually equal, hence, 'All disputes . . . for pre-eminence between the sexes have only for their object the poor precedence for a few short years.'[7] However, this did not mean that the exigencies of temporal society were to be ignored. Both the political upheaval of the revolution in France – which she partly blamed on growing female infidelity – and the increasing influence of German rationalism, made it imperative that women should take responsibility for the education of their children. In the case of daughters, this meant that they should be taught 'to distrust their own judgement', and should 'early acquire a submissive temper and a forbearing spirit', not only for the good of society, but 'on the high principle of obedience to Christ'.[8]

Hannah More's distinction between sound English forms of instruction and suspect continental ones was useful not only in resolving the contradictions involved in both advocating and fearing female education, but also in coping with the ambiguity of her own position as a highly educated and gifted woman in a society that was suspicious of learning in women. Her talents, and those of other women, gave the lie to her cautiously expressed doubts about women's intellectual abilities, and provided they used their gifts in the interests of religion – and were as careful as Hannah More not to challenge publicly the conventional view of the relationship between the sexes – a small number of able women did receive encouragement and patronage from the Church.

One of the most prominent early eighteenth-century clerical supporters of women's education was the Non-Juror Dr George Hickes, the translator of Fénélon and a noted Anglo-Saxon scholar. In 1684, when he was Dean of Worcester, Hickes preached a sermon advocating the creation of schools or colleges for young women 'much like unto the Universities, for the Education of young men'. With the memory of the religious radicalism of the 1640s and 1650s still very much alive, Hickes's aims were conservative: if such a scheme were carried out it would, he believed, root out 'Enthusiasme, with her Daughter Schisme', which were particularly promoted by women 'who are so silly and deceivable for want of Ingenious and Orthodox Education, and not for want of Parts'.[9] Hickes's belief in women's intellectual abilities led him to promote and support their work whenever he could. In the Preface to his *Thesaurus* published in 1705, he praised Susanna Hopton as 'an outstanding example of Christian piety and a great glory to the Church of England, who having acquired no common knowledge of the sacred Scriptures, has put forth not a few anonymous books which are worn to pieces in the hands of pious men and women'. Hopton was a writer of devotional works, the second of which Hickes himself revised and published in 1701; she was also schooled in theological controversy, having become a Roman Catholic and then returning to the Church of England, and Hickes published her reasons for doing so after her death in the second volume of his *Controversial Letters*.[10]

By far the most eminent writer whom Hickes championed was the Anglo-Saxon scholar Elizabeth Elstob. Born in Newcastle in 1683, she received early encouragement in her education from her mother, but after her premature death she lived with her uncle, the Rev. Charles Elstob, who did not believe in women's education and thus hindered her linguistic studies. From 1702 until his death in 1715, she lived much more congenially with her brother William, who was the incumbent of two London churches and a linguist and antiquary who supervised her studies. In 1709, her parallel English and Anglo-Saxon text of the *Homily on the Birthday of St Gregory* was published, and in the dedication to the dean and chapter of Durham Cathedral in 1713 of his collected sermons, Hickes praised her incredible industry in preparing a collection of the Saxon Homilies of Archbishop Aelfric – a work that she was unable to complete as a result of the years of poverty and insecurity that followed her brother's death.[11]

Mary Astell's career was also made possible by clerical support and encouragement. She was the daughter of a Newcastle coal merchant, and her early studies were influenced by her uncle, who was curate of St Nicholas's Church. Later, after the death of her family, she moved to London and was helped by the Non-Juror Archbishop Sancroft, who provided her with money and contacts.[12] Her first published work was *A Serious Proposal to the Ladies for the Advancement of their True and Greatest Interests*, which appeared in 1694 and had reached its fourth edition by 1701. This advocated the creation of places of 'Religious Retirement' for women, where they would not only undertake works of devotion and charity, but would also receive an education. Astell emphasized that the purpose of such studies was as an aid to devotion, and not to equip women to preach in church or usurp male authority. However, she was aware that such was the hostility to learning in women that even her modest scheme required some defence:

> The Ladies, I'm sure, have no reason to dislike this Proposal, but I
> know not how the Men will resent it to have their enclosure broke
> down, and Women invited to taste of that Tree of Knowledge they
> have so long unjustly *Monopoliz'd*. But they must excuse me, if I
> be as partial to my own Sex as they are to theirs, and think Women
> as capable of Learning as Men are, and that it becomes them as
> well. For I cannot imagine where the hurt lies, if instead of doing
> mischief to one another, by an uncharitable and vain Conversation,
> Women be enabled to inform and instruct those of their own Sex at
> least; the Holy Ghost having left it on record, that *Priscilla* as well
> as her Husband, cathechiz'd the eloquent *Apollos* and the great
> Apostle found no fault with her.[13]

As we have seen, objections to the creation of houses for female
celibates aroused hostility, and Astell's vision of institutions of higher
education for women was not to be realized until the late nineteenth
century.

Astell's own intellectual interests were wide-ranging, and
encompassed theology and ecclesiastical controversy as well as works
on the position of women in society. Her *Letters Concerning the Love
of God* (1695) was the result of a correspondence with John Norris,
the rector of Bemerton near Salisbury, and showed her abilities as a
philosopher and theologian. Norris's theology posited a God who was
the source and ground of all human life and all sensations, and ought
therefore to be the sole focus of our love. This was a view that led
Mary Astell to raise the problem of evil and suffering in Norris's
thought – an objection that surprised him, coming as it did from a
woman.[14]

One of the best-known female Anglican intellectuals of the next
generation was Elizabeth Carter, the daughter of a clergyman from
Deal, and whose fame rested on her translation of the Greek
philosopher Epictetus that appeared in 1758. Carter's father, the Rev.
Dr Nicholas Carter, who was perpetual curate of St George the
Martyr in Deal and one of the six preachers at Canterbury Cathedral,
gave his sons and daughters the same rigorous classical education –
teaching all of them Greek, Latin, and Hebrew, and encouraging
them to study French and German. He also helped to launch his
daughter on a literary career by sending her to London to work for
the *Gentleman's Magazine*, whose editor, Edward Cave, was a personal friend.[15]

The other important clerical influence on Elizabeth Carter was the Bishop of Oxford, and future Archbishop of Canterbury, Thomas Secker. Carter met Secker through her friendship with Catherine Talbot, who had lived in the Bishop's household since the early death of her father. Catherine Talbot encouraged Elizabeth in her translation of Epictetus, and since both were devout Christians they discussed their misgivings about publishing the work of a pagan philosopher.[16] Bishop Secker also spent a month reading her work, and offered advice on points of translation and on the content of the notes. Following Catherine Talbot's death in 1770, Elizabeth repaid her debt of gratitude for her friend's help and encouragement by publishing her *Reflections on the Seven Days of the Week*, which set out the nature of the Christian life, and the hope of immortality that was its true foundation.

The friendship of other women writers was also of great importance to Elizabeth Carter; and her nephew and executor, the Rev. Montagu Pennington, while going out of his way to present her as the epitome of eighteenth-century conservative Christian femininity, was not unaware of her dissatisfaction with the lack of educational and social opportunities for women. Pennington was quick to point out that despite her severely intellectual training, the 'more feminine accomplishments' (such as needlework and music) were not neglected, and that her formidable erudition was always at the service of 'a calm, rational, and constant devotion', which eschewed any interest in controversial theological questions. Her social outlook was also reassuringly conservative, as from its inception she recoiled from the French Revolution as 'a tissue of injustice, impiety and rebellion against lawful government and entirely agreed with Mr Burke'. Yet in discussing what he dubbed 'her extreme partiality for writers of her own sex', her nephew was forced to depict a less conventional aspect of her thought:

> She was much inclined to believe that women had not their proper station in society, and that their mental powers were not rated sufficiently highly. Though she detested the principles displayed in Mrs Wollstonecraft's wild theory concerning the 'Rights of Women', and never wished them to interfere with the privileges and occupations of the other sex, yet she thought that men exercised too arbitrary a power over them, and considered them as too inferior to themselves.[17]

As Pennington indicates, Carter, like Hannah More, was a staunch opponent of Mary Wollstonecraft. This has led some historians to see the nineteenth-century women's movement as the product of separate and essentially antagonistic traditions: on the one hand, an ideal of orthodox Christian womanhood that gave women a new role within both family and society, but one that was also restrictive in its definition of femininity and in the limits that it placed on women's participation in political life; and on the other hand, of a radical, rational feminism exemplified by Mary Wollstonecraft, whose inspiration lay in the Enlightenment rather than in Christian pietism and tradition. Such a view can, however, easily suggest that Christian thinking, even within Anglicanism, was more monolithic than was in fact the case.

As we have seen, Hannah More's belief in women's mental capacities, and her insistence on the importance of an intellectually rigorous education, was very different from the Rev. John Bennett's emphasis on acquiring polite social accomplishments. It can also disguise how much the evangelical More and the free-thinking Wollstonecraft had in common. Both argued that women's education should be improved, both were keen to emphasize the need to provide women with a rational education – and both were correspondingly suspicious of many aspects of the late eighteenth-century cult of sensibility and feeling for encouraging false and trivial notions of women's natures and capacities.[18]

The charges of immorality and infidelity levelled at Mary Wollstonecraft can also obscure the extent to which she and Hannah More shared a stern moral earnestness, which appealed for its authority to a religious conception of the world. Wollstonecraft's religion was undogmatic, and her optimistic belief in the meliorative power of human reason as an emanation of divinity was far removed from the evangelical sense of man's sinfulness, and of Christ's place in the economy of salvation; but her condemnation of women created by God for a high moral purpose, who spend their lives in 'playful dalliance' to the appetites of men, and her indignant surprise that any woman 'can consent to be occupied merely to please him; merely to adorn the earth, when her soul is capable of rising to thee', could equally have been uttered by Hannah More.

What Wollstonecraft could not have subscribed to was the eighteenth-century Anglican programme of education for the poor, in which women played a prominent part. The charity school movement was inspired and co-ordinated by the High Church Society for Promoting Christian Knowledge, which was founded in 1698, and until the creation of Sunday schools in the last quarter of the century provided the chief form (and often the only form) of education for poor children. The primary function of the schools was religious: they aimed to give children a reading knowledge of the Bible and the catechism, and sometimes to teach them to write and do accounts; and although clerical initiative was important in the creation of schools, so too was that of the laity. As the historian of the movement has noted, among lay activists women were prominent as subscribers to societies, and as managers, trustees, and school teachers.[19]

Wealthy aristocratic women, and those of lesser means (particularly if they remained single or were widowed), often took the lead in the founding of schools. For example, Mary Astell described the part played by Lady Anne Hastings in the creation of the Chelsea Charity School for the daughters of Hospital veterans: 'She subscribed five guineas April 5th 1709, and her example had so good an influence on several ladies and others in the parish, and many out of it that their subscriptions together with the Reverend the Rector, the Governor, Lieutenant Governor and others of Chelsea College, amounting to about £50 the school was open'd June 6 1709.' The management of the school was in the hands of seven female trustees, chosen 'out of the Ladies and other Gentlewomen who are subscribers; & is always to be under the Direction of Women', though such a stipulation was unusual.[20]

Women were also prominent in the creation of schools outside of London. In Cheshire, only a handful of girls received a grammar school education in the eighteenth century – most had to rely on the provision of charity schools. One of the earliest schools mentioned in the county by the SPCK was that founded at Little Budworth by a wealthy widow who left £20 per annum to educate eight poor children, while the episcopal visitation returns of Bishop Gastrell in 1719 describe a school at Eccleston where children were taught 'at the charge of a charitable lady and the minister of the parish'. On a far grander scale was the £1,000 given in 1760 for a school at Dunham Massey by Lady Mary Booth, Countess of Stamford and heiress of the Earl of Warrington, who personally drew up the rules governing the pupils and the mistress, laid down the curriculum, and kept the accounts.[21] Another prominent aristocratic patron of education was Lady Elizabeth Hastings, a wealthy heiress who had never married and was noted for her piety. She not only founded a boarding school for twenty poor orphan girls on her estate, but also assisted Bishop Wilson in the opening of thirteen schools on the Isle of Man, where attendance was encouraged by the imposition of fines on parents who neglected to send their children.[22]

Charity schools placed great emphasis on the religious as well as the intellectual capacities of their teachers, and did much to establish elementary education as a profession on a secure full-time footing. The average salary for a master in London in the early part of the century was £30, while a woman might receive £24 per annum including accommodation – a not unattractive remuneration at a time when many clerical stipends did not exceed £40.[23] The qualities required of a schoolmistress were set out in the minutes of the Charity School for girls in the parish of St Martin-in-the-Fields in London in 1700. She was to be a regular communicant member of the Church of England, 'of an ingenious mind, willing to learn and apt to teach', having 'a command of her passions' and 'solidly grounded in the true Principles and Practice of Christianity so as to give a good account thereof to the Minister of the Parish upon examination'. Such a paragon was duly found: a Mrs Harbin, a single woman of about forty who received the sacrament weekly, and who proved to be an indefatigable mistress of the school for sixteen years – until its managers were reluctantly forced to dismiss her in 1716 as a Non-Juror who could not bring herself to teach her pupils to pray for King George. The cost of following her conscience is not recorded, for her subsequent fate is unknown.[24]

The curriculum for charity school pupils laid heavy emphasis on teaching both girls and boys to read the Bible and to learn the Church catechism. Boys were also taught to write and do elementary calculations, but this was rarely the case for girls, who instead were given instruction in needlework, knitting, and spinning to prepare them for apprenticeship or domestic service. Social discipline and obedience to one's social superiors were also inculcated in the children. The prayer that opened the day in the girls' charity school in Sheffield began, 'Make me dutiful and obedient to my benefactors, and charitable to my enemies. Make me temperate and chaste, meek and patient, true in all my dealings and content and industrious in my station.'[25] In a sermon preached for the Asylum for Female Orphans in 1773, the Bishop of Chester, Beilby Porteus, reassured his audience that education would not make girls 'forward and insolent, vain of their acquirements and dissatisfied with their condition', but would encourage 'all those meek and self-denying virtues, which are particularly suited to the lowness of their situation and the gentleness of a female mind'.[26] Richard Steele claimed that charity schools were the greatest examples of public spiritedness of which his age could boast, and that their supporters were moved by Christian piety and benevolence as well as by more prudential social considerations.[27] If the latter now seem rather less attractive, it should not be forgotten that in advocating education for the poor, its supporters faced fierce opposition from those who felt that they needed no schooling at all.

The Sunday school movement involved similar issues of class and social control, and again women played a prominent part in its organization and running.[28] The beginnings of the work are usually associated with the work of a devout layman Robert Raikes, who opened Sunday schools at Gloucester in 1780, but Raikes's importance lies more in the publicity and impetus that he gave to the idea, for there is evidence of Sunday schools before 1780 – some of them the result of the initiative of women. For example, Mrs Cappe was impressed by a Sunday school opened in Catterick by the Rev. Theophilus Lindsey, and commenced her own at Bedale in 1765 to teach poor children to read the Bible. At High Wycombe in 1769, Hannah Ball opened a school where children were taught on both Sunday and Monday and taken to worship at the parish church.[29]

Another early enthusiast was Sarah Trimmer. She was born in 1741 and was given a thorough education at a boarding school in Ipswich before moving to London at the age of fourteen, where her father was employed in teaching drawing to the Prince of Wales. This gave her the opportunity to meet many of the intellectual and artistic giants of the day, including Hogarth and Johnson. In 1759 she married; and despite bringing up a family of twelve, found time to interest herself in educational matters. In 1780, Trimmer published her *Easy Introduction to the Knowledge of Nature and Reading the Holy Scriptures*, which was based upon the lessons that she gave her own children. In May 1786, she organized a number of Sunday schools for the poor in Brentford, and in November of the same year Queen Charlotte consulted her about the running of similar institutions in Windsor. This led to the publication of her *Oeconomy of Charity; Or, an Address to Ladies Concerning Sunday Schools*, which established her reputation as an authority in the field.[30] Trimmer was writing at a time she regarded as one of moral crisis for the hierarchy of society, when the handiwork of an 'all-wise and beneficent CREATOR' was being called into question. The work of combating insubordination was, she felt, particularly suitable for unmarried ladies of the middle and upper classes, whose 'hours often hang heavy on their hands', and also for young ladies, who, since they will in future be able to sleep easy in their beds 'without the dread of being disturbed by the nightly robber', will be the chief beneficiaries of attempts 'to train up to religion and virtue, servants, labourers, and mechanics'.[31]

It was true that the work could be demanding, but Trimmer dealt robustly with the fear that 'it will endanger health to sit down in a room surrounded by a parcel of dirty children' by pointing out that 'there is no such contagion in dirt as many people are apt to imagine'.[32] In suggesting that women who had often had experience of educating their own children might be well suited to do the same outside the home, she was careful not to challenge male control of the new institutions; instead, she argued that since 'women are undoubtedly best able to judge of the faults and mismanagements of their own sex and of their peculiar wants', she hoped that at least 'the worthy conductors of Sunday-Schools will allow us to be helps meet for them'.[33]

In fact, the Sunday school movement was one of the earliest examples of a pattern of activity that involved women in applying what Sarah Trimmer called 'the tenderness which is allowed to our sex' to social problems outside the home, and which was to become widespread in the Victorian era. In the case of recruiting pupils for Sunday schools, male authority was circumvented at more than one level: although the initial proposal at Brentford came from the vicar of Ealing, it was thought best to send ladies around the parish to persuade women to send their children 'in those hours when daily labour engages working men from home'.[34]

The provision of Sunday schools for the poor aroused the same kind of opposition as had the earlier charity schools, as Hannah More discovered when she and her sister Martha opened a school in Cheddar in 1789. One of the leading farmers in the area objected to educating the poor on the grounds that 'it made them lazy and useless', and it took Hannah More eleven further visits to win the opposition round to her view that, on the contrary, the inhabitants 'would be more industrious as they were better principled'.[35] The school opened with 120 pupils, and the schoolmistress and her daughter, who received a salary of £30, also undertook parish visiting – an early example of the way in which evangelical zeal for the salvation of souls gave women opportunities to undertake work outside of their own domestic sphere:

The mother or daughter visited the sick, chiefly with a view to their spiritual concerns; but we concealed the true motive at first; and in order to procure them access to the houses and hearts of the people, they were furnished, not only with medicine, but with a little money, which they administered with great prudence. They soon gained their confidence, read and prayed with them, and in all respects did just what a good clergyman does in other parishes.[36]

A further extension of the work involved the creation of benefit clubs for women, similar to those already in existence for men in an area where women working in agriculture earned only 1 shilling a day. The subscription was three half-pence a week, and sums were paid out to women who were unable to work through illness or pregnancy.[37] The same pattern of activity initiated in Cheddar was pursued in a number of neighbouring parishes, though opposition was never entirely quelled, and flared up again after the opening of a school at Blagdon. This resulted in a bitter and prolonged pamphlet war against the work of More and her supporters.

Both Hannah More and Sarah Trimmer also played an important part in the writing of educational works for the poor, which were designed to promote religion and social order while at the same time combating what they regarded as the infidelity and subversion of popular literature, which went so far as to familiarize the lower classes with the political radicalism of Paine and Godwin. As one of Hannah More's biographers explained, 'To teach the poor to read, she now saw, was putting a dangerous engine into their hands, unless safe and salutary reading was also provided.'[38] From 1788 to 1789, Trimmer produced *The Family Magazine*, a monthly publication for 'lower-class readers', which contained gardening and housekeeping advice as well as hymns, sermons, 'instructive tales', and 'descriptions of foreign countries, in which care was taken to make the lower orders see the comforts and advantages belonging to this favoured land, and also to render them contented with its laws and government'.[39] She also wrote a series of children's books designed for use in charity schools, even though establishing a career for herself as an author was not easy. She waited anxiously while these books were vetted before being accepted by SPCK, since 'this honour, she was sensible, could not easily be attained by a female writer'.[40]

Hannah More began writing works with a similar anti-revolutionary purpose at the instigation of the Bishop of London, Beilby Porteus, whom she met in Bath in 1792. This encouragement led to the publication of her first tract, *Village Politics, by Will Chip, a Country Carpenter*, and culminated in the series of popular moral tales for the edification of the poor, entitled *Cheap Repository Tracts*, which began to appear in 1795 with financial support organized by Henry Thornton, who was one of the leaders of the Evangelical Clapham Sect. Hannah More herself wrote 19 of the first 114 tracts, and in one year over two million were bought for distribution among the poor – though how many were read is another matter.[41] The best-known and most characteristic of More's efforts in the genre of the pious counter-revolutionary tale was *The Shepherd of Salisbury Plain*. Here More uses all her skill to paint a vivid picture of the hardships faced by an agricultural labourer and his family living in a two-roomed cottage on a meagre diet of potatoes, and dependent on clerical charity for the provision of medicine for his sick wife; the conclusion to be drawn, though, is not that the social and political order is in need of reform, but that the shepherd is a model Christian in so far as he accepts the status quo as God-given. In this task, religion proves to be of great value, since it makes the poor aware that they are exposed to fewer temptations and vices than the rich, and teaches them 'the vanity of all earthly possessions' while holding out the prospect of eternal happiness in the world to come.[42]

The saccharine-coated didacticism of works of this kind are not much to the taste of a more democratic age, and one can understand why Gordon Rupp somewhat dismissively dubbed Sarah Trimmer 'a sanctified Enid Blyton'. However, this fails to convey the sense of real alarm felt by conservative upper-class Anglican ladies at the political and social upheavals of the late eighteenth century, and the earnestness with which they regarded the obligations imposed upon both rich and poor for the maintenance of a divinely ordained hierarchical ordering of society.

The Church and popular culture

As the history of women's education in the Georgian Church makes clear, class distinctions meant that the life experiences and values of women were far from being homogeneous, and this was also true of the way in which women understood religion and viewed the Church as a social institution. Eighteenth-century episcopal visitation returns and clerical diaries indicate that the Church was often an important source of charitable aid in times of hardship and sickness, but how far this implied an acceptance of its doctrinal teaching is open to doubt.

Parson Woodforde's diaries, which record the life and work of an eighteenth-century clergyman who was rector of Weston Longville in Norfolk from 1776 until his death in 1803, show that while the average number of Easter and Christmas communicants did not rise above thirty out of a population of about 360, the numbers of old people claiming the traditional St Thomas's Day dole of sixpence averaged over fifty, while as many as ninety children came to receive the St Valentine's Day gift of a penny in 1798.[43] At Over Stowey in Somerset, the vicar, William Holland, found the same discrepancy between the alacrity with which his parishioners claimed their traditional rights and their reluctance to make use of the ministrations of the Church. In December 1799, he complained of being 'much harried by the poor of the parish who come for Christmas gifts', but the following Ash Wednesday the church was virtually empty for prayers; and he was lamenting that devotion was dead, though it might again revive, he hoped, 'as French principles begin to be exploded'.[44]

The problem was not in fact a new one, and one of the aims of the charity school movement had been to overcome what was perceived to be the widespread religious ignorance and indifference of ordinary people. As Samuel Wesley wrote to his Bishop in 1700, the creation of a school for the poor at Epworth would be 'a mighty advantage, for the people are so extream [sic] ignorant that not one in twenty can say the Lord's Prayer right, nor one in thirty the Beliefs'.[45] The same obstacles thwarted Archbishop Secker's attempts to increase the frequency of communion in the Georgian Church, for, as he complained, 'Some imagine that the sacrament belongs only to persons of advanced years, or great leisure, or high attainment in religion, and it is a very dangerous thing for common people to venture on.'[46]

However, the difficulty facing the Church was not simply ignorance of its doctrines, but the fact that popular culture surrounded orthodox religious practice with a penumbra of folklore and magic.[47] In an age when medicine could offer little effective relief from the sufferings occasioned by accident and sickness, resort to practitioners of white magic was common, and often such practitioners were women. As one observer of rural life in Suffolk recalled, 'There were several old people, indeed there are some still of my acquaintance chiefly old women, who "bless" and "charm" different maladies, especially wounds from scalding and burning.'[48] The darker side of such practices was the continuing belief in witchcraft. In 1712, a poor and unpopular old woman in the village of Walkern in Hertfordshire, Jane Wenham, was sentenced to death as a witch, though she subsequently received a royal pardon. Despite the abolition of the offence of witchcraft in 1736, assaults on women continued.[49] At Leicester Quarter Sessions in 1760, two men were put in the pillory and gaoled for attempting to subject a woman to an ordeal by water, while as late as 1827, four men were found guilty of assaulting a woman whom they believed had used occult powers to bring about the death of cattle.[50]

It would have been easier for the Church if clear distinctions could have been drawn between popular superstition and its own rituals, but this was not always the case. It was widely believed, for example, that unbaptized infants were vulnerable to supernatural attack and illness, and in parts of the North of England it was customary when a child was taken to church to be christened to engage a small boy to meet the child upon leaving the house 'because it is deemed an unlucky omen to encounter a female first';[51] while at the ceremony itself it was said in Shropshire that if one of the sponsors looked into the font, the child would grow up like him.[52]

One of the most important rites of passage for women was the ceremony of churching following the birth of a child. Parson Woodforde frequently performed the ceremony, usually charging sixpence, but waiving the fee for poor women.[53] The Prayer Book of 1549 described the service as 'the Order for the Purification of Women', which echoed the association of women and childbirth with ritual uncleanness that can be traced back in the Judaeo-Christian tradition as far as the Book of Leviticus.[54] The 1552 Prayer Book renamed the service 'the Thanks Giving of Woman After Childbirth', but the continued insistence that the woman should wear a veil suggests that the penitential aspects of the rite had not disappeared.[55] This stipulation was ended after the Interregnum, and the eighteenth-century Church emphasized that the purpose of the rite was 'To bless God for restoring Persons to their Strength', and was at pains to repudiate earlier notions:

> We do not indeed pretend to debar People Admittance upon any Pretence of Pollution; for we know that Marriage is honourable, and the Children of Christians are a Holy Seed. We prescribe no Number of days, but leave that to Custom, and Convenience; and would Health and Decency permit, should not scruple to receive them the very next Day into our Churches. We expect no Sin-

Offering, nor a lamb for a burnt-Offering, because all Bloody Sacrifices ended in Christ.[56]

Given the high rates of mortality for both women and infants in childbirth, there was every cause for such thanksgiving, but it is clear that older associations did not necessarily disappear from popular consciousness. In Shropshire, for example, it was said that 'colliery people think it very unlucky for the mother to go out of doors even over the door-step, till she goes to be churched'.[57]

There were two other important areas where the official teaching of the Church was often in conflict with popular culture. The first was the increasing hostility shown by some churchmen towards the continuance of traditional sports and pastimes, and calendar customs such as harvest suppers, plough Monday, and sheep-shearing festivities. Celebrations based upon the agricultural and ecclesiastical calendar provided opportunities for commensality and goodwill that did much to reinforce the social order. One such occasion was at Rogation Tide, when villagers processed round the parish boundaries. At Shalstone in Buckinghamshire in May 1740, for example, the local landowner, Henry Purefoy, laid out 10 shillings and sixpence for beer and bread for the festivities that accompanied the event.[58] Another occasion for festivities was the annual dedication feast of the parish church. In Herefordshire, according to one observer, 'The feast of the Church is observed with great conviviality and ale-house balls, and dinners; nor do they separate till the money, which they lay up for weeks before is spent; cock-fighting is at such seasons a favourite amusement.'[59]

Many of the country clergy also supported the traditional round of parish life with enthusiasm. Parson Woodforde recorded in his diary for 25 May 1801 that 'This being Whit-Monday there was plowing, rafling etc., at the Heart in Church Street in the Afternoon. . . . It was a cheering day for the happy villagers.'[60] However, not all of the clergy saw matters in this light. Evangelicals in particular were suspicious of many aspects of traditional culture as being no more than apolaustic excesses that were incompatible with the serious business of working out one's salvation with fear and trembling.[61] For example, the Rev. Samuel Walker, one of the early leaders of the evangelical revival in Cornwall, founded a religious society in Truro for men and married women, but taking part in card playing, dancing, drinking in taverns, parish feasts, and sports festivals were deemed to be grounds for exclusion.[62] To educated churchmen, many popular customs were more than unseemly affronts to genteel behaviour: they seemed to threaten not only immorality, but also social anarchy. For example, the widespread custom of 'lifting' or 'hocking', which took place on the Monday or Tuesday after Easter, when villagers would unceremoniously carry their betters and demand money for their release, often involved the 'lifting' of men by women and seemed to subvert the hierarchy of gender as well as class.[63]

The second (and undoubtedly the greatest) gulf between Anglican attitudes and popular belief was in the area of sexual morality. As we have seen, chastity was regarded by the Church as the bedrock of family morality, and sexual relations outside of marriage were uniformly condemned. The Church courts had the power to prosecute offenders, and sometimes did so by imposing an act of public penance upon transgressors to be carried out in their parish church. A case occurred in the diocese of Exeter in 1764:

> It is ordered that Mary Cutting of Pyworthy in the county of Devon . . . shall upon some Sunday before the Day of the Return hereof in the forenoon immediately after the reading of the second lesson come into the Parish Church aforesaid, bare-headed with a white sheet about her shoulders, bare-footed and bare-legged, with a white rod in her hand, and shall stand before the Ministers' seat or pew until the end of the Nicene Creed, and shall openly confess and acknowledge that she hath been delivered of a male child unlawfully begotten on her body, and shall show her hearty sorrow and repentance and shall desire God to forgive her, and the Minister and the People to pray for the amendment of her life for the future, Promising by her own endeavours to certify her repentance by a Holy and Circumspect Conversation, and no more to give the like occasion to the Church.

An important part of the ordeal consisted of a confession in which the father was named, so that the magistrate could charge him with a contribution towards the child's maintenance.[64] Although the ecclesiastical courts were less powerful and less active in the eighteenth century in the sphere of public morals than in earlier centuries, they did not lack teeth; failure to carry out the order of the court led to excommunication, which could be followed by imprisonment by the civil courts. James Woodforde recorded similar cases of public penance in Norfolk and also instances of what he called 'compulsory' marriages, since under the Bastardy Act of 1733 a woman having named a father on oath before a justice of the peace could have him imprisoned for non-payment of maintenance to the parish, a punishment that was avoided if he agreed to marry her.[65]

The actions of the ecclesiastical courts and the functions of public penance were a typical example of the way in which in the eighteenth century the concerns of civil society (to ensure that the father was identified and made liable for the child's support) and the spiritual concerns of the Church (the maintenance of Christian moral standards) were interwoven. However, with regard to the latter, working-class custom viewed matters very differently. Illegitimacy rates were rising, and whereas in the first half of the eighteenth century 25 per cent of brides were pregnant at time of marriage, the figure had risen to 38 per cent a hundred years later.[66] Sexual relations before marriage were often regarded as a part of courtship, and provided the couple married, no opprobrium attached to them.[67] The regulation of marriage in this way, though far removed from the standards of evangelical morality, was part of a wider moral economy which, when its rules were broken, led to communal sanction: for example, 'rough music', which involved parading noisily outside a neighbour's house with indecent effigies, was a way of shaming cuckolded husbands into putting their affairs in order. That the Church was unable to recognize, much less to support, the morality of the crowd is an indication of the gulf that increasingly separated it from the lives of ordinary men and women.

Women in the life of the Georgian Church

Despite the limited education that most women received in the eighteenth century, and the oft-repeated claim that they should not meddle in such public matters as politics and theology, a number of exceptional women did engage in theological controversy and the defence of Anglicanism, though this was truer of the early part of the century. The most notable writer was again Mary Astell, who took part in the bitter pamphlet war of the early 1700s espousing the High Church Tory cause against the toleration of dissenters; and in particular, the practice of Occasional Conformity, by which dissenters were able to evade the restrictions of the Test and Corporation Acts on their holding public office by attending an Anglican service once a year.[68] In 1705, she published her *The Christian Religion as Professed by a Daughter of the Church of England*. Astell's work was the most substantial contribution to eighteenth-century Anglican theology by a woman writer until the appearance of Hannah More's *Thoughts on the Importance of the Manners of the Great to General Society*, which appeared in 1788, and her *An Estimate of the Religion of the Fashionable World*, which followed in 1790. Astell's spirituality is different, though, from More's, and reflects the Christianity of Tillotson, with its emphasis on the reasonableness of Christian belief and the life of charity, benevolence, and decorum that it entailed. Not that Astell's writing is bloodless, particularly when discussing women's alleged inferiority to men, which she tartly dismissed by saying that 'my blind Soul can't discern it: Since the duties of a Christian are as much our Business as theirs.'[69]

Authors such as these were exceptional: many more women were involved in the day-to-day life of the Church as clerical wives and daughters. In his study *The Eighteenth Century Country Parson*, A. T. Hart has suggested that clerical wives were less active in parochial affairs than was later the case, and he quotes the Rev. William Cole's ideal as being that of a Mrs Drayton, 'a very fine woman and a proper Parsons' wife, visiting nowhere and taking care of her family concerns'.[70] But while it might be true that systematic parish visiting and philanthropy were more characteristic of the Victorian Church, in other respects Hart's emphasis is misleading. For one thing, the maintenance of family life and the running of the household were arduous and fundamental contributions to clerical life, and these can easily be overlooked when unpaid housework is not recognized as 'work'.[71] Moreover, women were involved in both Sunday schools and the distribution of charity. Henry Venn, for example, became vicar of Huddersfield in 1760, and the burden of bringing up five children and meeting the needs of the poor out of an income of £100 a year fell largely upon his wife, Mira, who made the family's clothes, supervised the work of two maids, and gave away clothing and meat to the poor.[72] With a stipend of £100 per annum, the Venns were by no means among the poorest of Georgian clerical families – the Rev. William Ford and his wife struggled to make ends meet at Seathwaite in Lancashire in 1754 on less than £30 a year.[73]

As well as their responsibility for household management, women were also sometimes more directly involved in clerical business. The Rev. John Lonsdale, who was vicar of Darfield near Barnsley, not only deferred to his wife in matters concerning the upbringing of their children, but during his absence expected her to manage the farming of his glebe and to find suitable clergy to take services for him.[74] Women also provided their husbands with emotional and intellectual support in their work. Albinia, the wife of the Rev. George Woodward, the rector of East Hendred in Berkshire, not only managed the household and treated the poor for miles around with medicines of her own devising, but, as he confided in a letter, 'she amongst other great qualifications is a very good Divine; for she is a perfect mistress of the Bible and several books of divinity; which makes the reading of such books much more agreeable to me . . . and by conversing together upon these sort of topics, she makes herself the best companion to me, as well as the best of wives'.[75] Well-to-do women could also play a part in the appointment of clergy through their exercise of lay patronage. For example, Lady Elizabeth Hastings bought up advowsons near her estate, took care to appoint clergy of exemplary piety, and refused to countenance the widespread practice of clerical pluralism.[76] Equally influential was the Countess of Huntingdon, who kept a firm control over her chaplains and who went on to found her own denomination.[77]

Nevertheless, there were very clear limits to what it was thought proper for Anglican clerical wives and patrons to undertake in the way of pastoral duties. When, during the absence of her husband at Convocation in 1712, Susanna Wesley began holding a house meeting for prayer and sermon reading – which began with her family but was soon attended by two hundred parishioners – the curate accused her of holding a 'conventicle', and her husband also expressed his unease.[78] Susanna's self-defence expresses something of the frustrations felt by a woman keenly aware of the limitations imposed upon her by social and ecclesiastical convention: 'At last it came into my mind though I am not a man, nor a minister of the gospel, and so cannot be engaged in such a worthy employment as they were yet . . . I might do something more than I do.'[79] Nothing more was heard of her experiment, which presumably ended on her husband's return.

Samuel Wesley himself had earlier inaugurated a lay society that met once a week for prayer, and whose members gave time and money for charitable purposes. The society followed the pattern begun by Anthony Horneck in 1678 as part of a High Church religious revival that also involved the setting up of Societies for the Reformation of Manners, which employed agents as informers to bring about prosecutions of blasphemous or pornographic publications and of individuals accused of immorality, and the creation of the SPCK and SPG.[80] The religious societies, which met weekly for spiritual instruction and devotion, were evidence of widespread lay religious aspirations that the Church was endeavouring to meet;

however, as their historian has noted, the needs of women were largely overlooked, since 'It was not thought proper for women to form any sort of religious associations of their own, or take any part in the work of the Societies.'[81] The creation of a separate society for women at Wolverhampton in 1711 was exceptional – more typical was Samuel Wesley's stipulation that women were not to attend the meeting at Epworth because of the risk of scandal, but were instead to content themselves with receiving instruction at home.[82] The High Church impetus for religious and moral reform petered out in the early part of the eighteenth century, and it was left to the new breed of Evangelical clergy to experiment with house meetings and less rigid forms of devotion. As we have seen, the Rev. Samuel Walker began a society at Truro in 1754 with two separate groups meeting weekly, one for single men and one for married men and women. He also organized smaller, more informal, single-sex lay meetings led by the members themselves, and similar organizations were created by Richard Conyers while vicar of Helmsley.[83]

Such innovative methods were not widespread among Georgian churchmen, and it was Samuel Wesley's son John who inherited and developed the aims and methods of the High Church revival. The organization of local Methodist societies into weekly classes and bands for the more spiritually advanced gave religion a more domestic focus with which women could identify, and they often outnumbered men in the early societies. At Frome in Somerset in 1759, for example, the society had thirty-eight members, twenty-five of whom were women.[84] Visiting sick members was also work that they were encouraged to undertake. In his *Plain Account of the People Called Methodists* published in 1748, Wesley argued that such ministrations were a revival of the role of deacons and deaconesses in the early Church, and cited the example of Phoebe as a visitor.[85]

The class and band meetings also encouraged women to contribute by offering edifying testimony about their spiritual state. Exhortation of this kind involved women in leadership roles, and the experience of conversion and the sense of God's saving presence in their lives gave them the courage to speak in public to men as well as women. Thus in October 1776 Wesley wrote to Mrs Dorothy Downes, telling her that she could lead a class of men provided she did not act 'as a superior, but as an equal; and it is an act of friendship and brotherly love'.[86] The experience of spiritual empowerment was described by one class and band leader, Hester Anne Roe Rogers, in her manuscript journal in 1781:

I opened the Hymn book on that precious hymn, 'O for a Heart to praise my God' etc - and in singing it, was filled indeed with the Divine Presence and love unprintable. Prayer was as a Gate of Heaven, and I sensibly felt the words given me to speak were not my own. I think I never was so entirely led out of myself and influenced by a divine power - while the dear people seemed as melting wax before the fire.[87]

The most significant enlargement of women's participation in Methodism was into the field of preaching, which was a logical extension of their work in class and band meetings. In February 1761, Sarah Crosby wrote to Wesley - explaining that since her class meeting had expanded to include two hundred people, she was in effect preaching in public. He did not feel that she had done anything wrong, but advised her to preface any future remarks on such occasions with the words, 'You lay me under a great difficulty. The Methodists do not allow of women preachers; neither do I take upon me any such character. But I will just nakedly tell you what is in my heart.'[88] In 1771, Mary Bosanquet wrote to Wesley, arguing that Methodist women should be given the right to preach. Part of her case rested upon a now familiar biblical exegesis in which she pointed out that the prohibitions on women speaking in 1 Timothy 2 and 1 Corinthians 14 do not imply a blanket prohibition on women speaking in church, but must be directed at specific matters of discipline, since they are contradicted by 1 Corinthians 11, in which women are mentioned as praying and prophesying. In his reply of 13 June 1771, Wesley conceded the principle, accepting that her case rested upon her having 'an *extraordinary* call'.[89] Once begun, more formal recognition followed.

By the 1780s, women proved to be popular and effective open-air preachers, and in 1787, on Wesley's instructions, the senior minister of the Norfolk circuit formally authorized a woman to preach.[90] Wesley's willingness to make use of women's abilities is an example of the way in which his burning concern to preach the gospel, and his capacity for pragmatism and innovation, overrode traditional forms of Anglican ecclesiastical organization, and it was an experiment that largely died with him. In 1803, the Wesleyan Conference passed a resolution allowing women to preach only on the basis of an extraordinary call, and then only to other women, a stipulation that was to remain unchanged until the twentieth century.[91] The practice of itinerant female preachers continued in the nineteenth century among the breakaway Primitive Methodists, though such activity was increasingly discouraged, especially after 1836 when women were no longer able to claim from the itinerant preachers' fund.[92]

As is well known, the Wesleyan experiment provoked strong hostility within Anglicanism, but historians have tended to pay more attention to the challenges posed by its disregard for the traditional parochial structure and ministry by the use of itinerant lay preachers, and the Establishment's refined dislike of the more emotional manifestations of popular religious revivalism, than to its unsettling implications for traditional assumptions about the family and gender. Although in one sense the class meeting could be seen as a more domestic style of religion than the cold formalism of worship in the parish church, the intense spiritual bonds forged among its members could also provide an alternative focus for social life and emotional fulfilment to that offered by the family unit. Charles Wesley was uneasily aware of this when he wrote to Susanna about the class system:

Their societies are sufficient to dissolve all societies but their own. Will any man of common sense or spirit suffer any domestic to be in a band engaged to relate to five or ten people everything without reserve that concerns the person's conscience how much soever it may concern the family? Ought any married persons to be there unless husband and wife be there together?[93]

In her study of women in early Methodism in Cheshire, Gail Malmgreen has highlighted the higher proportion of unmarried women who joined the societies in comparison with male members, and has suggested that whereas for the latter, religious commitment may have been part of a 'settling down' process, for the former it may often have involved an assertion of independence quite separate from the responsibilities of marriage and family life.[94] Thus the young Hester Ann Roe defied both her mother and her uncle by her Methodist allegiance, recalling in her journal that 'I now reasoned with my mother, and entreated her not to confine me any more; telling her in humility, and yet plainness, I must seek the salvation of my soul, whatever the consequences.'[95] This was a classic example of the tension that has always existed within Christianity between the human demands of family life on the one hand, and the transcendental referent of faith on the other; and it was one which, as we have seen, was also to be found within more mainstream Anglicanism, though critics of Methodism were quick to seize upon it as a characteristic fault of Wesley's revivalist movement. For example, Nathaniel Lancaster's *Methodism Triumphant* describes the attitude of women converts towards traditional family obligations:

> And Nature's fond, connecting Ties disdain.
> Domestic Sweets, Parental Charites,
> Filial Endearments, Conjugal Delights,
> The Passions of mere carnal Men, deriv'd
> From feeble instinct, they with scorn reject;

And these women conclude by asserting that 'We had relations – we disclaim them now.'[96] The same line of attack was pursued by James Lackington, who claimed that 'I am informed from good authority that there are now in Mr Wesley's society, in London, some women who ever since they were converted, have refused to sleep with their husbands, and that some of those will not pay the least attention to any temporal concern whatever, being as they term it, wholly wrapped up in divine contemplation having their souls absorbed in divine love, so as not to be interrupted by the trifling concerns of a husband, family, etc.'[97]

Female preaching was another cause of Anglican ire. It had been attacked by the Church as a Puritan irregularity in the 1620s – an instance of that spiritual and social anarchy that led ultimately to the collapse of the political order in the Civil War and Interregnum. For example, in the early 1620s, the Bishop of Bath and Wells, Arthur Lake, preached a sermon in St Cuthbert's church 'when certain persons did penance for being at conventicles where a woman preached', scornfully upbraiding them for showing themselves 'unworthy to be men, that could be so weak as to become scholars to a woman'.[98] The links with seventeenth-century radical dissent were continued in the eighteenth century by the Quakers, whose women continued to preach in public, but Methodist women preachers represented a new and more direct challenge to the established Church.[99] According to Bishop George Lavington, the people most likely to 'fall into Methodist enthusiasm' were young people and women, 'who (notwithstanding some exceptions) may without offence, be called the weaker vessels', and it was from among these that preachers were chosen:

> Hence they take upon them, I do not say to ordain but to appoint, and give authority to, persons who (in their own words) are *neither* Bishops, Priests, *or* Deacons, to preach the word; common

mechanics, *women* and *boys*, are actually employed in *this Ministry of Publick Preaching*, without any *human qualifications*.[100]

Critics of Methodism such as Lavington regarded the convulsions, visions, and hysteria that sometimes accompanied revivalist preaching and conversion, and to which they felt women were particularly susceptible, as evidence of 'enthusiasm', which Dr Johnson defined in his dictionary as 'a vain belief of private revelation; a warm confidence of divine favour or communication'. More bluntly, the epitome of eighteenth-century rational Anglicanism, Bishop Butler, denounced such claims to special revelation as a 'very horrid thing'.[101]

As such unfavourable reactions indicate, the ideal of Georgian spirituality for both men and women was calmer and more dispassionate. In a letter to Mrs Vesey in 1769, Elizabeth Carter encapsulated the faith of upper-class Anglican women, a faith that now often only survives in the marmoreal coldness of innumerable family epitaphs:

A steady attention to the rule of duty as such, is the sweetest path to conviction. The natural feelings and interests of a good heart and the divine assistance will sooner or later subdue any mere constitutional scepticism to such a degree, as will be sufficient to calm the mind into tranquility, and encourage it by cheerful hope. This is all that is necessary to comfort and to virtue; and high transports of divine enthusiasm, though a great blessing when founded on real principles of true religion, can like other distinguished advantages, fall to the lot of very few.[102]

This too was the religion of Jane Austen, socially conservative, strongly patriotic, and in whose novels heroines such as Elizabeth Bennet and Fanny Price are commended for their control of their passions through self-government, reason, and unwavering adherence to duty and principle.[103]

It was in fact a commonplace of eighteenth-century writing about women and religion that the particular trials and social disadvantages to which they were subjected made them more in need than men of a spirituality that encouraged the qualities of self-denial and resignation. As a doctor, John Gregory explained:

Your whole life is often a life of suffering. You cannot plunge into business, or dissipate yourselves in pleasure and riot, as men often do, when under the pressure of misfortunes. You must bear your sorrows in silence, unknown and unpitied. You must often put on a face of serenity and chearfulness, when your hearts are torn with anguish, or sinking in despair. Then your only resource is in the consolation of religion. It is chiefly owing to these that you bear domestic misfortunes better than we do.[104]

Religion as opium was not only necessary in the face of illness and childbirth, but also to cope with the injustices of a patriarchal society. As a writer in the *Gentleman's Magazine* pointed out in 1788, women were not only often forced into loveless marriages, but because of the laws of primogeniture they were often abandoned and ill-treated in old age. Faced with such hardships, it was important that their minds should be 'seasoned with principles of religion; for these principles will best support the soul when all human comfort is ineffectual'.[105] Such an emphasis could encourage a spirituality of almost masochistic self-martyrdom, as in the case of the young Mary Astell, who was painfully aware that she possessed talents for which the Church had no use. She expressed her frustrations in a poem written in 1687 when she was twenty-one:

> How shall I be a Peter or a Paul?
> That to the Turk and Infidel,
> I might the joyful tydings tell,
> And spare no labour to convert them all:
> But are my sex denies me this,

She concludes that through religion she can at least become 'a Martyr in desire'.[106]

To what extent did the evangelical revival introduce a new element into the religious lives of eighteenth-century churchwomen accustomed to a piety of resignation and self-denial? As we have seen, the belief in women's moral and religious superiority could be a source of empowerment, and it encouraged their involvement in philanthropic and educational work outside the home. For example, Faith Gray, the wife of a York solicitor who was a friend of Wilberforce, threw herself into a ceaseless round of Sunday school teaching, school management, and the creation of friendly societies.[107]

The strength of evangelical conviction in the reality of human depravity, and the assurance of righteousness to be found in Christ, could provide women with powerful motives for action. This was the case with Sarah Trimmer, who prayed for God's help in overcoming opposition to her plans to open Sunday schools – resistance that she saw not in earthly terms, but as evidence of 'the malice of the Devil'.[108] On the other hand, there is some evidence that the evangelical stress on sin and guilt did not always offer comfort and solace, even in areas of life where women were felt to be most in need of it. Faith Gray recorded in her diary the loss of a daughter as God's punishment for 'vain trifling, and wandering thoughts';[109] while Sarah Trimmer drew comfort from her belief that her dead child was in heaven, but not before struggling with the self-lacerating thought that her death might have been God's way of punishing her for her sins.[110]

The consequences for women of evangelical attitudes to sexuality are also far from clear, and have been variously interpreted by historians. While Nancy Cott has suggested that the new ideology of pious femininity had considerable appeal to women as it enhanced their power and self-respect both by repudiating the traditional derogatory image of woman as the fallen Eve, and by advocating an education that was not based purely on the need to appear attractive to men, Patricia Spacks has made use of eighteenth-century novels and autobiographies to suggest ways in which such attitudes also helped to create patterns of emotional repression in women's lives. In this view, the cost of placing women on a moral pedestal was to be the denial of female sexuality and the psychic traumas often endured by the Victorian 'angel in the house'.[111]

Historians have also suggested that the new evangelical emphasis on domesticity, and the inculcation of the values of thrift, sobriety, and education, may have had a particular attraction to women who were concerned for the physical and moral welfare of their families.[112] On the other hand, the cult of pious domesticity did much to reinforce patriarchal and hierarchical forms of thought and practice within both the family and society. A good example of this process was the revival of family prayers, which became an essential feature of evangelical households. Cowper recorded that in 1768 he was called upon to lead prayers at Olney, while Wilberforce resolved in 1788 to begin constant morning and evening prayer and Bible reading in his family. Such a responsibility was clearly the prerogative of husbands as the heads of their households, and although evangelicalism preached a doctrine of radical spiritual equality, in that all were sinners and in need of redemption, the ritual of family prayer – at which servants were also expected to be present – re-enacted the hierarchy of the whole temporal and spiritual order in microcosm.

Notwithstanding the dynamic and innovatory aspects of evangelicalism, its impact upon women's lives was varied and in some respects contradictory, while the theology of subordination that was at the heart of eighteenth-century Anglican theology and spirituality was evidently also carried over into evangelical modes of thought. In fact, throughout the eighteenth century, within all shades of Anglicanism, the theological discourse and social praxis of patriarchy were mutually reinforcing: when Sarah Trimmer recalled her dead father, it was natural that she should take comfort from the fact that he was with 'the universal Parent, the Great Governor of the Universe'.[113]

Notes

1. For a brief introduction to these debates and a selection of contemporary texts, see V. Jones, *Women in the Eighteenth Century: Constructions of Femininity* (London, Routledge, 1990), pp. 98–139.

2. Jones, *Women in the Eighteenth Century*, p. 102.

3. *The Gentleman's Magazine*, vol. 5 (1735), p. 589, and vol. 7 (1737), pp. 553–554. In his *The History of Pompey the Little: Or, The Life and Adventures of a Lap-Dog* (London, M. Cooper, 1751), p. 60, Francis Coventry ridiculed a learned woman in the guise of Lady Sophister, who visited France where 'the Ladies affect a reputation of science, and are able to discourse on the profoundest questions of theology and philosophy'. It was a common refrain in the eighteenth and nineteenth centuries that women lacked the aptitude to study theology.

4. T. Gisborne, *An Enquiry into the Duties of the Female Sex* (London, T. Cadell & W. Davies, 3rd edn, 1798), p. 286.

5. H. More, 'Strictures on the Modern System of Female Education', in *Works* (8 vols, London, T. Cadell, 1801), vol. 8, p. 33. More was a supporter of the Clapham Sect's campaign against the slave trade, hence her allusion to the question of the innate abilities and rights of Africans. In discussing this passage in *The Eighteenth-Century Feminist Mind* (Brighton, Harvester Press, 1987), pp. 176–178, Alice Browne suggests that it is indicative of the way in which debates about women's education had altered in the course of the century. Women's rationality is now accepted, and More's reference to African slavery points to an awareness that she shared with Wollstonecraft of the real possibilities of social and political change affecting women's lives. This, however, is to underplay the extent to which the outlook and activities of Anglicans, including Evangelicals, were a reaction against change, and one that was largely successful until the constitutional reforms of the late 1820s.

6. More, 'Strictures', in *Works*, vol. 8, pp. 17–24.

7. More, 'Strictures', in *Works*, vol. 8, p. 35.

8. H. More, 'Address to Women of Rank and Fortune on the Effects of Their Influence on Society', in *Works*, vol. 7, pp. 183–184. The image of women as the mainstay of Christian faith in an age of unbelief was to be a recurring one in the nineteenth century, though its proponents differed as to whether this was best achieved by their receiving a sound education or by avoidance of the masculine world of sceptical intellect in favour of a spirituality of sympathy and emotion.

9. Quoted in M. Reynolds, *The Learned Lady in England 1650–1760* (Boston, Houghton Mifflin, 1920), pp. 290–291.

10. D. M. Stenton, *The English Woman in History* (London, George Allen & Unwin, 1957), pp. 235–236.

11. Stenton, *The English Woman in History*, pp. 238–239.

12. R. Perry, *The Celebrated Mary Astell, An Early English Feminist* (Chicago, University of Chicago Press, 1986), pp. 46–68.

13. B. Hill (ed.), *The First English Feminist. Reflections Upon Marriage and Other Writings by Mary Astell* (Aldershot, Gower/Maurice Temple Smith, 1986), p. 155.

14. Hill (ed.), *The First English Feminist*, pp. 7–8.

15. For the details of Carter's career, and the significance of her life and friendships, see S. H. Myers, *The Bluestocking Circle: Women, Friendship, and the Life of the Mind in Eighteenth-Century England* (Oxford, Clarendon Press, 1990).

16. M. Pennington, *Memoirs of the Life of Mrs Elizabeth Carter* (London, Rivingtons, 1807), pp. 118–127. Elizabeth Carter found no difficulty in identifying with the stoical self-discipline and self-restraint of thinkers such as Epictetus and Marcus Aurelius, while acknowledging the absence of the Christian scheme of salvation in their thought. It was for this reason that Catherine Talbot suggested the addition of explanatory notes to her translation of Epictetus, commenting that it was 'terrifying to think what effects a book so mixed up of excellence and error might have in this infidel age' (p. 118).

17. Pennington, *Memoirs*.

18. More's suspicion of the cult of feeling places her firmly within the tradition of eighteenth-century evangelicalism. Partly under the influence of the Romantic movement, and partly in response to the growing intellectual threats to faith posed by biblical criticism and scientific thought, an emphasis on the importance of the emotions became more characteristic of nineteenth-century evangelicalism. The difference between the two periods is obscured by describing the eighteenth-century evangelical revival as purely a reaction against the aridities of rationalism and Latitudinarianism.

19. M. G. Jones, *The Charity School Movement* (Cambridge, CUP, 1938), p. 6. Perry, in *The Celebrated Mary Astell*, p. 235, concludes that 'The participation of large numbers of women in planning and managing these schools was also revolutionary, in as much as it was the first time that women, on such a scale, were involved in the work of the church.'

20. Perry, *The Celebrated Mary Astell*, p. 239.

21. D. Robson, 'Some Aspects of Education in Cheshire in the Eighteenth Century', *Chetham Society*, vol. 13, 3rd Series (1966), pp. 117–157.

22. Jones, *The Charity School Movement*, p. 64.

23. Jones, *The Charity School Movement*, p. 100.

24. Jones, *The Charity School Movement*, pp. 99–107.

25. Jones, *The Charity School Movement*, p. 75.

26. Quoted in B. Rodgers, *Cloak of Charity: Studies in Eighteenth-Century Philanthropy* (London, Methuen, 1949), pp. 12–13.

27. D. F. Bond (ed.), *The Spectator* (5 vols, Oxford, OUP, 1965), vol. 3, p. 108.

28. In his *Religion and Respectability: Sunday Schools and Working Class Culture 1780–1850* (New Haven, Yale UP, 1976), Walter Laquer claims that Sunday schools were often attended, staffed, and run entirely by the working class, and should be seen as part of popular culture rather than as a hegemonic imposition upon it – though he does not deny the importance of social control as a motive in the eighteenth century. In his more recent *The Rise and Development of the Sunday School Movement in England 1780–1980* (Nuffield, Surrey, National Christian Education Council, 1986), Philip Cliff argues that Laquer uses the words 'working class' too loosely, and doubts whether the teachers and organizers of Sunday schools ever really came from the same social stratum as their pupils.

29. Cliff, *The Rise and Development of the Sunday School Movement*, p. 22.

30. For the details of her life, see *Some Account of the Life and Writings of Mrs Trimmer, with Original Letters and Meditations and Prayers, selected from her Journal* (2 vols, London, Rivingtons, 1814).

31. S. Trimmer, *The Oeconomy of Charity; Or, an Address to Ladies Concerning Sunday Schools* (London, T. Longman, 1787), pp. 24–26.

32. Trimmer, *Oeconomy*, p. 43.

33. Trimmer, *Oeconomy*, p. 23.

34. Trimmer, *Oeconomy*, pp. 132–133.

35. W. Roberts, *Memoirs of the Life of Mrs Hannah More* (2 vols, London, Seeley & Burnside, 1836), vol. 1, p. 450.

36. Roberts, *Memoirs*, pp. 489–490.

37. Roberts, *Memoirs*, pp. 491–492.

38. Roberts, *Memoirs*, p. 552.

39. *Some Account of the Life and Writings of Mrs Trimmer*, vol. 1, p. 50.

40. *Some Account of the Life and Writings of Mrs Trimmer*, vol. 1, p. 54.

41. M. Hopkins, *Hannah More and Her Circle* (New York, Longmans Green, 1947), pp. 205, 211–213. Hopkins's biography tends to the adulatory, concluding that in their educational work 'the More sisters helped raise the standards of living, of techniques, of ethics, and of grace, in generations then unborn' (p. 220).

42. H. More, 'The Shepherd of Salisbury Plain', in *Stories for the Middle Ranks of Society and Tales for the Common People* (2 vols, London, T. Cadell & W. Davies, 1818), vol. 2, pp. 1–68.

43. Quoted in A. Smith, 'Popular Religion', *Past and Present*, vol. 40 (1968), p. 182.

44. J. Ayres (ed.), *Paupers and Pig Killers. The Diary of William Holland, A Somerset Parson, 1799–1818* (Harmondsworth, Penguin Books, 1986), pp. 23, 27. The following year was much the same: while 'a vast number of the poor of the parish came for boiling pease which were distributed among them' on Christmas Eve, the following day 28 received the sacrament (pp. 53–54).

45. Jones, *The Charity School Movement*, p. 64.

46. Quoted in F. C. Mather, 'Georgian Churchmanship Reconsidered: Some Variations in Anglican Public Worship 1714–1830', *Journal of Ecclesiastical History*, vol. 36 (1985), p. 273.

47. For the period before 1700, the classic work is K. Thomas, *Religion and the Decline of Magic* (Weidenfeld & Nicolson, 1971), while the nineteenth century has been explored by J. Obelkevich, in *Religion and Rural Society: South Lindsey 1825–1875* (Oxford, Clarendon Press, 1976). Popular religious beliefs in the eighteenth century have been less studied, but see A. Smith, *The Established Church and Popular Religion 1750–1850* (London, Longman, 1971), and R. Bushaway, *Ceremony and Community in England 1700–1800* (London, Junction Books, 1982).

48. G. Gomme, *The Gentleman's Magazine Library: Being a Classified Collection of the Chief Contents of the Gentleman's Magazine from 1731 to 1868. Popular Superstitions* (Boston, Houghton, Mifflin & Co., 1885), p. 129.

49. Jane Wenham's case is discussed by P. Guskin in 'The Context of Witchcraft: The Case of Jane Wenham (1712)', *Eighteenth-Century Studies*, vol. 15 (1981–1982), pp. 48–71. As Guskin points out, the trial did not straightforwardly involve a division between educated and popular culture, since two of those who testified against Wenham were clergymen. This was still the thought world of Newton, who uneasily held together a belief in scientific law and occult powers. As the century wore on, the growth of a more scientific and materialistic view of the world widened the gap between popular and elite culture, though religion, particularly in its popular

revivalist forms, remained uneasily suspended between the two.

50. Gomme, *The Gentleman's Magazine Library . . . Popular Superstitions*, pp. 248–250.

51. G. Gomme, *The Gentleman's Magazine Library: Being a Classified Collection of the Chief Contents of the Gentleman's Magazine from 1731 to 1868. Manners and Customs* (London, Elliot Stock, 1883), pp. 17–18, 20–21.

52. Smith, 'Popular Religion', p. 183; C. Burne (ed.), *Shropshire Folk-Lore, A Sheaf of Gleanings* (London, Turner & Co., 1883), p. 286.

53. J. Beresford (ed.), *The Diary of a Country Parson: The Diary of the Reverend James Woodforde 1758–1781* (5 vols, London, OUP, 1924–1931), vol. 1, pp. 28, 36.

54. Leviticus 12.4 enjoined that after the birth of a child, a woman 'shall touch no hallowed thing, nor come into the sanctuary, until the days of her purifying be fulfilled'.

55. W. Coster, 'Purity, Profanity, and Puritanism: The Churching of Women, 1500–1700', in W. J. Sheils and D. Wood (eds), *Women in the Church*, Studies in Church History 27 (Oxford, Basil Blackwell, 1990), pp. 377–387.

56. G. Stanhope, *A Paraphrase and Comment upon the Epistles and Gospels, Appointed to be used in the Church of England on all Sundays and Holy-Days throughout the Year* (4 vols, London, 7th edn, 1751), vol. 4, p. 144.

57. Burne (ed.), *Shropshire Folk-Lore*, p. 286. J. Lewis, in *In the Family Way: Childbearing in the British Aristocracy, 1760–1860* (New Brunswick, New Jersey, Rutgers UP, 1986), pp. 200–202, provides evidence that aristocratic women did regard churching as a means of expressing gratitude to God, though she points out that they increasingly demanded that the ceremony be performed at home rather than in church.

58. L. G. Mitchell (ed.), *The Purefoy Letters* (London, Sidgwick & Jackson, 1973), p. 5.

59. Gomme, *The Gentleman's Magazine Library . . . Manners and Customs*, p. 18.

60. Beresford (ed.), *The Diary of a Country Parson*, vol. 5, p. 316.

61. For the attack on popular pastimes, see R. Malcolm, *Popular Recreations in English Society 1700–1850* (Cambridge, CUP, 1973).

62. G. C. B. Davies, *The Early Cornish Evangelicals 1735–1760* (London, SPCK, 1951), pp. 68–69.

63. Bushaway, *Ceremony and Community*, pp. 172–176. Burne, in *Shropshire Folk-Lore*, p. 336, records that because of objections to the custom, 'The heaving of men by women was already in my old Ludlow informant's youth, confined to servants and others of the poorer classes.' Whether these perceptions of the significance of popular rituals were accurate is another matter. Historians and anthropologists have stressed that rituals of status reversal and carnival might embody elements of social protest, but could also be ways of

releasing social tension and of acknowledging the normality of the everyday social order even by its abnormal suspension in moments of ritual play. For this theme, see Bushaway, *Ceremony and Community*, pp. 167-171, and S. Kaplan (ed.), *Understanding Popular Culture: Europe from the Middle Ages to the Nineteenth Century* (Berlin, Mouton Publishers, 1984), pp. 10-11.

64. A. Warne, *Church and Society in Eighteenth-Century Devon* (Newton Abbot, David & Charles, 1969), p. 77. The charge was known as ante-nuptial fornication when couples married after the offence, and the penance was carried out less humiliatingly in private before the minister and churchwardens in normal clothes – and this, in any case, ceased to be a presentable offence after 1787 (p. 79).

65. Beresford (ed.), *The Diary of a Country Parson*, vol. 2, p. 297. Woodforde was critical of enforced marriages, though the system provided a means of ensuring financial support for women and children, and compares not unfavourably with recent government attempts to make social security payments for unmarried mothers dependent on their naming the father. The position of unmarried women deteriorated in the nineteenth century when bastardy and poor relief were effectively separated in 1844, and the responsibility of seeking redress from the father was laid upon the woman (p. 298).

66. L. Davidoff, 'The Family in Britain', in F. M. L. Thompson (ed.), *The Cambridge Social History of Britain 1750-1950* (3 vols, Cambridge, CUP, 1990), vol. 2, p. 91.

67. A. G. Crosby (ed.), 'The Family Records of Benjamin Shaw Mechanic of Dent, Dolphinholme and Preston, 1772-1841', *The Record Society of Lancashire and Cheshire*, vol. 130 (1991), provides a detailed insight into the attitudes to sexuality of a chapel-going mill worker and his family. Illegitimacy and sexual freedom were commonplace among the young and unmarried, and provoked no moral condemnation, while Shaw's own values are evident from his attitude towards one of his wife's brothers: 'It is indicative of his concept of "respectability", and his view that financial rectitude was of far greater moral importance than sexual restraint that the youngest son, James Leeming could be described in the same sentence as the father of a bastard child and as the most respectable man of any of the younger Brother's' (pp. xlii-xliii).

68. Astell's works, which were all published in 1704, were *Moderation Truly Stated*; *A Fair Way with the Dissenters and their Patrons*; and *An Impartial Enquiry into the Causes of Rebellion and Civil War in this Kingdom*. For a discussion of their content and context, see Hill (ed.), *The First English Feminist*, pp. 43-49.

69. M. Astell, *The Christian Religion As Professed by a Daughter of the Church of England* (London, R. Wilkin, 1705), p. 297.

70. A. T. Hart, *The Eighteenth Century Country Parson* (Shrewsbury, Wilding & Son, 1955), p. 92.

71. A. Oakley, in *The Sociology of Housework* (Oxford, Basil Blackwell, 1985),

pp. 21–28, discusses the reasons for this bias in the work of academic sociologists.

72. M. Hennell, *John Venn and the Clapham Sect* (London, Lutterworth Press, 1958), p. 25.

73. Lady Llanover (ed.), *The Autobiography and Correspondence of Mary Granville Mrs. Delany* (London, Richard Bentley, 1861), pp. 371–372.

74. *The Publications of the Surtees Society*, vol. 188 (1973), pp. 53, 90.

75. D. Gibson (ed.), *A Parson in the Vale of the White Horse: George Woodward's Letters from East Hendred, 1753–1761* (Gloucester, Alan Sutton, 1982), pp. 25, 62.

76. Perry, *The Celebrated Mary Astell*, pp. 258–261.

77. H. Rack, *Reasonable Enthusiast: John Wesley and the Rise of Methodism* (London, Epworth Press, 2nd edn, 1992), pp. 282–285.

78. Rack, *Reasonable Enthusiast*, pp. 53–54.

79. Quoted in P. Chilcote, *John Wesley and the Women Preachers of Early Methodism* (Metuchen, New Jersey, Scarecrow Press, 1991), p. 19.

80. For the history of the late seventeenth-century Anglican religious revival, see E. Duffy, 'Primitive Christianity Revived; Religious Renewal in Augustan England', in Derek Baker (ed.), *Renaissance and Renewal in Christian History*, Studies in Church History 14 (Oxford, Basil Blackwell, 1977), pp. 287–300; and T. Isaacs, 'The Anglican Hierarchy and the Reformation of Manners 1688–1738', *Journal of Ecclesiastical History*, vol. 33 (1982), pp. 391–411.

81. F. Bullock, *Voluntary Religious Societies 1520–1799* (St Leonards-on-Sea, Budd & Gillat, 1963), p. 157.

82. Bullock, *Voluntary Religious Societies*, pp. 146–147.

83. Bullock, *Voluntary Religious Societies*, pp. 205–222.

84. Chilcote, *John Wesley*, p. 60.

85. Chilcote, *John Wesley*, p. 72.

86. Chilcote, *John Wesley*, p. 71.

87. Quoted in E. Brown, *Women of Mr Wesley's Methodism* (New York, Edwin Mellen Press, 1983), p. 48.

88. Brown, *Women of Mr Wesley's Methodism*, p. 26.

89. Brown, *Women of Mr Wesley's Methodism*, pp. 26–30.

90. Rack, *Reasonable Enthusiast*, p. 244.

91. J. Field-Bibb, *Women Towards Priesthood: Ministerial Politics and Feminist Praxis* (Cambridge, CUP, 1991), p. 14.

92. Field-Bibb, *Women Towards Priesthood*, p. 23.

93. Quoted in A. Armstrong, *The Church of England, the Methodists and Society 1700-1850* (London, University of London Press, 1973), p. 67.

94. G. Malmgreen, 'Domestic Discords: Women and the Family in East Cheshire Methodism, 1750-1830', in J. Obelkevich *et al.* (eds), *Disciplines of Faith: Studies in Religion, Politics and Patriarchy* (London, Routledge & Kegan Paul, 1987), pp. 55-70.

95. Malmgreen, 'Domestic Discords', p. 65.

96. N. Lancaster, *Methodism Triumphant, or the Decisive Battle between the Old Serpent and the Modern Saint* (London, J. Wilkie, 1767), pp. 92-95.

97. J. Lackington, *Memoirs of the first forty-five years of the life of James Lackington* (London, 2nd edn, 1792), p. 235. For other examples of similar charges, see A. Lyles, *Methodism Mocked: The Satiric Reaction to Methodism in the Eighteenth Century* (London, Epworth Press, 1960), pp. 97-98.

98. Chilcote, *John Wesley*, pp. 8, 29.

99. For eighteenth-century Quaker women preachers, see S. Wright, 'Quakerism and its Implications for Quaker Women: The Women Itinerant Ministers of York Meeting, 1780-1840', in Sheils and Wood (eds), *Women in the Church*, pp. 403-414. Wright also points out that there were limits to the equality of men and women within Quakerism, since the Men's Meeting, from which women were excluded, exercised all real power over the Society's property and finances (p. 413).

100. G. Lavington, *The Enthusiasm of Methodists and Papists Compar'd* (London, J. & P. Knapton, 1749), pp. 126, 193. The question of ordination was of course to assume greater importance in the gradual separation of Methodism from Anglicanism, which became formalized in the 1795 Plan of Pacification, four years after Wesley's death. In the debates of the 1750s, Wesley had declared it to be lawful but inexpedient for Methodism to separate from the Church of England, but his ordination of Methodist preachers to serve in America in 1784 has been seen as an important step along the road to establishing an independent Methodist identity.

101. Rack, *Reasonable Enthusiast*, p. 276.

102. M. Pennington (ed.), *A Series of Letters between Elizabeth Carter and Miss Catherine Talbot from the Year 1741 to 1770* (4 vols, London, 1809), vol. 3, p. 374.

103. Jane Austen's religious beliefs have been much discussed, and particularly the question of how far *Mansfield Park* was influenced by evangelicalism. For an overview of this subject, see D. Monaghan, 'Mansfield Park and Evangelicalism: A Reassessment', *Nineteenth Century Fiction*, vol. 33 (1978-1979), pp. 215-230. In his *Jane Austen. Real and Imagined Worlds* (New Haven, Yale UP, 1991), Oliver MacDonagh agrees with Monaghan in seeing Austen as a representative of Anglicanism as 'a median religion' (p. 14).

104. J. Gregory, *A Father's Legacy to His Daughter* (Dublin, Thomas Ewing,

1774), p. 7.

105. *The Gentleman's Magazine*, vol. 58, no. 2 (1780), pp. 862–864.

106. Perry, *The Celebrated Mary Astell*, p. 61.

107. E. Gray, *Papers and Diaries of a York Family 1764–1839* (London, Sheldon Press, 1927).

108. *Some Account of the Life and Writings of Mrs Trimmer*, p. 133.

109. Gray, *Papers and Diaries*, p. 81.

110. *Some Account of the Life and Writings of Mrs Trimmer*, p. 107.

111. N. Cott, 'Passionless: An Interpretation of Victorian Sexual Ideology, 1790–1850', *Signs*, vol. 4 (1978), pp. 219–252; P. Spacks, 'Ever'y Woman is at Heart a Rake', *Eighteenth-Century Studies*, vol. 8 (1974–1975), pp. 27–46.

112. D. Hempton and M. Hill, *Evangelical Protestantism in Ulster Society 1740–1890* (London, Routledge, 1992), pp. 129–142.

113. *Some Account of the Life and Writings of Mrs Trimmer*, p. 20.

CHAPTER THREE

Anglican Theologies of Womanhood in the Victorian and Edwardian Church: Sources and Themes

The development of an Anglican theology of gender relations in the nineteenth century was intimately connected with the economic and social changes that had begun in the previous century, but whose full impact was only felt in the Victorian period. The Church of England was part of an increasingly powerful and self-confident middle-class world, whose definition of respectability was based upon a clear separation between the spheres of work and domesticity, and upon its ability to sustain a lifestyle in which women were above the necessity of undertaking paid employment – a crucial distinction between 'ladies', and the 'women' upon whom they often depended for domestic labour.

This is not to say that theological conviction was not a significant variable in church attitudes. There were, for example, sharp differences between Evangelicals and Broad Churchmen on the one hand, and Anglo-Catholics on the other, over such issues as priestly celibacy and the creation of female religious orders. Nevertheless, the social context in which such theologizing was undertaken, if not determinative, exerted a powerful influence on its outcome. This is evident, for example, in the fact that even in sections of the Church less wedded to traditional ideas of biblical inspiration that seemed to reinforce the notion of women's subordination, beliefs about the social roles of men and women in society were not significantly different nor more radical.

In one other important respect, the experience of all sections of the Church – Evangelical, Liberal or Anglo-Catholic – was the same: they all advocated and witnessed the increasing involvement of women in church life. However, what has been called the feminization of the Church had important implications for its theology, and the tensions and ambiguities that this process created reveal a great deal about the centrality of gender in church doctrine and practice.

Evangelicalism and the theology of true womanhood

As we have seen, by the end of the eighteenth century William Wilberforce had outlined an evangelical theology of Christian femininity that saw women as endowed with particular qualities of devotion and self-sacrifice, qualities that found their natural sphere of operation in homemaking and motherhood. This also implied a rigid and clearly defined view of male and female gender attributes, such that the division of labour between the sexes was grounded not only in Scripture, but also in the divine ordering of nature. According to this view, men and women were different, but complementary. As *The Christian Observer*, the leading Evangelical journal of the period, put it:

> One fact we hold to be indisputable, that our wise Creator purposed man and woman to hold different positions in the universe wherein he placed them. The knowledge of the difference in their physical structure, which we have acquired through science, proves incontestably man was created for strength, woman for beauty, whether of body or mind: man's life is of necessity active, woman's quiescent.[1]

The emphasis on women's greater religiosity still sat rather uneasily beside the belief in her original sin and disobedience, which explained and justified her subjection to male authority – a doctrine that could also be derived from the Genesis account of woman's secondary creation from Adam's rib. Evangelicals believed that such a theology was clearly to be found in Scripture, particularly in the opening chapters of Genesis and in St Paul's discussion of their implications in 1 Corinthians 11 and 1 Timothy 2. Thus the Rev. Thomas Scott, in his widely read biblical commentary, argued that 'the original creation of the man, and then the woman; and the entrance of sin by the woman, who "being deceived was first in the transgression" concur in showing the reasonableness of that subjection, humility, and teachableness, prescribed in Scripture to the woman'.[2] Such contradictory images of women, as being potentially more sinful than men, and at the same time potentially more pure, were often resolved by making an absolute distinction between the chaste, innocent, and passionless middle-class Christian woman, and the sexually depraved and voracious fallen woman of the streets.

Scripture also (in Ephesians 5.22-24) enjoined subordination upon women within marriage, as *The Christian Lady's Magazine* repeatedly pointed out, though here too biblical warrant and woman's innate attributes were largely, if not entirely, mutually reinforcing in their effects, since 'the female mind . . . is so constituted, as to render this subjection comparatively easy to some; and the warmth and disinterestedness of a woman's affection will often change the performance of this trying duty into a delightful enjoyment'.[3]

The subordination of women to men in marriage also had wider implications for the ordering of society. Reviewing an anonymous pamphlet written in 1866 by a woman – entitled *A Few Thoughts on Woman's Rights* – *The Christian Observer* commented that the work was in a tradition that derived from Mary Wollstonecraft's plea for sexual equality, but that from a Christian viewpoint it was fatally flawed:

Now this lady entirely forgets an eternal truth, which, since the world's creation, has never with the slightest degree of success been once evaded, – 'Thy desire shall be to thy husband, and he shall rule over thee.' Till this text shall be removed from Scripture, it is pure folly to talk about the equality of the sexes.[4]

John Stuart Mill's *Essay on the Subjection of Women*, with its claim that the supposedly innate female characteristics to which upholders of the doctrine of Christian femininity appealed were in fact artificially created by society, and his support for female suffrage, predictably received 'an emphatic and uncompromising negative' in the pages of *The Christian Observer*. In this instance, the case was grounded on the imagery of Ephesians 5, which likened the relationship between man and wife to that of Christ and his Church. The context of Mill's unwelcome ideas was the beginnings of an organized women's movement that campaigned not only for the vote, but for a Married Women's Property Act giving women some control over their income within marriage. Far from welcoming such ideas, *The Christian Observer* argued that women would do better if legal and social discrimination were maintained, since they otherwise stood to lose 'the privileges which chivalry and courtesy have, in consequence of those disabilities, accorded to women'.[5]

Evangelical theology was, then, in a number of important respects, conservative and limiting in its definitions of femininity and of women's role in society. However, it also provided a powerful justification for Christian women's involvement in social reform and philanthropy as an appropriate extension of their maternal and spiritual tasks into the public realm. This case was all the more irresistible, since it was based upon impeccably conservative premises that seemed to confirm rather than confront contemporary expectations about gender. As one writer in *The Christian Observer* enthusiastically proclaimed:

By maintaining the most kindly intercourse with the poor, by alleviating sorrow beyond the little circle of the home, by guiding the work of education, by using life for its highest and most beneficent purposes, by self-dedication to God, by labours in the mission field as well as in their own country, women are employing an influence scarcely acknowledged until we see it in detail, but the aggregate of which entitles it, when comprehensively surveyed to rank amongst the highest human agencies which a merciful God is blessing to the benefit of men's souls and bodies.[6]

Faced with a movement that was so contradictory in its results, historians have tended to make varying assessments of its impact upon women's lives, and such assessments also tend to reflect their overall degree of sympathy towards religious belief. Thus in his history of evangelicalism, David Bebbington supports the view that 'Evangelical religion, despite its emphasis on the domestic role of women, was more important than feminism in enlarging their sphere during the nineteenth century.' This argument fails to attach sufficient weight to the power of evangelical theology in the construction of limiting gender stereotypes for both men and women, or stress sufficiently the difficulties created for women by a spirituality that constantly emphasized the desirability of feminine submission, passivity, and self-abnegation.[7] On the other hand, Barbara Taylor, in her study of nineteenth-century socialism and feminism, tends to see any liberating consequences of evangelical religion as unintended, and while she admits that claims about women's regenerating mission within society could be used to make feminist demands, 'in general the effect was to detach sexual egalitarianism from the new middle-class canons of respectability'.[8]

What is interesting about both these approaches is that they accept definitions of feminism that derive from a secular and liberal equal rights tradition, while it might be more helpful to see a pluriformity of feminist initiatives and ideologies within the nineteenth-century women's movement, of which a genuinely Christian feminism was one. As Olive Banks has suggested, evangelicalism was a significant factor in the development of feminist consciousness: conservative in that it reinforced rather than challenged traditional constructions of femininity and domesticity, but also radical in that it sought to bring feminine influence and activity into important areas of public life.[9]

Anglo-Catholicism

The Anglo-Catholic wing of the Church, which grew out of the Oxford Movement of the 1830s, shared many of the theological assumptions of Evangelicalism – particularly its view of biblical inspiration and authority. Thus both wings of the Church could make common cause in 1860 against the liberal theology of *Essays and Reviews*, with its call to treat the Scriptures like any other book, and the doubts that it cast upon the doctrine of the eternal torment of the wicked. Anglo-Catholics therefore appealed to the same exegesis of Scripture as Evangelicals in seeking to understand and expound the Christian doctrine of womanhood. In his commentary on 1 Timothy, Pusey's disciple and biographer H. P. Liddon took exception to a passage in Mill's *Essay on the Subjection of Women* that suggested the Apostle's acceptance of slavery was only one example of the way in which he was influenced by the society of his day; but, as with Evangelical expositions of Scripture, what purported to be plain readings of its meaning were in fact interpretations that were framed and reinforced by contemporary gender expectations. For example, in discussing Eve's role in the Fall, Liddon felt that 'the experience of all ages that woman is more easily led away than man, is warranted by what is said of the first representative of the sex'.[10] The literal acceptance of Genesis was also important in the thinking of another prominent Anglo-Catholic, the novelist Charlotte Yonge, who wrote that she had 'no hesitation in declaring my full belief in the inferiority of woman, nor that she brought it upon herself', since 'it was the woman who was first to fail, and to draw her husband into the same transgression'.[11]

Yet if Anglo-Catholicism shared the conservative Evangelical vision of Christian femininity in certain respects, in others its theology affected women in ways that Evangelicals found unacceptable. This was true of the High Church enthusiasm for sisterhoods and priestly celibacy, both of which seemed to challenge the Victorian belief in marriage and family life as the highest form of Christian vocation. The practice of auricular confession was also seen not only as Popish and prurient, but as an insidious attack upon patriarchal authority within the family. According to Bishop Wilberforce, the confessional superseded 'God's appointment of intimacy between husband and wife, father and children';[12] while to the Rev. S. A. Walker, writing in 1877, it was a cause for astonishment 'that fathers and husbands have tolerated for an hour a system by which the purity of their wives and daughters is so grossly outraged, and even the secrets of their own domestic life are extracted from the female members of their family under the moral rack of the Confessional'.[13] As in Catholic Europe, the priest was seen as a rival focus of authority to the male head of the household, a perception that helped to stir up anti-clericalism.[14]

The Anglo-Catholic devotion to the Blessed Virgin Mary also aroused Protestant ire. Historians of the sixteenth century have sometimes seen the loss for women of access to the example of female piety in the lives of the saints and of Mary as contributing to the patriarchalism of a Protestantism that offered its adherents only male images of the divine; but Anglo-Catholic devotion to Mary in the nineteenth century served only to reinforce the conservative ideals of femininity and of woman's domestic vocation. In a sermon preached at St Paul's Cathedral, H. P. Liddon warned women against their so-called new friends who were encouraging them to compete with men, whereas they were much better advised to look to the Virgin Mary – and in particular to her 'sweetness, her grace, her modesty, which so admirably adorn her rank'.[15] According to the Honourable Lady Acland, 'the Bible gives us two contrasted pictures of women – Eve, the natural woman, governed by impulse, self-indulgent and inquisitive; and Mary, the spiritual woman, pure, unselfish, patient, humble'. Following this model was, she believed, 'the secret of a woman's power – sympathy, the subtle mixture of imagination and experience, which makes her realise the worries, ambitions, interests, hopes, disappointments of her husband and her children, her friends and her servants'.[16] Here, as in other aspects of its thought and practice, the feminization of Anglo-Catholicism was not so much a contribution to Victorian feminism, but rather an alternative to it.[17]

Liberal theological attitudes

It is by no means easy to characterize Victorian Anglican theological liberalism as a coherent movement. The term 'Broad Church' was applied to a wide range of thinkers that included Coleridge, Dr Arnold, and F. D. Maurice, and the term 'liberalism' was later in the century extended still further to include the new school of biblical criticism, and thinkers such as Matthew Arnold whose theological opinions were far from those of Maurice.[18] While theological liberals were less wedded than Evangelicals or Anglo-Catholics to a biblical fundamentalism that reinforced patriarchal attitudes within the Church, they often shared many of the traditional expectations about gender that were common to the middle class of their time. Thus F. D. Maurice, who lost his chair at King's College, London, in 1853 for rejecting the doctrine of the eternal punishment of the wicked, and was the moving spirit behind the creation of Queen's College for women in 1848, held in other respects to the conventional view that women's highest gifts were best exercised in motherhood; and he sharply rejected claims for women's independence as failing to appreciate the complementarity of the sexes.[19]

Another supporter of women's higher education, and even more of a *bête noire* of conservatives than Maurice, was Benjamin Jowett, contributor to *Essays and Reviews* and Master of Balliol College, Oxford. Yet Jowett's views were far from being free of class and gender assumptions, as when he wrote to Florence Nightingale that 'for the mass of women I doubt whether any change in the subjects of Education would do any good – a second rate mind intellectualized and crammed with information is very useless and disagreeable. . . . With women even more than men it seems absolutely necessary that education should bear some proportion to original power.'[20]

This is not to suggest that the impact of biblical critical methods in the second half of the century was irrelevant to the debate about the nature of Christian womanhood. For instance, in an article with the somewhat incongruous title 'Women's Suffrage and the Teaching of St Paul', in *The Contemporary Review* for May 1896, the Honourable and Rev. E. Lyttleton claimed that Christians no longer accepted the literalist view of Scripture, neatly characterizing its proponents as 'professing a literal adherence to the New Testament injunctions while, at the same time, ignoring some of them without knowing why'.[21] Lyttleton was a good example of the way in which, through the exertions of Westcott and Hort, English churchmen had accepted German biblical critical methods, but had warded off their more radical and threatening implications. He was therefore in no doubt that while modern research, by placing some of the apostolic teaching in its true historical setting, had invested 'certain precepts with more or less authority than others', it had also been the means of 'establishing on an even firmer basis than ever the incomparable universality of all the teaching of our Lord'. This meant that in St Paul's case his teaching about women 'was not only tinged but saturated with Jewish ideas', and that 'his precepts on the relation of the sexes are not necessarily authoritative for us to-day'.[22]

Yet Lyttleton's attitude to women's emancipation was just as much coloured by contemporary assumptions as the Evangelical and Anglo-Catholic fundamentalists whom he castigated. St Paul, it appeared, was not in fact wrong to stress that while man was made in God's image, woman was made in man's, since translated into plain language this was meant to illustrate the truth that 'something of a creative power belongs to one sex and is wanting in the other; that whereas the faculty of making a beginning which we call genius has in all ages and among all the progressive nations of the earth been frequently shown by men, women's powers are those of receiving life and storing it; and that this broad distinction is an ordinance of Nature, and applies not only to physical but to mental attributes'. He was, however, prepared to admit that women had not had the opportunities granted to men, and that the past was no guide to the future; and even if women's intellectual inferiority to men's did turn out to be permanent, this was not a justification for denying them the vote.[23] Lyttleton's critical method might be anathema to *The Christian Observer*, but much of his thinking about gender was not that dissimilar.

The feminization of the Victorian Church?

A number of historians of American religion have commented on the way in which women became from the eighteenth century onwards, if not earlier, the mainstay of the worship and philanthropic enterprise of modern Protestantism, and on the implications that this had for the formulation of Christian theology. According to Ann Douglas, the feminization of the Church was part of a process of economic and intellectual change that resulted in the marginalization of both the clergy and women from the economic and political centres of power, and about which the former were bound to feel highly ambivalent.[24] It also resulted in significant changes in the Church's theology and spirituality, with a greater emphasis on the more gentle, 'feminine' aspects of the Godhead and on the domestic and private aspects of religiosity.

This approach can also help to illuminate the history of Victorian Anglicanism, though one must be wary of applying a general sociological formulation too sweepingly to particular historical contexts and institutions. For one thing, the Church of England endeavoured to maintain a far greater hold on the public sphere than was possible for American denominations, a task that was made easier by its close identification with the upsurge in imperialist sentiment. An emphasis upon the feminization of Christian belief and practice can also oversimplify a process of theological negotiation and redefinition that was bound to be both complex and contradictory given the ideologically polarized definitions of gender in existence in nineteenth-century society.

Certainly in England, as elsewhere, women seized the opportunities afforded by the belief in the socially regenerative power of their unique religious and maternal attributes to undertake a wide range of philanthropic activities; this ranged from the education of children to the reclamation of prostitutes. At the same time, it became a commonplace that the Church's pews were filled not by men but by women. The *Daily News* survey of religious attendance in London during the period from November 1902 to November 1903 gave some substance to this claim. In West London, women formed 66 per cent of those attending morning and evening worship, while the figure for the Church of England was 69 per cent; however, women made up only 58 per cent of the adult population. In East London, which was on the whole much poorer, overall attendances were lower, but there were still significant differences between the sexes; in Shoreditch, for example, male attendances were estimated to be one in twenty-three of the population in the morning and one in nineteen in the evening, while for women the comparable figures were one in nineteen and one in ten.[25] William Booth's *Life and Labour of the People in London* reached a similar conclusion, noting that 'throughout London the female sex forms the mainstay of every religious assembly of whatever class'.[26]

However, given the patriarchal structure of the Anglican Church, and the very clear definitions of gender with which the Church operated, the feminization of the Victorian Church and its theology involved considerable tension and ambiguity. In a society that accepted that leadership, rationality, and creativity in the public domain were male attributes, too close an association of the Church with the feminine implied its marginalization. In his *Directorium Pastorale*, a handbook for the clergy, the Rev. John Blunt warned of the dangers of 'the too common idea that a clergyman is principally concerned with the charge of women and children', and he went on:

It should, therefore, be recognised as a first principle of parochial action, that men are by the laws of Providence the leaders of the society in which they live; and that if they are not gained, very little real work has been done. The susceptible mind of the weaker sex is naturally open to personal influence, but let it be also remembered that the personal influence of the clergyman is not the power of religion. As a rule, the substantial tone of a family, whatever appearances may be, will follow the tone of its head.[27]

Women's religiosity and large-scale involvement in church work also had implications for the way in which Christ's nature was understood. The nineteenth century saw a growing interest in the quest for the historical Jesus, and the portrayal of his humanity was attempted in a number of biographical lives. But if Jesus was the perfect pattern of humanity for both men and women, how were questions of gender to be negotiated in depicting him? In a sermon preached at St James's, Paddington, to the Church of England Zenana Missionary Society in 1885, which was one of the most active of the women's organizations created in the nineteenth century, the Archbishop of Dublin considered Christ's humanity in the context of the growing contemporary demand for women's rights:

But when Christ stood on the Mount of Beatitudes and singled out for His benediction certain special graces of the Christian life whom did He then describe as blessed? The strong, the brave, the just, the learned, the wise? No! His first blessing was for the poor in spirit, the mourners, the meek, the pure, the peace-makers, the down-trodden, and the persecuted. . . . Here was a consecration, an enthronisation [sic], of Humility, of Mercy, of Sympathy, of Purity, of Gentleness, of Resignation, as deserving of a place beside, if not above, the sterner virtues of a former code. Here, in

85

other words, was manifested for the first time, in the development of the Divine purposes, a recognition such as had never been vouchsafed, of those heavenly graces which may be said to form the distinctive glory of Womanhood.[28]

In Christ, he went on, was to be found 'a mysterious union of those distinctive qualities of manly and womanly excellence respectively', the former evinced by the way in which he put to flight 'by one glance the craven recreants who came to seize Him in Gethsemane', the latter at the grave of Lazarus where 'the loving, tender heart gives way and tears of woman-like sympathy unrestrainedly flow forth'.[29] As a staunch Protestant, the Archbishop also attached particular importance to the need for women to identify with Christ, and not – as in Roman Catholicism – with the Virgin Mary, which had led, in his view, to a form of worship directed towards a 'one-sided ideal of womanly tenderness uncombined with manly strength' – the result being that 'the faith of too many a woman in that Church has degenerated into an effeminate and sentimental emotionalism, and the faith of too many a man, finding nothing manly whereon to lean has been hopelessly lost'.[30]

However, in a society that differentiated so sharply between masculinity and femininity, the kind of balance that the Archbishop tried to strike was not that easy to maintain. The sturdy muscular Christianity popularized by Charles Kingsley, and by Thomas Hughes in *Tom Brown's Schooldays* and *Tom Brown at Oxford*, attempted to tailor the Christian ethic to the values of a competitive and militaristic society, but it sat uneasily beside the bi-polar image of Christ favoured by the Archbishop. Thus the writer of *Christian Manliness: A Book of Examples and Principles for Young Men*, published by the Religious Tract Society, condemned the popular misconception that 'feebleness is characteristic of the religious man', and bemoaned the fact that '"fit for woman and children and soft men", is the idea of religion which has too generally prevailed, and which, unhappily, many Christians have helped to justify'. The antidote to such erroneous views was an appreciation of Christ's true manly nature, whereas 'too often we leave out of sight the element of strength in his character, and associate with our idea of him only the gentler aspects of humanity'.[31] F. D. Maurice was similarly concerned to counteract 'the passive or feminine character which has often been ascribed to the Sermon on the Mount'.[32]

The attempted reconciliation of such apparently contradictory gender expectations lay in the concept of chivalry, that interplay of masculine strength and feminine weakness that reinforced both. Thus Maurice was prepared to acknowledge in Christianity 'a Spirit which makes men feminine, if feminine means courteous, deferential, free from brutal and insolent pretensions but which also gives women manliness, if manliness means the vigour to live for the cause of Humanity and die for it'.[33] In *The Manliness of Christ*, which he published in 1879, Thomas Hughes took a similar line, stressing that 'there must be no flaw or spot on Christ's courage any more than on his wisdom and tenderness and sympathy'.[34] As the author of *Christian Manliness* put it, courtesy was the sign of that true combination of strength and gentleness that made up Christian manhood, and he quoted with approval the dictum that 'A Christian is God Almighty's gentleman.'[35] With leadership in the Church still largely an all-male preserve, and the Godhead portrayed as the epitome of the Victorian gentleman, the feminization of the Church had, to say the least, its limits.[36]

Notes

1. *The Christian Observer* (1865), p. 547.

2. T. Scott, *The Holy Bible; Containing the Old Testament and New Testaments According to the Authorized Version; With Explanatory Notes, Practical Observations, and Copious Marginal References* (6 vols, London, James Nisbet & Co., 1866), vol. 6, n.p.

3. *The Christian Lady's Magazine*, vol. 5 (1836), p. 169.

4. *The Christian Observer* (1866), p. 721.

5. *The Christian Observer* (1869), p. 626.

6. *The Christian Observer* (1859), p. 446.

7. D. Bebbington, *Evangelicalism in Modern Britain. A History from the 1730s to the 1980s* (London, Unwin Hyman, 1989), p. 129.

8. B. Taylor, *Eve and the New Jerusalem: Socialism and Feminism in the Nineteenth Century* (London, Virago Press, 1983).

9. O. Banks, *Faces of Feminism: A Study of Feminism as a Social Movement* (Oxford, Martin Robertson, 1981), pp. 13–27.

10. H. P. Liddon, *Explanatory Analysis of St Paul's First Epistle to Timothy* (Oxford, privately printed, 1877), pp. 12–13. Liddon was at the forefront of clerical opposition to the Victorian women's movement. As his fellow Anglo-Catholic Henry Scott Holland recalled, 'On few subjects was he more

vehement in denunciation than on that of "Women and the Universities". It was one of his surest draws' (H. S. Holland, *Personal Studies* (London, Wells Gardner, Darton & Co., 1905), p. 164).

11. C. Yonge, *Womankind* (London, Walter Smith & Innes, 2nd edn, 1889), p. 1.

12. Quoted in J. Bentley, *Ritualism and Politics in Victorian Britain: The Attempt to Legislate for Belief* (Oxford, OUP, 1978), p. 31.

13. Quoted in J. S. Reed, '"A Female Movement": The Feminization of Nineteenth-Century Anglo-Catholicism', *Anglican and Episcopal History*, vol. 57 (1988), pp. 199–238.

14. Theodore Zeldin comments that in nineteenth-century France the priest often appeared as 'the great enemy or rival of the husband' (T. Zeldin, *Conflicts in French Society* (London, George Allen & Unwin, 1970), p. 50).

15. H. P. Liddon, *Christmastide in St Paul's, Sermons Bearing Chiefly on the Birth of Our Lord and the End of the Year* (London, Rivingtons, 1889), p. 84.

16. *Report of the Women's Meetings Held in Connection with the Pan-Anglican Congress of 1908* (London, SPCK, 1908), pp. 25–27.

17. Reed, '"A Female Movement"', p. 238.

18. For a brief discussion of the problems of defining liberal religion, see N. Vance, *The Sinews of the Spirit: The Ideal of Christian Manliness in Victorian Literature and Religious Thought* (Cambridge, CUP, 1985), pp. 42–46.

19. F. D. Maurice, *Social Morality: Twenty-One Lectures Delivered in the University of Cambridge* (London, Macmillan, 1869), pp. 61–65.

20. V. Quinn and J. Prest (eds), *Dear Miss Nightingale: A Selection of Benjamin Jowett's Letters to Florence Nightingale 1860–1893* (Oxford, Clarendon Press, 1987), p. 7.

21. E. Lyttleton, 'Woman's Suffrage and the Teaching of St Paul', *Contemporary Review*, vol. 365 (May 1896), pp. 680–691.

22. Lyttleton, 'Woman's Suffrage', pp. 685–686.

23. Lyttleton, 'Woman's Suffrage', pp. 688–689.

24. A. Douglas, *The Feminization of American Culture* (New York, Avon Books, 1977). See also B. Welter, 'The Feminization of American Religion: 1800–1860', in M. Hartman and L. Banner (eds), *Clio's Consciousness Raised: New Perspectives on the History of Women* (New York, Harper & Row, 1974), pp. 137–157, and R. Shiels, 'The Feminization of American Congregationalism 1730–1835', *American Quarterly*, vol. 33 (1981), pp. 46–62. For a discussion of the same theme in nineteenth-century France, see R. Gibson, *A Social History of French Catholicism* (London, Routledge, 1989), pp. 180–190. Gibson sees the Church as 'an essential centre of sociability' (p. 189). Less helpful is B. G. Smith's eloquent but essentialist

assertion that 'The mathematical explanation of life proposed by modern science appeared as a patent fatuity to the visibly bleeding, swelling pained women of the nineteenth century. They preferred theology and the pre-Copernican vision of the universe' (B. G. Smith, *The Ladies of the Leisure Class: The Bourgeoises of Northern France in the Nineteenth Century* (Princeton, New Jersey, Princeton UP, 1981), pp. 95–96).

25. R. Mudie-Smith, *The Religious Life of London* (London, Hodder & Stoughton, 1904), pp. 91, 27.

26. W. Booth, *Life and Labour of the People in London, Third Series: Religious Influences*, vol. 7 (New York, AMS Press, 1970), p. 424. This is a reprint of the 1902–1904 edition.

27. J. H. Blunt, *Directorium Pastorale. Principles and Practice of Pastoral Work in the Church of England* (London, Rivingtons, 1864), p. 91.

28. *Fifth Annual Report of the Church of England Zenana Missionary Society, 1884–1885*, pp. 13–22.

29. *Fifth Annual Report of the Church of England Zenana Missionary Society*, p. 15.

30. *Fifth Annual Report of the Church of England Zenana Missionary Society*, pp. 16–17.

31. S. S. Pugh, *Christian Manliness: A Book of Examples and Principles for Young Men* (London, Religious Tract Society, 1867), pp. 120–129.

32. Maurice, *Social Morality*, p. 460.

33. Maurice, *Social Morality*, p. 460.

34. Quoted in P. Gay, 'The Manliness of Christ', in R. W. Davis and R. J. Helmstadter (eds), *Religion and Irreligion in Victorian Society, Essays in Honour of R. K. Webb* (London, Routledge, 1992), pp. 102–116. Gay discusses the way in which at the end of *Tom Brown at Oxford*, Mary Brown seems to be endowed with a manly concern to set right the wrongs of the world, and suggests that this and other examples raise 'some serious questions about the absolute distinctions that we have long thought differentiated the sexes in Victorian ideology' (p. 113). He fails, however, to relate his discussion to its specifically religious context and the tensions created by the feminization of the Church.

35. Pugh, *Christian Manliness*, pp. 122–123.

36. As usual, it was Florence Nightingale who agonized most deeply over the problems that Christianity seemed to put in the way of women's fulfilment, writing to Jowett that 'a female Christ' was needed if women's lot in society were to be improved (Quinn and Prest (eds), *Dear Miss Nightingale*, p. xvii).

CHAPTER FOUR

Marriage, Morality, and Motherhood

Victorian Anglicans were in no doubt that the family was the key to Christian socialization, that it was essential for the well-being of society, and that women had the primary role in its maintenance. This belief led many of them to espouse a wide variety of public causes in the defence of the sanctity of family life. Thus the Divorce Act of 1857 was generally regarded as a retrograde step, and divorce itself was stigmatized as unchristian, while the double standard of sexual morality for men and women – epitomized by the Contagious Diseases Acts, child prostitution, and pornography – was attacked in the name of a feminism that was distinctly Christian in its inspiration. At the same time, efforts were made to support family life, of which the most notable was the creation of the Mothers' Union.

One discordant note in the refrain of Christian familial praise was struck by the Anglo-Catholic movement's advocacy of celibacy as a desirable way of life for men and women, an ideal that seemed to challenge the primacy of marriage within the Christian scheme, and the terms of this debate reveal a great deal about the centrality of gender in the formulation of Anglican social theology.

Anglican attitudes to marriage

In 1895, Mrs Sumner, the founder of the Mothers' Union, underlined the vital importance of the family in the Christian vision of society: 'It is an institution above all other institutions, because it is the one founded by God Himself as the basis of human existence, the central institution upon which the life of the community rests and around which all social life vibrates, and in which, day by day, the character and habits of the coming race are being hourly formed.'[1] The responsibility for the well-being of the Christian family, it was believed, lay primarily with women. As the Bishop of Oxford told the Church Congress at Portsmouth in 1885, home was a woman's empire and 'nothing which is possible to the other sex can replace her influence or stand in her place'.[2]

The benefits of a home in which a woman was responsible for child-care, education, and the running of the household were regarded as flowing exclusively from the Christian gospel, which had not only placed women in a more favourable position than in any other culture past or present, but had also created a form of family life unknown in other societies. As the Honourable Lady Acland told the women's meeting of the Pan-Anglican Congress in 1908, home 'is a purely Christian invention, because it rests on the position of our women, which is entirely the result of Christian teaching', and she concluded, with the confident ethnocentrism characteristic of her age, that 'the Christian ideal of the home is the highest the world has ever seen'.[3]

This was not the case simply because it embodied a natural and appropriate division of labour between the sexes, but because it sustained a level of sexual purity and lifelong fidelity that was not the case in other religions, and Christian denunciations of Islam often characterized it as a faith that sanctioned polygamy and unbridled sensuality, while Hinduism was condemned for the practice of child marriage. Of course, it was true that the Pauline writings enjoined a wife to be submissive to the authority of her husband, but this was to occur within a context of mutual respect and love, and was again contrasted with the life of purdah, poor education, and arbitrary male power that was held to be a woman's lot in non-Christian societies.

However, as Lady Ackland was careful to point out, she was speaking about the Christian ideal, and, as its proponents were aware, not only was the reality often very different, but the very premises on which it was based were frequently challenged in the Victorian period. One threat seemed to come from the Owenite Socialist movement of the 1830s and 1840s, which called for the introduction of civil marriage and divorce, and which argued that the basis for marriage lay in the quality of the relationship between men and women, and not in externally imposed social and legal obligations. The advocacy of voluntary sexual liaisons and the equality of both partners within the relationship ('I affirm that divorce begins when

91

love ends', as Goodwyn Barmby succinctly put it) was condemned by the Church as leading to free love, immorality, and blasphemy.[4] Speaking in the House of Lords in 1840, the Bishop of Exeter demanded governmental action against what he described as 'doctrines that were hostile to the interests of morality and religion', and that exposed the institution of marriage 'to scorn and detestation'.[5] Owen was a particular target on account of his 1835 tract, *Lectures on the Marriages of the Priesthood in the Old Immoral World*; and when Lord Melbourne had the temerity to present him to Queen Victoria in 1840, he was denounced by *Fraser's Magazine* for the insult offered to women 'as virgins and matrons', while the *Christian Lady's Magazine* called upon women to organize themselves against so great an affront to the sanctity of Christian home life.[6]

At stake in this controversy were not just issues of sexual morality, but a whole Christian patriarchal theology – a point seized upon by a number of women preachers for the Socialist cause. Not only was the Bible incredible on historical and moral grounds, they claimed, but it was also responsible for the oppression of women. As Eliza Sharple told an audience in 1832, Eve's action in eating the apple should be commended, not condemned, and she went on to ask her hearers, 'Do you not with one voice exclaim, well done woman! LIBERTY FOR EVER!' Another woman contributor to the Owenite journal *The New Moral World* suggested that if Genesis had been 'penned by a woman' the myth of the Fall would have been written very differently.[7] Views such as these stood in direct contradiction to an Anglican theology that still appealed to Genesis as warrant for the belief in women's innate inferiority to men, and in her subjection as a justifiable consequence of the Fall.

Owenite Socialism, with its radical social and political critique of the existing order, had little influence on the debates surrounding the passage of the 1857 Matrimonial Causes Act. This swept away the old system by which a separation granted by the ecclesiastical courts did not allow the remarriage of the parties involved unless a separate act of Parliament was obtained, and replaced it by divorce granted by the civil courts. While religious considerations were not excluded from the parliamentary debates, much more attention was devoted to the dangers' to the existing structure of patriarchal family life and inheritance, and attempts were made to obviate this threat by instituting an unequal system of divorce – whereby a man could divorce his wife for adultery, but a woman had to prove some extra cause such as cruelty, desertion, or unnatural vice.

The other difficulty for the Church of England was that its bishops were unable to speak with one voice on the subject. The problem that they faced arose from the apparently contradictory evidence of Scripture, where Jesus is recorded as saying both that what God had joined together no man was to put asunder, and that divorce for a man was permissible where his wife had committed adultery.[8] In the debate on the second reading of the Bill in the Lords, the Archbishop of Canterbury made a distinction between the innocent and guilty parties, arguing that the former should be allowed to remarry, but not the latter, a position that the Bishop of Bangor was deemed to have supported as he spoke too quietly to be heard.[9] On the other hand, the Bishop of Salisbury, who clearly could be heard, argued that while Christ appeared to make a concession to human weakness in Matthew 19.9, such an interpretation went against the explicit Pauline prohibition of divorce and remarriage, and he believed that the passage was actually meant only to indicate that the rabbinic law in allowing divorce for adultery had gone beyond what God intended. As to the argument that divorce and remarriage already existed in practice for those who were wealthy enough to obtain a private Act of Parliament, the Bishop saw this as an argument for withdrawing the privilege from the rich – not for extending it to the poor. He also drew attention to another important aspect of the legislation: the law of the land, he believed, was being changed in a fundamentally unchristian direction – what he called 'the placing of God's people on that sloping path which might end in unbelief' – and this would put the clergy in a difficult position since civil law and Christian morality would no longer coincide. This was, of course, to recognize the anomalous position of the established Church in an increasingly secular and pluralist society, and it was a dilemma that churchmen were frequently to face in the future.

However, for the Bishop of London, the Divorce Act did not raise this particular issue, since he maintained – in what sounded remarkably like a Victorian version of situation ethics – that general biblical statements about divorce 'were seldom to be taken as holding in all cases' – as in the parallel instance of the injunction to honour one's father and mother, which no longer held 'in cases of utter iniquity'. As to the Bishop of Salisbury's appeal to the authority of St Augustine, he reminded the House that 'there was scarcely any subject on which a whole string of the Fathers could not be brought on one side and a whole string upon the other', though it was not in fact clear from the general tenor of the debate that the correct exegesis of St Augustine carried much weight with many peers.[10]

93

What emerged from the passing of the Act was an acceptance in some parts of the Church that a distinction could, and should, be drawn between the innocent and guilty parties in any marital breakdown. As Mandell Creighton, the Bishop of London, explained in 1895:

> We as Christians abhor divorce, but when a divorce has been judged necessary are we to refuse any liberty to the innocent and wronged party? It seems to me a matter for our discretion on equitable grounds in each case. I could not advise any of my clergy to refuse to solemnise a marriage of an innocent person who genuinely desired God's blessing. I prefer to err on the side of charity.[11]

However, there was also a widespread belief within the Church that divorce could never be acceptable among real Christians, and that while it might be true that some people were unhappily married, this was not itself sufficient justification for what Mary Sumner dubbed 'the miasma of the Divorce Act', which would encourage couples to separate.[12] Not unnaturally, this view of the matter gained ground in the late nineteenth and early twentieth centuries as the divorce rate rose. When, for example, the Church Congress at Shrewsbury in 1896 considered 'the Church's law of marriage in relation to divorce' (the subject was considered too delicate to allow for the admission of women to the proceedings), not one speaker could be found to speak in defence of the 1857 Act. Both the Dean of Lichfield and the rector of Marylebone endeavoured to dismiss the apparent acceptance of divorce by Jesus in Matthew, the latter claiming that the text was corrupt, while Viscount Halifax, the President of the English Church Union and the leading Anglo-Catholic layman of the day, concluded that nothing could ever justify the clergy in remarrying divorcees in church.[13] To those who thought like this, the Church's duty was not to be swayed by legal and secular definitions of marriage, but to assert its sacramental character.

The problem with such a stance was that it involved a refusal to face up to the multifarious psychological and social pressures confronting men and women in marriage, and it was a stance that was often combined with a bitter condemnation of contemporary literature that did so. Marriage, Mrs Sumner claimed, was under assault from the forces of 'Ibsenism' and 'Decadentism',[14] while Thomas Hardy's *Jude the Obscure*, the theme of which was in part a working out of Hardy's own belief that 'marriage should be dissolvable as soon it becomes a cruelty to either of the parties', was burnt as 'garbage' by the Bishop of Wakefield, who urged the pious bookseller W. H. Smith not to stock it.[15] However, the insistence of most church people on seeing marital difficulties and divorce in narrowly moral terms, without reference to changing demographic patterns and cultural expectations, was to ensure much further agonized wrestling with the question in the twentieth century.

A very different kind of challenge to the Christian idea of marriage as the divinely ordained role in life for both men and women was presented by the Anglo-Catholic enthusiasm for clerical celibacy and the monastic life. As the Rev. James Vaux admitted in 1866, the hostility aroused by the ideal of a celibate clergy went far deeper than any Protestant distaste for Popish practices: it arose from a sense that the doctrine was an affront to the ideal of family life and to the rigidly enforced patterns of gender differentiation on which it depended. 'Of all the human race', he observed with a coolly ironic sense of understatement that must have infuriated his opponents, 'English people are probably the most essentially and thoroughly domestic; and any proposition which clashes with this peculiarity in our social system is likely to be received at first with but a moderate degree of favour.' He went on in an apparently more conciliatory vein to emphasize that marriage was indeed an honourable state, and that celibacy considered from a practical point of view left a priest freer to devote his time and energies to his parochial duties; however, he could not resist observing that his case did not rest upon regarding celibacy as a higher state than marriage, 'though St Paul teaches us to believe this to be the case'.[16] As Benedicta Ward has observed of the early leaders of the Oxford Movement, all the Christian writers they proposed to their fellow Christians came from the milieu of monasticism, and this was a source of inspiration that not only fired the Anglo-Catholic wing of the Church of England with a vision of chastity, pastoral devotion, and the beauty of holiness, but also imported into its life the much more dubious legacy of morbid asceticism and misogyny that characterized the teaching and practice of Newman's beloved Early Fathers.[17]

Charles Kingsley's crusade against celibacy, which was partly the cause of his dislike of Newman and Catholicism in general, is one indication that issues of sexuality and gender were at stake, and not simply theological questions. Passionate and highly sexed, as his letters to his future wife (and, still more, his drawings) reveal him to have been, Kingsley had a deep-seated need to exorcize the guilt that he felt over his sexual feelings, a guilt that he blamed on the Church's long-standing denial of the flesh and human sexual expression. 'Matter is holy', he told Fanny, in words that may not strike the modern reader as best calculated to unleash libidinous urges, 'awful glorious matter. Let us never use those words *animal* and *brutal* in a degrading sense. Our animal enjoyments must be religious ceremonies.'[18]

Kingsley's brand of exuberant sensual Christian manliness regarded celibacy as both theologically and socially wrongheaded. In his novel *Yeast*, the hero Lancelot Smith grows into a more mature Christian Socialist faith with the aid of Argemone, whom he has rescued from a misguided devotion to Puseyite monasticism, but his cousin Luke, by becoming a Roman Catholic priest, turns his back on his duties as a 'Parent, Englishman, Citizen'. The attack is pursued even more pointedly in his historical novel *Hypatia*, set in early fifth-century Alexandria, in which the young monk Philammon, described by Kingsley as 'full of life and youth and health and beauty . . . a young Apollo of the desert', is fascinated by the pictures of women and dancing girls that he stumbles across in a pagan temple, only to be severely rebuked by his abbot for even looking at the face of women, who are 'the first fruits of the devil, the authors of all evil, the subtlest of all Satan's snares'.[19] Notwithstanding this diatribe, and a peremptory order that he is not to leave the precincts of the monastery, Philammon successfully asserts his right to travel to Alexandria and to be his own judge of the narrow monastic view of the world.

Kingsley's condemnation of celibacy also included veiled charges of homosexuality against its practitioners. For all their brutality, the Goths in *Hypatia* are more sympathetically portrayed than the Alexandrine monks, since the former are 'untainted by hereditary effeminacy'.[20] In 1851, during the outcry surrounding the restoration of the Roman Catholic hierarchy, Kingsley wrote of Catholics and Tractarians that, among them 'there is an element of foppery – even in dress and manner; a fastidious, maundering, die-away effeminacy, which is mistaken for purity and refinement'.[21]

The controversy surrounding the early days of Cuddesdon Theological College provoked similar uneasiness. Its regime of elaborate ritual and an austerity that found no place for the cult of athleticism in the curriculum was condemned as unmanly, and eventually the Bishop of Oxford, Samuel Wilberforce, was forced to intervene, admitting to a friend that 'Our men are too *peculiar* –

some, at least, of our best men', and going on to complain of 'a want of vigour, virility and self-expressing vitality of the religious of young men'.[22] In his novel the *Way of All Flesh* published in 1903, Samuel Butler also hints obliquely that celibate Anglo-Catholic clergy were given to homosexuality.[23] By the time of the publication of Evelyn Waugh's *Brideshead Revisited* in 1945, the supposed connection between the two had become a commonplace, with the novel's hero Charles Ryder being warned on arriving at Oxford to 'Beware of the Anglo-Catholics – they're all sodomites with unpleasant accents.'[24]

The association of celibacy and Anglo-Catholic ritual with 'effeminacy' – that is to say, masculine behaviour that was deemed to be in some way inappropriately feminine – is indicative of the way in which gender boundaries were sharply defined in the mid-Victorian period. However, determining whether homosexuality was a significant component in the growth of the Anglo-Catholic movement – and, if it was, what its significance was for the development of clerical attitudes towards women – raises a number of thorny problems. Suggestions that leading Victorian Tractarians such as John Henry Newman, or Anglo-Catholics such as Edward King, the Bishop of Lincoln (who was prosecuted on charges of ritualism in 1889), were homosexual inevitably lead to verdicts of not proven for lack of evidence.[25] This is hardly surprising since buggery remained on the statute book as a capital offence until 1861, and the substitution of legal and medical definitions of homosexuality as an innate condition for previous concepts of individual sexual acts as sinful did little to change attitudes, and in 1885 all male homosexual acts, whether in public or in private, were criminalized. This still leaves the possibility that homosexual feelings were sublimated into intense homoerotic friendships within an all-male subculture, and that those who experienced such feelings were attracted to Anglo-Catholicism with its religious sanctioning of celibacy.[26]

Such judgements are, however, further complicated by changing constructions of masculinity in the Victorian period, and certainly until mid-century a more overtly passionate style of male friendship was less suspect than it later became.[27] In this respect, the celibate wing of Anglo-Catholicism might best be seen as only one of a number of all-male subcultures in the nineteenth century, including the public schools, the older universities, theological colleges, clubland, and the professions, from which women were excluded. What is striking is that while, however tentatively, most social change in the Victorian and Edwardian era worked against such exclusivism, Anglo-Catholicism, with its high doctrine of an all-male priesthood, was a creation of the period. This was in fact just one of a number of ways in which the movement was self-consciously a radically conservative response to modernity, a stance that became even more marked in the twentieth century, despite the efforts of Gore and others to win over Anglo-Catholics to a more progressive and incarnational style of theology.[28]

Christian feminist morality and the defence of family life

Religiously inspired celibacy remained an irritant rather than a major challenge to the Victorian ideal of married life, and one of the most striking examples of churchwomen's involvement in the public sphere in the defence of traditional family values was in the area of social purity campaigns to enforce Christian moral standards of sexual behaviour for both men and women. As early as 1802, Wilberforce had founded the Society for the Suppression of Vice, which brought prosecutions against those selling obscene publications or profaning the Sabbath; however, the main thrust of such efforts was aimed at the protection of the young from exposure to what were considered to be corrupting influences. Much more significant was the campaign against the Contagious Diseases Act, in which Josephine Butler played a leading part.

Josephine Butler was the daughter of a Northumberland farmer and estates manager who was a cousin of Earl Grey; the latter had steered through the Parliamentary Reform Act of 1832. She married an Anglican clergyman, George Butler, the eldest son of the Dean of Peterborough, Dr George Butler, who had been headmaster of Harrow. Her husband also pursued a career in education, and became Examiner of Schools at Oxford University, where Josephine experienced something of the discomfort and hostility caused by a woman's presence among celibate male academics. On one occasion, for example, she recalls hearing a work by Raphael dismissed as insipid by a distinguished don on the grounds that 'a woman's face when engaged in prayer could never wear any other expression than that of insipidity'.[29] Subsequently, George became Deputy Principal of Cheltenham Boys' College. This was a happy period in their life that ended brutally when their youngest daughter fell to her death from a balcony before their eyes, a tragedy that haunted Josephine Butler for the rest of her life.

It was with a sense of relief that the couple moved to Liverpool, where George Butler became Principal of Liverpool College for boys. While there she began visiting the Brownlow Hill workhouse, and became aware of the plight of the many destitute prostitutes within its walls; she then went on to establish a house of rest 'for dying Magdalens'. Concern over the plight of prostitutes also led her to study the effects of the Contagious Diseases Acts of 1864, 1866, and 1869, which set up a system of compulsory examination of suspected prostitutes in designated garrison towns and ports, and allowed the imprisonment and treatment of women found to have venereal disease. To Parliament, the Acts were a public health measure designed to tackle the problem of unacceptably high levels of sexually transmitted disease within the armed forces; to Butler, they were a brutal demonstration of the hypocrisy of the double standard of sexual morality for men and women – subjecting women to punishment, while condoning male sexual licence.

Alongside other groups working for the repeal of the Acts, Butler organized a National Ladies' Association, and was tireless in speaking at meetings and in the 1870 by-election at Colchester when the repealers succeeded in defeating the government candidate. The repeal campaign managed to mobilize widespread support from the growing trade union movement and from sections of the churches, most notably from the Quakers and the Wesleyan Methodists; however, Butler's own Church was more lukewarm, with the Archbishop of York twice refusing to receive deputations, claiming that the subject was obscene.[30] Nevertheless, it was possible to organize a clerical petition of 1,500 signatures against the Acts in 1871 and one containing 4,300 names in 1883–1884. By this date, the Acts were suspended; they were finally repealed in 1886, an achievement that owed a great deal to the skill and experience of the liberal politician James Stansfield.

The social purity movement within Anglicanism campaigned in other ways too. The ideal of overcoming the evils of prostitution not by state regulation or by taking coercive action against its victims, but by insisting upon Christian standards of sexual morality among men, also lay behind Jane Ellice Hopkins's Church of England Purity Society and the White Cross Army, created in 1883, whose male members pledged themselves 'to treat all women with respect', and 'to maintain the law of purity as equally binding on men and women'.

Hopkins was the daughter of a Cambridge mathematician, and came to national prominence after gaining experience through the typical round of evangelical philanthropy as a Sunday school teacher and missioner to navvies and public houses; and in 1866, after moving to Brighton, she became involved in the work of a rescue home for prostitutes.[31] Her fervent belief in 'the irresistibility of the moral sense, which is God's voice within us' did not, it seemed, preclude the need for firm action, since she also observed that 'If God is teaching us anything, He is teaching us that we are not going to quench this pit of hell in our midst by emptying out our scent bottles upon it.'[32] She was also instrumental in the setting up of the Ladies' National Association for the Care and Protection of Friendless Girls, which set up associations throughout Britain to provide accommodation for girls seeking work who might otherwise be lured into prostitution.

Another leading figure in the defence of Christian moral standards was Mrs Laura Ormiston Chant, who was closely associated with the work of the National Vigilance Association. This was set up in 1885 to ensure the enforcement of the provisions of the Criminal Law Amendment Act of 1885. This legislation had been hurriedly passed through Parliament in the wake of W. T. Stead's revelations in the *Pall Mall Gazette* of the existence of child prostitution and of the rape of young girls, whom he described as 'snared, trapped and outraged either when under the influence of drugs or after a prolonged struggle in a locked room'.[33] The new legislation raised the age of consent from thirteen, where it had been fixed in 1875, to sixteen, and attempted to close down brothels by fining and imprisoning those running them, a provision that the National Vigilance Association attempted to enforce through information provided by its members. Mrs Chant also turned her attention to the activities of London's music halls, gaining considerable public notoriety for her attempts to stop the granting of licences to what she regarded as places of 'demoralising' entertainment.[34]

Not surprisingly, activities such as these have led some historians to characterize the social purity movement as no more than an example of repressive Christian puritanism. Thus Constance Rover, writing in 1970, charged Josephine Butler and her middle-class allies with being 'charitable rather than emancipated', and explained the context of the campaign against the Contagious Diseases Acts as one in which 'the country was suffering from one of its cyclical attacks of puritanism, partly as a result of religious revival'.[35] Both Josephine

Butler's Christian beliefs, and her insistence on pre-marital chastity rather than on sexual expression, found little sympathy within the secular feminist movement of the 1960s and 1970s. Increasing concern over the issues of pornography and rape, and a greater willingness among social historians to take religion seriously, have tended to modify such simplistic assessments, and there are good grounds for regarding at least some aspects of the social purity movement as not only Christian in their inspiration and objectives, but also feminist.[36]

In the case of Josephine Butler, it is quite clear that it was her religious faith that was at the centre of her being and of her view of the world. As she wrote late in life, she believed passionately that 'God has not and will not forsake any part of His redeemed world, tho' He will sternly purge, and burn out all that cannot and must not continue'. This was a vision of the social order as both redeemable and under God's judgement, and was the inspiration behind a great deal of Victorian Christian philanthropy.[37] Like many Victorian women, Butler drew inspiration from the lives of Christian women from the past, and her perception of St Catherine of Siena (whose biography she wrote) as someone whose life was founded on her 'constant converse with God' was equally applicable to herself.[38] It was this inner resource that empowered Josephine Butler to undertake work that was arduous, unpleasant, and, on occasions, dangerous. At the time of the Colchester by-election, where she successfully led a campaign to defeat the candidate in favour of the Contagious Diseases Acts, she recalled that she was present at 'a series of devotional meetings, gathering together chiefly women, in groups, to ask of God that the approaching events might be over-ruled for good'.

Butler's faith was soon tested even further when she was forced to leave her hotel after receiving word that her opponents had threatened to burn it down, and she was warned against speaking in public. As she wrote to her family: 'For a moment a cowardly feeling came over me as I thought of you all at home; then it suddenly came to me that now was just the time to trust in God and claim his loving care.'[39] Equally striking was Josephine Butler's insistence that the campaign against the Contagious Diseases Acts had to be largely conducted by women, and hers was one of the many examples of the way in which Victorian women used the belief in their particular feminine qualities of care and compassion within the home to argue for their extension and application in the wider community. As she put it with her usual bluntness: 'So far as I have been able to study history, I have never found that there was a strong, virtuous and free nation in which the

101

women of that nation were not something more than mere appendages to men in domestic life.'[40]

Of equal importance from a feminist viewpoint was Butler's sense of solidarity with women whom she regarded as the victims of the double standard of sexual morality, a point made with equal force by Mrs Chant, who regarded the Contagious Diseases Acts as a prime example of the prejudice 'that unchastity is necessary for men – that it is the masculine prerogative'; and she went on with devastating clarity to expose the class-based hypocrisy of a society that taught that 'My wife, and sister, and daughter, may not for the world be thought capable of doing what I pay someone else's wife, or sister, or daughter, to do.'[41] This sense of the injustice done to women was deeply rooted for Mrs Chant in the theological conviction that 'God is the Father of every man and woman born into the world', and she quoted in this context the claim in Galatians 3.8–9 that in Christ there is neither male nor female. Fired by this insight, she believed that it was inevitable and necessary that the purity movement should be 'essentially active and aggressive'.[42]

Of course, not all aspects of the social purity campaign were uncontroversial, or are easily translatable into the perspective and sympathies of a later age. Deborah Gorham has suggested that the campaign for moral reform failed to come to terms with the reality of poverty, which made prostitution seem an inevitable recourse for destitute young girls and women.[43] Equally problematic was the assumption that women were inevitably passive and passionless victims of male sexuality. This belief in exploited innocence was partly the result of the widely held notion that women were in comparison with men lacking in sexual drives, and while it was an attitude shared by most secular feminists of the period, it was strongly reinforced by a Christian theology of women as, in the poet Coventry Patmore's phrase, 'the Angel in the House'. Since middle-class Christian morality made an absolute distinction between the pure and chaste woman and the indelibly stained woman who had fallen, a great deal of the success of the campaign sparked by Stead's revelations depended upon arousing sympathy for young girls who were essentially innocent, but seduced by predatory men. However, as Judith Walkovitz has shown, within working-class culture the distinction between absolute innocence and defilement made little sense; many women resorted to prostitution out of economic necessity; and, despite the lurid images of inevitable downfall and ruin that so reassured their middle-class audience, prostitution was often no more than a temporary expedient, and involved no inevitable loss of status or marriage prospects within the community.[44]

From a late twentieth-century vantage point, one of the most interesting difficulties facing social purity campaigners was the potential contradiction between their passionate Christian belief in individual moral reform, and the role of governmental action in providing solutions to social problems. Josephine Butler based her whole campaign on what she called 'the force of a spiritual and moral revival as an agency for political reform'; indeed, one of her basic objections to the Contagious Diseases Acts was that they substituted coercive legislative action for moral principle and individual responsibility.[45] It was for this reason that she became increasingly lukewarm towards the efforts of the National Vigilance Association to enforce morality by legal enactment. Nowhere do the implications of this attitude stand out more starkly than in her evidence to the Royal Commission set up in 1871 to consider the operation of the Contagious Diseases Acts. Confronted by the argument that some practical solution to the spread of venereal disease was urgently needed, she replied that 'men and women can avoid that disease by voluntary self-control, and I think it is a mischief to meddle with it at all' – an attitude that still finds echoes in contemporary Christian objections to the provision of adequate sex education and condoms to combat the spread of HIV on the grounds that these are incitements to promiscuity, when sexual continence provides the real answer to AIDS.[46]

Issues such as these indicate that the motives and methods of social purity campaigners were deeply influenced by contemporary notions about class and gender, yet to define their work as a distinctively religious form of feminism is to recognize that the women's movement was far from uniform in its inspiration, and that what were in many ways conservative definitions of womanhood are as much a part of its history as the more secular equal-rights feminism of Mill and Harriet Taylor.[47]

The support of Christian motherhood

One of the most significant institutional embodiments of conservative Christian constructions of womanhood was the Mothers' Union, which began in 1876 as the brain-child of Mary Sumner. The daughter of a prosperous banker, and married to a clergyman whose father was Bishop of Winchester and whose uncle was Archbishop of

Canterbury, she threw herself into the normal round of high Victorian parochial activity at Old Alresford, which included parish visiting, Sunday school teaching, men's Bible classes, and a branch of the Church of England Temperance Society. She also organized special meetings for 'cottage mothers' and out of these – and her day-to-day experience of the problems facing poor families – grew the idea of an organization to uphold the values of Christian family life. Cards were distributed that urged mothers to bring up their children in the Christian faith, to make prayer and Bible reading a part of daily family life, to keep children from reading 'bad books or police reports', and to keep girls from 'unsafe companions and from any dangerous amusement'.[48]

Mary Sumner's view of gender difference was a conventional one, and she believed that 'chivalry is innate in a boy, as modesty is in a girl', and that it was a mother's duty to foster and cultivate these instincts.[49] Her ideas received a publicity boost when she spoke at the Church Congress at Portsmouth in 1885, and two years later she was able to tell the first Mothers' Union Diocesan Conference in Winchester that there were fifty-seven branches, and that seventeen other dioceses had taken up the idea. In 1888 the quarterly *Mothers' Union Journal* was founded, which set out the two objectives of the Union as 'awakening in mothers a sense of their responsibility in the training of their boys and girls (the future Fathers and Mothers of England) and to organise in every place a band of Mothers who will unite in prayer, and seek by their own example to lead their families in purity and holiness of life'. In 1892 an important third objective was added, 'to uphold the sanctity of marriage'.

The success of the Mothers' Union should not, however, merely be seen in terms of the charismatic leadership of its founder, who also articulated fears and concerns that were widespread within late Victorian society. Writing in the mid-1890s, she saw the Mothers' Union as an attempt to check the growth of immorality, which she claimed had 'increased tenfold in recent years', as evidenced by the alarming rise in the divorce rate, which now ended one marriage in 577; and, as an awful warning as to what might happen in the future, she pointed to France 'where the moral law is in a far lower stage of decadence' and where one marriage in sixty-seven was dissolved.[50] Staunchly patriotic, Mary Sumner was also representative of a late Victorian Anglicanism that benefited from the upsurge of imperialist sentiment, and she allied the theme of Christian motherhood to the growing preoccupation with nationalism, eugenics, and Social Darwinism. Quoting Benjamin Kidd's 1894 bestseller *Social Evolution*, she warned that cultures 'which place religion in the background, will be weeded out in the process of natural selection'.[51]

A further threat to national greatness lay in increasing class conflict. It was not Mary Sumner's aim to abolish class distinctions, for she believed that 'reformation of life and morals comes from the higher classes', and the Union produced two separate publications, *The Mothers' Union Journal*, and *Mothers in Council*, which was edited by Charlotte Yonge and aimed at upper- and middle-class women whose role was to aid and teach the Union's lower-class members. Owen Chadwick has argued that despite such distinctions, the Mothers' Union succeeded in crossing class boundaries, and created an organization where 'the cottage mother and the mother of the great hall met in the same meeting and undertook the same duty', but how far the Mothers' Union can be regarded as an example of a Christian-inspired feminism, with a vision of sisterhood where gender rather than class was the unifying factor, is debatable.[52] Of course, no one involved in its work could fail to be aware for long of the problems of poverty, poor housing, and long hours worked by many mothers, but finding remedies for these evils drew the Union into a much wider argument within the Church of England as to the relative merits of individual philanthropy over against state legislation – a debate that clearly revealed that its members had radically different analyses of the causes of poverty and of the means to alleviate it. Mary Sumner's initial response to these problems was to stress the importance of individual parental responsibility for the instruction and actions of their children, and she was critical of educationalists and philanthropists, whom she accused of telling poorer parents, 'these are your children, it is true, but you are too ignorant, or too busy, or too wicked to train them yourselves. We will do it for you.'[53]

Differences over the appropriate balance between individual responsibility within the family, and state legislative action in the combating of social and moral ills, were very evident at the Women's Meeting of the Pan-Anglican Congress of 1908. Louise Creighton, the widow of the Bishop of London, Mandell Creighton, spoke of a crisis within poor homes and of a situation in which state legislation was undermining parental responsibility, but much of the problem stemmed, she believed, from working-class women going out to work for up to nine hours a day, which had the effect of undercutting male wages. The solution was to provide 'a living wage for the men', which would enable women to stay at home and care for their children. There was also the problem of poor housing to be overcome, since four-fifths of families lived in overcrowded conditions 'where it is almost impossible to bring up a family in the decencies of life'.

Just how middle-class standards of living were to be brought within the reach of the majority of the population Mrs Creighton did not make clear, but Miss Gertrude Tuckwell, President of the Women's Trade Union League, made some more concrete suggestions for state legislation to limit the hours and raise the pay of overworked women in factories and shops, and she called for the encouragement of trade unions to help to achieve these objectives. Such proposals were, she believed, in line with the thinking of Bishop Gore's Christian Social Union, and she urged her female audience to seek 'what is Christian in Socialism, and not to turn aside because misrepresentation and exaggeration may mislead us as to the true character of this'.[54]

Very different in approach was the contribution of another speaker, Dr Chilcot, who laid emphasis on improvidence as the sin of the poor, and who objected to the provision of free education by the state.[55] He was also something of a neo-Malthusian, castigating members of the educated middle classes for adding to social problems by having fewer children than the poor.[56] With its belief in the primacy of the home in moral formation and of a woman's responsibility to oversee her children, the Mothers' Union was also wary about state intervention, but it was on occasions prepared to intervene more publicly in social questions, as in 1903 when the Central Committee agreed to appoint a representative to the Council of the National Union of Women Workers, and in 1905 when it decided to organize a petition to the London County Council and the Metropolitan Police on the need to register all registry offices for the employment of domestic servants.[57] However limited, such initiatives involved a recognition that the Christian ideal of motherhood and the family, which was its matrix, could not exist divorced from a harsh economic and social context that often did little to ensure that they could thrive.

Notes

1. *Mothers in Council*, vol. 5 (1895), p. 194.

2. *Report of the Church Congress held at Portsmouth* (London, Bemrose & Sons, 1885), p. 160.

3.   *Report of the Women's Meeting Held in Connection with the Pan-Anglican Congress of 1908* (London, SPCK, 1908), p. 25.

4.   This account is based upon B. Taylor, *Eve and the New Jerusalem: Socialism and Feminism in the Nineteenth Century* (London, Virago Press, 1983).

5.   Hansard, 3rd Series, 51, 514–532.

6.   Taylor, *Eve and the New Jerusalem*, p. 188.

7.   Taylor, *Eve and the New Jerusalem*, p. 146.

8.   Matthew 5.31–32.

9.   Hansard, 3rd Series, 155, 495–496, 522.

10.   Hansard, 3rd Series, 155, 531–533.

11.   L. Creighton, *The Life and Letters of Mandell Creighton* (2 vols, London, Longmans Green, 1906), vol. 2, pp. 68–69.

12.   *Mothers in Council*, vol. 12 (1902), p. 84.

13.   *The Official Report of the Church Congress Held at Shrewsbury* (London, Bemrose & Sons, 1896), pp. 263–287.

14.   *Mothers in Council*, vol. 5 (1895), p. 196.

15.   R. Gittings, *The Older Hardy* (Harmondsworth, Penguin Books, 1980), p. 118. The novel provoked Mrs Oliphant to publish a celebrated article entitled 'The Anti-Marriage League', while a former Wesleyan missionary to China accused Hardy of facing 'filth and defilement . . . with the calm, unshrinkable countenance of a Local Board Labourer'. Hardy's statement of his intentions in writing the book was contained in a postscript to the 1912 edition of his works.

16.   J. Vaux, 'Clerical Celibacy', in O. Shipley (ed.), *The Church and the World: Essays on Questions of the Day* (London, Longmans Green, 1866), pp. 141–177.

17.   B. Ward, 'A Tractarian Inheritance: The Religious Life in a Patristic Perspective', in G. Rowell (ed.), *Tradition Renewed: The Oxford Movement Conference Papers* (London, Darton, Longman & Todd, 1986). This is not the interpretation placed upon this inheritance by Sister Ward, who observes that 'these men proposed religious consecration specifically as a parallel to their own consecration through their ordination to the priesthood', which begs a number of questions about power and gender within the Church. For the early Church Fathers' denigration of women's sexuality, see R. Ruether, *Religion and Sexism: Images of Woman in the Jewish and Christian Traditions* (New York, Simon & Schuster, 1974). In his 'Women in the Writings of the Fathers: Language, Belief, and Reality', in W. J. Sheils and D. Wood (eds), *Women in the Church*, Studies in Church History 27 (Oxford, Basil Blackwell, 1990), pp. 1–13, Graham Gould takes a less hostile view, but still concludes that in the long run attitudes like Augustine's – which identified women with the irrational and sexual sides of human nature – were damaging.

18.   Quoted in S. Chitty, *The Beast and the Monk: A Life of Charles Kingsley* (London, Hodder & Stoughton, 1974), p. 80.

19.   C. Kingsley, *Hypatia or New Foes with an Old Face* (London, Macmillan, 1882). The abbott goes on to argue that 'A woman first opened the gates of hell; and until this day, they are the portresses thereof', an allusion to Tertullian's description of a woman as 'the devil's gateway'.

20.   Kingsley, *Hypatia*, p. xii. N. Vance, in *The Sinews of the Spirit: The Ideal of Christian Manliness in Victorian Literature and Religious Thought* (Cambridge, CUP, 1985), has a fine discussion of Kingsley's horror of celibacy and its wider context.

21.   F. Kingsley, *Charles Kingsley: His Letters and Memories of His Life* (2 vols, London, C. Kegan Paul, 7th edn, 1880), vol. 1, p. 201.

22.   R. G. Ashwell, *The Life of the Right Reverend Samuel Wilberforce* (3 vols, London, John Murray, 2nd edn, 1881), vol. 2, pp. 367–368.

23.   Butler has the young Anglo-Catholic priest, Pryer, opine that 'no practice is entirely vicious which has not been extinguished among the comeliest, most vigorous, and most cultivated races of mankind in spite of centuries of endeavour to extirpate it' (S. Butler, *The Way of All Flesh* (London, Jonathan Cape, 2nd edn, 1913), p. 239).

24.   E. Waugh, *Brideshead Revisited* (Harmondsworth, Penguin Books, 1962), p. 28.

25.   Geoffrey Faber's study of the leaders of the Oxford Movement speculated that 'both Froude and Newman may have derived the ideal of virginity from a homosexual root', while in Newman's case he sees 'the strength and the emotional depth of his friendships with men' as the natural counterpart of his 'indifference to women' (G. Faber, *Oxford Apostles* (Harmondsworth, Penguin Books, 1954), pp. 47, 213). Faber's study was first published in 1933 to coincide with the 150th anniversary of the beginning of the Oxford Movement. It has understandably not found favour with those who see Newman as a candidate for canonization. It is interesting to note, however, that in the standard modern biography of Newman, Ian Ker is still influenced by questions of gender stereotyping, setting out not to deny the 'feminine' aspect of his character, but to stress also the other highly 'masculine' side of his temperament (I. Ker, *John Henry Newman* (Oxford, Clarendon Press, 1988), p. viii). For King, see J. A. Newton, *Search for a Saint: Edward King* (London, Epworth Press, 1977). Newton discusses the suggestion in Lord Elton's 1958 biography 'that King's aura of radiant love was homosexual in origin', and notes that rumours of this kind were sufficiently prevalent for misgivings to be expressed about a commemorative bronze statue to King in Lincoln Cathedral, which was to have included the figure of a young boy whom he is confirming. He concludes that the celibate King was devoted to his mother, 'though not abnormally so', and that there is not a shred of evidence to justify such charges (pp. 45–48).

26.   The best discussion of this whole subject is D. Hilliard, 'Unenglish and Unmanly: Anglo-Catholicism and Homosexuality', *Victorian Studies*, vol.

25 (1982), pp. 181–210.

27. For this theme, see D. Newsome, *Godliness and Good Learning* (London, Cassell, 1961), pp. 83–84.

28. For a critique of Anglo-Catholicism as a counter-cultural movement, see V. Pitt, 'The Oxford Movement: A Case of Cultural Distortion?', in K. Leech (ed.), *Essays Catholic and Radical* (London, Bowerdean Press, 1983), pp. 205–224.

29. J. Butler, *Recollections of George Butler* (Bristol, J. W. Arrowsmith, 1892), p. 99. In many respects, this remains the best account of her life. Modern studies include E. Bell, *Josephine Butler, Flame of Fire* (London, Constable, 1962); N. Boyd, *Josephine Butler, Octavia Hill, Florence Nightingale: Three Victorian Women Who Changed Their World* (London, Macmillan, 1982); M. Forster, *Significant Sisters: The Grassroots of Active Feminism 1839–1939* (London, Secker & Warburg, 1984).

30. P. McHugh, *Prostitution and Victorian Social Reform* (London, Croom Helm, 1980), pp. 188–190.

31. I have taken the details of her career from S. Jeffreys, *The Spinster and Her Enemies: Feminism and Sexuality 1880–1930* (London, Pandora Press, 1985), pp. 9–15.

32. E. Hopkins, *The Present Moral Crisis; An Appeal to Women* (London, Dyer Brothers, n.d.), pp. 2–3.

33. D. Gorham, 'The "Maiden Tribute of Modern Babylon" Re-examined: Child Prostitution and the Idea of Childhood in Late-Victorian England', *Victorian Studies*, vol. 21 (1977–1980), p. 353.

34. L. Bland, '"Purifying" the Public World: Feminist Vigilantes in Late Victorian England', *Women's History Review*, vol. 1 (1992), p. 398. I am grateful to Sue Morgan for drawing my attention to this article.

35. C. Rover, *Love, Morals and the Feminists* (London, Routledge & Kegan Paul, 1970), p. 83. This is also the perspective of E. J. Bristow, *Vice and Vigilance: Purity Movements in Britain Since 1700* (Dublin, Gill & Macmillan, 1977).

36. For a more nuanced approach, see Jeffreys, *The Spinster and Her Enemies*, pp. 6–7.

37. Josephine Butler to Miss Forsaith, 8 January 1905, Butler Papers, Fawcett Library, London.

38. J. Butler, *Catherine of Siena: A Biography* (London, Horace Marshall, 4th edn, 1895), p. 39.

39. J. Butler, *Personal Reminiscences of a Great Crusade* (London, Horace Marshall, 1896), pp. 45–49.

40. Butler, *Personal Reminiscences*, p. 76.

41. L. Chant, *Chastity in Men and Women: A Woman's Answer to a Woman in*

Regard to the Equality of the Moral Law (London, Dyer Bros, 1885), pp. 4–8.

42. Chant, *Chastity in Men and Women*, pp. 8–10.

43. Gorham, 'The "Maiden Tribute of Modern Babylon" Re-examined', pp. 376–377.

44. J. Walkovitz, *Prostitution and Victorian Society: Women, Class and the State* (Cambridge, CUP, 1980).

45. This aspect of the social purity movement is discussed in B. Harrison, 'State Intervention and Moral Reform in Nineteenth-century England', in P. Hollis (ed.), *Pressure from Without in Early Victorian England* (London, Edward Arnold, 1974), pp. 289–322.

46. Rover, *Love, Morals and the Feminists*, p. 78.

47. In his *Essay on the Subjection of Women* published in 1869, Mill went to the heart of the problem of religiously inspired definitions of true womanhood when he pointed out that 'what is now called the nature of women is an eminently artificial thing', though in other parts of his argument he is far from abandoning traditional views about the role of men and women in family life. For a discussion of the potential contradictions within the work, see G. Tulloch, *Mill and Sexual Equality* (Hemel Hempstead, Harvester Wheatsheaf, 1989).

48. O. Parker, *For the Family's Sake: A History of the Mothers' Union 1876–1976* (Oxford, Mowbray, 1975), pp. 9–10.

49. M. Sumner, 'The Responsibilities of Mothers', in Baroness Burdett-Coutts (ed.), *Woman's Mission: A Series of Congress Papers on the Philanthropic Work of Women by Eminent Writers* (London, Sampson Low, Marston & Co., 1893), pp. 65–78.

50. *Mothers in Council*, vol. 5 (1895), p. 198.

51. *Mothers in Council*, vol. 5 (1895), p. 197. The popularity of Kidd's book owed a great deal to its virulent attack on Socialism. In both this and his later work *The Science of Power*, he stressed the key role played by women in social regeneration.

52. O. Chadwick, *The Victorian Church* (2 vols, London, A. & C. Black, 2nd edn, 1972), vol. 2, p. 193. This is the view of G. Wilton in his 1992 MA thesis, 'Mary Sumner's Mothers' Union (1876–1901)', Cheltenham and Gloucester College of Higher Education, and Trinity College, Bristol, p. 19. I am grateful to Gary Wilton for allowing me to read his thesis and for discussing it with me.

53. Burdett-Coutts (ed.), *Woman's Mission*, p. 66.

54. The Christian Social Union was founded in 1889. For a detailed, if hostile, account of its aims and the debate within Anglicanism between proponents and opponents of governmental intervention in the regulation of the free market in the interests of alleviating poverty, see E. R. Norman, *Church and*

Society in England 1770-1970 (Oxford, Clarendon Press, 1976), pp. 175–260. The similarity of these debates to those heard a hundred years later, particularly with regard to the breakdown in family life and the alleged link between crime and single-parent families, indicates the success of Mrs Thatcher in reintroducing at least one Victorian value into contemporary Britain: the belief in a clear and ascertainable distinction between the deserving and undeserving poor, and the adoption of a harsh punitive moralism towards those who are considered to fall into the latter category.

55. See *Report of the Women's Meeting Held in Connection with the Pan-Anglican Congress of 1908* (London, SPCK, 1908), pp. 1–40, for this debate.

56. For the importance of eugenicist preoccupations with the differential birth rate between the upper and lower classes and the potential dangers of racial 'degeneracy' in arguments about sexuality and family life, see J. Weeks, *Sex, Politics and Society: The Regulation of Sexuality Since 1800* (London, Longman, 2nd edn, 1989).

57. Mothers' Union Central Committee Council Meetings, 2, ff. 26, 50.

CHAPTER FIVE

The Church and Women's Education

Both through the provision of schools and Sunday school teaching, the Church of England made a significant contribution to the education of girls at elementary level, even though the advent of state provision in 1870 indicated that the churches in general were increasingly unable to meet the growing educational needs of the country. More controversial was the movement for secondary and higher education, with churchmen expressing a wide spectrum of views – from outright opposition, cautious or qualified approval, to enthusiastic and practical support.

Elementary education

As we have seen, the charity school movement in the eighteenth century faced considerable hostility from those who feared that the education of the poor would lead to discontent by giving them ideas above their station, and such views were still voiced in the early nineteenth century. This was not the stance of the Church, though, which regarded the ability to read the Bible as the foundation stone of true religion and morality, and set out to combat what it saw as a dangerous flood of immoral and blasphemous literature with the works of Hannah More and Sarah Trimmer and the publications of the Religious Tract Society. In fact, the aims of those favouring the education of the poor were as conservative as those who opposed it. The National Society for Promoting the Education of the Poor in the Principles of the Established Church throughout England and Wales stated in its first annual report in 1812 that it sought to give children religious instruction in the doctrines of the Church of England, and other knowledge sufficient to equip the poor for life 'in their proper stations'. The Society was also conservative in its attitude to gender roles, reassuring its supporters that it had no desire 'to make girls little Newtons, little Captain Cooks, little Livingstones, little Mozarts and Handels, and little Sir Joshua Reynoldses', but rather to train them 'to make and mend shirts, to make and mend pinafores, and darn stockings and socks'.[1]

The provision of schools for working-class girls was haphazard at the beginning of the nineteenth century, and included private dame schools, often of a low standard, and a network of charity schools largely created by the Church in the eighteenth century. Thus the establishment of the National Society was an attempt to put Anglican teaching on a more systematic footing. Anglican schools made use of the monitorial method developed by Andrew Bell, which required only one teacher to instruct the older children, who in turn taught the younger – a system that, whatever its limitations, at least had the advantage of cheapness. The reports of the Parliamentary Commissioners who examined the state of charities in England for the education of the poor in 1819 indicate that there were wide variations in the quality of provision for girls, depending upon the use or misuse of the original endowments and the zeal of the current trustees, who usually included the local clergyman. For example, Archbishop Tenison had made provision in his will in 1715 for a school in Lambeth to educate twelve poor girls. In 1819, this school was educating and clothing twenty girls using Bell's method; they were admitted at eight, stayed until they were fifteen, and were taught reading, writing, arithmetic, and needlework.[2] At the Blewbury school in Berkshire, however, where thirty boys and thirty girls were taught in a National School, there were complaints that the children were not well taught and fed. One girl, who had been a boarder for six years from the age of eight, recalled poor food and a dormitory in which ten girls shared four beds.[3]

Whatever the shortcomings of individual institutions, by 1847 the National Society was able to report that it had 20,350 schools, of which 6,659 provided a totally free education, and that overall it was educating 666,791 boys and 640,072 girls.[4] However, the National Society's figures also indicate that significantly fewer girls than boys received the more thorough education provided at weekday schools as opposed to Sunday or mixed schools, the figures being 107,211 as against 122,506, an imbalance confirmed by the Newcastle Commission in 1861.[5] This was not a reflection on the Church's disinclination to offer girls elementary education, but rather it was the result of the reluctance of parents to send girls to school in an age before compulsory schooling. Both cultural and economic constraints contributed to this situation. When girls in the Tottenham Court Road area of London were asked if they went to school in the 1850s, they replied that they did not do so, since their mothers expected them to look after the younger children; while in 1866, the Rev. W. Howard pointed out that with agricultural wages as low as 9 shillings per week in Devon and Dorset, families sent their young children out to earn a few pence as soon as they were capable of doing so.[6]

Sunday schools were another important aspect of the Church's educational effort, and nearly every memoir of a Victorian daughter or wife of the parsonage records their involvement in this work. In 1910 it was estimated that the Church of England had 2,437,000 pupils enrolled, compared with some 3,000,000 for the major Nonconformist denominations. However, by then, recruitment was already beginning to decline, for the movement had reached its apogee in about 1885, when some 19 per cent of the population was registered. The educational value of these schools has also been called into question, and in the most detailed modern account of their work, Philip Cliff, a by no means hostile historian, has concluded that at the end of the nineteenth century, 'The intensely biblical religiosity of the Sunday Schools gradually seemed to become light years away from the realities of the new century', and that 'the poverty of resources, untrained teachers and poor materials all assisted the decline'.[7]

Secondary and higher education for girls

If there was little dispute about the need to give working-class girls an elementary education, and little difference in the education they received in comparison with boys (apart from the teaching of needlework), the education of middle-class girls at secondary and university level was far more contentious, for it appeared to threaten the belief that home was a woman's primary sphere of duty.[8] Since women of this class were not expected to work for their own support, the education that they received in the early part of the century was very much a hit-and-miss affair. There were some excellent girls' schools, such as the one at Coventry that the young George Eliot attended. Run by two Baptist sisters, the curriculum included music, drawing, English, French, history, and arithmetic, and the pupils were encouraged to read widely with no prohibition on contemporary novels.[9]

George Eliot benefited from a Nonconformist tradition of secondary education that continued throughout the nineteenth century,[10] but Charlotte Brontë's experience of the Cowan Bridge boarding school for clerical daughters, run by the Rev. Carus Wilson, was much less happy – and many girls avoided the rigours of such a harsh regime by being educated at home either by governesses or by their parents.[11] As Margaret Bryant has pointed out in her study of female education in the nineteenth century, the schooling provided at home for daughters by clerical fathers was often of a high standard, and it is therefore not surprising that a significant number of the early leaders of the movement for women's higher education came from this background.[12]

This was the case with Elizabeth Wordsworth, the daughter of the Bishop of Lincoln, and the first Principal of Lady Margaret Hall in Oxford. She was encouraged in her studies by her father, who made use of her proficiency in Latin, Greek, and Hebrew in the writing of his own biblical commentary, and she always remained grateful for his help.[13] Mary Paley Marshall, one of the first five students to attend Newnham College, Cambridge, in October 1871, was the daughter of a strict evangelical clergyman who not only employed a German governess to educate his daughter, but himself taught her Latin, Hebrew, and Euclid, and introduced her to English and Classical literature, though with certain characteristically evangelical prohibitions – Scott's novels were acceptable, but Dickens's were forbidden.[14] Emily Davies, the first Mistress of Girton, was also the daughter of an evangelical clergyman (this time even Scott failed the test of godly rectitude), and recalled that she and her brother did weekly English composition exercises that were corrected by their father, and to which her biographer attributed her later effectiveness as a writer.[15]

Given the evident care that clerical fathers often gave to the education of their daughters, it is not surprising to find that out of the 112 women students who were educated at Oxbridge colleges in 1869–1880 whose family background can be traced, the highest number, thirty-two, were the children of Anglican clergymen.[16]

However, such an image of clerically inspired educational enterprise is far from being the whole picture. Many in the Church shared the widespread fear that higher education would lead girls away from the path of family duty. In 1869 Emily Davies wrote of the difficulties of finding suitable students for her new college at Hitchin, which later moved to Girton: 'I am more and more impressed with the difficulties of conscience in the way of young women, as I hear more about them. They think they ought not to urge their own wishes against those of their parents, who . . . "don't see the use of learning such a lot!"'[17] One writer to the High Church newspaper *The Guardian* in 1913, made a connection between female higher education and what she saw as growing and undesirable unrest among women. Most women would always, she claimed, find their true fulfilment at home because of 'elemental instincts which the most up-to-date feminism will never stamp out'. She also appealed to conservative medical prejudice, claiming that 'a woman's brain does not work in the same way as a man's and should not be trained in the same way'.[18]

The same reliance on supposedly scientific authority was made in 1892 by another writer in the Mothers' Union journal, *Mothers in Council*. This writer claimed, with touching faith, that 'our medical men are, as a class, too liberal-minded to cling to old-fashioned prejudices; so, if they tell us that an intellectual training which, to the stronger physique of men, would do no harm, may be of permanent physiological injury to women, ought we not to believe them?' Since a woman's social function was to be a helpmeet, she went on, 'we do not so much need her to be profound as sympathetic'. Sadly, things had come to such a pass that she had even heard a Girton MA make scornful remarks about the bible of conservative Victorian ideals of femininity, Ruskin's *Sesame and Lilies*.[19]

Added to such commonplace objections to women's higher education were more specifically religious qualms. Following the vote in April 1884 to admit women to Oxford University examinations, but not to degrees, the Rev. J. W. Burgon took the opportunity of preaching to the University on Trinity Sunday to denounce such a move by making direct appeal to Genesis and the Pauline texts to prove women's subordinate status as helpmeets, not intellectual rivals to men. However, Burgon – in the oleaginous words of his biographer, 'a more devoted and chivalrous admirer of the softer sex never existed' – was something of an ecclesiastical dinosaur, sure to be found in opposition to all the theological and social changes of his day, and such a crudely direct appeal to biblical fundamentalism was rare.[20] More common among clergymen beleaguered by evolution and biblical criticism was the fear that exposure to higher education would undermine the faith of women, whose qualities of unaffected piety and goodness were regarded as proof against the corrosive acids of the untrammelled male intellect.

Before the advent of higher education for women, such resistance had perhaps been easier to maintain: when Catherine Tait, the wife of the headmaster of Rugby and future Archbishop of Canterbury, arrived at the school in 1843, she discovered that its masters were infected with Arnoldian liberalism, but when one ventured to express an unorthodox theological view in her presence she was able to overcome temptation by shutting herself in a spare room and repeating aloud the words of the Apostle's Creed.[21] University education, it was feared, would open doors to free thinking, not shut them. Anna Lloyd, one of the first five students to attend Girton when it opened at Hitchin in 1869, recalled boarding a train only to be confronted by a clergyman who described the college to his two female travelling companions as 'that infidel place',[22] while a correspondent in the Mothers' Union journal *Mothers in Council* warned in 1892 against letting 'any girl enter on the battle-field of university life whose religious convictions are confused' – adding that 'the world does not want intellectual goddesses, but bright, loving, intelligent women'.[23]

Not surprisingly, parental attitudes such as these could create self-doubt and tensions in the minds of able women attracted by the thought of pursuing an academic life. One for whom this was so was Constance Maynard, who went to Girton in 1872 and later became the first principal of Westfield College in 1882, and who had internalized the ambivalent attitude of her evangelical mother towards education. She had begun teaching her daughter from the age of four, reminding her children 'that they were not only bodies but minds', but never let them forget that there was a vital distinction between saving faith and worldly knowledge. In 1872, Constance's cousin wrote to reassure her that she would be strong enough to withstand the trials of intellectual life:

In the present stir about Woman and her development, my heart would ache over an unspiritually-minded, unconverted girl going to a College, or even one who had merely a 'hoping' rather than a 'having' religion, heavenly and earthly aspirations get so easily confused together – while actual possessions assert their distinctness by their very nature and reality.[24]

Constance's faith ultimately withstood the test, as her cousin had hoped, and she ensured that Christianity was central to the life of Westfield, beginning a course of divinity lectures in the college in

1901. However, as her biographer indicates, this was not before a protracted and agonizing struggle against doubt, which contributed to the psychological and emotional problems that plagued her throughout her life and that could only partly be held in check by a life of hectic Christian activity.[25]

Christian anti-intellectualism took other forms, too. It was often suggested that pursuing higher education was unwomanly and un-christian in that it encouraged feelings of self-assertiveness and competitiveness rather than those of modesty, self-denial, and reserve. Despite educating his own daughter and seeing her become the first Principal of Lady Margaret Hall in 1879, the Bishop of Lincoln, Christopher Wordsworth, gave voice to these fears in a sermon on 'Christian Womanhood and Christian Sovereignty' published in 1884. Not only did education subvert the divinely ordained social order in which a woman's existence was 'a derivative one', since 'she has her being and authority from man', but it threatened what he saw as her most attractive grace: 'modest retirement and delicate reserve'. Stimulating the intellect would, he feared, blight a woman's heart, and it was therefore of paramount importance to 'shelter her from anything that may tend to rob her of those fair attributes of quietness, meekness, and gentleness with which God Himself has invested her'.[26] A similar view was taken by the High Churchman Nathaniel Woodard, the founder of a series of notable boys' schools that included Lancing and Hurstpierpoint.[27] Whenever the Reverend E. C. Lowe, who was for many years headmaster of Hurstpierpoint and later Provost of the Midland Division of the Woodard Corporation, suggested the creation of girls' schools, he was rebuffed by Woodard, who wrote gloomily in 1880 that public schools for girls were 'of very doubtful merit', and that 'knowledge without the grace of female gentleness and devotion, is another cloud in the gathering storm which is awaiting society'.[28]

Undoubtedly the greatest popular exponent of this view was the novelist Charlotte Yonge. Born at Otterbourne near Winchester, Yonge was prepared for confirmation by one of the founding fathers of the Oxford Movement, John Keble, who was a neighbour and fam-ily friend; and in both her life and works she exemplifies the ideals of early Tractarianism with its emphasis on a life of holiness and self-denial, and the exercise of a reverential reserve in the face of the mysteries of the faith – a spirituality well calculated to inculcate and sustain the qualities of modesty and unassertiveness among women. Of course for Charlotte Yonge, as for the poet Christina Rossetti who shared the same religious inheritance, there was a tension between their creative energies and desire for recognition, and the proscription of the self that their faith seemed to demand. Yet for both, religion, properly understood and channelled, became a warrant to write. In Charlotte Yonge's case this was ensured by the requirement that she submit all her work to her father, and later to Keble for approval prior to publication.[29] The result was a body of novels in which a young woman's highest duties are to home and family, and in which intellectual pursuits are more of a snare than an aid to the Christian life. Thus in *The Daisy Chain*, first published in 1856, the heroine Ethel May early learns from her mother the lesson that 'the love of eminence for its own sake' is sinful, and that caring to be clever and getting on are contrary to the teaching of the gospel for a woman; and Ethel, although intelligent and well educated at home, devotes her life to a round of Sunday school teaching and family duties. In so doing, she embodies Charlotte's own ideals of Christian womanhood, which centred upon 'all those obvious family claims that Providence marks out by the mere fact of there being no one else to undertake them'.[30]

The same fear of intellectual enquiry and where it might lead was expressed by another Tractarian writer, Elizabeth Sewell. In her autobiography she recalled her own childhood struggles against sceptical thoughts, which were overcome 'by a short quick prayer, and an almost physical effort to turn away from the suggestions', though sometimes it seemed there was no escape, as when she was able only to go through the motions of piano practice 'whilst reasoning upon the probability of the Jewish miracles till I was nearly wild'. Even later, the serenity of an untroubled faith was maintained only precariously, and she admitted that it was 'an immense comfort to have one's days so occupied as to leave little time for abstract thought'.[31] In fact, the remedy for doubt was not intellectual reasoning, which was really only a form of self-will, but obedience to religious authority.

However, in practice, anti-intellectualism of this kind was tempered not only for many Liberal Churchmen, but also for conservative Evangelicals and Anglo-Catholics, by the realization that ignorance might be more of a threat to religious conviction than knowledge in an age of biblical criticism and new scientific theories. Was it not better for young women to be able to learn of the reassuringly conservative conclusions of Lightfoot or Hort on the vexed question of the historicity of the Scriptures than to be exposed without such guides to the destructive conclusions of a Strauss? It was also argued that the consequences of female education need not be to lure women away from their traditional tasks, but rather to equip them to be better instructors of the young and better-informed philanthropists.

Typical of this cautious but very definite support of women's education was Josephine Butler's 1868 pamphlet *The Education and Employment of Women*. When she and her husband moved to Liverpool in 1866 they became involved in the work of the North of England Council for the Higher Education of Women. Butler became its President in 1867, taking a petition to Cambridge the following year requesting the university to set examination papers for women. Writing with the down-to-earth appreciation of unwelcome facts that also informed her crusade against the Contagious Diseases Acts, she began by highlighting the plight of the two and a half million women who had no husbands and were forced to work for their own subsistence, many of them as poorly paid governesses and teachers. Far from seeking education, as their critics claimed, in order to compete for academic distinction, she pointed out that 'for many women to get knowledge is the only way to get bread'.[32] She was also keenly aware, however, that the subject of women's education was a battleground, and she was careful to chart a path between the opposing forces. Those who feared that learning was a threat to women's sense of domestic duty were dismissed as hiding from harsh social realities behind a romanticized and idealized rhetoric of chivalrous protection, and one that denied women the right to exercise their God-given talents for the benefit of society:

> They argue in favour of all which is likely to make women better mothers, or better companions for men, but they seem incapable of judging of a woman as a human being by herself, and are superstitiously afraid of anything which might strengthen her to stand alone, prepared, singlehanded, to serve her God and her country. When it is urged upon them that the women who do and must stand alone are counted by millions, they are perplexed, but only fall back on expressions of a fear lest a masculine race of women should be produced, if we admit any theories respecting them apart from conjugal and maternal relationships.[33]

On the other hand, she had no time for those whom she saw as speaking slightingly of maternity, and who regarded intellectual competition and equality with men as an able woman's primary goal, an ambition that lost sight of the God-given truth that 'men and women were made equal indeed, but not alike, and were meant to supplement one another . . . each supplying force which the other lacks'.[34]

It was this cautious belief that men and women were equal but different, and could therefore both benefit from higher education – provided it was firmly based in sound religious doctrine – that characterized Anglican attempts to create and extend women's educational opportunities. One of the first efforts in this direction arose out of the same concern that had preoccupied Josephine Butler: the plight of unmarried women, and particularly governesses, who struggled to earn a living and were ladies in name, but condemned in practice to a life of genteel poverty at the hands of often capricious employers. Begun in 1829 as a mutual assurance society, the Governesses' Benevolent Institution attempted to alleviate their lot by providing temporary grants and annuities to those who were unable to continue working, and then turned its attention to raising the status and standards of governesses by improving their education.

In 1844, one of the society's most energetic supporters, David Laing, the vicar of Holy Trinity, St Pancras, raised with the National Society and the Archbishop of Canterbury the possibility of creating a system of examinations and certificates for governesses; and in 1848 Queen's College was opened in Harley Street in London.[35] Nearly all the members of the education committee were members of staff of King's College in the Strand and, with the exception of those who taught languages, were required to be communicant Anglicans, since King's had been founded as an Anglican college in response to the unsectarian University College in Gower Street. King's itself had made tentative attempts to allow women to attend its lectures, but when the wives and daughters of the professors had flocked to hear Charles Lyell's lectures on geology – which seemed to question the historical veracity of the Genesis account of creation – the college council passed a resolution banning them from attending, a decision that was not rescinded until 1878. Queen's was to suffer no such restrictions. Its courses were open to young women from twelve upwards, and at its fourth meeting the committee decided that attendance was not to be restricted to intending governesses only, but was to be made open to anyone.

Prominent among its early teachers and supporters were the Christian Socialists Charles Kingsley and F. D. Maurice, who was a professor at King's College and who became the first chairman of the education committee at Queen's. Maurice, as in his Christian Socialism, was the embodiment of the cautious Anglican reformer. In his prospectus for the college he explained that its aims had originally been to train governesses, but this aim had been widened with the realization that all ladies were in some sense teachers, whether of their own children, or of their siblings, or of the poor, and he assured his readers that the originators of the scheme had no intention of creating a utopian establishment along the lines of that in Tennyson's *The Princess*.[36] The curriculum was to include traditional female accomplishments such as music and drawing, while the academic subjects were modern languages, English literature, Latin, geography, theology, and arithmetic; but at this stage, Maurice's view of women's education was a severely limited one: in 1855, he rejected the idea of opening the professions to women and their admission to university degrees, though by 1870 he was involved in the programme of lectures that led to the creation of Newnham College, Cambridge.[37]

Despite the conservative ideals of its founders, Queen's played a role of considerable importance in the development of women's education. It proved to be the spur for the creation of Bedford College, the achievement of a wealthy Unitarian and Abolitionist, Mrs Reid, who determined that her new college should be non-denominational, and that women should play a prominent part in its government. It was also the institution where two of the pioneers of improved women's secondary education, Dorothea Beale and Frances Mary Buss, finished their studies – the former serving on the staff for seven years as the first female tutor.

In 1850, Frances Buss opened her North Collegiate School for Ladies in Camden Town, with the Rev. David Laing, the vicar of St Pancras, as its superintendent and Scripture teacher. The school was unusual in that it took children from a wider background than simply the upper middle class, for, as Miss Buss told the audience at the first prize day, a thorough education based on sound religious principles 'is as necessary for the daughters as for the sons of the large and influential portion of society consisting of Professional Gentlemen of limited means, clerks in public and private offices and persons engaged in Trade and other pursuits'. Although firmly based on Anglican teaching, the school was also liberal in its attitude to religious tests, with parents having the right to withdraw their children from some or all of religious instruction.[38] Carol Dyhouse has described Frances Buss as energetic, capable, and a first-rate entrepreneur, whose sense of mission was 'profoundly secular'; however, while this might appear to be the case in comparison with the devoutly High Church life of Dorothea Beale, religion remained the driving force behind Buss's life's work – as Dorothea recalled,

'How full of prayer was her life only a few intimate friends knew.'[39]

Dorothea Beale's faith was of an altogether more demonstrative kind. Cheltenham College had been founded in 1854; and its Committee of Management were not only all Anglican, but mostly strongly evangelical in their sympathies. Their first annual report was permeated by an intensely religious confidence in the restorative moral and social power of educated women that lay behind so much Victorian educational endeavour. Not only was a due cultivation of women's minds, they believed, desirable in itself, 'but the general welfare of society at large depends greatly upon it'. This was a vision fully shared by Dorothea Beale, but the College was anxious at first as to whether she might not hold High Church views on the subject of baptismal regeneration. Having satisfied them on this point, she made the teaching of Scripture the foundation of the education offered at Cheltenham. Not only was her faith the source of her own educational vision, it also sustained her through all trials and disappointments:

> How often I was full of discouragement. It was not so much the want of money as the want of ideals that depressed me. If I went into society I heard it said: 'What is the good of education for our girls? They have not to earn their living.' Those who spoke did not see that, for women as for men, it is a sin to bury the talents God has given; they seemed not to know that the baptismal right was the same for girls as for boys, alike enrolled in the army of light, soldiers of Jesus Christ.[40]

Her sense of being the agent of divine providence also made her formidable when faced by opposition to her own wishes. She identified herself closely with the powerful and scholarly Anglo-Saxon Abbess, Hilda of Whitby, and she behaved towards the College's governing council as if she were indeed the Mother Superior of a religious house when they opposed her plans to enlarge their membership and to take additional powers upon herself.

The Church was also actively engaged, both for and against, in the campaign to open university education to women. Foremost in the early stages was Emily Davies. She had met Miss Leigh Smith and her sister, Madame Bodichon, while nursing her sick brother on a trip to Algiers, and subsequently became involved in the work of the Langham Place circle. This campaigned for a Married Women's Property Act, and, through *The Englishwoman's Journal* and the Society for the Employment of Women, sought to increase the opportunities for employment open to women. Since Emily's brother

Llewelyn had been appointed rector of Christ Church, Marylebone, in 1856, it was possible for her to make frequent visits to London while still undertaking the tasks of a dutiful only daughter in her father's rectory in Gateshead. Inspired by the ideals of the embryo women's movement at Langham Place, Emily set out to introduce some of its ideas into her own parish work in the North East by creating a Northumberland and Durham Branch of the Society for Promoting the Employment of Women, with herself as Treasurer and the Bishop of Durham as President – an action that led her friend, Elizabeth Garrett, to describe her as 'a recognized worker for the cause'.[41]

In October 1862, Emily formed a committee to obtain the admission of women to the local examinations of Oxford and Cambridge, and after a trial examination at Cambridge, the subject was debated at a special meeting of the Social Science Association on 29 April 1864, and again at its regular meeting at York in September. At the latter, the proposal was opposed by the Archbishop of York and by Canon Norris, who accepted that women should study freely but in their own way – since the two sexes were in his view 'in mental constitution as in all else, marvellously, beautifully, and distinctly supplemental to one another'. Despite such fears, the University Senate accepted the proposal by fifty-five votes to fifty-one.[42]

A far bolder step was the creation of a women's college at Hitchin in 1869, which in 1873 moved to Girton. Again, Anglican opinion was divided as to the wisdom of the proposal. The General Committee that was formed to promote the project included two bishops and three deans, but approaches to Dr Pusey and Charlotte Yonge were predictably fruitless, as was one to Archbishop Longley's daughter – who told Emily Davies that the idea of a women's college was 'quite contrary to her notions of a woman's sphere'.[43] Despite such doubts, the success of a number of students in the University Little-go examination in October 1870 – which included a viva voce examination on the Gospel of St Luke in Greek, and was regarded as a qualifying examination for degree courses – did much to establish the academic credibility of the new college.

In October 1875, a second college, Newnham Hall, was opened – thanks partly to the efforts of Anne Clough, the poet's sister, and Henry Sidgwick. Part of the reason for the creation of a second college lay in differences between Sidgwick and Davies over the question of religious affiliation. The former was insistent that at Girton religious instruction would be given in accordance with the principles of the established Church, though students were excused these if they wished, and two of the first five students admitted were Quakers. Sidgwick had resigned his college fellowship in 1869, and opposed the regulation that all college fellows should be required to subscribe to the Thirty Nine Articles of the Church of England. Unlike Girton, Newnham had no chapel and was regarded as the upholder of intellectual liberalism, though in practice this made little difference to the education that was offered; and the historian of women at Cambridge, Rita McWilliams-Tullberg, has suggested that it was the more pious and conservative Girton that gained a reputation as an institution that favoured the women's rights movement.[44]

Anglican activism was also instrumental in the creation of women's colleges at Oxford.[45] The moving spirits behind the building of Lady Margaret Hall were the Rev. Edward Talbot, the first Warden of Keble College, and his wife Lavinia, the daughter of Lord Lyttleton and niece of Mrs Gladstone. 'Why', Talbot asked his wife, 'should the Church not be for once at the front instead of behind in this new development?' – an innovatory view of the role of the Church of England that found little favour with Canon Liddon of Christ Church, who thought the scheme 'an educational development which runs counter to the wisdom and experience of all the centuries of Christendom'.[46] As at Cambridge, there were tensions within the women's movement between High Churchmen such as Talbot who wished to establish a distinctively Anglican college, and others such as Dr John Percival, President of Trinity College and future Bishop of Hereford, who favoured an undenominational hall – a view shared by free-thinking supporters of women's education among the liberal intelligentsia, including Mrs Humphry Ward. The result was the opening of Lady Margaret Hall and Somerville College in October 1879. Anglican initiative, this time inspired by Evangelicalism, was also instrumental in the founding of Westfield College at London University, whose first Principal, Constance Maynard, was even able to enlist the support of the elderly Lord Shaftesbury in its favour.[47]

Of course, it is misleading to see the movement for women's higher education in narrowly denominational or religious terms: it was part of a growing sense among the middle classes that in an industrializing society that placed an increasing premium upon professional standards, their daughters too required a higher level of education. Religious ideals and social aspirations were also often combined, as for example in the case of the notable financial contributions that northern Unitarian textile families made to Newnham, Girton, and Somerville.[48]

125

However, the first generation of middle-class students found themselves uneasily caught between more traditional ideals of women's domesticity and newer visions of pursuing an independent career, and it was not coincidental that all the colleges with their strict system of chaperoning were described as conforming to the model of English family life in their organization and daily life. Nor is it surprising that many Anglican churchmen who supported higher education for women clung to the idea that it ought to be conducted along separate lines from that provided for men. Thus the Rev. G. F. Browne, who was Secretary of the Cambridge Local Examinations Board and one of the first lecturers at Hitchin, responded to the proposal in 1887 that women should be admitted to degrees at Cambridge by suggesting that a wholly separate and parallel institution should be created to teach and award degrees to women, an idea that continued to find favour with the eminent biblical scholar Westcott.[49] Attitudes and hesitations such as these help to explain why the proposal to admit women to degrees at Cambridge was rejected in 1897, and why women were not admitted to full membership of the University of Oxford until 1919, and not until 1948 at Cambridge.

In practice, the revolution in women's higher education in the nineteenth century was an extremely conservative one, and therefore well suited to find support as well as opposition from within the Church of England, but it was a revolution nevertheless. Even the Mothers' Union, the epitome of Victorian ideals of female domesticity, could find room in the first number of its journal *Mothers in Council* in 1891 for an article in favour of higher education for women, which admitted that 'the education of the past has had its day'.[50] Speaking at a conference at Westfield College in 1913 on the subject of women's education, Canon Masterman embodied both the essence of a Christian vision of higher education and the constraints of gender to which it was subject in the Victorian period. Women's and men's minds were and would remain fundamentally different, he began, but he was in no doubt also that 'our intellectual life was quite as much Divine and quite as much a part of God's gift as any other part of our lives'.[51]

Notes

1. Quoted in J. Purvis, *Hard Lessons: The Lives and Education of Working-Class Women in Nineteenth-Century England* (Oxford, Polity Press, 1989),

pp. 87-88.

2. Parliamentary Papers, 1819, Report from Commissioners, *Charities in England for the Education of the Poor*, vol. x, pp. 382-383.

3. *Charities in England for the Education of the Poor*, pp. 31-36.

4. C. Brown, *The Church's Part in Education 1833-1941 with Special Reference to the Work of the National Society* (London, SPCK, 1942), pp. 163-164.

5. Brown, *The Church's Part in Education 1833-1941*. The Newcastle Commission's findings are set out and discussed in Purvis, *Hard Lessons*, pp. 72-79.

6. Purvis, *Hard Lessons*, p. 78.

7. P. B. Cliff, *The Rise and Development of the Sunday School Movement in England 1780-1980* (Nuffield, Surrey, National Christian Education Council, 1986), p. 202.

8. As Gillian Sutherland explains, the distinction between elementary and secondary education in the nineteenth century was not one of age, but of social class. Elementary education was provided only for children of the labouring poor, and took children of all ages from 7 to 12; secondary schools provided for the middle classes took children from 7 to 20 (G. Sutherland, 'The Movement for the Higher Education of Women: Its Social and Intellectual Context in England, *c.* 1840-80', in P. Waller (ed.), *Politics and Social Change in Modern Britain: Essays Presented to A. F. Thompson* (Brighton, Harvester Press, 1987), pp. 93-94). Purvis is more doubtful than Sutherland as to whether girls received a comparable education to boys in National Society schools (Purvis, *Hard Lessons*, pp. 87-93).

9. G. S. Haight, *George Eliot* (Oxford, Clarendon Press, 1968), pp. 10-15.

10. For this, see C. Binfield, *Belmont's Portias: Victorian Nonconformists and Middle-Class Education for Girls* (London, Dr Williams Trust, 1981).

11. The Cowan Bridge school was the basis for Charlotte's savage attack on the hypocrisies and cruelties of evangelicalism in the shape of Lowood school and its tyrannical headmaster, Mr Brocklehurst, in *Jane Eyre*. Mrs Gaskell suggests that Charlotte later regretted that Lowood came to be identified so closely with Cowan Bridge, though she did not deny the truth of the picture that she painted (E. C. Gaskell, *The Life of Charlotte Brontë* (Edinburgh, John Grant, 1924), p. 51).

12. M. Bryant, *The Unexpected Revolution: A Study in the History of the Education of Women and Girls in the Nineteenth Century* (London, University of London Institute of Education, 1979), p. 31.

13. G. Battiscombe, *Reluctant Pioneer: A Life of Elizabeth Wordsworth* (London, Constable, 1978), pp. 21-22.

14. M. Marshall, *What I Remember* (Cambridge, CUP, 1947), pp. 6-7.

15. B. Stephen, *Emily Davies and Girton College* (London, Constable, 1927), p. 25.

16. Sutherland, 'The Movement for the Higher Education of Women', p. 101.

17. Stephen, *Emily Davies and Girton College*, p. 211.

18. *The Guardian*, 10 January 1913, p. 51.

19. *Mothers in Council*, vol. 2 (1892), pp. 43–49. A classic statement of the scientific opinion to which these writers appealed is to be found in George Romanes's *Mental Difference Between Men and Women* published in 1887, which claimed that the fact that women's brains were on average some 5 pounds lighter than those of men resulted in their exhibiting 'a marked inferiority of intellectual power'. Romanes was not in practice against the movement for women's higher education, so long as it did not lead to what he called 'an unnatural, and therefore an impossible, rivalry with men in the struggles of practical life'. The text is reproduced in D. Spender (ed.), *The Education Papers: Women's Quest for Equality in Britain 1850–1912* (London, Routledge & Kegan Paul, 1987), pp. 10–31.

20. For Burgon's sermon and his career, see E. Goulburn, *John William Burgon* (2 vols, London, John Murray, 1892). In Goulburn, a former Dean of Norwich, Burgon found a sympathetic biographer and kindred spirit, who described the admission of women to university examinations as a 'dislocation of the Divinely constituted order of Society', and who warned darkly of 'the frightful social mischiefs' that would follow (vol. 2, p. 238).

21. *Catherine and Craufurd Tait, A Memoir* (London, Macmillan, 2nd edn, 1881), p. 144.

22. E. Lloyd, *Anna Lloyd: A Memoir* (London, Cayme Press, 1928), pp. 57–58. Anna came from a Quaker background, and recalled that members of her family regarded her going to Hitchin as both unnatural and unchristian.

23. E. Robson, 'University Education', *Mothers in Council*, vol. 2 (1892), p. 36.

24. Quoted in J. Burstyn, *Victorian Education and the Ideal of Womanhood* (London, Croom Helm, 1980), pp. 108–109. The whole chapter 'Religion and Women's Education' is a helpful, if somewhat one-sided, account of this theme.

25. C. B. Firth, *Constance Louisa Maynard* (London, George Allen & Unwin, 1949).

26. C. Wordsworth, *Christian Womanhood and Christian Sovereignty* (London, Rivingtons, 1884).

27. J. Kamm, *Hope Deferred: Girls' Education in English History* (London, Methuen, 1965), p. 220.

28. J. Otter, *Nathaniel Woodard. A Memoir of his Life* (London, Bodley Head, 1925), p. 274.

29. For the details of her life, see G. Battiscombe, *Charlotte Mary Yonge: The Story of an Uneventful Life* (London, Constable, 1943).

30. *The Daisy Chain* was republished in 1988 by Virago Press. The quotations

are from pp. 6–7 of this edition. Apart from her emphasis on the primacy of domestic duty, Charlotte Yonge also held the widespread belief in women's innate intellectual inferiority, claiming that 'A woman of the highest faculties is of course superior to a man of the lowest, but she never attains to anything like the powers of a man of the highest ability.' Where, she asked, was the woman who had written an oratorio or built a cathedral? (C. Yonge, *Womankind* (London, Walter Smith & Innes, 2nd edn, 1889), pp. 2, 233).

31.   Quoted in J. E. Baker, *The Novel and the Oxford Movement* (Princeton, Princeton UP, 1932) p. 122.

32.   Spender (ed.), *The Education Papers*, p. 72.

33.   Spender (ed.), *The Education Papers*, p. 79.

34.   Spender (ed.), *The Education Papers*, pp. 83–84.

35.   This account is based upon E. Kaye, *A History of Queen's College, London 1848–1972* (London, Chatto & Windus, 1972).

36.   F. D. Maurice, *Queen's College, London: Its Objects and Method* (London, Macmillan, 1848), pp. 8–11.

37.   Kaye, *A History of Queen's College*, p. 87.

38.   J. Kamm, *How Different From Us: A Biography of Miss Buss and Miss Beale* (London, Bodley Head, 1958), pp. 47–49.

39.   C. Dyhouse, 'Miss Buss and Miss Beale: Gender and Authority in the History of Education', in F. Hunt (ed.), *Lessons for Life: The Schooling of Girls and Women, 1850–1950* (Oxford, Basil Blackwell, 1987), pp. 22–38. The quotation is from Kamm, *How Different From Us*, p. 243.

40.   Dyhouse, 'Miss Buss and Miss Beale', p. 57.

41.   Stephen, *Emily Davies and Girton College*, p. 53.

42.   Stephen, *Emily Davies and Girton College*, pp. 92–100.

43.   Stephen, *Emily Davies and Girton College*, p. 167.

44.   R. McWilliams-Tullberg, *Women at Cambridge: A Men's University – Though of a Mixed Type* (London, Victor Gollancz, 1975), p. 68.

45.   This phrase is used by Sutherland, 'The Movement for the Higher Education of Women', p. 112, to draw attention to the part played by the Church of England in the promotion of women's colleges.

46.   V. Brittain, *The Women at Oxford, A Fragment of History* (London, George Harrap, 1960).

47.   Firth, *Constance Louisa Maynard*, p. 184.

48.   Sutherland, 'The Movement for the Higher Education of Women', pp. 97–98.

49.   G. F. Browne, *The Recollections of a Bishop* (London, Smith, Elder & Co., 1915), pp. 309–310.

50. *Mothers in Council*, vol. 1 (1891), pp. 241–242.

51. *The Guardian*, 31 January 1913, p. 157.

CHAPTER SIX

Piety and Philanthropy: Women Volunteers in the Life of the Church

The Victorian age saw an explosion of charitable endeavour on the part of the Church, much of it undertaken by upper- and middle-class women – many of whom were the wives and daughters of the vicarage. Historians and contemporary observers have, however, taken widely differing views of the motivations behind, and consequences of, this endeavour – some seeing it as the working out of the Christian gospel of charity and compassion, while to others it appears as an instrument of social control in a class-ridden society. Both the limitations of female higher education, and the dominance of an all-male clergy, worked against women's involvement in theological questions in a direct way, though as religious novelists and hymn writers they contributed a great deal to the spirituality and theology of the age.

Women and philanthropy

Writing in 1869, Josephine Butler, soon to be the best-known Anglican social campaigner of her day, claimed for women the 'freedom and power to reach and deal with great social evils'. To those who feared that such a mission would be undertaken to the detriment of their family responsibilities, she responded by claiming that 'the extension beyond our homes of the home influence' would regenerate society and thereby strengthen family life itself; homes were not to be merely places of sacred seclusion, and it was the

Christian's duty to guard against what she called 'a selfishness of five or ten'.[1] If Anglicans needed any further persuasion that this was so, she went on, they had only to contemplate the example given by Quaker women. Mrs Butler was in fact by that date already preaching largely to the converted, for according to the Rev. John Blunt in 1864, 'the most available form of lay help which the clergyman will find at his disposal is that offered by ladies of the higher middle classes, many of whom do, and many more wish to devote themselves altogether to works of charity'.[2] Surveying the activities of unpaid women workers in the Church of England in 1893, the Bishop of Ripon's wife, Mrs Boyd Carpenter, listed a wide variety of organizations and activities in which they were involved. Some of the most important were: Sunday school teaching; Girls' Friendly Societies, which sought to provide accommodation and moral support for lower-class girls seeking work in large industrial cities; missionary auxiliary societies working to raise funds and send clothing and needlework overseas; the Church Mission to the Fallen, and a wide network of penitentiaries and houses of refuge for the reclamation of prostitutes; and district visiting in which all the families in a parish were visited, and the spiritual and material wants of each ascertained and alleviated.[3]

The nature of parochial visiting is well illustrated by the life of Maria Havergal, the sister of Frances Ridley Havergal, the hymn writer. The daughter of a clergyman, she was educated from the age of twelve at an evangelical school, where she underwent a conversion experience that she later described in this way: 'a very glimpse of eternity, of the reality of heaven and hell as real places, where each one of us must be for ever, burnt in me a new and powerful desire to help some at least to find the Lord Jesus I trusted in'.[4] As a result, she began distributing tracts to local cottages. When in 1845 her father moved to St Nicholas's, Worcester, she set about systematic visiting in the parish, and later recalled that 'My knowledge of the hundreds of poor, the names of every man, woman, and child, was a great help to my father, especially in the yearly distribution of the church gifts.'[5]

Devoutly evangelical – Maria Havergal only once read a novel, and regretted that trains and the postal service operated on a Sunday – she relied upon what she regarded as divine guidance to unmask immorality on the part of those whom she visited, as on one occasion when, on an impulse, she returned unexpectedly to a cottage and was able to upbraid a woman and man for living in sin.[6] She was also staunchly conservative in her political and social outlook, replying to a doubtless suitably chastened group of school boys who had asked her what she thought of Gladstone's disestablishment of the Irish Church, that 'No Church means no Queen, no God! no peace, no order. The example of our Lord in paying tribute to Caesar rivets the question of obeying the powers that be.' Like other Anglican women engaged in philanthropy, Maria Havergal also believed that it was important to draw a clear distinction between the deserving and undeserving poor, as when she countered the claim by a Jew whom she met at a music box factory in Geneva that money spent in trying to convert his co-religionists was better spent on the poor, by remarking, 'Granted they are poor, but with many it is their vice and their drunkenness, and English charities provide abundantly for the deserving.'[7]

Maria Havergal was not alone in seeing drink as one of the causes of vice and poverty, and Anglican women played a prominent part in the Temperance Movement. The best-known worker in this field was Julia Wightman, a clergyman's wife, who branched out from visiting the poor and sick in their homes to organizing a temperance hall for both men and women. Her account of her endeavours, *Haste to the Rescue*, published in 1859, ran to 26,000 copies in fourteen months, and was instrumental in the creation of the Church of England Temperance Society. In her introduction she appealed to 'the educated classes', and what her biographer called her 'patronizing spirit and kindly condescension' were typical of the ethos of middle-class Christian women undertaking charitable work.[8]

Along with Nonconformists, Anglican women were also heavily involved in the first national women's temperance organization, the British Women's Temperance Association founded in 1876.[9] Despite such efforts, the work proved to be an uphill battle, and at the Church Congress of 1899, the Treasurer of the Church Army, Edward Clifford, was lamenting the fact that 'from the factory girl to the leader of smart society, drinking stimulants has enormously increased among women', though whether this was the result of 'the increased strain of nerve' brought about by the pressures of modern life, or 'the fashion of women claiming every license and liberty which has hitherto been restricted to men', he was unsure.[10] As the Bishop of Hereford realized, part of the trouble lay in the inadequacy of the traditional philanthropy of personal initiative and face-to-face contact; what was needed was legislative action by government, and this raised problems for the Church of England. For one thing, the Bishop was forced to ask his audience how many of them had shares in the brewing industry.[11] It was far easier for Nonconformists to be enthusiastic about the temperance cause, seeing it as crusade against an unholy alliance of the Conservative Party, the Church, and the brewers.

Unlike the temperance cause, the Girls' Friendly Society founded in 1874 by Mrs Townsend was unhampered by the tortuous complexities of politics and legislation, and became one of the largest Anglican charitable organizations for women. In 1884, it had 640 branches, 19,406 lady associates, and 71,181 members. By 1914, it had grown to 196,321 members and 39,433 associates, organized in 1,749 branches.[12] The Society was launched in 1874 after a meeting of ladies, including the Archbishop's wife, at Lambeth Palace; and according to its historian, Brian Harrison, it was the first Anglican organization designed for and run by women.[13] The division of the society into lady associates and ordinary members was central to the purposes of the society, which hoped that the moral and spiritual example of the former would rub off on the working-class girls whom it helped by running employment registries, clubs and recreation rooms, and homes of rest. Members also ran reception points at railway stations to try to prevent girls arriving in cities from the country from falling into evil ways, since as one member warned somewhat cryptically, 'there is a certain class of girls who lose their heads the moment they enter a railway station'.[14]

Unpaid but organized philanthropy of this kind gave many women with time on their hands, and who were bored by the stifling and repetitive round of domestic life, opportunities to acquire new interests and exercise their talents outside the home.[15] Despite seemingly endless pious encomiums upon the satisfactions of domesticity, there is evidence that for many women, particularly those who were single, it failed to provide a fulfilling way of life. As Florence Nightingale bitterly realized, 'The family uses people, not for what they are, nor for what they are intended to be, but for what it wants them for. . . . If it wants someone to sit in the drawing-room, that someone is supplied by the family, though that member may be destined for science, or for education, or for active superintendence by God, i.e. by the gifts within.'[16] Caroline Maitland wrote to the well-known Christian philanthropist Catherine Marsh, on reading her *The Daughter at Home*, of 'the drab-coloured picture of life' that she portrayed, and wondered if any unmarried woman who stayed at home could 'bear sixty years of sour sisters and Sunday schools'. Catherine's religious ideals and the life of charitable service that they suggested had given her 'comfort and beauty however, in the midst of this insufferable dullness'.[17] Florence Nightingale's driving ambition for a publicly recognized career – which led her to ask 'the Church of England has for men bishoprics, archbishoprics, and a little work. . . . For women she has what?'[18] – was less typical than the response of Caroline Maitland and Catherine Marsh, which was to seize the opportunities which voluntary philanthropy afforded.

The charitable exertions of Victorian women undertaken on behalf of the poor had a number of aims, which were set out by the Rev. J. H. Blunt in his manual on pastoralia.[19] Some of these were designed to meet physical need, preferably by promoting schemes that encouraged self-help, such as clothing clubs and penny savings banks, and by increasing 'the comfort of the poor by judicious advice on domestic subjects'. Direct giving of assistance was more problematic and required careful monitoring, since it was thought likely to foster what it is now fashionable to call a culture of dependence. Typical of this approach was the work of one of the most celebrated of Anglican female philanthropists, Octavia Hill, who set up a model housing project for the poor, and, along with John Ruskin and the Rev. Samuel Barnett, took a leading part in the creation of the Charity Organization Society in 1868. In a paper to the Society on 'The Importance of Aiding the Poor without Alms Giving', she warned of the dangers of indiscriminate charity, and throughout her life remained suspicious of proposals for state provision of housing, medical care, or pensions.[20]

Octavia Hill's approach was not popular with some clergy accustomed to a tradition of Christian charitable giving, nor – surprisingly – with the poor themselves, and it was one that militated against what Blunt regarded as among the most important objectives of philanthropy – namely, religious education and the hope of persuading the working class to go to church. But how successfully were these objectives accomplished, particularly the last? As we have seen, *The Daily News* survey of church attendance in London in 1902–1903 indicated that significantly more women than men attended Anglican places of worship in the East End of London, but overall they formed a small percentage of the female population – at best, no more than one in ten attended evening services.[21] However, the Church also provided for women's religious and social needs in other ways. In his *Life and Labour of the People of London*, Charles Booth saw the mothers' meetings, with their thrift clubs for saving towards Christmas expenses and annual day trips to the country, as providing a meeting place for often tired and harassed women who had little time to attend a place of worship on Sunday.[22]

It was also the case that the Church's campaigns against the abuse of alcohol and its provision of savings clubs often had direct relevance to the lives of women who were primarily responsible for the maintenance of domestic life, and were themselves the ones most likely to go without in times of need. Overall, he concluded, 'The women, however, have, nearly all of them, a strong though rather indefinite sense of religion which the mothers' meeting does something to satisfy, and which finds expression in other ways, such as may be found in the proprieties of the marriage rites and of churchings, and in respect for baptism.'[23] As Booth suggested, a rather diffuse religiosity expressed in terms of basic moral standards of care, neighbourliness, and endurance rather than in dogmatic propositions, and the rites of passage that marked and sanctioned the stages of family life, often had more relevance to women's lives than did regular churchgoing.

However, Booth was also at pains to emphasize that the women he was describing were poor, and while 'the wives of regularly employed labouring men may attend in some cases . . . those of the artisans hardly ever'.[24] For the latter, the class moralism and political conservatism of middle-class philanthropy were unwelcome, and a culture of deference was experienced as an affront to the sense of independence and self-improvement of the labour aristocracy. Historians have given widely differing interpretations of middle-class philanthropy, with Frank Prochaska emphasizing the Christian values of love and self-sacrifice that inspired it, while Jennifer Hart has seen the Church as an instrument of social control aimed at warding off fundamental change to the existing order – and from this perspective she concludes that 'It is not difficult to understand why the authorities were anxious that the working classes should go to church, nor why many of them did not.'[25] These two approaches need not of course be mutually contradictory, given the view of the right ordering of society and of the individual's place within it to which philanthropists adhered.

Certainly, industrialization, the growth of cities, and increasing class conflict led many in the Church to fear a breakdown in the social fabric. This was expressed luridly in a sermon by Bishop Browne of Winchester, who warned that 'beneath all government, and waiting to subvert and submerge all, lie hidden, or scarcely hidden, volcanic fires of communistic anarchy, joined in close affinity with agnosticism and atheism'.[26] Anglican middle- and upper-class ladies believed that the social order was God-given and beneficial, that, in the words of Mrs Alexander's classic hymn,

> The rich man in his castle,
> The poor man at his gate,
> He made them high and lowly,
> And ordered their estate.[27]

Through their charitable work, women were, it was claimed, in a unique position not to subvert class differences, but to make them more acceptable by softening their contours through kindness. As the Honourable Mrs Dundas told a meeting of the Girls' Friendly Society at Darlington in 1890, its members were to be 'a sort of golden bridge between the different classes of life'.[28]

The same theme was taken up at the 1908 Pan-Anglican Congress by a speaker on women's work in the Church, who claimed that 'It is women who guard those barriers of social life which mark the boundary between class and class. It is they mainly who must see that those boundaries are true – they who must reconcile those barriers with the sense of brotherhood and sisterhood within the Christian Church.'[29] This was no easy task. One of the agents of the Girls' Friendly Society, one of whose aims was described as the creation in its members of 'Happy and modest looks, Respectful and retiring manners', found by contrast that mill girls were 'undisciplined, impatient of reproof, and entirely wanting in self-control'.[30] Although as a Nonconformist preacher and agricultural trade union organizer Joseph Arch was a hostile witness, no one captured better the gulf of class divisions that no amount of philanthropy could bridge, and the bitterness that class moralism and patronage could engender even in a rural society, which the Church regarded as more congenial to social deference and cohesion than the large cities:

> I can . . . remember the time when the parson's wife used to sit in state in her pew in the chancel, and the poor women used to walk up the church and make a curtsey to her before taking seats set apart for them. They were taught in this way that they had to pay homage and respect to those 'put in authority over them', and made to understand that they must 'honour the powers that be', as represented in the rector's wife. You may be pretty certain that many of these women did not relish the curtsey-scraping and other humiliations they had to put up with, but they were afraid to speak out. They had their families to think of, children to feed and clothe

somehow; and when so many could not earn a living wage . . .[31]

Women in church life

Charitable work was undertaken strictly under the supervision of the clergy, but evangelical conviction could in some circumstances give women opportunities to preach in public, even though this was generally considered to be against the teaching of Scripture. The second evangelical awakening, which came from America via Ulster and spread to many parts of Britain in the 1860s, made use of women preachers – a number of whom, in Olive Anderson's words, 'achieved star status in the revivalist firmament'. One of these, Geraldine Hooper, was an Anglican who was encouraged to preach in public to mixed audiences by W. Haslam, the curate of Trinity Church in Bath, but female preachers found a much readier reception in other denominations, and mainstream Anglican opinion was expressed by Isabella Bird, who regarded women's preaching in public as among the 'excesses' of the Ulster revival in 1859.[32]

Philanthropic work could, however, provide Anglican women with other – and less controversial – opportunities to address mixed audiences in public. This was the case, for example, with Catherine Marsh, described by her biographer as 'one of the foremost pioneers of the goodly band of women philanthropists'. Catherine was the daughter of the vicar of St Peter's, Colchester. From an early age, she helped her mother with parish work, teaching a Sunday school class when she was only eleven. When later a railway line was built near the family home at Basingstoke, she began distributing religious tracts to the navvies, experience that later stood her in good stead for addressing over two hundred prisoners at Preston Gaol on the theme of the Prodigal Son.[33]

Work in support of missionary societies also sometimes allowed women a public speaking role in church life, even though it was mainly directed at children – one of the chief targets of missionary fund-raising. For example, Louise Byrd, a member of the Church Missionary Society's Gleaner's Union, reported in 1891 on the success of creating a missionary map of Africa on the beach of a north Wales seaside resort, with sand pies to mark the location of mission stations. Afterwards, she and her colleagues spoke for hours to the assembled crowd. Might not the same method, she wondered, be applicable to a vicarage lawn in spring using flowers and flags?[34]

Women's work in support of overseas missions also brought a much more tangible return to the societies. This was an area where domestic influence could be used directly to promote a public cause, since children were mobilized both as contributors and as collectors. In 1887 the Church Missionary Society recorded having received over 6 shillings from three sisters in Stepney, 'the money having been raised by enforcing a fine on not being down to family prayers each morning'.[35] Such sums mounted up: in the financial year 1898–1899, children contributed over £17,000 to the CMS from missionary collecting boxes alone.[36]

Many of those most actively engaged in church work were the wives and daughters of the parsonage, and the period before the slump in agricultural prices in the 1870s was – not only economically, but also pastorally – something of a golden age for clerical family life. Nowhere, too, was the complementarity of the sexes within a patriarchal family structure seen to better effect, with wives and daughters the enthusiastic agents through Sunday school teaching and parochial visiting of the spiritual authority vested in the clerical paterfamilias. Such women were expected to have no independent existence of their own, but to be incorporated into the profession of their husbands – albeit in a secondary capacity – for, as Mrs Creighton (herself a bishop's wife) observed, the parson's wife 'has a sphere, but it is an entirely subordinate one, more subordinate than that of any other wife'.[37]

As in the eighteenth century, by no means all clergymen were well off, and the idyll of clerical family life did not always correspond to the reality. Life for the Brontë family, for example, when Patrick Brontë became perpetual curate of a poor upland parish in 1820, was far from comfortable, and his three daughters had to take a succession of posts as governesses as well as coping with a heavy round of domestic duties when they were at home. Charlotte coped with all this philosophically, writing to a friend that 'I am much happier black-leading the stoves, making the beds, and sweeping the floors at home, than I should be living like a fine lady anywhere else.' Lack of congenial company and intellectual isolation were often further trials in rural areas, as for the wife of one Wiltshire rector who wrote sadly of the lifeline provided by books 'which transport us, as it were, into a theatre bright with lights and teeming with life, where we can forget for the time being what and where we are'.[38]

Intellectual outlets for women in the Church were generally limited, partly owing to their lack of higher education, and partly to

139

the feeling that theology was a male preserve (it was the one dangerous subject that women should not study, according to Ruskin), and engaging in doctrinal controversy was considered unladylike.[39] Ruskin's fear that theological speculation might lead to radical conclusions for the patriarchal ordering of society was not without foundation. Josephine Butler, for example, based her theology on her own reading of Christ's life and words, concluding that 'of those subtle subdivisions, physical, intellectual, and moral, in which the inferiority or equality of woman is so jealously defined and guarded in theory, I find no hint whatever in Christ's teaching'.[40] From the fact that Christ first revealed the resurrection to women, she drew conclusions for the future that went far beyond those prevalent in the Church of her day, speculating that 'It may be that God will give grace to some woman in the time to come to discern more clearly, and to reveal to others, some truth which theologians have hitherto to see in its fulness; for from the intimacy into which our Divine Master admitted women with Himself it would seem that His communications of the deepest nature were not confined to male recipients; and what took place during his life on earth may, through his Holy Spirit, be continued now.'[41] Butler's theology was strikingly similar to that of Florence Nightingale, who concluded from her own reading of Scripture that 'Jesus Christ raised women above the condition of mere slaves, mere ministers to the passions of man, raised them by His sympathy, to be Ministers of God', and she too looked to the future, to a day when 'there shall arise a woman, who will resume, in her own soul, all the sufferings of her race, and that woman will be the Saviour of her race'.[42]

In their attempts to read the Bible from a non-patriarchal perspective and to bring to the androcentric tradition of the Christian tradition the experience and spirituality of women, Butler and Nightingale prefigure some of the central themes of feminist theology a hundred years later; and given the social and intellectual restraints placed upon Christian women in the Victorian period (Nightingale's work was not published until 1928), their achievements as theological writers were exceptional. However, a number of women did achieve prominence as the authors of improving religious literature, including Catherine Marsh – whose *Memoirs of Captain Hedley Vicars*, a Christian hero of the Crimean War, became a bestseller. For Evangelicals such as the Marsh family, fictional works were suspect, but for the High Church Charlotte Yonge, the novel could be an appropriate vehicle for a woman writer – provided it was used for Christian purposes.

Hymn writing was another area in which a number of women achieved public recognition. The composition and singing of hymns popularized by the Wesleys was an important feature of the eighteenth-century evangelical revival, but although collections were published by Martin Madan, Augustus Toplady (the author of 'Rock of Ages'), John Newton, and William Cowper, hymns within the Church of England were regarded as more suitable for private devotion rather than public devotion, in which pride of place was given to psalm singing.[43] This meant that Anglicans played little part in the growth of hymn writing by women in the eighteenth century, to which Nonconformists such as Anne Steele and Mrs Barbauld made notable contributions.[44] By the early nineteenth century, the value of hymns as aids to worship was being increasingly realized, and in the preface to her volume of translations of the psalms published in 1829, Harriet Auber lamented the lack of suitable hymns for use in the Church of England. The missionary bishop Reginald Heber tried to meet this deficiency by attempting, unsuccessfully as it turned out, to persuade the Church to authorize a volume of its own. It was in fact to be Heber's friend, the poet Mrs Felicia Hemans, whose volume of children's hymns appeared in Boston in 1827 and in England in 1833, who gave a new impetus to Anglican women's composition.[45] The following year, Charlotte Elliott – whose mother was the niece of the Rev. Henry Venn, one of the leaders of the Evangelical Clapham Sect – took over the preparation for publication of a friend's hymn book for invalids. She added 112 of her own compositions to this hymn book, including 'Just as I am Without One Plea', which rapidly achieved great success.[46]

Women had several claims to be accepted as hymn writers. As Canon John Ellerton, one of the editors of SPCK's *Church Hymns* argued of such compositions, 'It is not enough that they *suggest* devotion, they must be capable of expressing it', and devotion was a quality increasingly associated with women.[47] Moreover, some of the most successful collections were compiled for children, and here too women were thought to have particular maternal insight on which to draw. In this field the most successful writer was the wife of an Anglican rector who became Bishop of Derry, Mrs Alexander, whose 1848 *Hymns for Little Children* ran to many editions in the course of the century. Both Charlotte Elliott and Mrs Hemans specialized in hymns in which individual and family suffering and bereavement figure prominently, themes that they had experienced personally in their lives, and that called for womanly compassion and understanding.[48]

Another notable contribution to Anglican hymnody was made by Catherine Winkworth, six of whose translations of hymns from German appeared in the 1875 edition of *Hymns Ancient and Modern*. By that date, nineteen women had contributed forty-seven hymns to the collection, of which thirty-four were original.[49]

Yet even as the poets of exalted Christian domesticity, women could experience conflicts between their ambitions as authors and the ideals of self-abnegation enjoined by Christian teaching. Thus Frances Ridley Havergal, some of whose hymns appeared in her edition of her father's psalmody, confessed to a friend in 1870 that she felt 'naughty and vexed' by her mother's wish that only her initials and not her name should appear beside her compositions, though she accepted the rightness of the decision.[50] The same struggle between ambition and a piety of self-denial and humility was also experienced by the Tractarian poet Christina Rossetti. In many ways, she lived the life of Charlotte Yonge's ideal Christian heroine: the dutiful spinster at home who also undertook penitentiary work. Yet her work also reveals something of the intense inner conflicts between sexual expression and its sublimation in the love of God, and between her desire for worldly recognition and the denial of self demanded by her faith – conflicts that contributed to the physical and mental ill-health from which she suffered throughout her life.[51] In one of her darkest poems, *The Lowest Room* written in 1856, she expressed something of the struggle 'Not to be first; how hard to learn / That lifelong lesson of the past.' The essence of this religious ideal of womanly self-abnegation was encapsulated in some lines of Lady Dorothy Neville, which were quoted approvingly in the literature of both the Girls' Friendly Society and the Mothers' Union. She was responding to the claims of the New Woman of the 1890s and to the talk about women's rights and the franchise:

> The Rights of woman, what are they?
> The Right to labour, love and pray;
> The Right to weep with those who weep,
> The Right to wake when others sleep.[52]

This was a piety that, as we have seen, could inspire and empower women to devoted charitable service, but its psychic cost could be high for Christian women who aspired to self-fulfilment for its own sake or in ways for which it provided no sanction.

Notes

1. J. Butler (ed.), *Woman's Work and Woman's Culture* (London, Macmillan & Co., 1869), pp. xvii–xxxix.

2. J. H. Blunt, *Directorium Pastorale. Principles and Practice of Pastoral Work in the Church of England* (London, Rivingtons, 1864), p. 323.

3. Mrs Boyd-Carpenter, 'Women's Work in Connection with the Church of England', in Baroness Burdett-Coutts (ed.), *Women's Mission: A Series of Congress Papers on the Philanthropic Work of Women* (London, Royal British Commission, 1893), pp. 111–130. The best modern treatment of this subject is F. K. Prochaska, *Women and Philanthropy in Nineteenth-Century England* (Oxford, Clarendon Press, 1980).

4. J. M. Crane (ed.), *The Autobiography of Maria Vernon Graham Havergal* (London, James Nisbet & Co., 1887), p. 38.

5. Crane (ed.), *Autobiography of Maria Vernon Graham Havergal*, p. 53.

6. Crane (ed.), *Autobiography of Maria Vernon Graham Havergal*, pp. 141–142.

7. Crane (ed.), *Autobiography of Maria Vernon Graham Havergal*, pp. 108, 197.

8. L. Shiman, *Women and Leadership in Nineteenth-Century England* (London, Macmillan, 1992), pp. 109–111.

9. Shiman, *Women and Leadership in Nineteenth-Century England*, p. 159.

10. *The Official Report of the Church Congress Held at London, October 1899* (London, Bemrose & Sons, 1899), p. 167.

11. *The Official Report of the Church Congress Held at London, October 1899*, p. 177.

12. B. Heeney, *The Women's Movement in the Church of England 1850–1930* (Oxford, Clarendon Press, 1988), p. 40.

13. B. Harrison, 'For Church, Queen and Family: The Girls' Friendly Society 1874–1920', *Past and Present*, vol. 61 (November 1973), pp. 108–134.

14. Harrison, 'For Church, Queen and Family', p. 119.

15. In her *Silent Sisterhood: Middle-Class Women in the Victorian Home* (London, Croom Helm, 1975), Patricia Branca has warned against taking descriptions of middle-class idle gentility at their face value. Particularly for families on relatively low incomes, household management and the care of children could be an exhausting full-time occupation.

16. F. Nightingale, *Cassandra*, 1852, quoted in J. M. Golby (ed.), *Culture and Society in Britain 1850–1890* (Oxford, OUP, 1986), p. 248.

17. L. E. O'Rourke, *The Life and Friendships of Catherine Marsh* (London,

Longmans Green, 1917), p. 35.

18. C. Woodham-Smith, *Florence Nightingale* (London, Constable, 1950), p. 98.

19. Blunt, *Directorium Pastorale*, p. 333.

20. There are good accounts of Hill in R. Symonds, *Far Above Rubies: The Women Uncommemorated by the Church of England* (Leominster, Gracewing, 1993), pp. 23–44; and in N. Boyd, *Josephine Butler, Octavia Hill, Florence Nightingale: Three Victorian Women Who Changed Their World* (London, Macmillan, 1982), pp. 95–163.

21. See Chapter 3, p. 84, above.

22. C. Booth, *Life and Labour of the People in London, Third Series: Religious Influences* (New York, AMS Press, 1970), vol. 7, pp. 18–19.

23. Booth, *Life and Labour of the People in London*, p. 19.

24. Booth, *Life and Labour of the People in London*.

25. J. Hart, 'Religion and Social Control in the Mid-nineteenth Century', in A. P. Donajgrozki (ed.), *Social Control in Nineteenth Century Britain* (London, Croom Helm, 1977), pp. 108–177.

26. Quoted in Harrison, 'For Church, Queen and Family', p. 127.

27. This verse of her hymn 'All Things Bright and Beautiful' does not usually appear in modern hymn books.

28. Harrison, 'For Church, Queen and Family', p. 129.

29. *Report of the Women's Meeting Held in Connection with the Pan-Anglican Congress of 1908* (London, SPCK, 1908), p. 110.

30. Harrison, 'For Church, Queen and Family', p. 120.

31. Quoted in P. Horn, *Victorian Countrywomen* (Oxford, Basil Blackwell, 1991), p. 95.

32. O. Anderson, 'Women Preachers in Mid-Victorian Britain: Some Reflections on Feminism, Popular Religion and Social Change', *Historical Journal*, vol. 12 (1969), pp. 467–484. Anderson notes that the employment of female preachers was part of the sensationalist methods adopted by revivalists, but also that it sprang from the theology of nineteenth-century pietism, in which the emphasis on perfect love and obedience to God empowered women to undertake public activities while fitting in with expectations about women's greater purity and religiosity.

33. O'Rourke, *The Life and Friendships of Catherine Marsh*, pp. 125–132, 162–163.

34. *The Church Missionary Gleaner* (November 1891), p. 175.

35. *The Church Missionary Gleaner* (February 1887), p. 21.

36. Prochaska, *Women and Philanthropy*, p. 81.

37. Heeney, *The Women's Movement in the Church of England 1850–1930*, p. 23.

38. Horn, *Victorian Countrywomen*, pp. 84–85.

39. J. Ruskin, *Sesame and Lilies* (London, George Allen, 1904), pp. 107–108. While Ruskin did not object to women studying subjects other than theology, their aim in doing so and the methods they employed should be different, since 'a man ought to know any language or science he learns thoroughly – while a woman ought to know the same language or science, only so far as may enable her to sympathize in her husband's pleasures, and those of his best friends'.

40. Butler (ed.), *Woman's Work and Woman's Culture*, pp. liv–lv.

41. Butler (ed.), *Woman's Work and Woman's Culture*.

42. Quoted in J. M. Golby (ed.), *Culture and Society in Britain 1850–1890: A Source Book of Contemporary Writings* (Oxford, OUP, 1986), p. 254.

43. S. Drain, *The Anglican Church in the Nineteenth Century: Hymns Ancient and Modern 1860–1875* (Lampeter, Edwin Mellen Press, 1989), pp. 76–83.

44. M. Maison, '"Thine, only Thine!" Women Hymn Writers in Britain, 1760–1835', in G. Malmgreen (ed.), *Religion in the Lives of English Women, 1760–1930* (London, Croom Helm, 1986), pp. 11–40.

45. Maison, '"Thine, only Thine!"', pp. 31–32.

46. *Selections from the Poems of Charlotte Elliott with a Memoir by Her Sister* (London, Religious Tract Society, 1874), p. 32.

47. Drain, *The Anglican Church in the Nineteenth Century*, p. 42.

48. For the preoccupation with suffering in Mrs Hemans's work, see H. F. Chorley, *Memorials of Mrs Hemans* (2 vols, London, Saunders & Otley, 1836), vol. 2, pp. 43–44.

49. Drain, *The Anglican Church in the Nineteenth Century*, p. 265.

50. *Letters by the Late Frances Ridley Havergal edited by her Sister* (London, James Nisbet & Co., 1885), p. 95.

51. Two biographies that bring out this theme very clearly are G. Battiscombe, *Christina Rossetti, A Divided Life* (London, Constable, 1981); and K. Jones, *Learning Not To Be First: The Life of Christina Rossetti* (Moreton-in-Marsh, Windrush Press, 1991).

52. *Mothers' Union Journal* (1908), p. 59.

CHAPTER SEVEN

Full-time Church Workers

Anglican sisterhoods, revived in 1845, and the deaconess movement dating from 1861, were two of the most important ways in which women could undertake full-time church work in the nineteenth century. The re-creation of convent life within the Church of England was one of the earliest results of the Oxford Movement, and one that provoked bitter hostility from some evangelicals at what they saw as a prominent instance of a programme aimed at undoing the work of the Reformation by Romanizing the Church. For this reason, they preferred to promote the parochial deaconess as the model of female church worker, untainted as it was by conventual life and the taking of lifelong religious vows.

Yet the deaconess movement and (even more so) the religious life, were controversial for other reasons too. Both offered middle-class women the prospect of a life of Christian service beyond the confines of the Victorian home at a time when career opportunities for women were extremely limited, and when marriage and the care of children and relatives were regarded as a woman's proper sphere. Both forms of life also raised questions about women's status within the Church, and the extent to which they could undertake work that was free of male clerical control. This was less true of other forms of full-time work undertaken by women, since Biblewomen, parochial mission workers, and (from 1887) Church Army sisters were generally not drawn from the middle class, and therefore did not offend against its standards of leisured gentility and domesticity.

Sisterhoods

As we have seen, the dream of the celibate religious life for women was not altogether lost, even in a Georgian Church hostile to Popery and anything that smacked of religious enthusiasm, but interest in monasticism quickened appreciably in the early nineteenth century for a variety of reasons. The influx of monks and nuns fleeing from the French Revolution aroused interest and sympathy in some quarters, while the vogue for Romantic medievalism, exemplified by the Gothic Revival in architecture and the popularity of Sir Walter Scott's novels, also helped to mellow Protestant reactions to the Catholic heritage.[1] At the same time, the growing material and spiritual destitution of increasingly large urban populations – to which the nostalgic appeal to a medieval Christian social order was one response – suggested that there was vital work that middle-class women could undertake in caring for the poor.

It was to meet such needs that in 1826 the Rev. A. R. Dallas published a pamphlet entitled *Protestant Sisters of Charity*, which aimed to improve the nursing care of the poor who were sick by the creation of an organization similar to that of the Soeurs de Charité, whose work Dallas had seen at first hand while living in France. More influential was the Poet Laureate Robert Southey's advocacy of sisterhoods in the second volume of his *Sir Thomas More, or Colloquies on the Progress and Prospects of Society* published in 1829, the year of Catholic Emancipation. Southey shared the by now conventional belief in women's superior religiosity, convinced that 'if religion were everywhere else exploded, it would retain its place in the heart of woman', and he went on to urge the creation of Protestant convents that would undertake charitable and educational work, and offer homes to those women of genteel birth who were lacking adequate financial means.[2]

It was left to the leaders of the Oxford Movement to give concrete form to such aspirations. That their thinking owed something to the new-found enthusiasm for the Middle Ages is evident from the activities of John Mason Neale who, with Benjamin Webb, founded the Cambridge Camden Society in 1839 for the study and promotion of the Gothic style in church architecture. Neale also, in 1843, published a novel entitled *Ayton Priory; Or, the Restored Monastery*, which set out to show the religious and temporal benefits that society might derive from the reintroduction of monastic life into England.[3]

To Newman and Pusey, however, it was not a romantically charged vision of the Middle Ages but the more austere example of the early Church that was the inspiration behind their efforts to revive monasticism. In 1840 Newman published *The Church of the Fathers*, in which he not only described the growth of monasticism historically as a response to the increasing worldliness of the Church, but saw it as indicative of a recurring search for holiness, an abandonment of secular life that was 'often allowable, and when allowable praiseworthy'.[4] At the same time, Dr Pusey was also working to bring about the revival of the religious life. In 1839 he had written to the Tractarian vicar of Leeds, Dr Hook, suggesting the creation of one or more sisterhoods for women, which would, he believed, 'foster a high tone in the church', give 'holy employment to many who yearn for something', and – as an additional benefit – would channel feminine religious zeal, which might 'otherwise often go off in some irregular way, or go over to Rome'.[5]

In 1841, before any plan for a community could be realized, Marion Hughes, the daughter of a Gloucestershire rector, dedicated herself to the religious life under Pusey's direction, and it was not until Easter Week 1845 that the first Anglican sisterhood came into being at Park Village West near Regent's Park in London. This was at the instigation of a group of prominent High Church laymen – including Lord John Manners, the leader of the Tory Young England Movement, and the future Prime Minister Gladstone – and its purpose was stated to be to bring together women 'called by the grace of God to a life of devotion and charity' to relieve distress in the capital by assisting in hospitals, workhouses, and prisons, and by feeding, clothing, and instructing destitute children.[6]

Three years later, Priscilla Sellon, with Pusey's support, founded the Sisterhood of Mercy in response to the Bishop of Exeter's plea for help in working among the poor in the towns of Devonport, Plymouth, and Stonehouse.[7] From small beginnings, the work in and around Devonport expanded until it included an orphanage, a home for delinquent boys, a refuge for training girls for domestic service, an industrial school, a soup kitchen, and a home for old sailors. Later still, the activities undertaken by Priscilla Sellon's sisterhood extended overseas when in 1854 five of the sisters joined Florence Nightingale's party of nurses in the Crimea, while in 1864 three members of the order were sent to Honolulu as missionaries. Despite controversy and setbacks in the life of individual communities, sisterhood life continued to grow in the Victorian Church; and whereas in

1861 there were only 86 Anglican sisters, by 1900 the number had risen to between two and three thousand.[8]

As the prospectus for the Park Village Sisterhood indicates, charitable work among the poor was one of the primary aims behind the creation of female religious orders, and whereas some historians have tended to draw a contrast between the philanthropic orientation of most of the nineteenth-century orders and the increasingly contemplative nature of twentieth-century communities, this is not a distinction that the founders of most sisterhoods would have recognized.[9] For them, the inner strength and vision needed to meet the arduous demands of active philanthropy grew out of the life of prayer and self-discipline of the community. As Emily Ayckbowm, the founder of the Community of the Sisters of the Church in Kilburn, observed, the Eucharist and round of monastic Offices were central to the religious life for, she believed, the sisters' 'work for others will be fruitful only in proportion as they advance in the work of conquering themselves'.

Properly understood, the life of prayer and meditation flowed naturally into that of active compassion, for action was itself a form of prayer, and she had harsh words to say about a kind of so-called spirituality that 'would hear an orphan say its prayers, but leave it dirty and hungry', or would 'read the Bible to a sick man but object to binding up his wounds or making his bed'.[10] Harriet Monsell, the first superior of the Community of St John the Baptist, Clewer, was equally insistent that the life of prayer should not be divorced from that of active charity. In reply to a sister's inquiry on this point, she said that 'they must always be ready to leave God in devotion to work for God in those for whom He shed his blood. . . . I don't think that Martha's work will hurt Mary's contemplation in this life, so that both are really about our Lord.'[11]

Emily Ayckbowm's vision of the religious life as one of total surrender of the self to God was attractive to many young women whose family upbringing had already taught them the values of self-denial in the interests of others, and obedience to authority. Something of this single-minded sense of dedication can be gleaned from the entry that Marion Hughes made in her diary on the day of her religious profession:

> This day Trinity Sunday, 1841, was I enrolled one of Christ's Virgins, espoused to Him and made His handmaid and may He of His infinite mercy grant that I may ever strive to please Him, and to

keep myself from the world though still in it, and should it be most mercifully granted that an opportunity may be given me to separate myself entirely from it, make me to rejoice in the means of taking the burden of His cross more closely to myself . . .[12]

It was this sense of dedication that one nun, Margaret Goodman, saw as being at the heart of the religious life, and she was keen to rebut the suggestion that 'sisterhoods were a mode of existence for ladies who, after every effort on their part, from the supply not equalling the demand, are unable to find husbands; or a refuge for the woe-worn, weary and disappointed'.[13] Margaret Goodman's own experiences of convent life were not altogether happy, and it would be naïve to suppose that the motives of women entering the sisterhoods were not varied, but she was right to suggest that the life was rigorous and demanding. The *horarium* of the first Anglican sisterhood at Park Village in 1845 was built round the recital of the daily office, with charitable work filling the remaining waking hours. The sisters rose at 5.00 a.m. for Matins and Lauds, made their beds and did household cleaning until Prime at 7.00, and after breakfast and Terce at 8.55, spent the morning visiting the poor. After Sext, lunch, recreation, and Nones at 3.00, the rest of the afternoon was again spent in visiting, and the day ended with Vespers at 6.00, supper, religious reading, and Compline, and self-examination at 9.00 p.m.[14]

However, the formation of communities and the regulation of the religious life in a church that had not experienced it since the sixteenth century was not without difficulty. In 1840, the Anglican Newman felt as strongly as Pusey that sisterhoods were 'the only means of saving some of our best members from turning Roman Catholic', but that they could only be formed on the basis of inward principle, and could not be made merely by external regulation.[15] Yet this was bound to be the case with Anglican orders, since they could initially only draw upon Roman Catholic experience at second-hand. For example, in founding her community at Kilburn, Emily Ayckbowm visited the Continent to observe convent life at first-hand, as well as reading extensively from Catholic sources including St Augustine, St Ignatius, and St Vincent de Paul; but even after such careful research, the drawing up of the rule for her sisterhood was a task that involved much thought and many revisions during the first sixteen years of the community's existence.[16]

As Emily Ayckbowm's activities indicate, the success of the sisterhoods depended a great deal on the abilities and temperaments of their mother superiors. Even her own painstaking efforts could not prevent discontented groups from leaving her order in 1894, and again the following year, to found their own communities, while Priscilla Sellon was accused by former members of her sisterhood of imposing a regime of tyrannical self-aggrandizement and harsh disciplinary regulations – a 'despotic monarchy without a Parliament', as one sister described it.[17] The problems facing the early sisterhoods were further exacerbated by one of their leading advocates, Dr Pusey, whose enthusiasm for prolonged fasting and the use of both hair shirts and the 'Discipline' (a thin whip cord with five knots) helped to create a situation at the Park Village community that resulted in the death of one of the sisters.[18] Another of the Park Village sisters, who had been despatched to Plymouth to help Priscilla Sellon's work in the cholera epidemic of 1849, turned out to be too weak to leave her bed as a result of having kept a fast 'suggestive of the monks of the Egyptian Desert' – partly in imitation of Dr Pusey's practice.[19]

Extreme instances such as these provided ammunition for Protestant critics of the sisterhoods, who regarded convent life as a prime example of the sacrifice of reason and conscience demanded by Roman Catholicism. Part of the appeal of this particular manifestation of Victorian anti-Catholicism was to sexual prurience: copies of *The Awful Disclosures of Maria Monk*, which was published in New York in 1836, were available in England, and they held their readers enthralled by what purported to be the memoirs of a renegade nun from Montreal, who alleged that female religious regularly satisfied the sexual needs of priests while the resulting offspring were murdered and buried in a pit under the convent.[20] At a higher social level, the popularity of pictures of convent life, of which Charles Collins's *Convent Thoughts* of 1851 is perhaps the best-known example, owed something to their depiction of young postulants who fascinated and tantalized the viewer by a beauty at once virginal and unobtainable.[21] Understandably, Protestant attacks on sisterhoods did not appeal overtly to such pornographic enthusiasms, but concentrated instead on the supposed unnaturalness of perpetual celibacy, and on the ways in which the taking of vows was an assault on both the physical and emotional liberty of the individual. Attacks of this kind were not without effect: such was the force of popular anti-Catholic feeling that the festivities to mark the laying of the foundation stone of the Devonport sisterhood's new church in 1850 were disrupted by a mob that pelted the sisters and clergy with potatoes and plates – this in spite of the heroic work that they had done to relieve the sick during the cholera epidemic of the previous year.[22]

Anglican bishops viewed the more rowdy manifestations of popular anti-Catholicism with distaste, but they shared much of its hostility to Catholic forms of worship and practice, particularly the taking of perpetual vows; and for this reason, episcopal recognition of the sisterhoods was slow in coming. One bishop who was vociferous in expressing his opposition to lifelong vows was Samuel Wilberforce, who greatly disliked what he called 'a semi-Romanist system, with its *direction*, with its development of self-consciousness and morbid religious affection, with its exaltation of the contemplative life, and its un-English tone'.[23] While the Bishop of Oxford was prepared to support Anglican sisterhoods, this was on condition that no binding vows of celibacy should form part of the sister's profession, since these were, he told the 1862 Church Congress, unscriptural, unsanctioned by the Church of England, and an unwarranted interference with religious liberty.[24]

Yet in practice it was precisely the ideal of a wholehearted lifelong commitment that attracted women to the religious life. As the founder of the Community of St John the Baptist at Clewer near Windsor, the Rev. Thomas Thellusson Carter, argued in response to the Bishop of Lincoln's objections, 'celibacy is a vocation of a high spiritual order, and of a permanent character, to which some are called in the providence of God, though without disparagement to others not so called'. However, he was careful to draw a distinction between the practice of taking such vows and their obligatory imposition.[25] Despite such advocacy, suspicion about the nature and consequences of perpetual vows continued to hinder formal recognition of sisterhoods by the Church, and it was not until February 1891 that regulations for the governing of Anglican sisterhoods were finally agreed by the Upper House of Convocation. These allowed for 'life-long engagements' by women of at least thirty years of age from which release could be granted by the bishop. The form of this engagement was to be a promise made before the bishop. Although the offending word 'vows' was nowhere mentioned, it had originally been stipulated that the promise be made to the bishop rather than as it finally appeared – one made in his presence – an equivocation that the sisterhoods were able to take as sanctioning a vow made directly to God.[26]

One other important clause in the 1891 resolutions stipulated that no conventual statute was to contain any provision that interfered with the right of a sister to dispose of her property as she saw fit, which points to the fact that objections to sisterhoods had important social dimensions as well as doctrinal ones. Many critics of female religious orders saw them as a direct challenge to the authority of the patriarchal family, since they encouraged women to forgo both the prospect of marriage and the obligation to care for elderly relatives if they remained at home. In his novel *Yeast*, published in 1851, Charles Kingsley voiced such fears in his usual pugnacious style, declaring that one of the chief attractions of sisterhoods for young women was the hope of entering 'a higher place in heaven than the relations whom they had left behind them', while in the meantime, life could be carried on 'unshackled by the interference of parents, and other such merely fleshly relationships'. In the light of such fears, one of the most damaging allegations made against Priscilla Sellon was that she had persuaded a young woman to join her order without parental consent, and had attacked one of the central shibboleths of Victorian society by arguing that 'the love of home is also another idol, – a very sweet and honourable one, but one which, alas, comes often between us and high duties to our church, the poor, and our Lord himself'.[27] Speaking at the Church Congress in Dublin in 1868, the Bishop of Oxford described the reception of young women into convent life as a great evil, since it went against what he regarded as a woman's 'primary obligation', which was to marry, an obligation that in his view was 'distinctly laid down by the Holy Ghost, through the pen of the apostle St Paul'.[28]

Proponents of sisterhoods were well aware of such charges, and attempted to rebut them, but in so doing only succeeded in making it still clearer that women might indeed experience a conflict between the demands of the gospel and those of domestic duty. Thus having stressed that his support of sisterhoods would lead him to do nothing 'to lower the sacredness of marriage, or to encourage the idea that the plain and urgent duties of home may voluntarily be set aside for any work, or rule of life, however holy', the Rev. Thomas Carter went on to suggest that in his own society 'our danger lies in the opposite direction, in narrowing too much the range of female service, as if domestic duty were woman's only calling; as if there were no bonds and sympathies beyond those of home . . . no happiness but such as centres in the family circle; no unseen Hand felt all powerfully at times, beckoning the children of our love away to serve God in some special office of His Church'.[29]

The issue of parental authority was of course at its most acute, as the Anglican bishops realized in 1891, with regard to a woman's right to dispose of her property to a religious community. This was highlighted in 1857 when a young woman who had entered the Society of St Margaret, founded at East Grinstead in Sussex by John Mason Neale, died, leaving £400 to the community. This led her father to launch a bitter attack on the order, which resulted in an unseemly riot at her funeral and the subsequent withdrawal of the Bishop of Chichester as Visitor.[30] To understand the feelings aroused by this case, one should remember that it was not until the end of the century, with the passage of the Married Women's Property Acts of 1870, 1882, and 1893, that women finally gained the right to control their property upon marriage.

The issue of women's independence within the sisterhoods was also partly an ecclesiastical one. In the early days of their existence, a number of bishops experienced uneasy relations with communities founded in their dioceses and withdrew their support as Visitors. This was the case at Devonport where, having invited Priscilla Sellon to begin work, the Bishop of Exeter – Henry Phillpotts – resigned as Visitor in 1852, unhappy at what he described as 'the extravagance of the Superior's claim on the obedience of the Sisterhood'.[31] As one anonymous critic of the new communities recognized in 1850, it was partly the kind of woman who might be attracted to the religious life that potentially posed problems:

> I regret the necessity of thus hinting that communities of pious ladies may ever become otherwise than perfectly submissive to authority, and perfectly manageable; but the stern firmness of purpose which has placed so many members of the 'Homes' within their walls, naturally creates some misgivings on the subject.

Much safer in the view of this writer was the organization of middle-class women as district visitors, who would thereby still remain within the confines of their families and be under the direction of the parochial clergy.[32] The formal recognition of sisterhoods by the bishops in 1891 had in fact as much to do with the perceived need to gain control of the orders as with any sense of the value of the religious life or of the quality of the work that they undertook.

Within the context of Victorian patriarchal society, the subversive nature of the call to the religious life has led historians to consider the extent to which the sisterhoods might be considered as feminist institutions in their assertion of women's independence from family and clerical control. Thus A. M. Allchin sees their development as 'an important move in the early stages of women's emancipation', and their activities as constituting a 'silent rebellion against worldly values and standards (and the waste of women's lives often involved)'.[33] This is also the more tentatively expressed emphasis of Michael Hill's study *The Religious Order*, when he argues that 'supporters of sisterhoods worked with an incipiently feminist conception of the role of women'.[34] With equal caution, Susan Casteras writes that 'the decision to enter a convent was one of the rather few assertions of independence that a female might be able to demonstrate and as such might be considered a quasi-feminist statement'.[35] On the other hand, John Sheldon Reed, while fully recognizing 'the affront to Victorian family values that sisterhood life . . . presented', suggests that it would be a mistake to link the Anglo-Catholic movement too closely to the ideals of Victorian feminism, because it embodied patriarchal assumptions to such an extent that it 'might almost be better to regard it as an *alternative* to feminism'.

The ambiguity of sisterhood life in terms of women's self-fulfilment is also brought out by Martha Vicinus, who says that their history 'reveals a complicated picture of institutional subordination and self-determination'.[36] Part of the difficulty of assessing the significance of sisterhood life in the context of women's emancipation, which such diverse and qualified judgements reveal, has to do with the definition of feminism that one adopts. By the standards of late twentieth-century secular socialist or liberal feminism, Victorian convent life might seem more like a flight from women's oppression than a significant challenge to it; moreover, in the context of nineteenth-century attempts to gain women the vote, equality of treatment before the law, and entrance to the professions, the sisterhoods appear as singularly uninterested in such issues.

This point was not lost, for example, on *The Athenaeum* in 1861. Reviewing together Miss Goodman's accusations about the way in which Priscilla Sellon ran her order, and Caroline Dall's plea for female suffrage in America, the writer concluded that whatever mistakes Miss Sellon had made, her way of 'self-abnegation and devotedness' was infinitely preferable for women to that advocated by Caroline Dall.[37] If, however, one follows Karen Offen's distinction between an individualist feminism seeking the implementation of Mill's programme of equal rights for men and women and an older and more relational form of feminism rooted in sexual difference and complementarity, the role of the sisterhoods in fostering a distinctively female spirituality and communal life can appear more significant.[38]

Part of the difficulty facing the historian also stems from the problem of assessing the impact of religion upon women's lives. Here, the sisterhoods provide a particularly pertinent example of the difference between the Church's assumptions about the circumscribed role of women in its life, and their own – very different – responses to those limitations. In this respect, Reed is surely right to emphasize the patriarchalism that lies behind the Anglo-Catholic championing of female religious orders. It is true that Pusey could argue passionately for the independence of sisterhoods from control by the parochial clergy, as in 1864 when this stance led to a heated correspondence with the Rev. Arthur Stanton, whom he wished to work at St Saviour's in Leeds in conjunction with Priscilla Sellon's sisterhood. Ignoring Stanton's objections, he repeatedly denied that the clergy had 'any right to interference or check or wish to control any work which religious women wish to set about in their parish'.[39]

However, Pusey also had very clear ideas about the kinds of work that sisterhoods could undertake, and the clear distinction between these and the responsibilities of the clergy. As he told the Church Congress that met in Oxford in 1862, 'the Sister of Mercy is the pioneer for the parish priest'; in other words, she could reach women and children more easily than the male priesthood, and the range of work that she undertook in nursing and education was an acceptable extension of a woman's role within the home. Pusey was also quite clear that women had particular feminine qualities that fitted them for such tasks, and that these differed from those that men exercised in their calling. As he told the Congress:

> The longing for the religious life is deeply and widely spread amid our Christian ladies. Women are guided not by controversial arguments, but by instinctive feeling. Controversy they leave to us.[40]

Not surprisingly, Pusey's biographer Maria Trench was later to complain that 'Dr Pusey certainly always seemed to me to understand and to try and satisfy, any amount of devotional and spiritual craving in women, but to have neither understanding of or sympathy for the most moderate intellectual craving on their part.' He believed, she concluded, in 'the antithesis between bonnets and brains'.[41] Another defender of sisterhoods was concerned, like Pusey, to make it clear that Anglican sisters knew their place, and she quoted the views of Dr Jenner, a physician at University College Hospital London, on the difference between having a sisterhood and the other women working there: 'I found before they came to the Hospital that the ladies would (as I had heard of others doing) step out of their province in various

ways, and so interfere with the general usefulness of the charity.'
Happily, this was now no longer the case.[42]

Other aspects of Anglo-Catholic thought also reinforced the
tendency to allot distinctive roles to men and women. As we have
seen, the inspiration for the revival of religious orders came from the
early Church, and the misogynist tradition of the Fathers, with its
adulation of submissive virginal femininity, was incorporated into the
ideal of sisterhood life – as was the emphasis upon the authority of an
exclusively male priesthood. Indeed, for those who regarded gender
differences of the kind to which Pusey alluded as God-given, the discipline of convent life seemed particularly suited to bringing out the
qualities of compassion and self-sacrifice that belonged especially to
women. It was true, of course, that obedience and self-denial were
essential parts of the religious life for both men and women, but as
the Rev. Thomas Carter told the sisters at Clewer, this was so for
them in a special sense. In contemplating the nature of the holy angels
– into whose nature Carter seems to have felt he had some privileged
insight – he could see that they exhibited two 'special characteristics
of woman's true vocation', especially in her relation to man:
'unselfish love and submissiveness of will'.[43] However, it was Priscilla Sellon who put this distinction between the sexes, and its consequences for sisterhood life, as clearly as anyone:

> . . . it may be for men to argue for truth, to reason with the
> learned of the nineteenth-century, to preach to the refined
> sensualist or the intellectual philosopher as the noble penitent of
> old from the hill of Mars: but for us, Mary Magdalene of blessed
> memory has taught us our place; we are to lie at the foot of our
> Lord in silence; in tears, in love.[44]

Yet at this point the disjunction between the Church's view of the
religious life and its reality for women like Priscilla Sellon is obvious.
The founders and heads of religious houses were in positions that
allowed them to exercise considerable power and authority, and, at a
time when women were discouraged from undertaking any kind of
theological education, far from sitting in devotional silence they were
often involved in very public doctrinal debate in defence of their religious ideals. Priscilla Sellon herself was forced to defend her order
from charges of indulging in Roman Catholic practices before an
enquiry set up by the Bishop of Exeter in 1848, while two years later
she entered into a sharp exchange of letters with Lord Campbell,
insisting that he withdraw his financial support for her sisterhood as

she held him responsible for the Gorham Judgement, which seemed to call into question the High Church doctrine of baptismal regeneration.[45]

As both their supporters and critics were aware, sisterhoods were one of the most public manifestations of the Catholic revival within nineteenth-century Anglicanism, and in the face of Low Church polemic they could on occasion give as good as they got. Thus in a description of sisterhood life published in 1867, one anonymous sister answered those critics who preferred the pattern of deaconess life to that of the religious orders by describing the former as more suitable to the subjective religion of 'the pious German', and concluded in a somewhat triumphalist vein that 'as the Catholicity of the Church of England is being continually widened and deepened, there is less and less probability that those who have once drunk of its refreshing waters will deliberately turn away to the barren land of Protestantism'.[46]

Emily Ayckbowm was another superior whose position was as ambiguous as Priscilla Sellon's. In her instructions to her sisterhood she warned that 'women as a rule are neither logical nor deep thinkers, and in consequence are far more liable than men to be led astray by inaccurate and sophistical arguments', yet she herself was a tireless and effective public campaigner against the development of non-sectarian state education at the expense of church schools. She started the Religious Education Union in 1885, and in 1888–1889 she organized nation-wide petitions to Parliament and to the Royal Commission on Education in defence of the voluntary principle. She was also unyielding in the defence of the autonomy of her order, refusing Archbishop Benson's request to undertake an investigation into allegations about the improper treatment of orphans by her sisterhood, a decision that led to the withdrawal of episcopal patronage of the order.[47]

The contradictions evident in the lives of women such as Priscilla Sellon and Emily Ayckbowm between their adherence to conventional views of women's subordinate place in the Church and their own very different public lives might appear at first sight to be rather puzzling, but, like Florence Nightingale in a different sphere, they created for themselves roles of leadership and responsibility in a male-dominated Church more by manipulating Victorian theological and social prescriptions for correct female behaviour than by deferring to them. In Priscilla Sellon's case, the extent of her success was not lost upon her critics: the Evangelical *Christian Observer* included in its lengthy catalogue of her faults 'the gross assumption by one of their sex of rights and powers which the language and still more the spirit of the Holy Scriptures seems to deny to the female sex'.[48]

Much of the authority claimed by mother superiors like Priscilla Sellon was exercised in undertaking a wide range of charitable activity; and, as one historian of the Oxford Movement has pointed out, it is not the self-sacrificing life of the Anglo-Catholic priest in the inner city that marks the beginning of the Victorian Anglo-Catholic concern for the poor, but the work of the Devonport sister-hood.[49] Sisters spent much of their time running schools and orphanages, and nursing, and the devotion and method that they brought to such work was widely recognized even by some of those who, for other reasons, were critical. Thus in his study of the religious life of London, Charles Booth illustrated the extent and variety of the work undertaken by the sisterhoods by outlining the work of the Community of St John the Baptist, Clewer, in the capital. This included house visiting of the poor and sick and the organization of parochial Bible classes; girls' clubs; Sunday schools and missions, and the running of an orphanage and industrial training school in Pimlico; of two refuges for prostitutes; of two girls' training schools; of a home for poor working-class girls; and of a fee-paying secondary school for girls in Hampstead.[50]

How far, however, such efforts won the allegiance of the poor for the Church may be doubted. As the founder of the Community of St Mary the Virgin, Wantage – the Rev. W. J. Butler – noted in 1861, recruits to the religious life were for the most part drawn from the upper class.[51] Class distinctions were indeed woven into the fabric of most female religious communities, which usually consisted of two types of sister: the choir sisters, and those drawn from a lower social strata who did much of the daily menial work. This meant that the social vision of the communities tended to be a conservative one: they shared a belief in a deferential social order in which the rich had obligations to the poor, but it was one that could envisage no fundamental change in the existing class structure of Victorian society.

Thus one of the impulses behind Priscilla Sellon's work was the threat of social disorder in 1848, a year of revolutionary uprisings in many of Europe's capitals. The daughter of a naval officer, and of independent means, she had been 'startled by the want of deference of manner which one always meets with in agricultural districts', and she responded by embarking upon a vigorous educational campaign – the significance of which was not lost on Pusey. Writing to a friend at

Eton, in December 1848, he described the boys whom she attempted to reach as either 'the materials of earnest and good citizens or of Socialists and Chartists'. Happily, all was well: Miss Sellon's protégés were soon singing the national anthem – 'a substitute for some Chartist song of wickedness'.[52] Help that was given from such a perspective, *de haut en bas*, however self-sacrificially, could of course often provoke resentment. In 1860, for example, Miss Sellon's scheme to send unemployed weavers from the East End of London to the north of England where work existed, foundered on the refusal of the would-be beneficiaries to move.[53]

Yet far from regarding class distinctions as a hindrance to their work, the sisterhoods saw the gulf that existed between the life of the sister and those people she attempted to aid as essential both in inoculating her against the contagions of working-class vice, and as a way of providing the poor with suitable examples of moral and spiritual elevation. As a former sister in the Devonport community recalled:

> It was Miss Sellon's impression, judging from the whole tone and spirit of the training of the sisters, that very little could be done towards elevating the working classes by persons whose tastes, habits, and general cultivation of mind were very little above those they would raise; and she sought most carefully to keep up in her sisters a taste for the beautiful, and altogether to retain amongst them a refinement of mind.[54]

This sense of distance from the world was also reinforced by one of the most notable features of the early sisterhoods: a pervasive archaizing medievalism. This was most evident in the architectural and liturgical styles of Tractarian spirituality. Most of the first convents were designed by the leading architectural exponents of the Gothic revival, William Butterfield for the Devonport Sisterhood, George Edmund Street, Butterfield, and John Loughborough Pearson at Wantage, and Butterfield's pupil Henry Woodyer at Clewer. The latter's work is not untypical, a Puginesque conglomeration of narrow cloisters, high-pitched roofs and picturesque turrets, and an interior described by Peter Anson as consisting of 'endless cloisters and corridors with lancet windows, dark-stained pitch-pine panelling and cream distemper [that] manage to achieve the requisite medieval atmosphere without which the majority of the Tractarians felt it was impossible to be a good Christian'.[55]

The ethos of medieval spirituality that suffused the lives of the sisters not only provided a haven of tranquillity and beauty from the appalling conditions they encountered on the streets, it also extended to the work itself, helping to create a sense of *noblesse oblige* among those who undertook it. Not untypical was the approach of Sister Katherine Warburton, the first superior of St Mary's Priory in the East End of London, who worked with Priscilla Sellon during the cholera epidemic of 1866. Brought up on a heady educational brew of Arthurian legend, lives of the medieval saints, and the history of the Stuarts – 'whose charm, and unworthiness, and romance alike appealed to her' – her biographer rather improbably likens her work in London to a medieval crusade in which she was to be found 'serving her Prynce, and following Him to the East in far away Haggerston'.[56]

The distinctions of class and gender in the lives of Anglican sisterhoods were at their most obvious in one particular form of philanthropic endeavour in which they specialized: the care of prostitutes. A number of the early sisterhoods undertook penitentiary work, the environment of a convent providing a total institution safely removed from the temptations of the streets in which a programme of penitence, moral guidance, and reformation could be attempted. Not only was there a great gulf fixed between the sister and the prostitute in terms of both purity and class, but it was important from the viewpoint of mid-Victorian sexual respectability that it should be rigidly maintained. This point was insisted upon by the Rev. Thomas Thellusson Carter, whose house of mercy at Clewer was one of the first institutions to undertake this work, and who was a prominent publicist for their benefits. One of the most important advantages of sisterhood penitentiaries, he argued, was that fallen women received there 'the personal service of women of birth, of education and refinement'; however, this also meant that women of a very different social class lived in closer proximity than was normally the case, and there was therefore some danger that such arrangements might 'interfere with due distinction of rank and so injure both parties'. This problem even existed among the women themselves, and in order to meet it, a separate area was created for 'lady penitents', who were 'altogether separated from the rougher elements', and who were subjected to a far more genteel regime of embroidery rather than the harsh discipline of domestic work and training imposed upon most of the women.[57] The real dangers of moral pollution, however, concerned the sisters, and these were avoided partly by careful control of living arrangements – the sisters had their own rooms and ate separately from the inmates –

and partly by the attitude adopted by the former:

> The Sisters will be careful to show towards the Penitents in their manner, speech, etc., such tenderness and pity as would become a forgiving parent dealing with a prodigal child returning home, yet nevertheless they will preserve such distance and propriety of demeanour as become ladies dealing with persons of an inferior rank, fallen even from that rank by their sins.[58]

Though penitence and reformation might be achieved by such methods, the distinction between the fallen and the pure would always remain. After a period of reclamation, which usually lasted two years, some women chose to stay in the sisterhoods, joining an order of Magdalens who gave advice and encouragement to new arrivals, but whose life, Carter stressed, was quite different from that of the sister of mercy.[59]

Such successes were not that common. As Charles Booth noted, they were 'practically confined to the newly fallen', and he went on to suggest that the sisterhood regime that exposed women to a particularly heightened and intense form of religiosity, which it was impossible for most women to sustain, was itself one of the reasons for failure.[60] Another was the harsh and punitive stance adopted towards the prostitute. Women with children were expected to give them up for adoption; and when one woman went on hunger strike in order to leave and rejoin her children, she was punished by being put in solitary confinement before the mother superior agreed to release her.[61]

Martha Vicinus has argued that this exclusively moral approach to the problem of prostitution was both reassuring to respectable public opinion and inadequate, since it concentrated entirely on the victim and not the seducer, and did not result in any public campaigning by the sisterhoods against the double standard of sexual morality and the harsh economic circumstances facing many Victorian women.[62] These issues were not, however, altogether ignored. Thomas Carter realized that many women faced 'an organized system of female malignity', in which they were often seduced 'in moments of difficulty or discontent, when ill-paid perhaps or ill-fed';[63] nor was he unaware of the Victorian double standard, commenting sharply that 'though fallen woman has not sinned alone, how entirely in the world's eye has the undivided burden of guilt fallen upon her!'[64]

Too much can perhaps be made of the shortcomings of the sisterhoods in their approach to philanthropy, failings that characterized many of the charitable efforts undertaken by Victorian Christians. There were, after all, only some two thousand sisters engaged in tackling the immense economic and social problems of late Victorian England. However, even though their numbers were small, both for the women who dedicated themselves to the religious life and for the example that they gave to their society, the sisterhoods had a significance out of all proportion to their numbers. At the time of their creation, so powerful was the Victorian ideology of married domesticity and compulsory motherhood for middle- and upper-class women, that those who either chose not to marry or who increasingly were unable to do so for demographic reasons could be labelled as 'redundant', and suggestions made that such women might be shipped like surplus merchandise to the colonies.[65] By contrast, sisterhoods upheld the ideal of voluntarily chosen celibacy as worthwhile for women, and offered an example of a life lived in community in which the highest ideals of personal holiness were combined with a practical outreach of Christian love and charity that encouraged women to do meaningful and significant work.

Deaconesses

The revival of the order of deaconess within the Church of England sprang from some of the same concerns that led to the creation of sisterhoods. Their most influential early supporter, the Rev. John Howson, was as aware as the early leaders of the Oxford Movement of the mass of poverty and spiritual destitution in Victorian society. He believed that this was a problem that could often only be solved by women's particular gifts and abilities, since 'in nursing the sick, in visiting the mothers of the poor, in caring for neglected children, women are not likely to fail, and men can hardly interfere with advantage'.[66] Howson was also conscious of the debate raised by the findings of the 1851 census, which suggested that for demographic reasons many women were prevented from fulfilling their appointed social and religious destiny in marriage; and in urging the need for professionally trained and paid deaconesses in the Church, he charted a careful course among the conflicting expectations about gender that were involved in advocating remunerative employment for middle-class women. Like the advocates of sisterhoods, he argued that it was mistaken 'to limit the Divine law of woman's mission on the earth to the mere relation of marriage', and he reminded his readers that the

'Scripture is far wider than our prejudices'. At the same time, though, he was keen to reassure them that he was not here discussing the rights of women in any liberal feminist sense that appealed to the notion of the equality of the sexes. Men and women were, he was sure, different in their capacities and duties, and he quoted with approval Mrs Jameson's distinction between the masculine intellect whose task was 'to rule through power' and the feminine calling 'to minister through love'. The office of deaconess, he pointed out, was ideally suited for this purpose, since its original Greek meaning was 'helpful service' and its revival would therefore involve 'no feminine intrusion into the other sphere'.[67]

In other respects, the origins of the deaconess movement were quite separate – not to say antithetical – to those of the sisterhoods. Howson was careful to stress that his proposals for the creation of institutions for deaconesses were for training purposes only, and had nothing in common with High Church sisterhoods, and many of their early supporters saw them as an acceptable Protestant alternative to the life of the cloister. Thus the Bishop of London, Archibald Tait – who formally 'set apart' Elizabeth Ferard as the first Anglican deaconess in 1862 – was known to be a strong opponent of perpetual vows and, for this reason, had refused to serve as Visitor to a number of religious communities; and the Rev. William Pennefather, the founder of the Mildmay Deaconess Home in London, was said by his biographer to be 'most anxious to prove that it was possible to develop woman's power for practical service, in a happy communion of love and labour, without any approach to the evils of conventual life'.[68]

Differences between High and Low Church conceptions of women's work also emerged when Convocation met in 1884. While all could finally agree on a motion that 'the extension of the ministry of women is an urgent need of the Church of England in the present day', the Dean of Chester's support of deaconesses included an attack on vows, and he urged the need for episcopal control of any women's organizations within the Church – remarks that were greeted with calls of 'hear hear' from the floor, but that angered Canon Body, who dismissed such charges against convent life as ill-founded.[69]

For those who were opposed to what they saw as the crypto-Romanism of the sisterhoods, the model and inspiration for the deaconess movement was a reassuringly Protestant one. In 1836, Theodor Fliedner, pastor of the Evangelical church in Kaiserwerth in Germany, founded an order of deaconesses, and its aims and methods were introduced to the British public by a pamphlet written by Florence Nightingale, who stayed there in 1850 and again the following year, and who took part in the nursing work and the religious life of the community.[70] In 1861 the Rev. William Pennefather, vicar of Christ Church, Barnet, and his wife, Catherine, founded a missionary training home for women, Mildmay Park. After his appointment to St Jude's, Mildmay Park became the Mildmay Deaconess Institution, and was run on similar lines to Kaiserwerth, having its own hospitals, orphanages, dispensaries, and old people's home. The deaconesses took no vows, but wore a distinctive dress and returned to the home at night. By 1884, the institution numbered some two hundred deaconesses and fifteen hundred associates. Pennefather was an early supporter of ecumenism, and the Deaconess Superintendent and Treasurer were Presbyterians; most of the women trained at Mildmay were not Anglican deaconesses formally set apart for their work by a bishop, but Pennefather's example was influential within the Church of England and in 1917 the Mildmay Institution became a fully recognized deaconess house.[71]

The example of Kaiserwerth was also important in the life of Elizabeth Ferard, who visited the community in 1858, and who modelled her own North London Deaconesses Institution upon it. The emphasis that was thus placed upon the communal aspects of deaconess life led to the community becoming a fully fledged sisterhood, and in 1887 the title of Head Sister was changed to that of Mother Superior, and the Deaconess Community of St Andrew subsequently combined the religious life of prayer with the work and training of deaconesses.[72] This pattern was to be the exception, and more usual was that of the Rochester Deaconess Institution: here, women were trained for two years, and then, after acceptance by the bishop, were sent to undertake parish work under the direction of the incumbent.

The first head of the Institution was Isabella Gilmore. The sister of the artist William Morris, and a recent widow who was working as a nursing sister in Guy's Hospital, Gilmore typified the able, well-connected, self-confident women who contributed so significantly to the life of the late Victorian Church. Like most of them, she was a woman of strong convictions, and she fully agreed with Bishop Thorold in rejecting any style of life that savoured of the convent. Except for periods of rest, the deaconesses were to reside in their parishes, and the whole tenor of the training was designed to create self-sufficient and obedient parochial workers: 'We were sending out women and not children; if our training was worth anything they ought at the end of their two years to do well, working entirely under the parish priest, to receive their own stipend, live in their own house or rooms, and order their own lives.' Such stern attention to duty was not, however, to be pushed to unreasonable lengths, and she was insistent that the deaconess was to have a month's holiday and twenty-four hours' break each week, since 'she is not a cast-iron machine' – a sentiment with which many hard-pressed parochial workers would still concur.[73]

The work undertaken by deaconesses was similar to that done by the sisterhoods. The North London Deaconess Institution was responsible for the provision of nursing at the Great Northern Hospital, where it was claimed that 'the presence of women of education and refinement gives a tone to the hospital'. Its members also undertook house visiting in poor parts of London, and ran day and evening schools for children and adults. This was also the scope of the work with which Fanny Eagles was entrusted by Bishop Browne when she became deaconess in the parish of St Peter's, Bedford, in 1869, where she was enjoined to 'seek out the sick, poor and impotent folk and intimate their names to the curate; . . . instruct the young, in school or otherwise, minister to those in hospitals, prisons, or asylums; and setting aside all unwomanly usurpation of authority in the Church, should seek to edify the souls of Christ's people in the faith'. In 1872 the faithful discharge of her duties involved nursing the sick and dying during an outbreak of smallpox, and helping to carry the dead to carts for collection during the middle of the night.[74]

Bishop Browne's warning against 'unwomanly usurpation of authority' indicates one of the limitations placed upon the deaconess movement from its inception. As the Rev. William Pennefather's biographer records, his aim in starting the Mildmay Deaconess Institution was 'to make the ministry of Christian women as efficient as possible, without tempting them out of the lowly sphere assigned to them by God', and he therefore shrank from anything that might make the order 'too formal or self-asserting'.[75] While Victorian church leaders generally welcomed the revival of the office of deaconess, they were reluctant to specify the exact nature of the work – and even more wary of defining it as an official form of ministry. In 1891, the Upper House of the Convocation of Canterbury went so far as to state that 'a Deaconess should be admitted in solemn form by the Bishop, with benediction, by laying on of hands', and that she should only be allowed to work in a parish after receiving an episcopal licence issued at the request of the incumbent.[76] However, crucial ambiguities remained concerning the nature of the deaconesses' ministry and its relationship with the ordained priesthood, and these were to hamper its effectiveness and hinder recruitment far into the next century.

Other forms of paid employment created fewer problems of status and function. The Biblewomen's movement founded by Mrs Raynard was nondenominational, but gained Anglican support. Its members engaged in evangelism and set up clothing clubs and mothers' meetings in the poorest parts of London. Inspired by their example, in 1860 the Honourable Mrs J. C. Talbot created an organization of specifically Anglican parochial mission women. The granddaughter of a duke, a friend of Mrs Gladstone, and the mother of E. S. Talbot (the first warden of Keble College, Oxford), Jane Talbot was both capable and energetic. However, her son was careful to emphasize that her organizing zeal did not go beyond the bounds of womanly decorum, since although she was 'masculine in understanding', 'her strength did not unsex her', and 'in doing her work she preserved a womanly modesty, and showed no ambition to thrust herself forward, or to claim for her sex unusual functions'.[77]

As she described them, the women whom she recruited for the work were 'quiet, unassuming poor women living in the steady discharge of their own religious duties as members of the Church of England, and ready to devote themselves with their whole hearts to the endeavour to benefit their poor neighbours, in their souls and bodies, under the guidance which is now offered to them'.[78] Parochial mission women often knew at first-hand the deprivations of poverty, for as one East London clergyman explained after praising the excellent work done by a woman in his parish in caring for the sick, he had decided to raise her weekly salary since 'she has been struggling hard to support herself and child, and this will just enable her to keep her head above water'.[79] Such women in fact acted as intermediaries between the working class and the Lady Superintendents who supervised their work, and who attended the weekly women's meetings for Bible reading and needlework. With proper training they also acted as agents for middle-class socialization, since many of the women whom they reached were not only unconnected with the Church, but also 'ignorant of the management, cleanliness, and order necessary for the right fulfilment of the duties of wives and mothers'.[80] By the late 1880s there were over two hundred women engaged in the work, and in 1922 – when the *Official Year-book of the Church of England* ceased to list the organization – there were about thirty-eight working in the dioceses of Southwark and London.[81]

Another organization that undertook similar work was the Church Army, which had been founded by Wilson Carlile in 1883 as an Anglican imitation of the Salvation Army. From 1887, there was a separate women's branch, and in 1889 Wilson Carlile's sister Marie became superintendent of its training home. The course lasted between six and sixteen months, and included nursing and slum visiting as well as preparation for evangelism. The candidates were described as women who 'For the most part have been engaged in some branch of domestic science, or in business, though there is always a percentage of those coming from a different class and of better education.'[82] Even more than in the case of deaconesses, who had at least some formal recognition conferred by the bishop's laying on of hands, the status of Church Army women remained unclear, and in April 1907 the Upper House of Convocation passed a motion 'that heartily appreciating the excellent work done by the Church Army mission women, while of opinion it would not be expedient to give any such recognition to them as the adoption of a form of licence would imply, we commend them to the sympathetic encouragement of the bishops in their several dioceses'.[83]

In the nineteenth century, the Church did provide opportunities for paid employment for women, including those of very modest means and education, but it did little to encourage their efforts by way of conferring status or recognition. It was to be in the mission field, far away from the institutional and social confines of Victorian England, that the greatest opportunities for women to exercise responsibility and initiative were to occur.

Notes

1.   The background to the revival of the religious life within the Church of England is discussed in A. Allchin, *The Silent Rebellion: Anglican Religious Communities 1845–1900* (London, SCM, 1958); and P. Anson, *The Call of the Cloister: Religious Communities and Kindred Bodies in the Anglican Communion* (London, SPCK, 1955).

2.   R. Southey, *Sir Thomas More: Or, Colloquies on the Progress and Prospects of Society* (2 vols, London, John Murray, 1829), pp. 304–319.

3.   J. M. Neale, *Ayton Priory; Or, the Restored Monastery* (London, Rivingtons, 1843). Neale regarded the dissolution of the monasteries as an accident

rather than as an essential part of the English Reformation (p. 82).

4. J. H. Newman, *The Church of the Fathers* (London, Rivingtons, 1840), p. 340.

5. H. P. Liddon, *The Life of Edward Bouverie Pusey* (4 vols, London, Longmans Green, 1894), vol. 3, p. 6.

6. Allchin, *The Silent Rebellion*, pp. 61–62.

7. T. Williams, *Priscilla Lydia Sellon. The Restorer after Three Centuries of the Religious Life in the English Church* (London, SPCK, 2nd edn, 1965), p. 11.

8. Allchin, *The Silent Rebellion*, pp. 119–120.

9. In one of the best modern treatments of the sisterhoods, Martha Vicinus suggests that as the state took over many of the functions of charitable organizations, 'a life consecrated to prayer and spiritual succour came to the fore' (M. Vicinus, *Independent Women: Work and Community for Single Women 1850–1920* (London, Virago Press, 1985), p. 83). For the same point, see M. Hill, *The Religious Order* (London, Heinemann, 1973), pp. 292–293.

10. Anon., *A Valiant Victorian: The Life and Times of Mother Emily Ayckbowm 1836–1900* (London, Mowbray, 1964), pp. 42–45.

11. Allchin, *The Silent Rebellion*, p. 314.

12. Allchin, *The Silent Rebellion*, p. 59.

13. M. Goodman, *Sisterhoods in the Church of England* (London, Smith, Elder & Co., 1863), p. 268.

14. Liddon, *The Life of Edward Bouverie Pusey*, vol. 3, p. 24.

15. Liddon, *The Life of Edward Bouverie Pusey*, vol. 3, p. 6.

16. Anon., *A Valiant Victorian*, pp. 34–41.

17. Quoted in S. Gill, 'The Power of Christian Ladyhood: Priscilla Lydia Sellon and the Creation of Anglican Sisterhoods', in S. Mews (ed.), *Modern Religious Rebels: Essays Presented to John Kent* (London, Epworth Press, 1993), p. 34.

18. K. Dennison, 'Dr Pusey as Confessor and Spiritual Director', in P. Butler (ed.), *Pusey Rediscovered* (London, SPCK, 1983), pp. 220–222.

19. Williams, *Priscilla Lydia Sellon*, p. 51.

20. J. Wolfe, *The Protestant Crusade in Great Britain 1829–1860* (Oxford, Clarendon Press, 1991), p. 125.

21. For this theme, see S. P. Casteras, 'Virgin Vows: The Early Victorian Artists' Portrayal of Nuns and Novices', in G. Malmgreen (ed.), *Religion in the Lives of English Women, 1760–1930* (London, Croom Helm, 1986), pp. 129–160.

22. Williams, *Priscilla Lydia Sellon*, p. 80.

23. Anson, *The Call of the Cloister*, p. 302.

24. Hill, *The Religious Order*, pp. 246-247.

25. T. Carter, *Are 'Vows of Celibacy in Early Life' inconsistent with the Word of God?* (London, Rivingtons, 1878), pp. 3-4.

26. Allchin, *The Silent Rebellion*, pp. 157-168.

27. Gill, 'The Power of Christian Ladyhood', p. 157.

28. *Authorized Report of the Church Congress Held at Dublin* (Dublin, Hodges, Smith & Foster, 1868), p. 210.

29. T. Carter, *Objections to Sisterhoods Considered in a Letter to a Parent* (London, Rivingtons, 1853), pp. 9-10.

30. Anson, *The Call of the Cloister*, p. 344; Vicinus, *Independent Women*, p. 63.

31. Williams, *Priscilla Lydia Sellon*, p. 101.

32. Anon., *Sisterhoods Considered, with Remarks upon the Bishop of Brechin's 'Plea for Sisterhoods'* (London, Rivingtons, 1850), pp. 15-16.

33. Allchin, *The Silent Rebellion*, p. 251.

34. Hill, *The Religious Order*, p. 271.

35. Casteras, 'Virgin Vows', pp. 137-138.

36. Vicinus, *Independent Women*, p. 48.

37. *The Athenaeum* (December 1861), p. 873, reviewing Margaret Goodman's *Experiences of an English Sister of Mercy* and Caroline Dall's *Women's Rights under the Law*, which were both published that year.

38. K. Offen, 'Defining Feminism: A Comparative Historical Approach', *Signs*, vol. 14 (1988-1989), pp. 119-157. This is also the context in which Vicinus places the sisterhoods.

39. G. Russell, *Arthur Stanton* (London, Longman, 1917), p. 60.

40. *Official Report of the Proceedings of the Church Congress of 1862* (Oxford, J. & H. Parker, 1862), pp. 142-143.

41. Maria Trench, 'Reminiscences, Pusey House Oxford', quoted in Gill, 'The Power of Christian Ladyhood', p. 159.

42. O. Shipley (ed.), *The Church and the World: Essays on Questions of the Day in 1867* (London, Longmans Green, 1867), p. 171. The writer was herself a member of an Anglican order.

43. Gill, 'The Power of Christian Ladyhood', p. 159.

44. Gill, 'The Power of Christian Ladyhood', pp. 159-160.

45. Gill, 'The Power of Christian Ladyhood', p. 154.

46. Shipley, *The Church and the World*, p. 167.

47. Anon., *A Valiant Victorian*, pp. 83–91, 150–165.

48. *Christian Observer* (1852), p. 392.

49. E. Peck, *The Social Implications of the Oxford Movement* (New York, Scribner's, 1933), p. 80.

50. C. Booth, *Life and Labour of the People in London, Third Series: Religious Influences* (New York, AMS Press, 1970), vol. 7, p. 352. This is a reprint of the edition of 1902–1904.

51. Allchin, *The Silent Rebellion*, p. 88.

52. Dr Pusey, *Sketch of the Devonport Sisterhood*, copy, Pusey Papers, Pusey House, Oxford.

53. Williams, *Priscilla Lydia Sellon*, p. 204.

54. M. Goodman, *Sisterhoods in the Church of England* (London, Smith, Elder & Co., 1863), p. 147.

55. Anson, *The Call of the Cloister*, pp. 304–305.

56. Gill, 'The Power of Christian Ladyhood', p. 150.

57. W. H. Hutchings, *The Life and Letters of Thomas Thellusson Carter*, (London, Longmans Green, 1903), p. 87.

58. T. Carter, *Is it Well to Institute Sisterhoods in the Church of England for the Care of Female Penitents?* (London, Rivingtons, 2nd edn, 1853), pp. 3–4.

59. Hutchings, *The Life and Letters of Thomas Thellusson Carter*, pp. 86–87.

60. Booth, *Life and Labour of the People in London*, p. 361.

61. Vicinus, *Independent Women*, p. 79.

62. Vicinus, *Independent Women*, p. 78.

63. Carter, *Is it Well to Institute Sisterhoods . . .?*, p. 9.

64. Hutchings, *The Life and Letters of Thomas Thellusson Carter*, p. 78.

65. This is the suggestion made in W. R. Greg's article 'Why are Women Redundant?' (*National Review* (April 1862), pp. 434–460). The demographic imbalance and its significance for the ideals of sisterhood life are discussed in A. Deacon and M. Hill, 'The Problem of "Surplus Women" in the Nineteenth Century: Secular and Religious Alternatives', *A Sociological Yearbook of Religion*, vol. 5 (1972), pp. 87–102.

66. J. Howson, *Deaconesses; Or the Official Help of Women in Parochial Work and in Charitable Institutions* (London, Longmans Green, 1862), p. 13. This was an enlarged version of an article that appeared in *Quarterly Review* in September 1860.

67. Howson, *Deaconesses*, pp. 15–18, 207.

68. R. Braithwaite, *The Life and Letters of the Rev. William Pennefather* (London, J. Shaw & Co., 2nd edn, 1878), p. 408.

69. *The York Journal of Convocation* (London, Rivingtons, 1885), pp. 112–129.

70. C. Prelinger, 'The Female Diaconate in the Anglican Church: What Kind of Ministry for Women?', in Malmgreen (ed.), *Religion in the Lives of English Women*, pp. 161–192. Fliedner's appreciation of the potential of women to undertake charitable work owed something to the example of the Quaker Elizabeth Fry's efforts in the field of prison reform, which he became familiar with on a visit to England.

71. This account of Pennefather's work is based upon Prelinger, 'The Female Diaconate in the Anglican Church', pp. 167–168; and J. Grierson, *The Deaconess* (London, CIO, 1981), p. 19.

72. Sister Joanna, 'The Deaconess Community of St Andrew', *Journal of Ecclesiastical History*, vol. 12 (1961), pp. 215–230.

73. Prelinger, 'The Female Diaconate in the Anglican Church', p. 173.

74. Grierson, *The Deaconess*, p. 24.

75. Braithwaite, *The Life and Letters of the Rev. William Pennefather*, p. 408.

76. Grierson, *The Deaconess*, p. 33.

77. J. G. Talbot, *Memorials of the Hon. Mrs John Chetwynd Talbot* (London, Spottiswoode & Co., 1876), p. 13.

78. Talbot, *Memorials*, p. 9.

79. J. C. Talbot, *Parochial Mission-Women: Their Work and its Fruits* (London, Rivingtons, 1862), p. 61.

80. *A Servant of the Poor: or, Some account of the Life and Death of a Parochial Mission Woman by a Lady Manager* (London, SPCK, 1874).

81. B. Heeney, *The Women's Movement in the Church of England 1850–1930* (Oxford, Clarendon Press, 1988), pp. 53–54.

82. Anon., *Ann Wilson Carlile and the Church Army* (London, Church Army Bookroom, 3rd edn, 1928), pp. 145–146.

83. Heeney, *The Women's Movement in the Church of England*, pp. 57–58.

CHAPTER EIGHT

Women in the Mission Field

Mary Astell's unrealizable dream of 1687, serving as a single woman missionary 'to the Turk and Infidel', became possible for Anglican women in the course of the nineteenth century as both the Evangelical Church Missionary Society and the High Church Society for the Propagation of the Gospel made use of their talents not only as missionary wives and sisters, but increasingly as workers in their own right. Whereas the CMS had only a few missionary wives and sisters associated with its work in 1830, by 1909, out of a total of 1,390 European missionaries on its staff, 414 were clergymen, 152 were laymen, 386 were missionary wives, and 438 were single women.[1] Not only were the majority of workers female, but single women had come to form the largest group working overseas.

The High Church SPG moved more slowly than the CMS in making use of women. However, although it did not open full membership to them until 1921, the Ladies Association for the Promotion of Female Education in India and Other Heathen Countries was established in 1866 under the energetic secretaryship of Miss Louisa Bullock. Its first missionary, Miss Emily Lawrence, was appointed the following year, and by 1900 there were 186 women missionaries in the field.[2]

These changes in policy did not come about without considerable opposition and debate, since they not only ran counter to the belief that women should not preach or hold authority in the Church, but also placed them in situations that called for initiative, bravery, determination, and administrative ability of a kind that went beyond what were regarded as appropriate womanly attributes. Such scruples were overcome partly because it was recognized that in Hindu and Muslim societies male missionaries would not be granted access to upper-class women, and partly because it was claimed that missionary work among women and children was an extension of the philanthropic work among the lower classes that women were engaged in in English society. Just as the power of respectable middle-class Victorian motherhood could be enlisted to transform the lives of the poor at home, so those same values and qualities could help to bring Christian civilization to the rest of the world by reaching the women who were the bearers and educators of the next generation. Such a role undoubtedly offered many women the opportunity to assume more power and responsibility within the life of the Church than they could have done at home, but it also gave them a pivotal role in sustaining and disseminating the ideology of cultural imperialism that helped to fuel the drive for missionary expansion in the heyday of empire.[3]

The debate over women missionaries

The Church Missionary Society was founded in 1799 at the end of a decade of evangelical missionary fervour that also saw the creation of the Baptist Missionary Society in 1792, and the interdenominational London Missionary Society in 1795.[4] From the beginning of its overseas work in Sierra Leone, women participated in the life of the CMS as the wives of missionaries and schoolteachers, but in 1815 – when three ladies from Clifton in Bristol offered to work in any capacity in any part of the world – the CMS ruled that it would not accept single women for missionary work, other than sisters accompanying or joining their brothers.[5] The attitudes prevalent in the SPG to the use of single women as missionaries are evident from a letter written by the Bishop of Calcutta, Daniel Wilson, in reply to an offer of a woman's help in 1842:

I object on principle to single ladies coming out unprotected to so distant a place with a climate so unfriendly, and with the almost certainty of their marrying within a month of their arrival. Imagine the beloved Persis, Tryphena, Tryphosa, Julia and others who laboured much in the Lord, remained in their own neighbourhoods and families, and that no unmarried female would have thought of a voyage of 14,000 miles to find out a scene of duty. The whole thing is against the Apostolic maxim, 'I suffer not a woman to speak in the Church.'[6]

In 1859, and again in 1863, the central committee of the CMS refused to countenance the training and employment of single female missionaries, now arguing that there were already in existence two societies that undertook such work – namely, the Society for Promoting Female Education in the East (founded in 1834), and the Indian Female Normal School and Instruction Society (founded in 1852).[7] It was also indicative of the marginal role offered to women in the missionary movement that the interdenominational conference held at Liverpool in 1860 had no female representatives. Speaking at the conference, the CMS Central Association Secretary, the Rev. J. B. Whiting, could only envisage making use of women's talents on the home front, either as members of missionary working parties raising money for overseas missions, or as the mainstays of Juvenile Associations, 'important not only on account of the large sums they produce, but also because they early enlist the sympathies of the heart'.[8] The Rev. C. B. Leupolt, a CMS missionary in Benares, was more forward-looking. He advocated 'the agency of female missionaries in India', though he was careful to circumscribe their role, arguing that 'It would not be their duty to preach in the bazaar; but to go from house to house, and speak to the native women of the love of Jesus, wherever they find access.'[9] Clearly, the issue of women preaching to men, and thereby assuming a role traditionally reserved for the clergy, remained a sensitive one.

Despite such reservations, it was the pressing need to reach Hindu and Muslim women, which was highlighted by Leupolt, that did most to gain acceptance for female missionary work in Anglican circles. At the missionary conference of the Anglican Communion held in 1894 (at which women had their own separate meetings), the wife of the Bishop of Ripon, Mrs Boyd Carpenter, pointed out that 'Work in the Zenanas of India and the harems of the Mohammedans is only possible to a woman, and through such work she may, by raising the tone and character of the women of a district, with God's blessing, regenerate the whole Eastern world.' Such a far-reaching outcome was possible, since women 'Through their children . . . have charge of future generations, and thus those who rock the cradles may be said to rule the world.'[10] Seen in this way, missionary educational work among women and children, and the provision of medical care, were appropriate extensions of the work that women undertook in

English society, for which their particular qualities of nurturing and compassion made them ideally suited. Speaking at the same gathering, Mrs Bannister, a member of the Church of England Zenana Ladies' Committee, went so far as to argue that the presence of women at Pentecost, and the work done by Priscilla and other women mentioned in Romans 16, showed that women had been divinely called to missionary service and that the great commission had not just been limited to 'the Apostles representing an ordained ministry'. She went on, however, to make it clear that most women were called to be 'home missionaries, and to fill as such an important place at the base of operations', while the role of women overseas was to bring the gospel to other women whom men could not reach.[11]

However, for proponents of the traditional view of complementary but distinct gender roles, work in the mission field posed more acute problems than in any other area of the Church's life, since it seemed to require women to be in possession of a fair number of supposedly masculine attributes – most obviously, courage in the face of danger and hardship, considerable powers of organization, and independence of judgement. The Bishop of Grahamstown, Allam Beecher Webb, writing in support of missionary sisterhoods in 1883, was aware that this was unusual and demanding work that required a particular kind of 'womanly strength', but he went on to stress 'how far this ideal of the valiant woman . . . is from any approach to what is commonly called a "strong-minded woman"'.[12] What this meant in practice was that women undertaking Zenana work should be skilled in needlework, music, and drawing, and – since there was no supply of suitable servants in South Africa – in housework, where missionary women had a particular vocation in following the Virgin in rising above crude materialism by showing 'the compatibility of rude household work with the spirit of recollection and adoration'.[13] The missionary sister also needed 'some intellectual training in systematic theology and Church history, in order to meet inquiries', though hers was not in essence an intellectual role, as 'she does not, as a rule, originate great ideas'.[14]

In his *Women in the Mission Field: Pioneers and Martyrs*, a series of brief biographical sketches of prominent nineteenth-century women missionaries, the Rev. Augustus Buckland was more fulsome than the Bishop in his appreciation of women's work overseas. Writing in the aftermath of the murder of seven women missionaries at Ku-cheng in August 1895, and anxious to reject suggestions that women should either not be sent abroad or only to places where their safety could be guaranteed, Buckland employed the standard argument that native women could only be reached by women, and pointed to the 1894 Anglican missionary conference as evidence that 'Women's work had no longer become a mere adjunct; it was itself a power.'[15] The result was that 'We are more accustomed now to the independent activity of women than we were a quarter of a century ago. We believe more in their organising power and in their capacity to think for themselves.'[16] Yet in his portraits of women missionaries in the field, these were not the aspects of their lives that he was anxious to highlight. In the case of Miss Charlotte Tucker, the well-known CMS missionary in India, it was 'A life so gentle, so humble, so averse from the clamour and display of striving womanhood in some of its recent aspects' that he held up for his readers' emulation. Missionary work was not to be conceived of as an extension of employment and responsibility for women within the Church comparable to changes occurring in secular society; rather, it was a call to submissive service, an antidote to the demands of contemporary 'striving womanhood', not a response.

Yet if female missionaries could be encompassed within traditional expectations of appropriate gender roles, doubts still remained about the advisability of sending them to some parts of the world. This was especially the case with regard to Africa, where it was considered that white women faced particular perils. Writing in *The Nineteenth Century* in 1887, H. H. Johnston argued that female missionaries provided the natives with influential examples of Christian wives and mothers; moreover, celibacy had its dangers in such a climate, since an unmarried missionary 'young and in the prime of manhood is prone to be restless and discontented, or to find a consolation which arouses scandal'.[17] Yet, in Johnston's opinion, there were also serious disadvantages in allowing women to live in such circumstances. Both the climate and childbirth exacted a high physical toll, while the moral and spiritual risks were equally hazardous, since 'rude contact with coarse animal natures and their unrestrained display of animal instincts tends imperceptibly to blunt a modest woman's susceptibilities – especially where she may have been brought up stupidly innocent'.[18] Overall, he concluded that the benefits of sending out married women as missionaries outweighed the difficulties – provided they were not allowed to venture too far into the interior.

This view was sharply opposed by Dr Robert Needham Cust, who had served as Commissioner in Amritsar and as a member of the Committee of the CMS, though by 1890 he had become more critical of missionary policies. Cust had been an enthusiastic advocate of the employment of women missionaries by the CMS, and in 1885 had written an article on the subject for the Society's magazine, the *Church Missionary Intelligencer*, which was only published after he agreed to leave out a passage that called for the creation of a CMS Women's Department.[19] Always a forthright writer, Cust bluntly rejected each of Johnston's arguments. The sending of young married women into Equatorial Africa 'with the possibility of maternity without the surroundings of decent civilized life' was, he concluded, 'a downright wickedness'. Nor was the example of white Christian motherhood as edifying as Johnston supposed:

> I heard this year (1891) on a Missionary platform a Colonial Bishop, who ought to have known better, say that the exhibition of a white Baby to the simple African or Indian people *was favourable to conversion*. This seems to my mind sheer folly. As a matter of surprise, and excitement of interest, the exhibition of a spaniel, or still more a ferret, would have the same effect. It seems monstrous to anticipate any spiritual advantage from a Missionary's Nursery.[20]

The details of human birth also seem to have upset Cust. Objecting to the description of a missionary mother's pregnancy being published in another journal, he argued that 'It was foolish to write such things, but still more foolish to put them in a serious religious journal and circulate it to subscribers: there should be a chaste reserve on such subjects: they are the accidents of material life, not the objects of spiritual life.'[21] As for Johnston's offensive suggestion that it was necessary for male missionaries to be married to avoid sexual impropriety, in Cust's experience, 'those who have made moral lapses, have all been widowers, or married men'.[22] Not surprisingly, in view of the pitfalls that he saw in the path of married women in Africa, Cust concluded that they were an unacceptable burden, and that the place for female missionaries was as members of celibate sisterhoods.[23] Isabella Bird, the well-known travel writer and publicist for the CMS, agreed with Cust in favouring unmarried women, objecting to 'the waste of working power, and the scandal amongst the natives caused by the ceaseless marryings and maternities of the missionary women making an end of work'. In China, she discovered, this also meant that much of the time and energy of single missionaries had to be devoted to nursing the mothers.[24]

Arguments such as these in support of single women in the mission field marked the complete reversal of attitudes that had been prevalent at the beginning of the century. However, the acceptance of women's work as an extension of their complementary role in Victorian domestic and social service restricted the tasks that they could undertake, and limited their access to power and decision-making within the missionary societies. Writing in 1912, Minna Gollock, whose sister was the first secretary of the newly created Women's Department of the CMS in 1895, summed up the sense of frustration that this situation created:

> It is unthinkable that Christian women should 'agitate' on such a subject, but few will ever know what it has cost them to see, for instance, their own best hopes and plans pass on a sheet of paper into a men's board-room, to return altered and excised by those who have not first-hand knowledge, and who frequently do not call first-hand evidence to guide them in their adjudication.[25]

Such a state of affairs was, she remarked (with perhaps more assertiveness than was compatible with true womanly submissiveness), 'traditional no doubt, but tradition is not invariably synonymous with truth'. Women of ability had far more scope for the exercise of their talents, she noted, on Royal Commissions and in University Senates than in the missionary societies to which they contributed so much.[26]

The lower status of women within the societies was also reflected in the preparation they received, which was less thorough than that accorded to men. Training was provided for CMS women at two institutions over which the Society had no direct control: from 1892 at the Deaconess Training Home, the Willows, run by Mrs Pennefather, and from 1894 at The Olives, a private institution run by Mrs Bannister; however, as Eugene Stock remarked in his history of the CMS, most of the first generation of middle-class lady missionaries were considered to be 'Christian women of experience, and needed no training before going out'. Typical of this type of self-supporting 'honorary missionary' was Irene Petrie, who served in Lahore and Srinigar, and in 1893 was given only two weeks' training in Urdu at the Willows and in bandaging at the Bethnal Green medical mission prior to her departure. Stock also noted that by 1899 there were very few female recruits from the newly founded Oxbridge colleges for women.[27]

Class distinctions were also important in the selection and education of women missionaries. In 1891, the CMS opened a new training home at Highbury for women who, 'through lack of means or of adequate educational advantages, or from other causes', were not suitable for admission to the Willows. Here a two-year course was offered that was largely practical in nature: apart from lectures on Scripture, doctrine, and Anglican Church principles, students studied basic medicine, singing, domestic crafts, nursing, and teaching.[28] This compared unfavourably with the much more academic four-year course given to ordinands at the Islington Institution, and the two-year course for laymen instituted in 1891 – which was a scaled-down version of the former, and still therefore more academic in content than that offered to women.[29]

The early training of SPG women missionaries was also sketchy. In 1875, the Women Candidates' Sub-Committee established a three-month training course at the London Deaconesses Institute, but subsequently had to withdraw a clause in its promotional literature offering 'a regular course in medicine and district work' when the head of the Institution said that it couldn't be done in such a short period of time. The General Committee of the SPG required of all women missionaries that they be examined after one year's service in their ability to read, write, and speak in the vernacular, but only made a vague provision that 'some opportunity' for study in England should be provided.[30] In 1895, the Women's Sub-Committee agreed to send candidates for preparation to St Thomas's Sisterhood in Canterbury for a period from six months to two years.[31] Such comparatively inadequate provisions were partly a result of the fact that women had only recently been recruited by the SPG, but they also reflected the mentality of an organization that saw overseas missionary work primarily in terms of the ordained ministry.

Not surprisingly, with attitudes such as these to be found in missionary circles, when Bishop Montgomery preached a sermon in Westminster Abbey in 1915 to mark the jubilee year of women's work for the SPG, he was forced to admit that although the work offered women 'the very noblest cause and the completest romance, and the utmost self-sacrifice', it was sadly the case that 'the Church of God and the Mission Field abroad are not attracting the best women, that is the most capable women, in sufficient numbers, because we have not yet quite understood them'. Part of the problem was caused by the fact that modern women were 'more critical, less submissive, in the sense we used the words 40 years ago'.[32] Despite these difficulties, he concluded with a rousing call to any woman who wished 'to breakaway from conventional English life' and to 'strike out for yourself'. Yet only the following year the SPG was describing the kind of qualities needed by a woman missionary in South Africa in terms that did not suggest much in the way of an escape from Victorian and Edwardian domesticity:

> She must not mind turning her hand to anything. She must certainly be able to do all kinds of needlework. She will probably be asked to make chasubles, cassocks, and surplices. Then in Mission stations where the priests are unmarried and there is no woman housekeeper, she will be called on to do all kinds of mending, repairing and darning. A slight knowledge of tailoring would be useful. You must certainly know how to cook properly and also be prepared to cook a dinner on an oil stove.[33]

Women's experience of the mission field

Despite the restricted view taken by the missionary societies of women's potential usefulness overseas, there is no doubt that such work offered opportunities for employment – particularly for unmarried middle-class women dubbed 'redundant' by a society that saw marriage and the care of a family as a woman's natural means of fulfilment. As John Isherwood has shown, before 1890, few (if any) of the single women sent abroad by the CMS came from working-class backgrounds, while in the decade after 1890 the figure was only 11 per cent; moreover, most of the single women who went overseas in the nineteenth century remained unmarried throughout the period of their service. This was the case with nearly two-thirds of those who served in West Africa, and nearly three-quarters of those sent to China and India.[34]

For the much despised Victorian middle-class spinster, the mission field could be an escape from a lonely or marginalized life in England. This was a point that was not lost on the Bishop of Liverpool in his anniversary sermon to the Church of England Zenana Missionary Society in 1883, when he claimed that 'many women fall into ill health at home, and break down in their nervous system for sheer want of occupation suited to their capacity, while much Christian work is to be done, and cannot be done for want of hands'.[35] This was the case with Anne Mackenzie, who went out to Natal in 1854 to recover her health and to assist her brother who had been appointed Archdeacon. Following her mother's death and the break-up of the family home, Anne had lived in lodgings with a maid, since – as her biographer put it – 'she did not seem especially wanted anywhere'.[36]

It was also the situation of Charlotte Tucker, who began work in the Punjab with the Indian Female Instruction Society in 1875 at the age of fifty-four.[37] She was the sixth child and third daughter of a Bengal administrator who became chairman of the East India Company. Even the conventionally improving biography written two years after her death reveals a great deal about the difficulties and tensions facing an able and energetic single woman caught between the demands of her family and the ideals of selfless femininity on the one hand, and her own need to find some outlet for her boundless energy and ambition on the other. Fearful of the dangers of infectious disease, her father at first refused to allow her to undertake work in Marylebone Workhouse, and even after his death in 1851 she was able to participate in fewer philanthropic enterprises than she would have liked in deference to her mother's wishes.

Although Charlotte Tucker achieved some fame as a writer of children's stories under the patriotic sobriquet A.L.O.E. (a lady of England), her biographer holds her up as a paragon of female Christian self-abnegation, content to regard her father's prohibition 'as in itself sufficient indication of the Divine Will'; and later, with her sister, to live the life of typical unmarried middle-class daughters, devoting 'their time, talents and energies to successive generations of juveniles and elder guests, without a murmur'.[38] Despite her dislike of housekeeping and nursing, following her mother's death she lived with a brother until his death in 1875, and then offered herself for missionary service, writing to her sister that she was not prepared to end up 'a third or fourth lady in – perhaps – a Curate's dear little home'.[39] Saved from this dismal prospect, she threw herself with relish into Zenana visiting in the Punjab – work, she wrote home in 1876, for 'ladies who fear nothing, grumble at nothing, and are ready to carry the Holy War into the enemy's camp'. This of course was a fair description of her own character (the family motto was *nil desperandum*), though her enthusiasm for the cause, and her tendency to apply the language of Christian warfare in a dangerously literal sense, hindered her heroic efforts at conversion, and were a potential source of embarrassment to the Society – as when she was with difficulty dissuaded from executing 'a daring plan for carrying off one brave young girl from her relatives'.[40]

Another woman for whom the mission field was both an extension of Christian service already undertaken at home, and at the same time an opportunity to do more than seemed possible there, was Fanny Woodman. She was born in Lichfield in 1860, and worked as a Sunday school teacher, as local secretary of the Children's Scripture Union, and as a District Visitor. Woodman was on the Evangelical wing of the Church and attended the Keswick convention in 1888. First held in 1875, the Keswick gatherings were a focal point for the dissemination of a style of spirituality that stressed the need for a renewed experience of conversion, in which a faithful resting in God brought a new sense of holiness to the believer.

Both at home and in the mission field, this emphasis on relying on God's power rather than on human effort led not to quietism, but instead to a reinvigorated Christian activism.[41] Fanny Woodman was a typical product of Keswick-style evangelicalism, though her efforts to preach the gospel, initially to the boys in the Scripture Union, and later to audiences of men – both during missions and on visits to a local barracks – forced her to wrestle with her own personal diffidence and with the theological constraints upon women taking such a role in the Church. In March 1889, she admitted to feeling 'a wave of ambition sweeping over me', but then found herself brought up short:

> I have been wanting to convert half the world, forgetting it's none of my work at all. Then came the chance question, 'should a woman speak publicly in face of 1 Timothy 2.12 and 1 Corinthians 14.34?' Of course we may deliver a message, but it seems to touch some of my doings a little closely. I feel inclined to say, 'Oh, that I were a man' for the minute, only the Master did not wish it, that is very clear, and then there flashed through my mind Who are God's great ones?[42]

The answer was both children and the lowly, who undertook a life of service 'doing the things nobody cares about doing, and nobody ever notices are done'. Later she repudiated her earlier ambitious dreams as evidence of unregenerate self-will, ruefully concluding that 'one's writing tongue, as well as one's speaking tongue, is a most unruly member unless He has complete control'.[43] Yet she continued to preach, sure that it was Christ who spoke through her, a conviction that allowed her to cope with both the charge of unwomanly self-assertion and with the Pauline prohibitions. In January 1890, she expressed her desire to become a missionary, finding that 'every word in the *Missionary Gleaner* about Africa is a call to me'. In 1895, she realized her ambition when she and her husband began work for Hudson Taylor's China Inland Mission. However, both died of cholera within months of beginning their work.[44]

Irene Petrie's career followed a similar pattern. The daughter of a colonel, she was presented at court, but was not satisfied with a life of upper middle-class gentility. As her sister noted in her biography of Irene, 'Her special temptation was to use life to achieve and win applause'. She first found outlets for her talents in Sunday school teaching, in work with the daughters of prisoners, and as a member of a missionary union of the SPG, and then of the CMS Ladies Union. Despite being himself a member of the Kensington branch of the CMS Union, her father refused to allow Irene to undertake missionary work in India; and it was not until his death in 1892 that she was free to do so, serving with the CMS in Lahore and Srinigar, where she died after only three years in India in 1897.[45]

The premature deaths of Fanny Woodman and Irene Petrie were not isolated instances, for the reality of missionary service often involved exposure to harsh climatic conditions, illness, and sometimes physical danger. This was particularly true in Africa, where even travel could prove hazardous. For example, the first party of women missionaries to arrive in Uganda in 1894 were forced to cross a flooded river by making use of a fallen tree, 'the women scrambling from branch to branch with great pluck and but little aid'.[46] In India, conditions were better, and the redoubtable Charlotte Tucker found travelling alone an exhilarating experience, supported as she was by 'a kind of instinctive persuasion that neither man nor beast would dare to attack one – except perhaps a vicious horse'.[47] However, even she found the climate trying – anything from burning heat to bitter cold or driving rain – and warned that 'anyone who in England suffers from headache, liver, back, and uneven spirits, I would rather entreat to avoid the Punjab . . . she would be one of the choice delicate palfreys, yoked to artillery, who break down and give extra work to the already fully-taxed horses'.[48]

Hostility to missionary work could also lead to violence. At Isfahan in Persia, attempts to open a medical dispensary led to the CMS missionary Mrs Bishop being threatened by angry crowds in 1890, and again four years later.[49] However, it was in China that the clash between mutually incomprehensible cultures led to the greatest danger. In 1896, Isabella Bird interrupted her travels near the Tibetan border to go to the aid of a female missionary who had broken down under the strain of escaping from anti-missionary riots; she and three companions had been forced to hide for eleven weeks in a windowless room in the hottest season of the year.[50] Despite such an ordeal, theirs was a lucky escape compared with the women who were killed at Kucheng the previous year, a prelude to the Boxer uprising in 1900 in which many missionaries lost their lives.

Less serious, but no less real, were the trials and disappointments that arose from the difficulty of accomplishing missionary objectives. Women missionaries undertook a variety of work, including attempting to preach the gospel to Muslim and Hindu women in seclusion (Zenana visiting), running schools, and working in hospitals. However, although medical and educational work were integral parts of missionary practice – valued both as a way of expressing Christ's love, and as a means of bringing the benefits of Western civilization to less fortunate parts of the world – they were not its *raison d'être*, which was conversion and the salvation of lost souls. Speaking at the missionary conference of the Anglican Communion held in 1894, Mrs Ball, a CMS worker from Sindh, made a sharp distinction between secular philanthropy and missionary work. Alluding to what she regarded as the growing belief (and in her view, mistaken belief) that Christian medical work could be undertaken by doctors 'solely as healers of the body', she was at pains to emphasize that 'there is no scope for such like mere philanthropy in the Church's missionary work among the heathen'.[51] Perplexing liberal theological speculation about the possibility of salvation for non-Christians was dealt with equally briskly as being 'far too subtle, insoluble, and mysterious a question for the limited human mind to solve', and one that 'we are nowhere in Holy Writ asked to decide'.[52] Anglican women who undertook missionary work usually came from theologically conservative backgrounds, and were – not surprisingly – particularly confirmed in their Christian faith and in the overriding necessity to convert those of other religious faiths.

The distinction between secular and religious motivation was most acutely felt in the area of education. In India, missionaries found that what they regarded as purely secular knowledge was often far more highly regarded than the spiritual truths they were so anxious to communicate. For example, in Madras, Miss Oxley was only able to gain access to the homes of thirteen Muslim women. According to the editor of *India's Women*, the magazine of the Church of England Zenana Missionary Society, this was because she refused to offer instruction only in English and needlework and insisted on preaching the gospel.[53]

Mary Billington, a reporter for the *Daily Graphic*, who visited

India for the paper, also commented on the difficulties missionaries faced in attempting to use education as a vehicle for proselytism. Billington described herself as an Anglican, but one who was critical of many aspects of missionary work. She admitted that even the sternest critic of the missionary societies must acknowledge the extent of their contribution to female education in India, and quoted figures to show that out of 333,043 girls in public or recognized private schools in 1890, 104,159 were receiving a missionary education. However, she also argued that 'more is being achieved as education than the preaching and conversion presented as going on on the platform of Exeter hall'; she then cited the example of a Parsee machinist in Delhi who, when asked why he sent his children to a missionary school, replied that a knowledge of English was useful, while the Christian instruction would be forgotten within a couple of months.[54] She also noted rather caustically that the missionary societies seemed to be aware of the problem, since the insistence on providing religious instruction was weaker in areas where there were government schools to provide competition. This was the case, for example, in Madras; but in Bengal, where the administration did next to nothing in providing for female education, 'a far bigger pill of Biblical and ecclesiastical learning can be and is given with the jam of general teaching'.[55]

Even where it was possible to reach women on a one-to-one basis, persuasion proved difficult. As Mrs Winter, the wife of an SPG missionary in Delhi, found in attempts to convert Muslim women, 'very tough discussions on the spuriousness of the Gospels, the Divinity of Christ, & the Trinity constantly arise'.[56] Miss Hooper wrote to the SPG from India in 1894 that she had had to contend with equally thorny objections, including the belief that 'if God caused them to be born Hindus, He meant them to remain Hindus', and the claim that she had encountered in every new home she visited that 'our religions and theirs are really the same, only we call God by a different name'.[57] This was also the experience of Charlotte Tucker, who noted sadly in her journal in 1889 that she had been turned away from four Zenanas in one week, and admitted that such a 'deliberate choosing of darkness instead of light, Barabbas instead of Christ' had put 'a strain upon the threefold cord of Faith, Hope, and Love'.[58]

Doctrinal impasses of this kind were not made any easier by the uncompromising hostility of the missionaries towards faiths that they regarded as heathen and idolatrous, and the lack of knowledge and respect for non-Christian religions that this mind-set usually produced. Candidates for the Church of England Zenana Missionary

186

Society were required to answer certain questions, briefly stating what they knew of 'the different idolatrous systems in India', and to be familiar with the arguments a Muslim would be likely to advance against Christianity; however, such an approach left no room for understanding Islam and Hinduism as living faiths with their own cultural contexts. Indeed, an article in the Society's magazine *India's Women* on 'Work amongst the Mohammedans' specifically repudiated this line of thinking, and warned missionaries against 'seeking to find educational, physical and mental reasons to account for Islamism and the Koran, and their sway over the 160 millions of the present population of our globe, besides all those who have lived and died under the blighting curse of such a faith during the last twelve centuries'. Rather, it was better to know it as 'Satan's instrument', and 'a spiritual wickedness' to be overcome 'in the power of the Spirit'.[59] Charlotte Tucker evinced the closed and non-negotiable style of evangelism that this attitude could produce, writing to her niece in 1880 that 'I do not find the women made angry even by what must startle them. Of course one's manner must be gentle and conciliating, even when meeting the question, "Do you think that Muhammad told lies?" with a simple straightforward, "Yes."'[60]

However well prepared Zenana visitors were to deal with the task of conversion at an intellectual level, they were also forced to come to terms with the formidable social obstacles in the way of success. As Agnes Giberne admitted, the impact of Christianity in India was socially disruptive: it meant 'wives separated from husbands, mothers separated from children'.[61] The second annual report of the Church of England Zenana Missionary Society for the year 1881–1882 recorded instances in central India where husbands had turned their wives out of their homes for wishing to convert to Christianity.[62] Not surprisingly, Miss Hooper cited women's fears of the persecution they would suffer alongside theological objections to Christianity as a serious obstacle to conversion.[63] In China and Japan there were equally intractable cultural barriers to be faced; the political context in Africa made missionary work easier, but physical conditions meant that Anglican women's efforts here had been on a smaller scale during the nineteenth century.

The diverse trials that women faced overseas led them to rely heavily on each other for inspiration and support. Although ultimate authority was vested in the bishop or missionary society, the day-to-day running of a school or the organization of Zenana visiting was left largely to the women themselves. At St Hilda's Diocesan Home in Lahore, for example, matins and evensong in the cathedral and a daily service in their chapel at noon were important focal points in the lives of the four women missionaries, but for the rest of their day the round of visiting Eurasian women in their homes, and the organization of Sunday schools, Girls' Friendly Societies, and Ladies' Bible classes was entirely in their hands.[64] The same was true of the CMS mission in Old Cairo, where the women engaged in Zenana visiting lived together over a shop opposite the Anglican church. CMS female missionaries were also responsible for the running of a large girls' boarding school that was attended by Muslim children.[65]

The need to create self-reliant communities was made greater by the suspicion with which missionaries often regarded other sections of expatriate society. Coming from a military family, and endowed with what her sister called 'the ease and graciousness and tact that came of birth undeniably gentle', Irene Petrie was unusual in taking part in the round of tennis and social events offered by the Punjab Light Horse in Lahore.[66] Charlotte Tucker took a more jaundiced view, comparing an invitation from the Commissioner's wife at Amritsar to 'an attack of cavalry', where one would be expected to put up with 'worldly folk, who are inclined to think Natives "niggers", Converts hypocrites, and Missionaries half-rogues and half-fools'.[67] Miss Macrae of the St Hilda's Mission in Tokyo was equally scathing, warning that 'a Missionary has to contend with the weakened morality of Christian Europeans as well as with the ignorant immorality of heathens'.[68] Miss Schroder, who ran the CMS Willows training home, told the Anglican missionary conference in 1894 that part of the preparation given to women was designed to enable them to 'seek innocent recreation' and to 'avoid being drawn into European society which had in the past often rendered them less useful'.

However, at the same time as this isolation solved some problems, it created others; and she went on to say that the inculcation of 'habits of self-abnegation' was also important if female missionaries were to work well with others, and avoid the dangers of intense personal friendships to which they were prone because of 'the clinging affection, natural to woman'.[69] Missionary sisterhoods often proved the best means of providing the kind of communal support that was needed, and, although hostile to them on theological grounds, the Evangelical CMS often organized its female missionaries into what were in effect very similar communities. Where this did not occur, difficulties could arise.

In 1868–1869, for example, two young women went out to India to assist Mrs Winter and her husband in Delhi. Mrs Winter was a formidable figure who seems to have regarded single women not so much as helpers, but as threats to the standing of missionary wives, and she complained that 'many missionaries' wives endure continued abuse' and 'in silence long for some one to relieve them of the ladies by marrying them'.[70] Not surprisingly, one of the new recruits, Miss Johnson, found Mrs Winter 'rather an eccentric individual very cold and reserved in her manners' and hoped that she would improve on further acquaintance.[71] However, relations deteriorated, with Miss Johnson's frequent bouts of fever being dismissed as ill-temper; and when she sought more congenial company among the wives of local officers as she battled against the heat and her feelings of spiritual inadequacy in undertaking Zenana work, Mrs Winter was scandalized – accusing her of an overfondness for croquet and fine clothes and demanding her transfer to Calcutta. Before the situation could be resolved, Miss Johnson died of the effects of dysentery, and Louisa Bullock, the Secretary of the SPG Ladies' Committee, was in no doubt where the blame lay, having written to Miss Johnson before her death, urging her to shut her eyes and ears as much as possible to what appeared to be spiteful actions, and coldly informing the Rev. Winter after her death that they had been totally satisfied with her work and were not prepared to send out a replacement.[72]

The truth was that women's experience of overseas mission was far more varied than the rather simplistic and idealized portrayals of missionary biographies issued by the societies might suggest.[73] Such work clearly brought a great deal of fulfilment to someone as resilient as the ebullient Charlotte Tucker, who found a new career for herself at the age of fifty-four, and served abroad until her death sixteen years later; to Miss Johnson – young, inexperienced, and ill-cared for – it brought only frustration and an early grave.

Women missionaries and the imperialism of motherhood

Until recently, studies of the impact of Christian missionaries on the societies that they sought to transform have rarely focused on questions of gender, and the specific contribution that women made in this area has been unduly neglected. Women missionaries themselves were sent abroad with the particular remit of reaching other women, and could not but be concerned with their social conditions. As Frances

May, an SPG missionary in India, wrote in 1903, 'I think one gets a kind of passion for one's own sex out here; it is so down trodden, and so much nicer than the other, in spite of everything.'[74]

In campaigning against both child marriage and the prohibition on the remarriage of widows in India, and for the extension of educational opportunities for women, missionaries saw themselves as working for the rights of women less fortunate than themselves throughout the world. They also became aware of the way in which women's lives were threatened and diminished by cultural constraints such as the practice of foot-binding, and by inadequate medical provision. As Isabella Bird found, 'native midwifery abounds in ignorant and brutal customs which in thousands of cases produce life-long suffering and, in many, fatal results'.[75] Not without reason could Baroness Burdett-Coutts proudly proclaim, in one of a series of papers on women's work written for the Chicago World Fair in 1893, that female philanthropy throughout the world was 'one of the great facts of the age', and one that was 'helping to break down those barriers of race, colour, and creed, which are opposed to the progress of true civilisation and the spirit of real religion'. Such endeavour, she concluded, was 'elevating womanhood, and making all countries, but especially ours, proud of their women'.[76]

These claims were part of the picture, but some historians have tended to follow this contemporary evaluation too readily and have over-emphasized the role of women missionaries as advocates of women's rights in non-European societies. For example, Margaret Donaldson sums up the achievement of the Society for Promoting Female Education in China, India, and the East in this way:

> The educational contribution of the society was notable, extending over many lands and opening many doors for women. The FES teachers brought not only literacy and western skills, but also courage for a new way of life. Women in Africa learned to make their own decisions about marriage, about schooling and clothing, and family life; women in China found the strength to refuse to have their daughters' feet bound; Zenana women in India gained a window on the world – and a place in the 1867 Paris Exhibition! And all had the opportunity for a new kind of education.[77]

The difficulty with judgements such as this is that they fail to take account of the immensely complex interaction of Western and non-Western cultures, which often resulted in consequences that were unwanted and unforeseen by the missionaries. A concentration on missionary achievement also too easily ignores indigenous movements for change that owed little or nothing to Christian precepts. Part of the problem is that a great deal more work needs to be done locally to supplement or correct the picture derived from Western missionary sources, but questions of ethnocentrism also arise in matters of inter- pretation. If, for example, it was the case that missionary education gave Indian women 'a window on the world', was the glass two-way? Did missionaries learn from the cultures they sought to transform? How far were their own values modified by their experiences? More- over, what kind of vision of the Western world did its missionary ambassadors seek to impart?

There is a great deal of evidence to suggest that both men and women who worked overseas had a highly ambivalent view of the society they had left behind, one that was at pains to underline the Christian basis of its achievements while being uneasily aware of its increasingly secular system of values and of the huge social problems that had been created by industrialization. As educated Indian and Chinese Christians who visited the West discovered, seeing through a glass darkly might be a better description of the educational process that they had undergone.

In his study of the work of SPG missionaries in Delhi and Lahore, Jeffrey Cox gives a more nuanced and penetrating analysis than Donaldson of the relationship between imperialism and the work of women missionaries. He stresses that the missionary movement was 'a channel for a large outpouring of goodwill by ordinary English people toward the people of India, and by English women toward the women of India', but while the male ideal of compassionate Christian service was lost in the progressive professionalization of the clergy, 'the female ideal took longer to abandon, but by the early twentieth century it too had been submerged, not in racism or ethnocentrism, but in a more complicated strain of imperialism, the heritage of late Victorian Christianity, with its conviction that the progress of Christianity is intimately related to bricks, mortar and educational qualifications'. In Cox's view, the hierarchical nature of missionary schools and hospitals in which Westerners held most positions of responsibility made them institutions that gave 'a subtle but powerful sanction for the British imperial presence'.[78] It might be argued, however, that the nature of missionary institutions and the values that they inculcated were prime examples of racist and ethnocentric assumptions that were from the very beginning bound up with the development of the nineteenth-century missionary movement, and ones that took a specifically gendered form.

The arguments in favour of sending both married and unmarried women overseas involved an emphasis upon their ability to exercise distinctively maternal qualities in the nurturing and education of children. Just as the moral and spiritual power of women in the home was held to be the basis of Christian civilization in England, so its re-creation in non-Western societies was seen as the key to their transformation. As the Bishop of Grahamstown put it in calling for single women to work overseas, 'home is the centre and fountain of social life', and 'to reach that centre, to purify it and consecrate it for the Kingdom of God is woman's special work'.[79] It was also firmly believed that only Christianity among the world's religions had given women this exalted station and responsibility. For example, preaching the fourth annual sermon of the Church of England Zenana Mission-ary Society in 1884, the Bishop of Ossory referred to the close and warm relationships that Christ had had with women, and went on to issue a fervent appeal to 'Christian women whom the Gospel has raised to the throne of domestic influence, and blessed with the affection and esteem of the husbands, sons, and brothers', to 'have pity . . . on the hundreds of millions of women in the East, who are sunk in ignorance and misery themselves, and are therefore hindrances and impediments to all spiritual and temporal progress amongst their kind'.[80]

Imparting family values that were held to derive uniquely from the Christian faith could also have political as well as purely spiritual benefits. As the Bishop of Grahamstown emphasized in 1883, 'The importance of work for and amongst native girls and women cannot be pressed home too strongly upon those who would avoid the expen-sive disaster of Kafir wars and chronic native restlessness.'[81] The same point was made by Mrs Fanny Patteson to the SPG Ladies' Association in 1894, when she alluded to rumours of disturbances in India, and asked her audience 'if the women were Christians where would be the danger?'[82] Following the shock of the Indian Mutiny in 1857, safeguarding the Empire more by persuasion than by direct military force became an important governmental objective – and one that women missionaries could help to implement.

The pattern of home-life that the missionaries sought to export was very much that of the English middle class from which they came. It was not 'women', but 'ladies', who were required for the task, for, as the wife of the Bishop of Ripon, Mrs Boyd Carpenter, explained to the Anglican missionary conference of 1894, 'In India, where it may be said there is no culture at all amongst the women, it has been found that the most refined and cultured English ladies, other things being equal, make the best missionaries even to simpler people.'[83] The Church of England Zenana Missionary Society was described in 1884 in similarly middle-class terms as an organization of 'Christian women of piety and culture, who go forth from their happy homes in England, to bring the blessings of our faith and civilisation to their less favoured sisters', blessings that included 'all the arts and accomplishments of an English home – its music, its painting, its needlework, its literature'.[84] Class assumptions were also evident in a missionary training that included the management of servants as an essential part of the curriculum.[85]

Middle-class English women thus brought to the mission field experiences and assumptions that they had gained from undertaking philanthropic work among the poor at home, and attitudes that cut them off from understanding working-class culture in England had the same effect overseas. Work among the lower classes at home conjured up powerful images of dirt, disorder, and darkness. Whereas in earlier periods, domestic cleanliness and personal hygiene had not been marks of status differentiation, by the nineteenth century they had come to be essential elements of middle-class respectability. Cleanliness was not only next to Godliness, it was the most obvious outer sign of an inner spiritual grace, and the poor were the 'great unwashed', whose physical condition was indicative of a more deeply-seated moral pollution. Typical of this conflation of physical and moral imagery was Mrs Gilmore's address on the training of deaconesses, given to the Anglican missionary conference in 1894. The building up of toughness, she warned, had to be an important aim of such courses, and anyone who doubted this had only to 'think of the woman just come from her own spotless home, whom society has protected from even the knowledge of evil, thrown into a filthy hell of a London slum'.[86]

The equation of poor physical conditions with moral and spiritual inadequacy, and the need to create a *cordon sanitaire* between the realms of chaos and disorder, became preoccupations that often isolated nineteenth-century missionaries from any true encounter with the societies they attempted to reach. In Kolapore in India, the presence of a Christian school run by two SPG women, it was claimed, brought with it 'civilisation, education, and all that belongs to the moral and material welfare of humanity'. The result was a total transformation of both the physical and the moral dimensions of life, and a reassuring contrast was drawn between the dirt and squalor of native girls and the converts, 'decently clothed in their graceful white draperies, their hair done up in neat, shining, glossy plaits, looking occupied, happy, well employed, and as if they could have but little in common with the little semi-civilised crew of heathen children we had seen outside'.[87]

The same contrast was evident in the CMS day school in Cairo, where 'when the first floor is reached the region of order and method is reached also', and where the children were learning to read and to be 'clean, orderly, and obedient'. The CMS in Cairo also ran a large girls' boarding school that educated Muslim children, as well as a mission hospital that treated over 10,000 cases a year. It was not just Christianity that made the difference in the education that the missionaries believed they could offer, however, but the inculcation of a whole value system that owed a great deal to the Victorian public school ethos and in which drill, games, and patriotic songs assumed a prominent part.[88] Sunday was also an important day in the life of the school, particularly the elaborately organized parade to the CMS church, with the pupils dressed in pink cotton frocks in summer and red in winter, pointing up the moral of the 'contrast between them and those they pass; the girls in their surroundings of purity and love, the others living in the tainted atmosphere of Moslem homes'.[89]

The last quotation indicates the extent to which women who saw themselves as the guardians of middle-class Victorian domestic values, on which civilization itself was felt to depend, found it difficult – if not impossible – to see any worth in cultures that differed from their own. This was particularly the case with regard to Africa, a Conradian heart of darkness for the Western missionary women who ventured there. One of these was Ruth Fisher, the sixth child of a prominent Exeter Hall evangelist who went out to Uganda with the CMS in 1900. In Toro, she wrote enthusiastically, 'Christianity has completely revolutionized child-life' among the pygmy people (girls who had come to school clean had been given presents of dolls), to such an extent that the children now made excellent domestics and led her to speculate 'whether the problem of the over-taxed English market could not be solved by exporting some of these small people'.[90] Uganda in general, she noted, was 'unmistakably in the grip of progress', and this would benefit native women who were little better than slaves forced to do both housework and work in the fields. Nor did they know any love or sympathy in their lives from the African male, who 'had three sources of revenue – goats, wives,

and children; neither of them he regarded with deep feelings of affection, unless we except the goats'.[91] In lurid terms, she invited her
readers to try to understand the condition of Africa before
Christianity:

> If one can imagine a people that has never possessed a literature in
> any form however crude; that has never produced a song, except
> the war cry and the shout of savage exultation; that has known no
> music save the din of the tom-tom with its sensual accompani-
> ments; if one can picture a land without any recognised code of
> moral laws; that provides no restraint to the exercise of the most
> evil passions; if one can think of a land from which, all through
> the ages, there has never arisen one prayer to God or any deity
> save devils, one can faintly see these districts of Africa before the
> light broke in upon darkness – that light that lighteth every man.[92]

Given such an erroneous view of African history and its culture, it
might be doubted how qualified Ruth Fisher was to make sweeping
judgements about the emotional quality of life to be found within
African marriage.[93]

Missionaries were less inclined to regard Asia as a continent
without culture and history, but their overall evaluations of its peoples
were much the same. The first number of the Church of England
Zenana Missionary Society in 1881 asserted confidently that 'the
daughters of India are unwelcomed at their birth, untaught in childhood, enslaved when married, accursed as widows and unlamented at
their death', while Miss Clay warned that village visiting was particularly trying in the Punjab because of the extreme ignorance of the
population; this led her in some exasperation to the conclusion that
'However degraded and ignorant a person may be in England, there is
at least something to work upon.'[94] In her *Persian Women and their
Creed*, published in 1899, Mary Bird, a CMS missionary at Julfa,
described Islam in stock Victorian terms as a religion of the sword
whose precepts had little practical effect, and then went on to describe
the social life of the people: 'I had almost written home-life, but this
does not exist; there is no word for home in the Persian language,
because it has not been required; the Moslems have none of the associations and tender memories which that word wakens in us.'[95] What
did not conform to English expectations could exist in no other form.

The journalist Mary Billington felt strongly that missionary ethnocentrism created a distorted and misleading picture of the social
position of women in India. She rejected claims that the ban on the

remarriage of Hindu widows led to their ending up in a life of prostitution, pointing out that concern for the good of the family's name prevented this. As for child marriage, this was where 'inaccurate sensationalism' reached its climax, with missionaries confusing betrothal at the age of five or six with the bride's home-taking later at the age of physical maturity. Zenana life was not the sentence of incarceration that Western missionaries portrayed it as being, but 'simply rather dull', and just as much affection was to be found in Muslim and Hindu family life as anywhere else – as one would expect, given that 'the primal elements of human nature do not greatly vary the world over'.[96] As for what she called the missionary slander that a Muslim man could divorce his wife merely by repeating a form of words, she quoted an Indian authority on Islamic law to show the stringent conditions under which divorce could be granted and the independent property rights that Muslim women retained on marriage.

Overall, she did not regard Indian women as economically worse off than those in England, and cited the example of an East End woman struggling to bring up three young children while earning 5s 6d a week in a matchbox factory.[97] Missionary attitudes to native craftwork and styles of dress were also roundly condemned as prime examples of 'the extraordinary inability to recognise anything that is admirable unless it be of the most conventional and villa-residential character, which seems a peculiarity of the Englishman, and even more particularly the Englishwoman abroad'.[98]

Mary Billington's mention of the harsh conditions suffered by working-class women in England highlights the deeply ambiguous and contradictory nature of Victorian missionary ideology. It was precisely because the gospel, and only the gospel, had elevated the place of women in society to its proper heights that women were in gratitude called upon to take its message to their less fortunate sisters throughout the world. Yet the Victorian ideal of Christian womanhood was a class one, from which most women were excluded; and indeed one that relied upon the exploitation of the majority of women who struggled to bring up their families while undertaking paid employment, and whose work in domestic service was the indispensable basis of middle-class comfort. Struggling with the evils of child marriage, prostitution, and the poverty and lack of education of women overseas might in one sense be a logical extension of the same work undertaken at home, but it sat uneasily with claims about the inherent superiority of the Christian societies from which the missionaries came.

Not only was the vision of liberation that missionary women offered an unrealistic one, involving the transplanting of Victorian middle-class domesticity to other societies without reference to the economic and political power of the West on which it rested, but it was also limited in two significant respects. First, the low view that was taken of the intellectual and moral endowments of non-Europeans implied that Western tutelage would be a long-term process. The first number of *India's Women* in 1881 stressed the need to build up native churches as soon as possible, but, because of the ignorance of Indian women, the writer envisaged that foreign help would be indispensable for a long time to come.[99] Second, the vision of liberated womanhood that the missionaries brought contained all the limitations of the Victorian ideal from which it sprang. As we have seen, within the missionary movement itself the emphasis upon the complementarity of male and female roles was in conscious opposition to the idea of secular feminist equality that was growing in the late nineteenth century; while the export of Victorian domesticity involved all the limitations on women that this implied. As the Bishop of Down, Connor, and Dronmore told the thirteenth anniversary meeting of the Church of England Zenana Missionary Society in 1893, women in foreign lands were oppressed in comparison with their Christian counterparts, who had been made 'by His divine appointment the weaker vessel, that so man should shelter and cherish and defend her by his strength, and look upon her as his most precious treasure, lying at the very centre of his heart and his home; a well-spring of happiness in his life of toil and conflict'.[100] This was a gilded vision of purdah, but purdah none the less.

It might seem ungenerous to conclude by emphasizing the extent to which the cultural myopia and hierarchical class assumptions of nineteenth-century Anglican women missionaries vitiated their attempts to make common cause with the women to whom they reached out, inspired by the highest ideals of Christian love and service. Not all their reactions were as black and white as those of Ruth Fisher, and because they were often reticent in their writings about the degree of hardship and difficulty that they had to bear, it is easy to highlight those passages that strike the modern reader as arrogant and overbearing.[101] Moreover, one should not overlook the context of Victorian racist discourse in which the missionaries operated. Charlotte Tucker's belief in the non-European, her claim that 'none was too degraded to be helped up', encapsulates both the nature of missionary ethnocentrism and its limits in comparison with a racist anthropology that often regarded non-Europeans as inherently lesser forms of humanity.[102]

In their introduction to a recent series of studies of Western women and imperialism, Nupur Chaudhuri and Margaret Strobel see these missionaries as being involved in a process of 'negotiating the converging and conflicting fields of gender, race, class, and nationality', and warn against finding any 'single pattern of mere cultural arrogance or cultural acceptance, no single pattern of maternal appropriation of indigenous women versus identification with them'.[103] Nevertheless, because of the nature of the Christian ideology of womanhood that inspired their efforts, in the case of the aims and methods of nineteenth-century Anglican women missionaries, 'the maternal appropriation of indigenous women' is an apposite description of their outlook and aims.[104] It also indicates the extent to which they were the products of the values of the society and religious subculture from which they came – values for which they were prepared to give up their lives.[105]

Notes

1. G. Gollock, *The Story of the Church Missionary Society* (London, CMS, 1909), p. 46.

2. H. P. Thompson, *Into All Lands: The History of the Society for the Propagation of the Gospel in Foreign Parts 1701–1950* (London, SPCK, 1951), p. 235.

3. The connection between the missionary movement and Victorian imperialism has been a controversial subject. An up-to-date, if somewhat defensive, account is given by B. Stanley in *The Bible and the Flag: Protestant Missions and British Imperialism in the Nineteenth and Twentieth Centuries* (Leicester, IVP, 1990). For a more critical overview, see J. Kent, *The Unacceptable Face: The Modern Church in the Eyes of the Historian* (London, SCM, 1987), pp. 177–202. *Women's Studies International Forum*, vol. 13 (1990) is devoted to the subject of women and imperialism, and contains a number of perceptive essays on women in the mission field.

4. The standard history of the CMS is E. Stock, *The History of the Church Missionary Society: Its Environment, Its Men and Its Work* (4 vols, London, Church Missionary Society, 3 vols, 1899, vol. 4, 1916). Stock was Secretary of the CMS, and his perspective in this centenary history of the society is less critical than that of post-colonial historiography, but his work is full of illuminating detail in typically exhaustive – and exhausting – Victorian style.

5. Stock, *The History of the Church Missionary Society*, vol. 1, pp. 124–125.

6. C. F. Pascoe, *Two Hundred Years of the S.P.G.: An Historical Account of the Society for the Propagation of the Gospel in Foreign Parts 1701–1901* (London, SPG, 1901), p. 617.

7. Stock, *The History of the Church Missionary Society*, vol. 2, p. 398.

8. *Conference on Missions Held in 1860 at Liverpool, edited by the Secretaries to the Conference* (London, James Nisbet, 1860), p. 63.

9. *Conference on Missions Held in 1860 at Liverpool*, p. 112.

10. G. A. Spottiswoode, *The Official Report of the Missionary Conference of the Anglican Communion on May 28, 29, 30, 31 and June 1, 1894* (London, SPCK, 1894), p. 579.

11. Spottiswoode, *The Official Report of the Missionary Conference*, pp. 580–583.

12. The Rev. A. B. Webb, *Sisterhood Life and Woman's Work in the Mission-Field of the Church* (London, Skeffington & Son, 1883), p. 10.

13. Webb, *Sisterhood Life and Woman's Work*, p. 13.

14. Webb, *Sisterhood Life and Woman's Work*, p. 60.

15. The Rev. A. R. Buckland, *Women in the Mission Field: Pioneers and Martyrs* (London, Ibister & Co., 1895), p. 15. Popular lives of missionaries that emphasized both the romance and heroism of their calling were common in the late Victorian and Edwardian period. Representative of the genre is E. C. Dawson's *Heroines of Missionary Adventure. True Stories of the Intrepid Bravery and Patient Endurance of Missionaries in Their Encounters with Uncivilised Man, Wild Beasts, and the Forces of Nature in All Parts of the World* (London, Seeley & Co., 1909).

16. Buckland, *Women in the Mission Field*, p. 16.

17. H. H. Johnston, 'British Missions in Africa', *The Nineteenth Century*, vol. 22 (1887), p. 717. See also H. A. C. Cairns, *Prelude to Imperialism: British Reactions to Central African Society 1840–1890* (London, Routledge & Kegan Paul, 1965), pp. 57–61, for a discussion of the debate about the desirability of sending women missionaries into the African interior.

18. Johnston, 'British Missions in Africa', p. 718. Johnston's projection of unbridled sexuality on to the African reveals a great deal about Victorian attitudes to sex. His real fear was not about Africans, but about the difficulties of imposing restraint on white middle-class Englishmen and the contradictions involved in maintaining that women should be both sexually knowledgeable and innocent at one and the same time.

19. Stock, *The History of the Church Missionary Society*, vol. 3, p. 321. In fact, 1885 saw the acceptance by the CMS of Miss M. W. Harvey, whom Stock describes as 'the first representative of the new race of C.M.S. women missionaries' (p. 367).

20. R. N. Cust, *Africa Rediviva. Or, The Occupation of Africa by Christian Missionaries of Europe and North America* (London, Elliot Stock, 1891), pp. 70–71.

21. Cust, *Africa Rediviva*, p. 71.

22. R. N. Cust, *An Essay on the Prevailing Methods of Evangelization of the Non-Christian World* (London, Elliot Stock, 1894), p. 211.

23. Cust, *Africa Rediviva*, pp. 69–70. For similar debates within the Baptist Missionary Society about the advisability of sending single women missionaries to Africa, see N. R. Hunt, 'Single Ladies on the Congo: Protestant Missionary Tensions and Voices', *Women's Studies International Forum*, vol. 13, no. 4 (1990), pp. 395–403. At the Congo missionary conference of 1907, the Rev. J. Whitehead argued that single women were useful, though 'owing to the practice of unrestrained speech and imperfect manner of dress on the part of the wild native the presence of unmarried ladies is sometimes very embarrassing'. What was perhaps more important was that 'real women would realise that they were not divinely appointed to be directors of the mission', since there was 'room for a Joan d'Arc sometimes, but not every day' (p. 400). In 1909, it became official policy to allow single missionaries to undertake work among women and children, provided they did not live and work alone.

24. A. M. Stoddart, *The Life of Isabella Bird* (London, John Murray, 1906), p. 319.

25. M. C. Gollock, 'The Share of Women in the Administration of Missions', *International Review of Missions*, vol. 1, no. 4 (1912), p. 683.

26. Gollock, 'The Share of Women in the Administration of Missions', p. 677.

27. Stock, *The History of the Church Missionary Society*, vol. 3, p. 371.

28. C. P. Williams, 'The Recruitment and Training of Overseas Missionaries in England Between 1850 and 1900', University of Bristol M.Litt thesis, 1976, pp. 320–321.

29. Williams, 'The Recruitment and Training of Overseas Missionaries', pp. 95–102. Williams, however, also doubts whether the training given to men was adequate for the missionary work they undertook.

30. USPG Archives, Rhodes House, Oxford, Women Candidates Sub-Committee Minute Book 1874–1885, CWW 27/1–2.

31. USPG Archives, Rhodes House, Oxford, Women Candidates Sub-Committee Minute Book 1886–1898, CWW 26.

32. H. Montgomery, *'With the Women'. A Sermon preached in Westminster Abbey on April 22nd 1915 on the occasion of the commencement of the Jubilee Year of Women's Work* (London, SPG, 1915), pp. 7–8.

33. *'Pilot Letters' Describing the Work of Women Missionaries of the S.P.G. reprinted from the Home Workers' Gazette* (London, SPG, 1916), p. 33.

34. J. Isherwood, 'An Analysis of the Role of Single Women in the Work of the

Church Missionary Society, 1804-1904, in West Africa, India and China', University of Manchester MA thesis, 1979, appendix tables 6b and 9a.

35. *Third Annual Report of the Church of England Zenana Missionary Society for 1882-3* (London, CMS, 1883), p. 16. I have made use of the volumes in the CMS archives at the University of Birmingham, CEZ/G EL1/1.

36. F. Awdry, *An Elder Sister: A Short Sketch of Anne Mackenzie, and her Brother the Missionary Bishop* (London, Bemrose & Sons, 1878), p. 33.

37. The CMS had worked with the Indian Female Instruction Society and had sent out missionaries under its auspices, but in 1880 the CMS took over much of its work and created its own Church of England Zenana Missionary Society.

38. A. Giberne, *A Lady of England. The Life and Letters of Charlotte Mary Tucker* (London, Hodder & Stoughton, 1895), pp. 83, 114.

39. Giberne, *A Lady of England*, p. 171.

40. Giberne, *A Lady of England*, p. 292. Her biographer notes that Charlotte achieved few results in terms of conversions because she was unable to offer systematic instruction in the vernacular, yet like Livingstone, who was equally unsuccessful, she came to be regarded as something of a missionary icon - and for much the same reason. Both epitomized the Victorian qualities of optimism, self-confidence, and cultural superiority.

41. For a helpful discussion of the Keswick holiness movement, see D. W. Bebbington, *Evangelicalism in Modern Britain. A History from the 1730s to the 1980s* (London, Unwin Hyman, 1989), pp. 151-180.

42. A. Hodges, *Love's Victory. Memoirs of Fanny Woodman 1888-1895* (London, Marshall Brothers, 1899), pp. 13-14.

43. Hodges, *Love's Victory*, p. 14.

44. Hodges, *Love's Victory*, pp. 99-128.

45. Mrs Ashley Carus-Wilson, *Irene Petrie Missionary to Kashmir* (London, Hodder & Stoughton, 1900).

46. A. P. Shepherd, *Tucker of Uganda Artist and Apostle 1849-1914* (London, SCM, 1929), p. 104.

47. Giberne, *A Lady of England*, p. 223.

48. Giberne, *A Lady of England*, p. 315.

49. M. Bird, *Persian Women and their Creed* (London, CMS, 1899), pp. 56-67.

50. A. M. Stoddart, *The Life of Isabella Bird* (London, John Murray, 1906), p. 319.

51. Spottiswoode, *The Official Report of the Missionary Conference*, p. 603.

52. Spottiswoode, *The Official Report of the Missionary Conference*. For a discussion of the predominantly negative evaluation of Hindu belief and practice by nineteenth-century Protestant missionaries in India, and of the beginnings

of a more liberal theology of fulfilment, see E. J. Sharpe, *Faith Meets Faith. Some Christian Attitudes to Hinduism in the Nineteenth and Twentieth Centuries* (London, SCM, 1977), pp. 1-31.

53. *India's Women*, vol. 1 (1881), pp. 10-11.

54. M. Billington, *Woman in India* (London, Chapman & Hall, 1895), pp. 26-29.

55. Billington, *Woman in India*, p. 29.

56. USPG Archives, Rhodes House, Oxford, letters received from India 1867-1868, CWW 230/2.

57. J. Cox, 'Independent English Women in Delhi and Lahore, 1860-1947', in R. W. Davis and R. J. Helmstadter (eds), *Religion and Irreligion in Victorian Society: Essays in Honour of R. K. Webb* (London, Routledge, 1992), p. 171.

58. Giberne, *A Lady of England*, p. 475.

59. *India's Women*, vol. 1 (1881), p. 313. The questions to candidates were printed in the *Third Annual Report of the Church of England Zenana Missionary Society for 1882-3* (London, CMS, 1883), p. 31.

60. Giberne, *A Lady of England*, p. 334.

61. Giberne, *A Lady of England*, p. 300.

62. *Second Annual Report of the Church of England Zenana Missionary Society for 1881-2* (London, CMS, 1882), pp. 12-13.

63. Cox, 'Independent English Women in Delhi and Lahore', p. 171.

64. Carus-Wilson, *Irene Petrie*, pp. 80-84.

65. M. C. Gollock, *River, Sand and Sun Being Sketches of the C.M.S. Egypt Mission* (London, CMS, 1906).

66. Carus-Wilson, *Irene Petrie*, p. 86.

67. Giberne, *A Lady of England*, pp. 267-268.

68. Spottiswoode, *The Official Report of the Missionary Conference*, p. 655.

69. Spottiswoode, *The Official Report of the Missionary Conference*, p. 594.

70. USPG Archives, Rhodes House, Oxford, letters received from India 1867-1868, CWW 230/1; Mrs Winter to Miss Bullock, 20 April 1868.

71. USPG Archives, CWW 231/2; Miss Johnson to Miss Bullock, 4 April 1869.

72. USPG Archives, CWW 154/1.

73. The need to raise funds and recruits often involved the missionary societies in the creation of images and myths that were far removed from reality. Thus Mrs Winter wrote to Louisa Bullock, urging that Miss Johnson's letters 'may not be read at working parties as if she writes all that she says she will I fear many at home may be discouraged' (USPG Archives, CWW 231/3).

74. Cox, 'Independent English Women in Delhi and Lahore', p. 177.

75. Quoted in L. Byrne, *The Hidden Journey: Missionary Heroines in Many Lands* (London, SPCK, 1993), p. 133. Lavinia Byrne's book is an illuminating anthology that succeeds in allowing missionary women to speak for themselves while giving due weight to critical historiographical questions of context, culture, and ethnocentrism.

76. Baroness Burdett-Coutts (ed.), *Woman's Mission. A Series of Congress Papers on the Philanthropic Work of Women by Eminent Writers* (London, Sampson Low, Marston & Co., 1893), p. 360.

77. M. Donaldson, '"The Cultivation of the Heart and the Moulding of the Will . . ." The Missionary Contribution of the Society for Promoting Female Education in China, India, and the East', in W. J. Sheils and D. Wood (eds), *Women and the Church*, Studies in Church History 27 (Oxford, Basil Blackwell, 1990), pp. 429–442. The quotation is from p. 442.

78. Cox, 'Independent English Women in Delhi and Lahore', p. 181.

79. Webb, *Sisterhood Life and Woman's Work*, p. 3. The Bishop was also anxious to dispel the charge that celibate sisterhoods were not compatible with Victorian family values, partly by insisting that only women who had no obligations as wives, mothers, or carers of elderly relatives were free to join them, and partly by arguing that sisters in South Africa were building up its home life by training the future wives and mothers of the colony (p. 54).

80. *Fourth Annual Report of the Church of England Zenana Missionary Society for 1881-2* (London, CMS, 1884), p. 16.

81. Webb, *Sisterhood Life and Woman's Work*, p. 43.

82. Spottiswoode, *The Official Report of the Missionary Conference*, p. 606.

83. Spottiswoode, *The Official Report of the Missionary Conference*, p. 577.

84. *Fourth Annual Report of the Church of England Zenana Missionary Society for 1881-2* (London, CMS, 1884), pp. 17–18.

85. Spottiswoode, *The Official Report of the Missionary Conference*, p. 593.

86. Spottiswoode, *The Official Report of the Missionary Conference*, p. 587. There is a good discussion of this theme by Leonore Davidoff in her 'The Rationalization of Housework', in D. Leonard Barker and S. Allen (eds), *Dependence and Exploitation in Work and Marriage* (London, Longman, 1976), pp. 120–151. This draws upon the anthropological perspectives in M. Douglas, *Purity and Danger. An Analysis of Concepts of Pollution and Taboo* (London, Routledge & Kegan Paul, 1966), who suggests that our behaviour in cleaning or avoiding dirt is not adequately explained by our ideas about disease, but that concepts of pollution 'are used as analogies for expressing a general view of the social order' (Penguin edn, 1970), pp. 12–14. This was true of Victorian England, where fears of dirt preceded understanding of disease mechanisms and the sanitary reform movement.

87. *The Grain of Mustard Seed, Or, Woman's Work In Foreign Parts*, vol. 1

(1884), p. 4. This was the magazine of the SPG Ladies' Association.

88. Gollock, *The Story of the Church Missionary Society*, p. 61. In Kashmir, Irene Petrie described a situation where the CMS school was in competition with a state school, but was in no doubt about 'the contrast between the ordinary State School trained Kashmirir and the manly courteous Mission School lad'. Unfortunately, the methods used to bring about this metamorphosis were not always popular, and the school lost pupils because of its insistence on compulsory games (Carus-Wilson, *Irene Petrie*, pp. 252–253).

89. Gollock, *The Story of the Church Missionary Society*, p. 65.

90. R. Fisher, *On the Borders of Pygmy Land* (London, Marshall Brothers, 1905), pp. 81–82.

91. R. Fisher, *Twilight Tales of the Black Baganda* (London, Frank Cass, 2nd edn, 1970), p. 43. The first edition was published in 1911.

92. Fisher, *Twilight Tales of the Black Baganda*, p. 52.

93. For general Western attitudes towards Africa, see the Nigerian writer Chinua Achebe's novel *Things Fall Apart*, published in 1958, which took as its central theme the fact that 'African peoples did not hear of culture for the first time from Europeans; that their societies were not mindless but frequently had a philosophy of great depth, and value and beauty, that they had poetry and, above all, they had dignity' (quoted in C. L. Innes and B. Lindfors (eds), *Critical Perspectives on Chinua Achebe* (London, Heinemann, 1978), p. 37).

94. *India's Women*, vol. 1 (1881), pp. 3, 141.

95. Bird, *Persian Women and their Creed*, p. 25.

96. Billington, *Woman in India*, p. xvi.

97. Billington, *Woman in India*, p. 136. Mary Billington may have condemned the ethnocentric vision of the missionaries, but she herself did not altogether escape from the prejudices of her class, denouncing English working-class women for marrying 'with reckless improvidence' and indulging in recreations 'which savour more of horseplay than refinement' (p. 173).

98. Billington, *Woman in India*, p. 179. As Mary Billington realized, such cultural blindness was not solely the preserve of the missionaries, though their religious pietism gave it a particular form and emphasis. For a wider view of Victorian attitudes, see J. Pemble, *The Mediterranean Passion: Victorians and Edwardians in the South* (Oxford, OUP, 1988). Pemble concludes 'that the level of international goodwill and understanding would not have been reduced, and might even have been enhanced, if the British had stayed at home to cultivate their gardens' (p. 274). Edward Said's *Orientalism* (Harmondsworth, Penguin Books, 1985) is a masterly study of nineteenth- and twentieth-century cultural chauvinism.

99. *India's Women*, vol. 1 (1881), pp. 261–262.

100. *Thirteenth Annual Report of the Church of England Zenana Missionary*

Society for 1891-2 (London, CMS, 1893), p. 21.

101. For a more sympathetic response to a non-Western culture and of the place of women within it, see Sister Katherine, *Towards the Land of the Rising Sun, Or, Four Years in Burma* (London, SPCK, 1900), though she is equally firm in the conviction that the missionaries are the pioneers of civilization.

102. Quoted in Dawson, *Heroines of Missionary Adventure*, p. 48.

103. *Women's Studies International Forum*, vol. 13, no. 4 (1990), p. 293.

104. Patricia Grimshaw comes to a similar conclusion with regard to American women missionaries, arguing that they could not be agents of genuine emancipation for women, since such an outcome 'awaited not only an assault on powerful domestic ideologies, but also an assault on a narrow vision of issues of race and class which was endemic to nineteenth-century middle-class women's struggle for sexual equality'. See her article '"Christian Woman, Pious Wife, Faithful Mother, Devoted Missionary": Conflicts of American Missionary Women in Nineteenth-Century Hawaii', *Feminist Studies*, vol. 9 (1983), pp. 489–521.

105. It is also worth pointing out that this kind of appreciation of the limitations of race and culture that created barriers between women in the past has increasingly preoccupied feminist historians and theologians. As the Asian theologian Kwok Pui-Lan points out, 'women are becoming more keenly aware that they too have the double identities of both the oppressors and the oppressed', in U. King (ed.), *Feminist Theology from the Third World: A Reader* (London, SPCK, 1994). In the case of feminist historiography, this is just one example of the way in which the history of woman and gender needs to be truly critical of the past if it is also to be liberating for the future.

CHAPTER NINE

Women and the Church in an Age of Change

Since 1900, profound and far-reaching social and intellectual changes have undermined the Victorian Christian synthesis of a hierarchical ordering of gender relationships, and the subordination of women in Church and society. Both the movement for democracy in political life, and the growth of professional paid work for women, have had repercussions on the Church of England's own involvement of women in its life. At the same time, contraception, rising rates of divorce, changing patterns of middle-class employment and attitudes to sexuality have forced the Church of England to reformulate much of its traditional teaching, and have also undermined the model of Victorian middle-class family life on which it was largely based. The growth of an articulate women's movement in the late nineteenth century, and even more the women's liberation movement of the 1970s, have also influenced theological attitudes to gender relationships, as has the growth of feminist theology; this has developed new critical methodologies and strategies that have called into question the androcentric and patriarchal nature of much of the Church's doctrine and practice.

The response within Anglicanism to such a bewildering array of challenges has been far from uniform: while to some they have betokened the collapse of Christian values in family life and society at large, to others they have been welcomed as signs of the times to which the Church, under the guidance of the Holy Spirit, is being called to make a positive response.

Democracy in Church and state

The campaign for women's suffrage effectively began in the 1860s with the organization of a number of regional committees, which in 1868 became the National Society for Women's Suffrage. As Brian Harrison has indicated in his study of organized anti-suffrage groups, central to their thinking was the belief in the ideology of separate spheres of activity for men and women; and since this tenet was common to nearly all sections of the Victorian and Edwardian Church, it is not surprising to find the majority of Anglicans were opposed to granting the vote to women.[1] Typical of this attitude was a letter written to *The Times* in 1910 by the eminent philanthropist Octavia Hill, which regretted the campaign for women's suffrage on the grounds that 'men and women help one another because they are different, have different gifts and different spheres, one is the complement of the other'.[2]

The previous year, however, the active minority of those who did not take this view of the question founded the Church League for Women's Suffrage, with the Rev. Claude Hinscliff as its secretary, Maude Royden as its first chairman, and the Bishop of Lincoln, Edward Hicks, as president.[3] The increasingly militant activities of part of the suffragette movement naturally found little sympathy within the Church, and in 1912 Gertrude Bell was able to prevent the subject being discussed at the Church Congress at Middlesbrough by warning the Archbishop of York in advance that the topic might be raised.

The following year, however, the Church Congress at Southampton discussed 'The Kingdom of God and the Sexes', and with such a remit the subject was difficult to avoid. Thus the Dean of Manchester, discussing 'the ideals of manhood', saw Jesus as the exemplar of Christian chivalry in his treatment of women as the weaker sex, and thought that if his teaching were followed more widely there would be no need even to raise questions about the suffrage for women; he also warned that the advantageous protection afforded to women by men was being endangered by the activities of militant suffragettes.[4] In reply, Miss Helen Sprott, a member of Mrs Pankhurst's Women's Political and Social Union, claimed that women were being unfairly criticized for taking up the suffrage cause, and she went on to emphasize that God had created men and women equal. Speaking more generally of the women's movement, Miss Ruth Rouse, who was Travelling Secretary of the Student Christian Movement, argued that its aims were 'approximate to the ideals of the Kingdom of God'.[5] Such statements received short shrift from the Dean of Durham, Herbert Hensley Henson, who acidly recorded in his diary that 'a succession of young women bleated the *suffragist-nonsense* in variant degrees of absurdity'.[6]

At the same time as the Church of England was deeply divided over the question of democracy within the state, it also faced similar issues much nearer home. In May 1897, the Upper House of Convocation voted in favour of the formation of parochial church councils, but stipulated that those elected should be communicant male members of the Church of England. This led 1,100 churchwomen to sign a petition protesting at their exclusion. This proved to be unavailing, as the Lower House of Convocation voted against women's admission by thirty-nine votes to eighteen, having heard Archdeacon Sandford of Exeter warn that since the new councils would be involved in the governing work of the Church, there was 'a real danger lest the distinction between sex and sex should be forgotten'.[7] Speaking at the 1899 Church Congress, Mrs Creighton warned that the move to exclude women from the new church councils would alienate thinking women from parochial work, and she reminded her audience that women had already had to fight 'for better education, freer opportunities for the development of their capacities, without getting much help from leading Churchmen, often the contrary'.[8]

In 1903, women received a further snub from the Church when Convocation voted to exclude them from participating in elections for the newly proposed national Representative Church Council – a decision that outraged such normally conservative churchwomen as Mrs Arthur Philip, honorary secretary of the Mothers' Union in Worcester, who described the decision as an insult to women for whom the Church was 'their whole life'.[9] Partly in response to such pressures, and also as a result of lobbying by Bishop Charles Gore, the Representative Church Council issued a report in July 1914 recommending that women be allowed to vote for parochial church councils on the same basis as men, and be allowed to serve on them. They still remained excluded from Ruridecanal and Diocesan Conferences, and from the Representative Council itself.

Not surprisingly, the Church League for Women's Suffrage took up the issue as being directly related to its main campaign for national democracy, and, in a petition presented to the Representative Church Council, protested that women's exclusion from the councils of the

Church was 'an infraction of that spiritual equality of the sexes which is a fundamental principle of the Christian faith'.[10] Justice was finally done on 26 February 1919, when the Bishop of Lichfield's motion was passed granting women full equality. As Brian Heeney points out, this was not so much a triumph for Christian feminism within the Church, as a recognition that the 1918 Parliamentary Reform Act, which granted some women the vote and allowed them to become Members of Parliament, left the Church in an anomalous position.

When the new National Assembly of the Church of England met for the first time in 1920, it had 646 members – of whom 357 were lay, and of these, 40 were women.[11] This was a tiny proportion, though as Charles Gore's biographer noted, between 1920 and 1935 nearly ten times as many women gained seats on the Church Assembly as won seats in Parliament.[12] By the mid-1970s, the same kind of comparison was still being made: Kenneth Medhurst and George Moyser produced figures to show that in 1975, 32 per cent of the candidates seeking places in the General Synod were women, whereas in the general election of October 1974, only 7.2 per cent of candidates were female – figures that they regarded as satisfactory, though not a cause for complacency given the importance of women in the Church's institutional base.[13] Moreover, the minority status of women overall in Synod at this time is even more obvious, given that both the Houses of Bishops and of Clergy were of course all male.

Even so, the introduction of partly democratic forms of decision-making within the life of the Church has been of considerable long-term significance for women, particularly over the issue of ordination. In 1981, a survey found that almost 50 per cent of the House of Laity favoured immediate change, a higher figure than among the clergy; and that although 27 per cent of the Synod's female membership opposed such a change, a large majority were in favour. Women members of Synod were in fact much more committed to this cause than their male colleagues.[14] Without the clearly expressed support for change from the House of Laity, who alone of the three Houses voted in 1975 for women's immediate ordination, implementing the measure might have been even harder than it turned out to be. The Church's democratic institutions, however imperfect in their form, were therefore of considerable importance in allowing the Church's rank and file membership to express their appreciation of women's ministry as they had experienced it, and their rejection of continued sexism within its structures.

Changing attitudes to sexuality and morality

In the course of the twentieth century, the Church of England modified its teaching in two areas that bore directly upon women's lives – namely, contraception and divorce. The 1930 Lambeth Conference ended the Church's traditional blanket condemnation of artificial methods of birth control, declaring that while complete abstinence from intercourse was still the preferred method of family limitation, 'where there is a morally sound reason for avoiding complete abstinence, the Conference agrees that other methods may be used'. The bishops were also very concerned to place restrictions on the availability and advertising of contraceptives in an attempt to restrict their use to married couples.[15]

This relatively cautious change of stance, which was the result of a sharply polarized debate and was passed by a vote of 193 to 67, outraged conservative opinion within the Church. For example, when an editorial in the *Guardian* in November 1935 rejected basing birth control on sexual abstinence, a lively correspondence ensued, some of which verged upon the lunatic – a not infrequent outcome when Christians discuss sex.[16] One anonymous correspondent asked, 'If, after two thousand years of so-called Christianity, the Church still teaches that sensual gratification is a gift from God instead of, as Nicholas Berdyaev teaches, the result of sin and separation from God, how can we hope or expect the young people of today to believe that there is any need for chastity?' In the case of this worried writer, self-control appeared to involve little struggle, since he regarded sexual gratification as one of those childish things mentioned by St Paul that should 'with the wife's consent "be put away" by mature Christians'.[17] Another writer in the same edition took a very different line, accusing the Church of being too negative in its attitudes, and pointing out that young couples often used contraception because of economic pressures on them to restrict the size of their families. There were also, he believed, sound eugenic reasons for birth control, which was needed 'in cases of physical and mental deficiency to prevent degeneracy'.

Concerns about racial health also taxed an Essex rector, the Rev. Montgomery Hitchcock, who argued that all birth control publications should be banned, and that the subject should never have been taken up by the Church, but was best left to doctors. Indeed, in his view, willingness to broach such a topic in public was in itself evidence of both moral and physical decay, since he had observed 'that people who discuss these subjects are wretched physical specimens – flabby, narrow chested, unwholesome to look at'. In some cases, divine retribution took a swifter course – as when Hitchcock correctly predicted that an elderly clergyman whom he heard reading a paper on this 'prurient topic' would be dead within the year.[18]

Less extreme but still conservative opinion within the Church gradually came to terms with the fact that increasing numbers of people were using contraception within marriage. The Mothers' Union Central Council, for example, unanimously passed a motion in 1913, stating that 'certain prevalent customs of limiting the family are contrary to Divine law and hostile to the best interests of the nation'.[19] In 1926, a special meeting of the Central Council reaffirmed this stance, and a motion that a wife's actions in this matter should be guided by her husband, even if his wishes were not those of the Mothers' Union, found no seconder.[20] In 1946, however, the Fundamental Principles on Marriage and the Family that had been drawn up at the time of the 1926 constitution were amended, such that the Union continued to support the avoidance of artificial means of contraception as an ideal, but stated that individual views on birth control were not, and had never been, a test of membership.[21]

The official change of attitude within Anglicanism was completed by the 1958 Lambeth Conference, which rejected the dualism between flesh and spirit that had often in the past led to the devaluation of human sexuality, and now regarded family planning as 'a right and important factor in Christian family life'.[22] Past opposition to birth control had often been based on beliefs in the need to maintain a large population for reasons of national and military security, considerations rendered obsolete by the development of nuclear weapons; and in a world faced with increasing problems of overpopulation, as well as the relative decline in middle-class incomes, family planning had come to seem the moral and prudent course of action. What was not part of Anglican thinking was any perception of the potentially liberating consequences of contraception on women's lives, still less any sympathy with the later feminist agenda in which it was one part of a woman's right to control her own sexuality and life choices.

Attitudes to divorce followed an even more protracted and halting course. One problem that had taxed the Church in the nineteenth century remained unresolved. Although the biblical witness was in most passages opposed to divorce, there was also the provision in Matthew for divorce where a wife had committed adultery.

Ironically, the methods of modern biblical criticism that offered the possibility of interpreting this passage as a later interpolation were anathema to conservative Christians who knew little of its findings, but saw liberal scholarship as an attack on traditional Christian values. Writing in the Mothers' Union journal *Mothers in Council* in 1918, the Rev. J. P. Whitney, who was Professor of Ecclesiastical History at King's College, London, refused to follow what he called the line of 'German reformers' in accepting that Jesus sanctioned divorce; and another clergyman described the government's divorce proposals as reducing marriage to a mere gratification, arguing that 'it is the permanence of marriage which now sets people patiently to complete the task of adjusting their characters to one another'.[23]

The concern expressed in 1918 was in response to a Bill that would have added five new grounds to the existing one of adultery – namely, desertion, cruelty, insanity, habitual drunkenness, and imprisonment under a commuted death sentence. Such proposals had their origins in the 1909 Royal Commission on Divorce and Matrimonial Causes, and it was clear from evidence given to it by liberal churchmen such as Dr Inge and Dr Herbert Hensley Henson that far from wrestling with the difficulty of Christ's contradictory words, they regarded his teaching as an ideal or a principle – not a binding law on which to base a doctrine of the indissolubility of marriage.[24]

Yet it was the principle of indissolubility that the Church chose to assert. The 1920 Lambeth Conference affirmed as 'our Lord's principle and standard of marriage a lifelong and indissoluble union', and the 1930 Lambeth Conference recommended that the Church should refuse to celebrate the marriage of a divorced person who had a living partner, while the admissibility of the innocent party to a divorce was left to the discretion of the bishop.[25] The 1937 Matrimonial Causes Act, which extended the grounds for divorce to include desertion, cruelty, and incurable insanity, legally affirmed the clergyman's right to refuse to marry a divorced person in church or to permit his church to be used for such a marriage.[26]

In 1951, Mrs Eirene White introduced a Bill into the Commons that made provision for divorce where a couple had lived apart for seven years and there was no prospect of a reconciliation – a proposal that was also in Leo Abse's Bill of 1963. Along with other church leaders, the Anglican archbishops opposed these measures on the grounds that they in effect introduced divorce by consent; however, speaking in the debate on Abse's Bill in the Lords, Michael Ramsey stated that he was not opposed to any improvement in the divorce laws, 'which conserved the point that offences and not only wishes are the basis of breakdown', and he set up a mainly Anglican group to report on the subject.

This group published its report, *Putting Asunder: A Divorce Law for Contemporary Society*, in July 1966. It stressed that in an increasingly secular society the law and practice of the Church might not be the same as that of the state, but Christians nevertheless had a duty to try to make the divorce law 'as equitable and little harmful to society as it can be'.[27] The report recommended that the old system based upon the concept of matrimonial offence should be replaced by that of irretrievable breakdown as the sole grounds for divorce. The chief objections to basing divorce upon the idea of matrimonial offence were that it took a superficial view of the relationship between the partners, since adultery might be as much a symptom as a cause of difficulty, and that in many cases it forced couples seeking a divorce 'to pretend that the wrongdoing of one is such that the other is forced to apply for relief'. To the charge that it was opening the way to divorce by consent, the report argued that it was the court and not the couple that would decide the issue of irretrievable breakdown, and it recommended a procedure of judicial inquest into the past and present state of the marriage. In February 1967, the Church Assembly voted to accept the report, but the Divorce Reform Act of 1969, although it was based on a number of the report's principles, was criticized by Michael Ramsey – particularly for permitting a divorce where one party had deserted the other for two years, or where the couple had lived apart for five years, in which case a divorce could be granted against the wishes of one of the parties. Nor did the law contain the elaborate procedures for an inquest that the Church had recommended.

In accepting the findings of the 1966 report, the Church Assembly also passed an amendment asking the Convocations to reconsider the Church's ban on the remarriage of divorced persons in church.[28] The rising divorce rate, and the change in the law that allowed a divorce even against the wishes of one party, made the question yet more pressing. In April 1971, a Commission chaired by Professor Howard Root of Southampton University recommended that the remarriage of divorcees in church should be permitted in certain circumstances. The report *Marriage, Divorce and the Church* was received, but not commended, by Synod in February 1972 by only 184 votes to 180; and the debate on its proposals revealed the difficulty of reconciling the demands of upholding a Christian ideal of marriage with the pastoral needs of individuals. A number of speakers drew attention to the uncertainties that the clergy would face in deciding between cases, while to others the whole report was leading the way to 'marriage on demand'. According to Mrs Lucas, what the Commission was saying to the Church was, 'If you want to satisfy what society wants in 1972, we will cook the books for you.'[29]

Yet appeals to biblical authority (which was in any case unclear) without reference to changing social circumstances were both unrealistic and self-defeating. Longer life expectancy, new patterns of employment, and the increasing pressure on the family to meet all the emotional and social needs of its members – a privatization of life that, ironically, the churches had done much to foster – all contributed to a rising level of marital breakdown and cohabitation that could not simply be dismissed as evidence of moral decline. The 1978 report *Marriage and the Church's Task* discussed all of these factors, as well as what it called 'a new analysis of gender-roles for both sexes which is at once challenging and disturbing'.[30] It recommended, though not unanimously, that the remarriage of divorced persons in church, including members of the clergy, should be allowed in suitable cases with the bishop's permission.

As in the case of contraception, the evolution of policy within the normally conservative Mothers' Union is again indicative of the pressure for change that the Church was faced with. According to its constitution, the first objective of the Union was to uphold the sanctity of marriage, an aim that was not held to be compatible with the liberalization of the divorce laws, and one that in effect banned divorcees from membership. At the time of the debate over the 1937 Matrimonial Causes Act, the Executive Committee did receive a memorandum from four officials in a northern diocese that argued that loyalty to the first object of the Union 'was not incompatible with believing that divorce is permissible in certain exceptional cases', but this view was rejected.[31] Writing in *The Mothers' Union Workers Paper*, the President, Nina Woods, stated that 'a belief in the permanency of the marriage relation must be in opposition to easier divorce', and this was so notwithstanding what she called a 'few sad cases'.[32]

Yet internally, the Mothers' Union was far more divided on the issue than its public statements suggest. At another Central Council meeting, the President reiterated the traditional line, claiming that 'it

214

was not the Mothers' Union but the world which had changed, and it would not help the world if the Mothers' Union weakened in its witness', while other members replied that divorce might often be the lesser of two evils, and wondered what they were to say to those who upheld the principle of permanence in marriage but could not accept its utter indissolubility.[33]

A fundamental change of heart came about as a result of the report *New Dimensions*, published in 1972, which was an attempt to completely re-think the purposes and update the organizational structures of the now world-wide body. It proposed five new objects, including the upholding of the lifelong nature of the marriage vows and the provision of help for those 'whose marriages have met with adversity', and recommended that membership should be open to all communicant Anglicans who subscribed to its statement of aims. At a meeting of the Central Council, this proposal was accepted by a large majority, and a number of other proposals – which would have excluded divorcees or granted them a separate form of associate membership – were heavily defeated.[34]

This was not to imply that the Union no longer regarded lifelong marriage and the family as aspects of Christian teaching fundamental to the well-being of society, but it was a recognition of the complexities involved in working towards these objectives in the late twentieth century. For example, in 1980, the Central Council received a report from Barbara Finney on the World Conference on the Family that met in Brisbane in 1979, and that had discussed the impact of longer life expectancy, greater social mobility, the women's movement, and the ethos of competitive materialism upon family life. However, she felt that the conference had not paid enough attention to the problems of single parents, and she suggested that family life could in some circumstances be 'destructive, crippling, lethal'. All this was very much to continue wrestling with the concerns of Mary Sumner a hundred years before, but the context and tone had changed almost beyond recognition.[35]

Women in the life of the Church

As we have seen, the nineteenth century witnessed a great increase in the activities undertaken by churchwomen, mostly in the field of voluntary charitable work. During the same period, many professions sought to impose higher standards of training and conduct on their members, a process from which the clergy were not exempt. Whereas the early Victorian parson had had little (if any) formal training in theology and pastoral work, and was likely to undertake a whole range of activities deemed appropriate to his status as a gentleman (such as being a justice of the peace), by mid-century, standards of training and service were beginning to rise, and the clergyman's specialized professional role as a man set apart from the world was much more sharply defined.[36] The process of professionalization both within and outside the Church left its women workers in an anomalous position. Did they, like others, require special training? What place was there for full-time paid female workers within church life?

Discussions of these questions in the late nineteenth century were still influenced by middle-class values that saw paid work for women as incompatible with gentility. Put into religious terms, this implied that work that was undertaken without reward was of greater worth than that done for remuneration. Thus at the 1899 Church Congress that met in London, and which devoted one session to the training and payment of women church workers, the Honourable Mrs Lyttleton referred to the objections of those who held that paid work tended to be done mechanically, that it was derogatory to receive payment for work done in God's service, and that there was a danger of making philanthropy 'a profession like any other'. It was, however, to precisely this professional ideal that Mrs Lyttleton referred, arguing that no one expected a doctor or a teacher to work less zealously because he or she was paid, and pointing out that 'Training and knowledge are recognised as essential in all things where people look for success, except in philanthropy, and here, and here alone, the mere desire to do good is often accepted unhesitatingly as sufficient.'[37]

As a result of concerns such as those expressed by Mrs Lyttleton, a number of different institutions and schemes developed in the pre-war period to prepare lay women for church work. The 1908 Pan-Anglican Congress led to the creation of a Central Council for Women's Church Work, while the Settlement movement, which tried to work in deprived areas of industrial cities, also offered women some training. Thus the Women's University Settlement, which was founded in 1887 by the women's colleges at Oxford and Cambridge and which worked in Southwark, set on foot a one-year training scheme in 1893, which included courses on subjects such as the Poor Law, the Public Health Acts, and the causes and relief of poverty.[38]

The trouble with such schemes was that they were all small, uncoordinated, and lacked official recognition by the Church.

Steps to remedy these defects were taken by the Inter-Diocesan Committee for Women's Work, which was created in 1919. The Committee set out to provide training in teaching, rescue work, and social work, and by the time of its dissolution in 1930, it had awarded some seven hundred certificates to women church workers who had passed examinations in theology, teaching, and social studies.[39] At this time, the terms of employment of full-time women workers remained very much second-class. According to the Rev. L. S. Hunter, the Archdeacon of Northumberland, 'The Church is not paying women-workers an adequate wage and is living too complacently on their sense of vocation', and he urged women with a high sense of duty not to come forward to be exploited in this way.[40] This gloomy view was borne out by a statement in Convocation in 1929, which said that women were working for starvation wages – receiving in most dioceses a salary of £100 to £120 at a time when £150 was needed to live on, and when some curates received more than £200. One response was to set up a contributory pension scheme, which was replaced with a non-contributory one in 1956. Yet conditions of service for women remained in some respects less favourable than for their male counterparts. Unlike curates, for example, they generally did not receive rent-free accommodation.[41]

In 1930, the Inter-Diocesan Committee became a part of the newly created Central Council for Women's Church Work, which in turn was merged in 1960 with the Council of Deaconesses to form the Council for Women's Ministry in the Church.[42] By that date, the CWMC provided a three-year training course for the Inter-Diocesan Certificate. In 1966, there were said to be 3,500 full-time female church workers, of whom 78 were deaconesses, 307 lay workers, 222 Church Army sisters, 434 church social workers, and 2,658 professed religious.[43] Yet despite these figures, there is evidence that women were seriously disadvantaged in the provision of training. In 1935, the Church Assembly called for the creation of training bursaries for women, but nothing was done until 1945. In 1937, for example, the Central Advisory Council of Training for the Ministry received a grant of £4,215 for training male ordinands, while the Central Council for Women's Church Work received only £250, and nothing for women's training. In 1944, a further report called for the creation of a large new training establishment for women; however, funds could not be found, and it was only with the opening of Cranmer

Hall, Durham, to both men and women for training in 1966 that conditions began to improve substantially.[44]

In 1968, the report on women's ministry also pointed out that many of the Church's social workers were involved in rescue work and child care, functions that were increasingly being taken over by the welfare state. It should also not be forgotten that the vast majority of women who continued the Victorian tradition of philanthropy, pioneered by women such as Octavia Hill, did so in the twentieth century by exercising their Christian vocation within the caring professions rather than directly through church agencies. Some other opportunities for direct service in the Church have declined for other reasons. In a post-colonial era, less confident in the soteriological exclusiveness of Christianity, the activities of the traditional Anglican missionary societies have become much smaller in scale. In 1991, the CMS was sending 295 missionaries overseas compared with 549 in 1972, and the corresponding figures for the USPG were 184 and 657.[45]

The relative decline in some forms of Christian work for women within the Church has led to the ministry exercised by the deaconess assuming increasing prominence, although for much of the twentieth century both her role and status have been shrouded in confusion. The Archbishop's Committee, in its 1919 report, rehearsed the history of the deaconess movement, and pointed out that beyond the vague episcopal definition of 1871 of a deaconess as 'a woman set apart by a bishop under that title for service within the Church', there was within the Church of England no formal definition of her powers, nor any authorized form of ordination.[46] This was an undesirable state of affairs, the Committee noted, since 'in recent years a feeling of unrest and dissatisfaction has arisen amongst the women of the Church', who were not only asking for professional terms and conditions of work comparable to those increasingly pertaining in secular employment, but also a share in responsibility and status.[47]

The 1920 Lambeth Conference attempted to meet these aspirations by passing a resolution that defined the status of the Order of Deaconess within the Church, and went on to recommend a form of ordination service and to suggest that deaconesses should be allowed to preach and lead in morning and evening prayer under episcopal licence.[48] However, although the Conference recognized the Order of Deaconess as an order of ministry with the seal of apostolic approval upon it, of greater significance were the restrictions placed upon her functions. It was emphasized that the office was in no way comparable to that of the all-male diaconate, to which was reserved the right to assist with the chalice at Holy Communion and to preach the gospel: 'The office of a Deaconess is primarily a ministry of succour, bodily and spiritual, especially to women, and should follow the lines of the primitive rather than of the modern Diaconate of men.'[49] This was to reiterate the Victorian ideal of the Anglican deaconess as a paid parish worker who assisted the clergy, to whom all liturgical functions and authority were strictly reserved. The subsequent history of the order was to see a gradual extension of her role, which aroused both hopes and fears that this might prove to be a stepping stone to women's ordination to the priesthood.

The restrictions imposed in 1920 were made even clearer in 1922 when the Lower House of Canterbury Convocation passed two amendments prohibiting deaconesses from reading morning and evening prayer and from leading in prayer and preaching at church services.[50] However, in 1924, the Upper Houses of the Convocations of York and Canterbury agreed on a form service for the making of deaconesses, which included the laying on of hands, and the presentation of a copy of the New Testament.[51] The Lambeth Conference of 1930, although it took a restrictive view of the overall status of the deaconess – describing it as an order *sui generis*, which was thereby distinct from the historic threefold male order of deacons, priests, and bishops – recommended the extension of her functions to include baptizing in church and officiating at the churching of women.[52]

In 1950, the Convocation of York, followed by Canterbury in 1964, allowed licensed lay workers as well as deaconesses to take part in services other than Holy Communion, and in 1968, in the report *Women in Ministry*, their functions were described as the preparation of children and adults for baptism and confirmation, the conducting of courses and missions, and the taking of funerals and baptisms. One London deaconess described her work:

My duties are wide and varied. As there is no curate on the staff the vicar expects me to do the work he would normally allocate to the curate, with the exception of the purely priestly functions such as the administration of the sacraments. In addition to the normal parish duties which fall within this scope, I help with services, leading the Offices during the week, preaching from time to time (about once a month), and in the absence of the vicar, taking Matins and Evensong on Sunday. I am also on the staff of a General Hospital assisting the chaplain.[53]

While this and other examples suggested that deaconesses obtained considerable satisfaction from their work, there was another side to the picture. As the report noted, there were still significant differences in what deaconesses were allowed to do depending on the attitudes of incumbents, and they had little job security (since only three months' notice was required to remove them) and an inferior pension scheme to that in existence for the clergy. It concluded by recommending that women be admitted to the diaconate.[54] Information obtained by ACCM, which interviewed 150 deaconesses, Church Army sisters, and lay workers when compiling its 1972 report on the ordination of women to the priesthood, suggested that it was not so much the less favourable terms and conditions of employment that created the most frustration as the uncertainties surrounding their status, and the limitations imposed upon their ministry by being unable to give absolution and celebrate the Eucharist. The report summed up the feelings of a number of women working in parishes by saying that 'because they are unable to offer a full ministry *people suffer*'.[55]

It was not until February 1987 that the recommendation that women be admitted to the diaconate was finally implemented, but even then difficulties and anomalies persisted. In its 1990 report *Deacons Now*, ACCM noted that at the end of the previous year there were 999 women licensed as deacons within the Church of England, yet only 63 of these could be identified as holding an appointment that included a pastoral charge of a parish; and that, on the whole, these were 'in those places . . . where it is hardest for the Church of England to sustain an infrastructure of ordained ministry'.[56] In an appendix on women's experience of the diaconate, it was revealed that some 55 per cent of women serving as deacons who were questioned had at some time raised a complaint about aspects of their work, and only one-third felt that they had seen a satisfactory resolution of the problem. The difficulties described ranged from dissatisfaction at the limited range of duties they were allowed to undertake, to poor relationships with male clergy – which could include their being shunned or ignored.[57]

Overall, the working party concluded that for the first time the Church had seriously addressed the career development of women in the ministry, but that while some positions of responsibility (such as rural dean and residentiary canon) were now open to them, there were too few of these to offer an adequate career structure. The admission that the Church was for the first time addressing the problem, 130 years after the revival of the office of deaconess, spoke volumes for its exploitation of their abilities – a misuse often thinly disguised in the past by sanctimonious appeals to self-sacrifice.

Since the upper middle-class Victorian clerical family epitomized the amalgam of social and religious values from which the Church of England had derived most of its thinking about gender relations, some of the most significant changes in the work of women in the Church in the twentieth century have occurred in the roles and self-perceptions of women married to clergymen. In the lives of families such as the Havergals, in which wives and daughters sacrificed self and ambition to be the devoted but subordinate parochial assistants of the clerical paterfamilias, was to be found the working out of Victorian expectations about gender; and their gradual relegation in the twentieth century to the pages of Charlotte Yonge's novels is indicative of far-reaching changes in middle-class lifestyles and values from which the parsonage has not been exempt.

In her autobiography, *The Shabby Paradise*, Eileen Baillie, the daughter of an Anglo-Catholic priest who worked in an East End parish in London in the years before the First World War, paints a vivid picture of her mother fulfilling the traditional role of the clergyman's wife. Herself the daughter of a clergyman, and a woman of considerable intellectual ability whose parents refused to countenance her attending one of the new female Oxbridge colleges (which they suspected of being breeding grounds for feminism and even the suffragette movement), she settled down to a life whose demands she had known since childhood, and which were wryly described by her daughter:

> She should be indefinite in personality, not too opinionated, aggressive or distinctive. Her protective colouring should be sub-fusc, therefore, she should be neatly, but not too smartly dressed; she should wear suitable clothes suggesting poverty and unworldliness, but not so shabby as to prove an embarrassment to those she is with. . . . Naturally, the wife should be willing to perform the less agreeable tasks about the church and parish that time and tradition have long ago allocated as her portion: mending the hassocks or the choir-boys' cassocks; polishing those awkward bits of brass; running the Mothers' Union Meeting and taking on the unattractive kind of stall at the annual Sale of Works.

In sum, what was required of the clergyman's wife was that she 'should be entirely functional, like a good, strong chair to be sat

221

upon'.[58]

Eileen Baillie was writing in 1958 of what she regarded as a long vanished world. Whereas her mother had had the services of a cook and a nanny, modern women, she pointed out, now had to do their own housework and were in revolt against being their husband's unpaid curates. While in some respects Baillie clearly thought that change had been for the better, in others she feared that the pendulum had swung too far and that clerical wives 'by dissociating themselves completely from their husbands' professional activities, as though they were the wives of stockbrokers or actuaries, bring just condemnation on their heads'. Yet both economic and social change were working against the traditional clerical pattern of family relationships. The reference to servants in Baillie's account was indicative of the ongoing decline in the living standards of the Anglican clergy. While not all Victorian clergymen had in practice lived the lives of gentlemen – Trollope's world had its Quiverfuls as well as its Grantlys – twentieth-century stipends no longer made a middle-class standard of living even possible without a working wife who was increasingly the principal breadwinner.

However, the decline in the patriarchal clerical family as the only pattern of family relationships was not simply a matter of crude economics: it also reflected an unwillingness on the part of many women to forgo an independent career and identity of their own. In an article published in *The Times* in August 1982, Rosalind Runcie, the then Archbishop of Canterbury's wife, accepted that many women still found fulfilment in the traditional role of homemaker and clerical wife, but that there were also many others with responsible jobs who earned more than their husbands, and many 'who have spent years in specialized training, who want to use whatever talent they have rather than give it all up to be an unpaid second curate'.[59] If gender roles and expectations were changing even within the traditional clerical family, they were doing so even faster in other sections of the middle class, a fact that robbed arguments against women's ordination of much of their resonance and social context.

As in the past, the life of the Church has continued to be enriched by the talents of exceptional women, of whom the most notable have been Evelyn Underhill and Dorothy Sayers. The former was born in 1875 and studied at King's College, London, where she became a Fellow in 1927. In her early life she was at one stage attracted by Roman Catholicism but deferred to her husband and did not become a convert. In 1911, she published a study of mysticism, the first of many works that established her reputation as a leading authority in this field – an achievement that was recognized by the award of a D.D. from Aberdeen University. After serving in naval intelligence during the First World War, she became the first woman to be invited to lecture on religion as an outside lecturer at Oxford University; and later in life she was much in demand as a retreat director.[60]

Dorothy Sayers came from a clerical family, and achieved prominence in the Church in 1937 when her play *The Zeal of Thy House* was performed in Canterbury Cathedral. In this work, and even more in her later cycle of plays entitled *The Man Born to be King*, she attempted to give expression to her passionate belief in the dramatic nature of Christian dogma, particularly the doctrine of the incarnation. Her success in portraying Christ's life by the use of colloquial language provoked hostility in some quarters, and her dramatic method was described by the Secretary of the Lord's Day Observance Society with characteristic overstatement as 'irreverence bordering on blasphemy'. During the war she was increasingly asked to speak on theological questions, and was in January 1941 the only woman to speak at William Temple's conference on the Church and post-war reconstruction. Here she called upon the Church to adopt 'a realistic and sacramental theology' that would encompass all spheres of human endeavour, and that would 'include a proper reverence for the earth and for all material things'. Such a spiritual vision, at once both down to earth and all-embracing, sprang from her own personality as much as from the incarnational theological tradition of Anglo-Catholicism; it has not lost its cutting edge today, as when she remarked that 'The Church is uncommonly vocal about the subject of bedrooms and so singularly silent on the subject of board-rooms' – words that may well have sprung from her own experience of having an illegitimate child. Although much in demand in church circles, she decided in 1943 to stop her public involvement in theology, and she also refused the offer of a Doctorate of Divinity from the Archbishop of Canterbury.[61]

Evelyn Underhill died in 1941 and Dorothy Sayers in 1957, and it is interesting that while very different in temperament and in their spiritual lives, both have since been frequently cited as examples of fulfilled and creative women who opposed the ordination of women to the priesthood. This was undoubtedly so, but in both cases their attitudes and positions as talented women within the Church were more complex than might at first sight appear. In 1948, C. S. Lewis had been alarmed by the threat to tradition posed by the desire of the Anglican Church in China to ordain women to the priesthood, and urged Dorothy Sayers to come out publicly against the suggestion. In reply she agreed with him that 'nothing could be more silly and inexpedient than to erect a new and totally unnecessary barrier between us and the rest of Catholic Christendom', but in refusing to do as he wished, she explained that he would find her 'a rather uneasy ally' since she could 'never find any logical or strictly theological reason against it'.[62] Evelyn Underhill told the Central Council for Women's Work in 1932 that she opposed women's ordination for the same reason as Dorothy Sayers – that it would jeopardize links with Rome – but in her recent study of Underhill, Dana Greene considers the significance of gender in her life and work from a rather different perspective; she argues that being a woman was an asset precisely because it marginalized her, and thus left her free to pursue her interests in unorthodox directions. However, the benefits conferred by such marginalization were bought at a high price, since it was also responsible for her constant 'devaluation of self and the failure to love oneself'.[63]

Feminist theology and the women's movement

The kind of critique of traditional Christian spirituality, and of the gender roles that the Church helped to impose upon men and women found at the end of Dana Greene's study of Evelyn Underhill, was very much a product of the new mood of feminist consciousness that emerged first in America and then in England in the late 1960s and the early 1970s. As we have seen, the women's movement that developed in the second half of the nineteenth century had a number of different strands, and consisted not only of liberal equal rights campaigners who stressed the fundamental similarities between men and women, but also a tradition, of which Christian feminism was an important part, that took the differences between men and women as the basis for asserting women's rights to education and participation in the public sphere in limited but important ways in the cause of defending family life.

These divisions were evident in the women's movement in the 1920s in the National Union of Societies for Equal Citizenship, which was the successor to the National Union of Women's Suffrage Societies, with feminists such as Ray Strachey urging that the Union work for equal opportunities for women, while so-called new feminists, led by Eleanor Rathbone, urged that the Union work for an equality that recognized sexual difference and women's distinctive needs. Whereas new feminists saw maternity as a woman's most important occupation, equal rights feminists held to a vision of a society in which differences based on gender would no longer have any significant place.[64] While the influence of traditional doctrines of motherhood meant that inter-war new feminists could fight for women's needs within the family by supporting family allowances and – somewhat more uneasily – birth control, they did not challenge the idea that women were bound to choose between motherhood and a career, nor the organization of work within the domestic sphere.

Given the conservative and reformist nature of Anglican Christian feminism, and the traditional attitude of the Church towards questions of gender differentiation, it was clear that the majority of people in the Church of England could live happily with most aspects of the new feminist agenda (birth control was a more contentious issue), and with the relatively quiescent nature of the women's movement between the 1920s and the late 1960s. However, the demands of the women's liberation movement that emerged in diverse small groupings in 1969, including full equality of opportunity in the workplace, equal pay, free contraception, abortion, and free child care, were based on the premise that the traditional divisions between the workplace and the domestic sphere, with a corresponding division of labour along gender lines, were oppressing women, not liberating them.[65] Not surprisingly, references to women's liberation within the Church, particularly in its debates on the ordination of women, were almost entirely hostile, and even supporters of women priests were careful to base their case on the idea of the priesthood as an extension of women's traditional qualities and roles rather than on a critique designed to subvert them. In religious terms, the Church's opposition to the women's liberation movement found expression in the idea that the assertion of women's rights was unchristian and unwomanly, when the language of the Gospels was that of self-denial, service, and duty. However, such an appeal contained a crucial ideological obfuscation over the issues of power and status, and the concomitant capacity to serve God within the Church, since these rights had long been exercised almost exclusively by men within Anglican ecclesiastical structures.

The issues of power and inequality between men and women in society focused attention on patriarchy as a social system that disadvantaged the latter, even though there was no real agreement between liberal, Marxist, and radical feminist groups on its origins, and therefore on the best way to eradicate it. Within the churches, conceptualizing and combating patriarchy gave rise to a new way of doing theology from a feminist perspective. Feminist theology drew attention to the way in which the Christian tradition had been largely formulated out of the needs and experiences of men, and showed that such androcentrism in both Christian thought and practice had denied or undervalued the spiritual insights and abilities of women. It also drew attention to the development of modes of masochistic spirituality, in which women were viewed as subordinate, secondary, passive, emotional, and self-denying, and which, far from being God-given and liberating, were the product of man-made and oppressive gender stereotyping. Like the women's liberation movement, feminist theology began as predominantly white, Western, and middle class in its orientation, but has increasingly become aware of the oppression and needs of women throughout the world and the way in which issues of class, race, and poverty are central to any theology that claims to be truly liberating.

How significant has the feminist theological programme been within the Church of England over the past twenty years or so? Here it is important to take note not only of inherited sexist attitudes, and the perception of many women in the Church that feminist ideas somehow undermine the worth of the traditional kinds of lives that they have led, but also of institutional constraints upon women in higher education. Until recently, no English university had a female professor of theology (there are currently four, none of them Anglican), and women remain under-represented among the staff of university departments and Anglican theological colleges. Despite the fact that ministerial training in the theological colleges is now open to both men and women, a 1983 report that questioned women staff spoke of 'the sense of aloneness and of a pioneering spirit which many of these women feel'.[66] The fact that the majority of students studying theology at degree level are now women is too recent a change to have had a significant impact on Anglican thinking, despite it being the case that most institutions now offer their students at least some exposure to feminist methodology and theology.

The number of works published by Anglicans that show the influence of feminist theology has been relatively small, though one of the first, Susan Dowell and Linda Hurcombe's *Dispossessed Daughters of Eve: Faith and Feminism*, which was published in 1981, was also one of the earliest expositions of feminist theological methodology to be published in England.[67] The volume *Feminine in the*

Church, published in 1984 and edited by Monica Furlong, who was then Moderator of the Movement for the Ordination of Women (MOW), was perhaps more cautious in its approach. It reflected the desire of MOW to be as broad as possible in its membership, and therefore less radical than the undenominational Christian Parity Group (which was also concerned with questions of gender), but it was written from a feminist perspective, in which the issue of women's ordination to the priesthood was seen as part of a broader 'evaluation of women within the Christian community, and maybe within society as a whole'.[68] A number of the contributors to the volume also started from feminist theological premises – for example, Janet Morley in her critique of exclusive language within the Church's liturgy, and the chapter by Anne Hoad, a deaconess in the Community of St Andrew, which discussed the case for a truly inclusive priesthood and the need to overcome a patriarchal religion that had reinforced women's powerlessness 'by ignoring their experience in the past and present, by speaking of God in the male image and by promoting systems of dominance that damage women'.[69]

Dispossessed Daughters of Eve and *Feminine in the Church* were written in the midst of the protracted debates within the Church over women's ordination, and both made a contribution to it – as did groups such as Women in Theology and the Feminist Theology Group. However, the final outcome was not, as embittered opponents were to claim, the triumph of feminist theology within Anglicanism, but of much deeper changes within British society that were rendering the Church's whole attitude to questions of gender and the priesthood increasingly implausible. In this sense, feminist theology was more of a symptom of change than a cause of change.

Notes

1. B. Harrison, *Separate Spheres: The Opposition to Women's Suffrage in Britain* (London, Croom Helm, 1978), p. 56.

2. Quoted in N. Boyd, *Josephine Butler, Octavia Hill, Florence Nightingale: Three Victorian Women Who Changed Their World* (London, Macmillan, 1982), p. 140.

3. S. Fletcher, *Maude Royden: A Life* (Oxford, Basil Blackwell, 1989), pp. 140-141.

4. *Report of the Church Congress held at Southampton in 1913* (London, George Allen, 1913), pp. 97-99.

5. *Report of the Church Congress held at Southampton in 1913*, pp. 104–115.

6. Harrison, *Separate Spheres*, p. 184.

7. Quoted in B. Heeney, 'The Beginnings of Church Feminism: Women and the Councils of the Church of England 1897–1919', *Journal of Ecclesiastical History*, vol. 33 (1982), pp. 89–109, on which this paragraph is based.

8. *Report of the Church Congress held at London in 1899* (London, Bemrose & Sons, 1899), p. 128.

9. Heeney, 'The Beginnings of Church Feminism', pp. 97–98.

10. Heeney, 'The Beginnings of Church Feminism', p. 102.

11. Heeney, 'The Beginnings of Church Feminism', pp. 104–105.

12. Heeney, 'The Beginnings of Church Feminism', p. 105.

13. K. Medhurst and G. Moyser, *Church and Politics in a Secular Age* (Oxford, Clarendon Press, 1988), pp. 145–146.

14. Medhurst and Moyser, *Church and Politics in a Secular Age*, p. 262.

15. Quoted in E. R. Norman, *Church and Society in England 1770–1970* (Oxford, Clarendon Press, 1976), p. 347.

16. *The Guardian*, 29 November 1935.

17. *The Guardian*, 6 December 1935.

18. *The Guardian*, 13 December 1935.

19. Mothers' Union Central Council minutes, 4, ff. 170–171.

20. Mothers' Union Central Council minutes, 7, ff. 206–207.

21. O. Parker, *For the Family's Sake: A History of the Mothers' Union 1876–1976* (Folkestone, Bailey & Swinfen, 1975), p. 91.

22. Norman, *Church and Society in England 1770–1970*, pp. 412–413. Here, as throughout his account of the development of Anglican social and political theology, Norman is both grudging and narrow in his focus, seeking to fit all aspects of change in Anglican theology into an overall interpretative schema, in which such changes are seen as capitulation to secular thought forms brought about by clerical members of the liberal intelligentsia who are largely out of touch with grassroots opinion in the Church.

23. *Mothers in Council*, vol. 28 (1918), pp. 3–4, 91.

24. A. R. Winnett, *The Church and Divorce: A Factual Survey* (London, Mowbray, 1968), p. 8.

25. Winnett, *The Church and Divorce*.

26. Winnett, *The Church and Divorce*, p. 10.

27. Winnett, *The Church and Divorce*, pp. 86–87.

28. *The Church Times*, 24 February 1967.

29. *The Church Times*, 18 February 1972.

30. *Marriage and the Church's Task: The Report of the General Synod's Marriage Commission* (London, CIO, 1978), p. 18.

31. Mothers' Union Central Council minutes, 11, ff. 20.

32. *The Mothers' Union Workers Paper* (1937), pp. 3-4.

33. Mothers' Union Central Council minutes, 12, ff. 417-421.

34. Mothers' Union Central Council minutes, 19, ff. 156.

35. Mothers' Union Central Council minutes, 20, ff. 289-294.

36. The professionalization of the clergy is discussed in B. Heeney, *A Different Kind of Gentleman: Parish Clergy as Professional Men in Early and Mid-Victorian England* (Hamden, Connecticut, Archon Books, 1976); and A. Russell, *The Clerical Profession* (London, SPCK, 1980).

37. *Report of the Church Congress held at London in 1899*, pp. 132-137.

38. *Report of the Church Congress held at London in 1899*, pp. 152-155.

39. B. Heeney, 'Women's Struggle for Professional Work and Status in the Church of England, 1900-1930', *Historical Journal*, vol. 26 (1983), pp. 329-347.

40. L. S. Hunter, *A Parson's Job* (London, SCM, 1931), p. 141.

41. B. Fullalove, 'The Ministry of Women in the Church of England (1919-70) Part II', *The Modern Churchman*, vol. 29, no. 3 (1987), pp. 41-50.

42. *Women in Ministry: A Study* (London, Central Board of Finance of the Church of England, 1968), p. 17.

43. *Women in Ministry*, p. 17.

44. B. Fullalove, 'The Ministry of Women in the Church of England (1919-70) Part I', *The Modern Churchman*, vol. 29, no. 2 (1987), pp. 41-50.

45. P. Brierley and D. Langley, *UK Christian Handbook 1992/93* (London, MARC Europe, 1991), p. 444.

46. *The Ministry of Women: A Report by a Committee Appointed by the Archbishop of Canterbury* (London, SPCK, 1920), p. 45. This section of a report that also dealt with the wider question of women's ordination to the priesthood, was largely the work of the Dean of Wells, Dr Armitage Robinson, and his sister, Cecilia, who was herself a deaconess.

47. *The Ministry of Women*, p. 38.

48. *The Lambeth Conferences 1867-1948* (London, SPCK, 1948), pp. 47-48.

49. *The Lambeth Conferences 1867-1948*, pp. 47-48.

50. B. Heeney, *The Women's Movement in the Church of England 1850-1930* (Oxford, Clarendon Press, 1988), pp. 132-133.

51. J. Field-Bibb, *Women Towards Priesthood: Ministerial Politics and Feminist*

Praxis (Cambridge, CUP, 1991), p. 78.

52. *The Lambeth Conferences 1867-1948*, pp. 78-79.

53. *Women in Ministry*, pp. 24-25.

54. *Women in Ministry*, pp. 31-47.

55. *The Ordination of Women to the Priesthood: A Consultative Document Presented by the Advisory Council for the Church's Ministry* (London, Church Information Office, 1972), p. 74. The limitations imposed upon women working as deaconesses are also discussed in A. Aldridge, 'In the Absence of the Minister: Structures of Subordination in the Role of Deaconess in the Church of England', *Sociology*, vol. 21 (1987), pp. 377-392.

56. *Deacons Now: The Report of a Church of England Working Party Concerned with Women in Ordained Ministry 1990* (London, ACCM, 1990), pp. 13-18.

57. *Deacons Now*, p. 79.

58. E. Baillie, *The Shabby Paradise: The Autobiography of a Decade* (London, Hutchinson, 1958), p. 105.

59. Quoted in S. Brown (ed.), *Married to the Church?* (London, Triangle/SPCK, 1983), p. 1. The book consists of ten very different accounts of the trials and satisfactions of women married to Anglican clergymen.

60. I have taken the details of her life from C. J. Armstrong, *Evelyn Underhill: An Introduction to Her Life and Writings* (London, Mowbray, 1975), and D. Greene, *Evelyn Underhill. Artist of the Infinite Life* (London, Darton, Longman & Todd, 1991).

61. This account is based upon B. Reynolds, *Dorothy L. Sayers, Her Life and Soul* (London, Hodder & Stoughton, 1993).

62. Reynolds, *Dorothy L. Sayers*, pp. 358-359.

63. Greene, *Evelyn Underhill*, pp. 149-150.

64. H. Smith, 'British Feminism in the 1920's', in H. Smith (ed.), *British Feminism in the Twentieth Century* (Aldershot, Edward Elgar, 1990), pp. 47-65; M. Pugh, *Women and the Women's Movement in Britain 1914-1959* (London, Macmillan, 1992), pp. 235-263.

65. For the early women's liberation movement and its agenda, see D. Bouchier, *The Feminist Challenge: The Movement for Women's Liberation in Britain and the USA* (London, Macmillan, 1983).

66. *Women in Training: A Report of a Working Party Set Up by Women Staff Members of Theological Colleges and Courses* (London, ACCM, 1983), pp. 29-30.

67. S. Dowell and L. Hurcombe, *Dispossessed Daughters of Eve: Faith and Feminism* (London, SPCK, 2nd edn, 1987), p. xiii.

68. M. Furlong (ed.), *Feminine in the Church* (London, SPCK, 1984), p. 1. The

moving spirit behind the Christian Parity Group was Una Kroll, a deaconess and GP in the diocese of Southwark. For this and the whole struggle for women's ordination from the perspective of an insider, see M. Webster, *A New Strength, A New Song: The Journey to Women's Priesthood* (London, Mowbray, 1994).

69.   Furlong (ed.), *Feminine in the Church*, p. 101.

CHAPTER TEN

The Ordination of Women
to the Priesthood:
An End or a Beginning?

The question of the admission of women to the priesthood is one which not only can, but one which ought to be indefinitely postponed.

Canon B. H. Streeter, 1917[1]

In the eighteenth and nineteenth centuries, Anglican thinking about the place of women in its life and work was not, as its exponents liked to believe, simply the product of detached scholarly enquiry into the historical and biblical record: it was also an expression of the Church's vision of a Christian social order, and of its perception of its own role in a changing society. In the Georgian era, a theology of female subordination was part of a wider emphasis on the need for a stable and hierarchical ordering of politics and society, and one that included a repudiation of the religious and social radicalism that in the seventeenth century had seemed to undermine authority in the family as well as in Church and state.

In the Victorian period, the Church's belief in women's capacity to regenerate society by extending the use of the special moral and spiritual qualities that they exercised in the home into the area of philanthropy was a product of economic and social change in an industrializing society; this had created a sharp division between the spheres of work and home, and a middle class growing in affluence, but fearful of the consequences of poverty, vice, and irreligion among large sections of the population.

In the twentieth century, the established Church's thinking has been more and more dominated by numerical decline in its membership, and what it perceives to be the marginalization of its voice in an increasingly secular and religiously plural society.[2] The self-confidence of the Georgian Church that it was a significant force in the maintenance of the social hierarchy, and of Victorian Anglicanism that the Christianization of England and the wider world was a daunting but not impossible challenge, has given way to a much more agonized wrestling with the seemingly intractable problems of modernity. In such an unpropitious social context, the theological divisions that arose in the nineteenth century between, on the one hand, conservative Evangelicals and Anglo-Catholics (who rejected the need to reformulate Christian theology in the light of new knowledge), and on the other, of Broad Churchmen (who attempted to implement Schleiermacher's project of defending Christianity by dialogue with the modern world), have become much more pronounced.[3]

Increasingly, the often very bitter disagreements between Victorian Evangelicals and Anglo-Catholics over the nature of the priesthood and the sacraments, and the role of Scripture and tradition in determining Christian truth, have been partially superseded by newer divides between conservatives, liberals, and radicals, who differ primarily in their perception of the extent to which Christian belief is in need of reformulation in the light of the drastic social and intellectual changes of the past two hundred years. However vociferous opponents and supporters of the ordination of women to the priesthood have been in putting forward theological arguments derived from biblical or historical precedent, or (in the case of some of those who have resisted the change) ecclesiological claims about the Catholicity of the Church of England, the social context in which theological thinking is undertaken remains a powerful force in shaping its agenda.

It is because the issue of the ordination of women to the priesthood highlights so clearly the challenge of modernity, that Evangelical and Anglo-Catholic opponents of the measure have been able to make common cause with one another, even though the grounds of their opposition are not in other ways theologically compatible.[4] The debates about women's ordination can therefore be seen as one in a series of controversies within Anglicanism that have greeted the publication of liberal theological manifestos from *Foundations: A Statement of Christian Belief in Terms of Modern Thought*, edited by B. H. Streeter in 1912, to *Honest to God* in 1963, the *Myth of God Incarnate* in 1977, and, most recently, the work of Don Cupitt.[5] To put the matter in this way is perhaps to imply that academic theology has been more avidly read and inwardly digested by churchgoers than seems likely, but as in the case of the mild furore created by the Bishop of Durham's remarks on television in 1984 about the nature of the virgin birth, the media have been influential in popularizing what might otherwise appear to be somewhat arcane academic disputes.

Of more significance in raising awareness of the problematical relationship between theological and doctrinal discourse and social change have been the debates surrounding the Anglican Church's reformulation of its traditional teaching on a range of social and moral issues including contraception, divorce and remarriage, and homosexuality. To a traditionalist such as the Social Services minister Anne Widdicombe, the ordination of women to the priesthood was not a question to be considered in isolation from others: it was the last straw in a whole bale, which together called into question the possibility of authoritative Christian doctrine in a period of rapid social change.[6] The Archbishop of Canterbury, on the other hand, pointed to the need to make the Church credible in a society where women were exercising leadership in every area of life except the ordained ministry.[7] On both sides, the interplay between theological conviction and its social context was abundantly clear.

Women and the priesthood: the early twentieth-century debates

As we have seen, in the early twentieth century the issues of democracy and women's suffrage, and the growing professionalization of women's work, began to affect significant aspects of the Church's life. The women's movement, conceived in broad terms as the attempt to secure greater equality and opportunity for women in society, found both clerical and lay support within the Church, and it was in this context that the question of women's ordination began to be raised. In 1913, Ursula Roberts, the wife of the Rev. W. C. Roberts of St George's, Bloomsbury, and a member of the Church League for Women's Suffrage, wrote to some 150 people asking for their views on the question of women's ordination, and the proposal to hold a conference on the issue.[8] The conference was never held, because of the advent of war, but news of it provoked a strong response from the *Church Times*:

The monstrous regiment of women in politics would be bad

enough but the monstrous regiment of priestesses would be a thousandfold worse. We are not inclined, however, to treat the proposed Conference as a sane scheme; we regard it as a piece with that epidemic of hysteria which has manifested itself in the violence of feminine militants. It will pass with time.[9]

The question of women's position within the Church was raised again in a different form in 1916 when the Archbishop of Canterbury, Randall Davidson, launched his National Mission of Hope and Repentance in an attempt to make use of the opportunities that the war seemed to provide to foster a religious revival. The mission relied on recruiting large numbers of 'archbishop's messengers' to give addresses in parish churches throughout the land, and it was intended that some of these should be women. The Mission Council also approved a report that argued in favour of women being allowed to serve on Church councils, and claimed that the aims of the women's movement were 'in harmony with the teachings of Christ and His Church as to the equality of men and women in the sight of God'.[10] However, the idea of allowing women to speak in churches during the mission aroused a storm of opposition led by Athelstan Riley, a prominent Anglo-Catholic layman, and a vice-president of the English Church Union. Riley attacked the proposal as an innovation that contradicted both Scripture and 'the common order of the Catholic Church', and claimed that it was part of a conspiracy aimed at opening the priesthood to women.[11] With some clergy stating openly that they would take no part in the mission if women were allowed to speak in church, the bishops drew back, and the Bishop of London, Winnington-Ingram, revoked the permission that he had earlier granted.

Maude Royden spoke soon after this débâcle at a meeting of the Church League for Women's Suffrage on the subject of the Church's relation to the women's movement. The Church, she claimed, 'is so anxious to see what is safe that she loses her leadership in what is right'. For this reason, she opined, the Church of England had failed to address any of the needs of the age: 'in the rise of democracy, in the advance of science, in bettering the condition of the people, in the coming of feminism – one chance after another we have thrown away'. However, this was not a matter of the Church simply responding to a secular agenda; the women's movement should, she believed, 'first be tried by the Church to see whether it is of God or not'.[12]

To test a woman's vocation in this way was not easy, and a number of women, most notably Maude Royden herself and Edith Picton-Turbervill, took matters into their own hands by endeavouring to preach in Anglican pulpits. Royden also accepted an invitation to become an assistant at the Congregationalist City Temple in London, but it was her preaching at St Botolph's Church that provoked the most trouble within the Church of England, with the Bishop of London formally forbidding her to preach at the Three Hours Service on Good Friday 1919. In the same year, the Convocation of Canterbury debated a proposal that would have allowed 'women to speak and pray in consecrated buildings under regulations and conditions laid down by the bishops at services or meetings other than the liturgical services of the church', but this was rejected – and it was finally agreed in 1922 that women could be given the right to preach and pray in consecrated buildings, but normally this permission was to apply only to their addressing congregations of women and children.[13]

The year 1919 also saw the completion of a report on the ministry of women by a committee set up by the Archbishop of Canterbury in 1917, whose brief was to consider 'the sanctions and restrictions which govern the ministrations of women in the life of the Church, and the status and work of deaconesses'.[14] The committee, which consisted of ten prominent clergymen and laymen and one woman, attempted to adopt what it called a 'purely historical' approach, and did not deal with 'questions bearing upon sex in comparative or speculative theology'. Its review of the historical evidence pointed out that although Jesus did not share the low view of women common in his society, and although women such as Phoebe undertook a ministry of service as deaconesses, the Lord's Supper was instituted entirely in the presence of men, and all twelve apostles were male. Despite the committee's professions of historical objectivity, it was heavily influenced by contemporary assumptions. Thus, in its handling of St Paul's claim in Galatians 3.28 that in Christ there is neither male nor female, the committee gave considerable weight to its own early twentieth-century ideas about sexual and racial differentiation:

> St Paul teaches that in Christ every barrier is swept away; in Christ there is no room for the distinctions of race, rank, or even sex. But these mundane differences are indelible; and each variety has its opportunity of special service. They do not disappear on earth although in Christ they are obliterated. In Him mankind is one

family. Race and sex have their respective gifts to be dedicated and used. The work and calling of the sexes continue different, although in Christ there is neither male nor female.[15]

Similarly, in its discussion of the normative status of early church practices for the present, and in its refusal to consider the possible implications of their cultural context, the committee based its conclusions on hermeneutical principles that were largely implicit and unquestioned:

The historic Ministry of the Church of Christ has been transmitted through the male sex from the days of the Apostles. This restriction of the priesthood may have been due to the fact that in those times women would not have been entrusted with official posts of public administration; it may have been due to the influence of Jewish usage in the Temple and Synagogue; it may have been due to the recognition of fundamental differences in function and calling inherent in the natural variety of sex. It is not our province to discuss these questions. We simply record the fact that the restriction of the Ministry of the priesthood to men originated in a generation which was guided by the special gifts of the Holy Spirit.[16]

The Lambeth Conference of 1920, although equally cautious in its discussion of women's position in the life of the Church, nevertheless saw the issue of inspiration and the authority of the past more clearly than the Archbishop's committee when it approached the subject by stating:

We are profoundly conscious that the Holy Spirit teaches Christian people by those age-long precedents which we believe to be the outcome of His guidance. But sometimes it becomes our duty, faithfully retaining the lessons of the sacred past, in a very special sense to trust ourselves to His inspiration in that present which is our time of opportunity, in order that He may lead us into whatsoever fresh truth of thought or of action is in accordance with the will of God.[17]

In putting the matter in this way the Conference set out the terms of the debate between traditionalists and advocates of change in the form that was to dominate discussions about women's ordination for the next seventy-two years.

As we have seen, part of the remit of the Archbishop's committee was to consider the history and status of deaconesses within the

Church; and in the context of debates about women's ordination to the priesthood, the office assumed new importance, since it was seen by supporters of change as a precedent and stepping stone, and by opponents as a stalking horse, and as evidence of the limitations placed upon women's ministry by the early Church. However, while the definition of the Order of Deaconess by the 1920 Lambeth Conference as 'the one and only Order of the Ministry which has the stamp of Apostolic approval, and is for women the only Order of the Ministry which we can recommend that our branch of the catholic church should recognise and use', seemed to hold out some promise for those who saw it as a path to women's ordination, that of the 1930 Lambeth Conference dashed these hopes.[18] This reaffirmed that it was 'for women the one and only Order of the ministry', but removed the phrase 'which has the stamp of Apostolic approval', and went on to define the office as 'an Order *sui generis*' – and therefore not part of the historic order of deacons, priests, and bishops.[19]

The bishops at the 1930 Lambeth Conference also received a submission from the newly created Anglican Group for the Ordination of Women to the Historic Ministry of the Church, which had taken up the fight for women's ordination following the demise of the League of the Church Militant – which had replaced the Church League for Women's Suffrage as the body campaigning for women's ordination in 1919.[20] The Anglican Group's submission included a series of anonymous letters from women who felt they had a vocation to the priesthood that they were unable to fulfil. One wrote of the terrible sense of bitterness that she felt, which she overcame by deciding that wherever she worshipped she would 'make an Act of Faith that one day a woman priest would stand and minister at that particular altar'; another spoke of 'the ardent and overpowering longing, when preparing the altar for Celebrations, to be a man, just to be able to celebrate the Divine Mysteries'.[21]

Appeals of this kind, however heartfelt, faced two kinds of difficulty in the inter-war years. One was the reluctance of most women in the Church to support them. In 1918, for example, the Bishop of Lincoln, Edward Hicks, recorded in his diary that he was dissuaded from attempts to organize a conference on the place of women in the Church because the women of the diocese would be too shy or too fearful of novelties to take part.[22] The other was the hostility of most of the episcopal hierarchy. When in 1925 Margaret Stansgate dined with the Archbishop of Canterbury, Randall Davidson, and explained her interest in women's ordination on the grounds that she wished her children to grow up 'in a world in which the Church gives equal spiritual status to women', she was firmly told that ordination could never be since it would be against the Catholic tradition of two millennia.[23]

It was in fact the continued concern to define the status and responsibilities of deaconesses that was the most pressing reason for the setting up of another Archbishop's commission on the ministry of women, which issued its report in 1935. It concluded that 'it should be recognised that a deaconess is in Holy Orders', and that the 'grace of orders is bestowed upon her by the Holy Spirit through the laying on of hands with prayer'; however, it went on to reaffirm the distinction that had been maintained in previous reports, arguing that 'this Order should not be regarded as equivalent with the diaconate of men, but rather as the one existing Holy Order for women'.[24] The commission also considered the theological arguments for and against the ordination of women to the priesthood, and while it rejected the medieval view propounded by Aquinas that women were by nature defective and incapable of being ordained, its overall conclusion was in the negative:

> While the Commission as a whole would not give their positive assent to the view that a woman is inherently incapable of receiving the grace of Order, and consequently of admission to any of the three Orders, we believe that the general mind of the Church is still in accord with the continuous tradition of a male priesthood. It is our conviction that this consensus of tradition and opinion is based on the will of God and is, for the Church of today, a sufficient witness to the guidance of the Holy Spirit. We are therefore of the opinion that the case for a change in the Church's rule has not been made out. The theological justification offered in support of such a change does not appear to us convincing, nor do we believe that the objections to the admission of women to the traditional Orders are mere prejudices based on outworn notions of the relations of man and woman to one another.[25]

The one significant dissenting voice was that of the Dean of St Paul's, Dr W. R. Mathews, who in a memorandum presented to the commission argued that while he accepted that it was inexpedient for the Church to ordain women at present, he could nevertheless see no basic theological objection to their ordination. He also considered an issue that was later to loom large in the debate: how far the Church of England had the authority to act unilaterally apart from the universal

Church. Here he stressed the essentially Protestant nature of the Church of England, which at the Reformation had made fundamental changes to its theology and practice by repudiating papal authority and abolishing the celibacy of the clergy.

Arguments of this kind were rejected by the Anglo-Catholic Church Union, which published a reply to the Commission's report. This was critical of the Dean of St Paul's, claiming that clerical celibacy and universal papal jurisdiction were not part of the 'primitive system of faith and discipline as it was universally accepted'. This was not true of something as fundamental as the nature of the priesthood, and to ordain women would be more like 'the bizarre innovations sanctioned . . . by the Anabaptist sect'.[26] The Church Union was also opposed to any suggestion that the order of deaconess was part of the threefold order of deacons, priests, and bishops that had existed in the early Church, and that had specific liturgical functions that were not performed by women. For this reason, it objected to allowing deaconesses to read morning and evening prayer, to preach, baptize, church women, or to administer the chalice. There was no objection, however, to deaconesses being regarded as part of the staff of a parish, since overall responsibility lay with the incumbent; nor to their using the title 'Reverend', which had been applied in the past to clerks in minor orders in the Catholic Church and to the heads of religious houses – though even if this practice could be defended on grounds of logic, 'there will appear to the ordinary Englishman to be something abnormal and bizarre in the use of this term in addressing for instance, a letter to a woman'.[27]

More serious questions of propriety were raised by the Church Union, when it considered the matter of women performing liturgical functions, and of their presence in the Sanctuary. The Archbishop's commission, despite concluding that the case against women's ordination was not based upon outdated assumptions about the relationship between the sexes, published a paper by Professor L. W. Grensted on the psychological dimensions of the debate in which he argued that the sense of shame with which some viewed the admission of women to Holy Orders was part of 'a non-rational sex-taboo'. The Church Union rejected this point, claiming that since this feeling was so widespread in the Church, it must rest on something more substantial than the 'psychological aberrations of some of its members'. This sense of inappropriateness had in fact to do with the essential nature of Christian worship, which, unlike pagan rites, 'has always been essentially sexless in its character and atmosphere' and therefore 'eschews all appeal to passions and emotions connected with man's animal nature'. This meant that 'the genius of the liturgical action of the Eucharist, or the solemn recital of the Divine Office, is more akin to that of military ceremonial functions, such as the trooping of the colour, than to the sensuous beauty of grand opera or the Russian Ballet', and its solemnity was easily debased by the introduction of over-sensuous music (such as Gounod's). The need to exclude eroticism from the liturgy made it impossible to contemplate female priests – not because of any failings on their part, but for quite the opposite reason:

> It is a tribute to the quality of Christian womanhood that it is possible to make this statement, but it would appear to be a simple matter of fact that in the thoughts and desires of that sex the natural is more easily made subordinate to the supernatural, the carnal to the spiritual, than is the case with men; and that the ministrations of a male priesthood do not normally arouse that side of female human nature which should be quiescent during the times of the adoration of almighty God.[28]

The problem of controlling unbridled male sexuality applied equally to female preaching, or even to mixed choirs, since in America (already the *bête noire* of Anglican traditionalists), where women had taken part in choral singing, the effect had been, in the opinion of the Church Union, to assimilate 'the rendering of divine service to the performances of the theatre or the concert hall'.[29]

The *Church Times* responded to the Archbishop's report in more measured terms, but supported its conclusions, and somewhat begged the question by adding that 'if we were faced by a great body of devoted women who had become ministers in all but name . . . the situation would be different'.[30] This provoked a letter from Ursula Roberts and five other women, pointing out that they had no opportunities to become anything like 'ministers in all but name', and reaffirming their sense of vocation to the priesthood.[31] To the Archbishop of Canterbury, William Temple, writing in 1943, the opportunity to test such vocations still seemed far away. In a letter that praised the work done by deaconesses, he added that 'I do not think the question of ordaining women to the priesthood in this country will become a live issue for a considerable time, if ever.' This was because he sensed that most members of the Church were opposed to the idea, 'and whether or not it ought ultimately to happen, there would have to be a very long educational campaign to change the mind of these folk before it could happen'.[32]

The post-war debates and the acceptance of women's ordination

Brian Heeney has suggested that the major period of feminism in the Church was during the First World War and the succeeding decade, but that 'the movement evidently stalled in the early 1930s, to regain momentum only with the renewal of militant feminism and the vigorous . . . drive for female ordination in the 1970s'.[33] It is undoubtedly true that some of the impetus associated with the women's suffrage campaign was lost, and that the Anglican Group for the Ordination of Women, which defined its objectives as 'to build up an informed public opinion which will lead the Anglican Church increasingly to understand the extent to which her life is impoverished by her refusal to make use of the gifts which God has bestowed upon women', and to argue for women's ordination 'from time to time', adopted less forthright tactics than its predecessors.[34] However, the traumatic events of the Second World War inevitably involved the Church in other priorities, and it would be wrong to underestimate the extent to which the question of women's ordination remained a live issue in the immediate post-war years, even if it was not within the realm of achievable policies.

It came to prominence at the end of the war following the action of the Bishop of Hong Kong and South China, Dr R. O. Hall, in ordaining a deaconess, Li Tim Oi, to the priesthood in 1944, since following the Japanese occupation of Hong Kong, Anglicans were deprived of access to the sacraments. Preaching in London in 1945, Bishop Hall said, 'There is no question that Li Tim Oi has the gift of priesthood. The only thing that remains is, is it going to be possible to ordain women with these obvious gifts and calling to the ministry? I am convinced myself that it is right.' The Church did not agree with him. A letter was sent by both archbishops repudiating the action as *ultra vires*, and Li Tim Oi withdrew from working as a priest following pressure from the Chinese bishops on Hall to force her to resign. She did so, she said, when she realized that the choice was between her own resignation and that of the Bishop, and she was not willing to see that happen to the man who had so bravely ordained her.[35]

The 1948 Lambeth Conference was further involved in the affairs of the Anglican Church in China, when it was asked to consider a new canon from the diocese of South China. This would have allowed, for an experimental period of twenty years, an unmarried deaconess of thirty years of age with 'the same theological, spiritual and pastoral qualifications as are required of a deacon before ordination' to be admitted to the priesthood. The three Chinese members of the episcopal committee appointed to consider the request, made use of an argument that was to be of increasing significance in the future when they claimed that 'since Anglican tradition and order are based on the autonomy of national churches, the adoption of the experiment proposed in the Church of China for a twenty-year period of testing should be regarded as a proper exercise of autonomy not entailing any breach of fellowship'. The committee did not feel able to accept this view, and concluded that 'an experiment of so radical an order' would not be compatible with Anglican tradition. In arriving at this decision, they referred to the formulation adopted by the 1930 Lambeth Conference that the Order of Deaconess was the only one open to women, and was an order *sui generis*, not to be confused with the historic threefold ministry of the Church, a position reaffirmed by resolutions adopted by both Houses of Convocation of Canterbury and York in the period 1939–1941. The committee did, however, admit that the hope expressed by the 1930 Lambeth Conference that the Church's formal recognition of the Order of Deaconess would provide opportunities for women's ministry had not been fulfilled, and instead 'there had been much hesitation, delay, and uncertainty'. With regard to the more fundamental principle of admitting women to the priesthood, the committee referred to the Archbishop's report of 1935, and did not think that the time was ripe to re-open the question.[36]

Nevertheless, within Anglican circles it continued to be debated. For instance, in 1948 C. S. Lewis published an essay entitled 'Priestesses in the Church'. This had all the apparent directness and lucidity of style that made him such a successful exponent of popular theology, but that masked a great deal of over-simplification and confusion in its handling of theological questions. For example, with regard to the significance of the symbolism of an all-male priesthood, Lewis claimed that the priest 'represents us to God and God to us', while admitting that God has no gender. On the other hand, he warned, if we came to accept that gendered language about God was 'quite arbitrary and unessential', the truth of Christianity itself would be threatened, and he concluded with a rhetorical flourish that 'in the Church we are dealing with male and female not merely as facts of nature but as the live and awful shadows of realities utterly beyond our control'.[37]

The following year, three sermons by the Master of St Peter's Hall, Oxford, Canon R. W. Howard, were published under the title *Should Women Be Priests?*[38] Howard argued that St Paul's prohibitions on women speaking in church were only local rules, and in deciding what weight to give to tradition he felt that it was important to see the Church as a living organism whose survival depended on its capacity to adapt to its changing environment.[39] He also considered a number of practical objections to women's ordination, which he admitted had some force. One was the problem of sex rearing its ugly head in divine worship, which had so preoccupied the Church Union in 1936. Not unreasonably, he pointed out that 'It is possible for men also, however involuntarily, to radiate sex atmosphere, as every handsome curate knows.' As for what might happen at the kiss of peace – which one bishop confessed himself scarcely able to imagine – Christians could avoid the dangers of moral turpitude by the exercise of 'sanctified self-control'.

A further problem was the fear that 'if the door to the priesthood were once opened to women, there would be so great a spate, so serious a landslide, of female ordinations that, the ministry being swamped by a feminine invasion, men would increasingly refuse to enter it'. Howard did not respond to the misogyny implied by such a scenario, but instead sought to allay fears on this score by pointing out that a woman's true role was at home as a wife and mother, and that 'only a very small percentage, indeed, could be spared from that supreme task'. This still left the further difficulty of married priests, which could be solved by allowing women a period of secondment to bring up their children.[40]

A less wide-ranging, and perhaps more severely academic, discussion of the issues occurred in *Theology* in 1954–1955. This was begun by Dr Sherwin Bailey, who published the substance of an address on 'Woman and the Church's Lay Ministry' that he had delivered to the Central Council for Women's Church Work in October 1953. Bailey argued that the Pauline view of the relationship between men and women, and the Genesis myth on which it was based, reflected the social organization of the societies in which they were written, and he went on to ask, 'Is this antique view of woman intrinsic to the Gospel; or does it simply represent a situation in the light of which St Paul and others had to legislate temporarily – a situation which they accepted just as they did that of slavery?'[41] In his discussion of the

Pauline doctrine of headship and its later application, Bailey also drew attention to the androcentricity of the Christian tradition and to the persistence of this way of thinking in contemporary society.[42] In the same issue of *Theology*, Miss M. E. Thrall, a classics mistress at St Alban's High School, directly addressed the issue of women's ordination to the priesthood, arguing that the subordination of women was a consequence of the Fall; the results of this were abolished by Christ's coming, which restored to woman an equal dominion with man, a dominion that involves priesthood. She ended with a plea that those responsible for ministerial training be willing to test a woman's vocation.[43]

These two articles provoked a short reply by the Rev. E. L. Mascall, then a Student of Christ Church, Oxford, and a longer article by the Ven. G. F. Hilder, the Archdeacon of Taunton.[44] Mascall based his case on the facts of the incarnation, in which the two sexes were involved in different ways, stressing that 'it was male human nature that the Son of God united to his divine Person; it was a female human person who was chosen to be his Mother'. From this followed the different roles of men and women in the life of the Church.[45] Hilder rejected the analogy that was frequently made by supporters of the ordination of women between the early Church's acceptance of slavery, which the Church no longer found acceptable, and its restrictive attitudes towards women. Whereas the relationship between the sexes was spoken of by the New Testament writers as 'rooted in the order of creation and affording an insight into the very nature of the godhead', this was not the case, he argued, with regard to slavery.[46] One of the most striking features of Hilder's treatment of the biblical doctrine of headship was the way in which it was coloured by contemporary assumptions about the proper relationship between men and women in marriage, and his own view of the constitutive qualities of masculinity and femininity. The result was a circular mode of reasoning in which the correctness of biblical ideas about headship could be proven by recourse to contemporary social norms, which were themselves justified by an appeal to the biblical order of creation. Thus in defence of a notion of headship based upon subordination, Hilder cited 'the testimony of not a few practising psychotherapists that marriages often break down today simply because the husband will not take the particular responsibility of "headship" which nature requires of him'. With regard to an all-male priesthood, Hilder concluded, though far less certainly than Mascall, that this seemed not only to follow from the headship given to man in creation, but from the fact that worship and preaching involved an 'element of formality and transcendence of what is personal and particular', which was 'characteristically masculine'.[47]

On the other side of the debate, Bailey's case was also strongly influenced by his own studies into the history and psychodynamics of sexuality and marriage, which led him to regard the traditional doctrines of headship and subordination as both unhealthy and unjust.[48] The extent to which supposedly theological arguments were in fact often derived from strongly held views about the nature and significance of gender differences, and about the right ordering of society, was to be an important element in the subsequent debates, particularly in a period of social and moral flux.

The changing attitudes to sexual relations in English society, and the gulf that separated these from the world of the early Church Fathers, formed part of the backdrop to the report of the Central Advisory Council for the Ministry, *Gender and Ministry*, which was presented to the Church Assembly in 1962. Like earlier reports, *Gender and Ministry* again referred to the confusion surrounding the function of the deaconess, and raised the whole question of the nature of the priestly office in relation to the place of the laity in the Church. Its language was more blunt in places than the more measured tone of most Anglican church reports. A small part of the opposition to the ordination of women came, it was suggested, from clergy for whom the priesthood was 'a compensation for their own sense of inadequacy as males, or a satisfaction of their desire for a protected status'; while it swept aside the arguments from tradition with the tart, and perhaps not wholly adequate, observation that 'our Lord invited us to let the dead bury their dead; our duty is to the living'.[49] The subsequent debate within the Church Assembly on the report ended with a motion asking the archbishops to appoint a committee 'to make a thorough examination of the various reasons for the withholding of the ordained and representative priesthood from women'.[50]

The resulting report, *Women and Holy Orders*, which was published in December 1966, gave as the context of its work the emancipation of women (which it somewhat optimistically claimed had resulted in the acceptance of women in nearly every profession); the spirit of the times, which required the Church to look again at a teaching and tradition underpinned by discredited biological and psychological notions about the inferiority of women; the Church's failure to provide women with a properly defined ministry; and the shortage of candidates for the priesthood. The commission decided that its method of working would be to set out as clearly as possible the arguments that had to be taken into account in deciding whether or not the Church should ordain women, and would print in an appendix a series of essays for and against doing so. In this way, it was able to present a unanimous report, which it would not otherwise have been able to do given that its members were deeply divided.[51]

The main arguments against the ordination of women were stated to be first, the witness of tradition from the Apostolic period, which did not arise merely from cultural conditioning, since Christianity's attitude towards women was far more favourable than that of contemporary Jewish society. Second, such a change would be divisive within the Christian Church. Third, the rejection of a philosophy of social evolution that would see the ordination of women as 'the logical outcome of a steadily growing recognition of woman's full humanity'. Fourth, the rejection of the claim that there is a sexless human nature underlying gender differences in favour of a view of the sexes as different and complementary, and of women having particular gifts and opportunities that would be lost if they were drawn into the ordained ministry. Fifth, the practical problems that would arise for a woman who attempted to fulfil her responsibilities both as a married woman and as a priest. Sixth, the belief that the question was in some sense 'obsolescent', both because women have been given full professional opportunities within society, and because of the 'general indifference to the question' on the part of most churchgoers.

On the other side, it was argued that neither the Pauline prohibitions, nor metaphorical language about the nature of the Godhead, should be regarded as proving that for all time the priestly function is to be exclusively male. It was also accepted that while there were significant differences between masculinity and femininity, these did not make women any less fitted to be priests on grounds of temperament, intelligence, or spiritual insight. The claim that the movement for women's ordination was the outgrowth of secular feminism was also rejected: instead, it was justified in terms of women's sense of vocation and commitment to the renewal of the Church's mission.[52]

Three essays were included in an appendix that set out the cases for and against women's ordination: with Mrs Kay Baxter, a member of the Central Advisory Council for the Ministry and a former Fellow of Newnham College, Cambridge, arguing for; and Professor V. A. Demant, Regius Professor of Moral and Pastoral Theology at Oxford, arguing against. Demant's essay, like Mascall's arguments, revealed the way in which supposedly theological propositions were largely derived from questionable assumptions about gender. While it was not true, Demant admitted, to suggest that 'the Deity has sex or maleness', Christianity was a Logos religion, a faith in the incarnate Word of God, and 'in so far as we can use gender imagery for these things the Logos is a masculine principle', since 'in general the Logos is the active, manifesting, creative-destructive, redemptive power of the godhead, and has commonly been regarded, at this level, as a masculine power'. Demant could expatiate so confidently upon the supposedly masculine nature of the Logos because he was crystal clear about the innate differences between men and women:

> Maleness is associated with law, order, civilisation, logos, clock time, and what Freud called the 'super-ego'. Femaleness is associated with nature, instinct, biological time, feeling, eros, and what Freud called the 'id'. Maleness stands for association, organisation and technique; femaleness for relationship, community and improvisation.

These distinctions had direct application, in Demant's view, to the question of the exercise of priestly functions, which required an element of detachment found in men but not in women, as well as a kind of loneliness which, he confidently asserted, 'women are not fitted to stand'.[53] Baxter did not dispute that there might be differences between the sexes, but denied that they were of a kind that unfitted women for ordination. The main thrust of her case was that Scripture and tradition reflected the social patterns of the patriarchal societies that produced them.[54]

The third essay by the Dean of York, Alan Richardson, took the view that while there were no decisive theological objections to women's ordination, it was inexpedient on ecumenical and other grounds to proceed at present. This was to become an increasingly important stance as the Church tried to hold together its warring factions, and one that Monica Furlong was later to dub akin to St Augustine's views on chastity – 'Give us women priests, Lord, but not yet.'[55]

The Church Assembly debated the report in its spring and summer sessions in 1967. Despite Professor Dennis Nineham's warning that if views like those of Canon Demant prevailed, the Church would be defining women as 'second-class citizens of the kingdom',[56] a motion by Miss V. J. Pitt that women be considered for ordination on the same terms as men was predictably heavily defeated in all three Houses (House of Bishops 1:8; House of Clergy 14:96; House of

Laity 45:103). This result caused the Bishop of Chester, Gerald Ellison, who had been chairman of the commission, to conclude that there was now a need for 'a long period of education in which the Church will learn whether it is right for women to be ordained'.[57] However, of greater long-term significance was the fact that Professor Lampe's motion that there were no conclusive theological objections to the ordination of women, and that the question should be referred to the joint Committee of Representatives of the Church of England and the Methodist Church, was only lost in the House of Clergy (House of Bishops 12:4; House of Laity 115:81; House of Clergy 70:96).[58]

The reference to Methodism was in the context of the ongoing discussions about union between the two Churches, and in May 1968 an Anglican–Methodist commission published a report on the implications for union of the ordination of women.[59] The report pointed out that the 1966 Methodist Conference had voted in favour of the principle of ordaining women to its ministry, and suggested that, while the Church of England might within the next five years declare that there were no conclusive theological objections to the ordination of women, it would probably be many years before it would be prepared to ordain women to the priesthood. It recommended that if the Methodist Church ordained women ministers, this need not be an obstacle to stage one of Anglican–Methodist union if there was an agreement that female Methodist ministers would not undertake priestly functions within Anglican churches.[60]

The report proved to be too sanguine on the question of Anglican–Methodist union, which failed to obtain the necessary two-thirds majority in the Houses of Clergy and Laity in General Synod in May 1972, but its insight into the slow pace of change within the Church of England on the issue of women's ordination proved to be more prophetic. The impetus for such a decision now came not from the Church of England itself, but from the wider Anglican Communion. The 1968 Lambeth Conference passed a resolution affirming that the theological arguments for and against women's ordination were inconclusive, and requested that every national or regional Church or province should study the question, and report its findings to the newly formed Anglican Consultative Council. It also recommended that Churches within the Anglican Communion should be encouraged to make canonical provision for duly authorized women 'to share in the conduct of liturgical worship, to preach, to baptize, to read the epistle and gospel at the Holy Communion, and to help in the distribution of the elements', but that before any Church made a decision to ordain women to the priesthood, the advice of the ACC should be sought and carefully considered.[61]

The first meeting of the ACC was held at Limuru in Kenya in February and March of 1971, and it called upon all Churches of the Anglican Communion to consider the matter and report their views in time for discussion at the next meeting of the ACC in 1973. In response to a request for advice from the Bishop of Hong Kong, Gilbert Baker, whose synod had passed a motion in favour of the ordination of women, the ACC passed a resolution by twenty-four votes to twenty-two. This stated that if he, or any other bishop acting with the approval of his Province, decided to ordain women, his action would be acceptable to the Council, which would use its offices to encourage all other Provinces to stay in communion with dioceses where this occurred.[62] This favourable response led the Bishop of Hong Kong on Advent Sunday 1971 to ordain two women priests, Jane Huang, the principal of a primary school and deacon in charge of Holy Trinity, Kowloon, and Joyce Bennett, a CMS missionary and school principal.[63] In his charge to his Diocesan Synod in November 1971, Bishop Baker said that 'if humanity is to be fully represented before God in the priesthood it is logical to suppose that the ministry which is not limited to people of one tribe or race should not be limited to one sex'.[64] Meeting in January 1972, the Synod of the Church of Burma also passed a resolution in favour of the ordination of women to the priesthood.[65]

In July 1972, the standing committee of the General Synod asked the Advisory Council for the Church's Ministry, and the Council for Women's Ministry in the Church, for their advice on the resolutions passed by the ACC at Limuru, which resulted in Miss Christian Howard preparing a consultative report for ACCM, entitled *The Ordination of Women to the Priesthood*, which was published in October 1972. This was a remarkably well-documented and wide-ranging discussion of the issues – considering the time available for its compilation.[66] It outlined the differing attitudes in the Church to both the nature of biblical authority and to the weight to be attached to tradition, and argued that the early Church developed its structures over time and in response to changing social and cultural conditions. This meant that there was 'no divinely appointed, unchanging "church order" valid for all ages and places', and it followed that 'We have to play it by ear, and all we can hope for in any given situation, especially in times of rapid social change is to be able to say (as Paul said)

with some confidence, "I think I have the mind of Christ"' – a conclusion hardly likely to find favour with those who regarded Revelation as providing a far clearer and more precise guide to questions of
ecclesiastical and social order.[67]

Miss Howard also considered the nature and importance of religious language and symbolism within the Christian faith, and asked
whether these were related to 'certain deep and basic male and female
archetypes which should not be disrupted'. It was the case, she
admitted, that 'some women, as well as some men, think in this way:
it cannot be brushed aside as no more than discrimination'. On the
other hand, changes in society and in the natural sciences led her to
ask, 'Is it not now very difficult to be clear about the absolute quality
of the distinctions between men and women; at least as to *where* such
distinctions lie and *what* they imply?'[68]

The debate on the report in Synod in November 1972 showed that
some of its members held very strong and precise ideas about sexual
differentiation. Presenting the report as chairman of ACCM, the
Bishop of St Edmundsbury and Ipswich, Dr L. W. Brown, argued
that 'God is giving us insights into the meaning of the new humanity
in Christ which have not hitherto been fully understood. It is possible
that such insights will make us believe that sex difference is as relevant or irrelevant to holy orders as racial or cultural differences.'
Other speakers, however, reasserted traditional views about gender.
Miss Pobjoy, for example, maintained that a woman's place was with
her family, and added 'that she should wish to become a priest is
insulting to her nature'. Whereas 'women from time to time are at the
mercy of their hormones', she claimed, and are basically in competition with one another, men have 'the quality of detachment' that
allows them to fulfil the representative function of the priest.[69] One
clear decision of the Synod, though, was that in order to give an answer to the ACC, the opinion of diocesan synods should be sought.

The General Synod, which debated the question in July 1975,
approached its task with all the enthusiasm of men and women asked
to cross a minefield wearing magnetic boots – and perhaps, in the
view of all sides, with the same inevitable result. It was reported that
thirty diocesan synods had passed a motion in all three Houses of
Bishops, Clergy, and Laity that there were no fundamental theological
objections to the ordination of women, but that a second motion to
remove the legal barriers to doing so had been carried in only fifteen.
These results led the religious affairs correspondent of *The Times*,
Clifford Longley, to speculate that 'the swelling tide that seemed to

be moving the Church of England towards the ordination of women may have turned', and to predict in his headline, 'Women priests unlikely in this generation', which, correctly as it turned out, did not augur well for the supporters of women's ordination.[70] The Bishop of Oxford, who opened the debate in favour of the motion, argued for a doctrine of progressive revelation through the Holy Spirit that was guiding the Church to see as God's truth new insights into male–female relationships; and both he and the Archbishop of Canterbury, Donald Coggan, spoke of the great contribution that women made in the life of the Church, particularly as deaconesses, but regretted the partial waste of their talents. On the other side, Eric Kemp, the Bishop of Chichester, stressed the primacy of a tradition that derived from Christ's choice of only male apostles, which was not 'to be explained solely by the prevailing circumstances', and asked whether this might not rest 'upon something deeper and more permanent in the order of creation on which our Lord and his Church have built?' Speaking from the Anglo-Catholic wing of the Church, he also doubted whether the Anglican Communion had the authority to make such a change unilaterally.

The vote in favour of the motion 'that there are no fundamental theological objections to the ordination of women to the priesthood' was passed (House of Bishops 28:10; House of Clergy 110:96, 2 abstentions; House of Laity 117:74, 3 abstentions). There then followed a series of confused debates in which motions against removing the legal barriers to women's ordination and in favour of doing so were both lost, though it was notable that the House of Laity voted in favour of women's immediate ordination in response to both. With some relief, Synod then agreed on a show of hands to leave it to the House of Bishops to bring forward proposals to ordain women priests when 'they judge the time for action to be right'.[71]

In its leader, the *Church Times* highlighted the importance of the decision that there were no objections in principle, and thought that 'the odds are that practice will one day follow', and its significance was clear from the fact that from this date, the arguments of those opposed, while they continued to assert that there were fundamental theological reasons for not proceeding, relied increasingly on claiming that the Church faced dissension and division if it did so. Fearful of such an outcome, the *Church Times* also pleaded for patience, courtesy, and restraint, but a bare recital of Synod debates and voting figures fails to convey the bitterness and anger increasingly felt on both sides, and the deep-seated suspicion of the other's motives. For example, in its letters column in the same issue, the Rev. John Stewart claimed that the campaign for women's ordination, like the proposals for Anglican–Methodist union, had been led by 'the voluble, with-it novelty-seekers, often unfortunately fashion-followers in high places', who had 'preferred expediency to principle, and sociology to theology'; while Mrs Brenda Wolfe portrayed the Church of England as 'in danger of becoming an atrophied anachronism, without principle or courage of vision', which was paying too much attention to the 'pain or outrage or offence or what you will' of 'those insecure little clergymen who cannot face the loss of their only remaining status symbol'.[72]

In the face of such uncompromising views, it was not clear when would be a propitious moment for the bishops to bring the issue forward again, but they did so in November 1978. In the meantime, there had been significant developments in other parts of the Anglican Communion. On 29 July 1974, three American bishops had ordained eleven women in the Church of the Advocate, Philadelphia, without the consent of the General Convention; but this body decided in 1976 to ordain women to the priesthood, and accepted the ministry of the eleven women. In 1975 and 1976, the Churches in Canada and New Zealand also accepted the principle of women's ordination to the priesthood. In America, the issue and the manner of its resolution had divided the Church, and in opening the General Synod debate in 1978, the Bishop of Birmingham attempted to show that discord would have been even greater had the measure not been passed. In opposing the motion, the Bishop of Truro, Graham Leonard, who as Bishop of London was to be one of the most prominent opponents of women's ordination, reiterated the view that while it was 'unthinkable to attribute gender to God', sexual differentiation was fundamental in the incarnation. He also attacked what he saw as the basic incoherence of liberal theology in its attitude to Scripture, characterizing it as 'an attitude which regards not only St Paul but our Lord himself as so conditioned by the cultural and social conditions of the time that they were incapable of transcending them', and he went on to ask, 'If both our Lord and St Paul were so conditioned, what about us? By what criteria do we judge that our conditioning in this century accords with the Divine will but that in the earlier generations does not?' At the end of the debate, the motion was lost (House of Bishops 32:17; House of Clergy 94:149; House of Laity 120:106).[73]

When the result was announced, Una Kroll, a London doctor, deaconess, and well-known campaigner for women's ordination, shouted her now famous comment from the public gallery, 'We asked you for bread and you gave us a stone'; and Monica Furlong has described the way she and other women felt betrayed and humiliated by the decision given that Synod had already declared in 1975 that there were no fundamental theological objections. In July 1979, the Movement for the Ordination of Women was founded, with the Bishop of Manchester, Stanley Booth-Clibborn, as its first Moderator, and Mrs Margaret Webster as its Executive Secretary.[74] MOW members took part in some highly publicized events, such as a banner-waving protest at an ordination service in St Paul's Cathedral in July 1980, and produced literature in favour of women's ordination that set out to present a vision of 'the liberating and fulfilling power of a priesthood more representative of the whole of humanity'.[75] From 1986, MOW produced its own journal, *Chrysalis*.

In 1985, opponents of women's ordination formed the Association for the Apostolic Ministry, which also produced its own literature, and from 1987 a newsletter, *Aambit*. Its membership included both Anglo-Catholics and Evangelicals. One of its aims was 'to educate Church opinion, and in particular those who will influence synodical decisions', and at its conference in 1987, members were urged to 'ensure that every vacancy is filled or contested by alert energetic like-minded people'.[76]

Another new organization was Women Against the Ordination of Women (WAOW), which was initially led by Margaret Hood and Margaret Hewitt. WAOW saw the demand for women's ordination as a product of secular feminism (its first aim was 'to combat misplaced feminism in worship and theology'), which threatened traditional Christian family values in a wide range of areas. If scriptural authority were to be set aside over this issue, it was feared, Christ's marriage laws, 'which entirely rule out re-marriage after divorce and homosexual relationships of every kind', would also be in jeopardy.[77] WAOW's stance implied a highly conservative vision of the complementary roles of men and women in society. Writing in *The Times* in January 1986, Margaret Hood rejected what she called 'the militant feminism that has entered the Church', and called instead for a 'Christian feminism' that recognized motherhood as the true fulfilment of a woman's God-given nature. From this it followed that 'those women who are denied the ultimate fulfilment of their womanhood offer their pain and loss and deprivation, back to God, acknowledging that it is his will'. This is a view of women's ontological status not far removed from Gregg's concern for the Victorian 'redundant woman', who, because of unwelcome demographical trends, could not find her true vocation in marriage.[78]

The year 1987 saw the launch of yet another body, Cost of Conscience, a grouping of clergy opposed to the ordination of women; from its inception, this body was pledged to fight for the future place of opponents of women's ordination within the Church of England, and for provision for those who felt unable to remain if the legislation were passed.

By 1987, such eventualities had become possible in the foreseeable future. A measure that would have allowed women ordained abroad to minister in another Province with the consent of its archbishop was defeated in the General Synod in July 1986. This received the required 50 per cent majority in the diocesan synods (thirty-five for, eight against), but failed to gain the necessary two-thirds majority in the final vote in the General Synod as article 8 business – the same final hurdle facing the proposal to ordain women to the priesthood.[79]

However, in November 1984 the General Synod had taken the first step in this process, which did not require a two-thirds majority, by passing a motion 'That this Synod asks the Standing Committee to bring forward legislation to permit the Ordination of Women to the Priesthood in the Provinces of Canterbury and York' (House of Bishops 41:6; House of Clergy 131:98; House of Laity 135:79). The Synod had before it another detailed background report compiled by the indefatigable Christian Howard, which drew attention among other matters to the position in other English Protestant churches. The Baptist Union was recorded as having fifty-eight women ministers, the Methodist Church – which had ordained women ministers since 1974 – had six female superintendents, and the United Reformed Church had 165 women out of 800 active ministers.[80]

Before the 1984 vote, Clifford Longley warned in *The Times* that the fierce opposition of about one-third of the active churchgoing membership of the Church of England raised the prospect of a split if the measure went through, and asked whether, faced with such a prospect, the uncommitted members of Synod would think 'the cause of "justice for women" is worth such mayhem'. In any event, he foresaw the final requirement of gaining a two-thirds majority as a decisive obstacle, and described the significance of the Synod debate for the supporters of women's ordination as no more than 'another gentle squeeze from which their daughters or grand-daughters may ultimately benefit'.[81] While nearly all of this proved to be wrong, his emphasis on the increasingly divisive nature of the issue was not, and

255

it was further highlighted by the subsequent report of the standing committee of the General Synod which, in proposing safeguards for bishops, clergy, and congregations that could not accept women priests, seemed to raise the spectre of division and bitterness being permanently and formally enshrined within the Church.[82] In accepting this report, Synod also accepted an amendment to enable the House of Bishops to present their own report before any legislation was drawn up. In July 1985, Synod debated and passed a motion allowing women to become deacons; and it was clear from the fears expressed by some speakers that this was seen as a further step towards the priesthood, but any further action waited upon the promised report of the House of Bishops.

This was presented to Synod in February 1987.[83] It dealt very briefly with the theological principles involved, seeing the central issue as whether the ordination of women to the priesthood was 'a legitimate development', and not 'a fundamental change' to the nature of the Church's ministry, which in turn depended on accepting 'that it does not belong to the nature of the ordained priesthood that it is necessarily male'.[84] The bishops went on to consider possible safeguards for incumbents, laity, and bishops who were opposed to the measure. Following formal acceptance of the report, the Archbishop of Canterbury's motion that the standing committee should be asked to bring forward legislation based on its principles was passed (House of Bishops 32:8; House of Clergy 135:70; House of Laity 150:67).

In June 1988, the bishops produced a much longer document, which dealt more fully with theological matters.[85] This made it very clear that they were not of one mind, and arguments for and against women's ordination were consequently outlined without any attempt to weigh their relative importance – much less to decide between them. The bishops declared themselves divided over 'the different weight we place upon the significance of the maleness of Jesus in the incarnation and the relation of that maleness both to the nature of God and also to the nature of men and women created in God's image'; divided over 'the thrust of biblical teaching'; and divided over the Church of England's authority to make such a change without the consent of the wider Church. In summing up these positions, it was clear that the issues involved were complex, interrelated, and, on both sides, involved making contemporary judgements about the significance of gender differences and about the right ordering of society. Thus opponents of women's ordination claimed that:

An all male priesthood will witness to those things about the nature and being of God which were signified in the particularity of Jesus' maleness: a male priesthood will continue more faithfully to represent the priesthood of Christ in the sacramental life of the Church: it will point to the role and status of men in relation to women according to the purposes of God in creation and redemption, by testifying to the headship of men over women and the proper subordination of women to men. Those of us who hold this view believe this to be an important witness to our society as men and women struggle to find new patterns of relationship and new roles for women.

On the other side, it was argued that 'the continuation of an exclusively male priestly ministry in twentieth-century England actually obscures the Gospel', and that 'the insights and the experiences of the society around us stand in judgement upon our continuing exclusive practice'.[86] The report was received by Synod, which then gave general approval to the Draft Priests (Ordination of Women) Measure (House of Bishops 28:21; House of Clergy 137:102; House of Laity 134:93).

The draft measure and draft canons were then referred to the diocesan synods, where thirty-eight out of forty-five approved the proposed legislation, and General Synod prepared to debate the final approval or rejection of the measure on 11 November 1992. Votes cast at York, when Synod met in July 1992, suggested that the final vote in November would be close in terms of gaining the necessary two-thirds majority in all three Houses, and that this might well not be achieved, since the House of Laity voted in favour at York, but only by 148:93, a majority of 61.4 per cent and thirteen votes short of the required number.[87] When it became clear that the outcome might depend upon the votes of a small handful of waverers, intense lobbying took place, and both MOW and WAOW placed large advertisements in the ecclesiastical press. Parliamentary-style whipping tactics were reported to have been used by the Rev. Peter Geldard, the leader of the Catholic group, while the chairman of the liberal Open Synod group spoke of 'continuous conversations' and signs of last minute 'movement in the clergy and laity'. Such shifts of opinion were most evident in the Evangelical wing of the Church, one of whose leaders spoke of 'an awful lot of lobbying and arm twisting'.[88]

The debate itself aroused a great deal of media interest, including the broadcasting of large parts of the afternoon's proceedings on television; however, in practice there was little new that could be said, and because of the large numbers of Synod members who wished to speak, individual contributions were necessarily short. Some opponents of the legislation tended to concentrate more on the motion's shortcomings, and the difficulties that a vote in favour would create for the Church, than on the fundamental theological issues involved. Thus the Bishop of London, David Hope, argued that notwithstanding the proposed rights of bishops to forbid the ordination of women, or their exercising priestly functions within his diocese, and of parochial church councils to make declarations against accepting a female incumbent or a woman celebrating Holy Communion in their parish, those who could not accept the legislation would find themselves 'ignored and marginalised'.[89] In his concluding speech against the motion, the Archdeacon of Leicester, David Silk, expressed the same fear. He not only argued that neither 'the plain meaning of Scripture' nor 'the faith and order that we claim to share with other great historic Churches' warranted such a step, but felt that 'in the end the legislation will ease out one particular point of view'.[90] In reply, the Bishop of Guildford contended that the Church of England had not only to consider its relations with Rome and the East, but with the rest of the Anglican Communion, and that 'ever since the Reformation . . . at times it is necessary to accept responsibility for our own decisions in the pursuit of truth'. The legislation itself he described as 'pastoral in its understanding and intention', and as for the appeal made to the authority of Scripture and tradition, he described the latter as 'a living and organic truth, grounded in Scripture as the Spirit of God leads us to put old truth into new terms'. In conclusion, he warned Synod that the question would not go away, and urged them to vote in accordance with the wishes expressed by a majority of the members of the Church of England.[91]

The motion was carried by 39:13 in the House of Bishops, 176:74 in the House of Clergy, and 169:82 in the House of Laity. Having gained the necessary two-thirds majority, the measure was scrutinized by the Ecclesiastical Committee of the House of Commons, as a result of which safeguards for those unable to accept the ministry of women were enshrined in an Act of Synod in November 1993. By then, on 29 October, the House of Commons had voted by 215:21 in favour of the legislation.[92]

On 22 February 1994, the final legal requirement for the ordination of women to the priesthood was completed when Canon C4B was accepted in Synod without a debate. Final approval was also given to the Act that allowed parishes to refuse to accept a woman priest, and to seek alternative episcopal oversight should their parochial church councils so desire. Despite an eirenic speech from Dr Carey that welcomed 'the rich and diverse gifts women will bring to the priestly ministry', while promising opponents of the legislation 'a full and honoured place within the church', controversy continued. Supporters of women's ordination were resentful at what they saw as undue concessions to the opposition, while Forward in Faith, the umbrella organization of those on the other side, predicted an exodus of over a thousand priests and bishops from the Church.[93]

On Saturday 12 March 1994, the first thirty-two women priests were ordained in Bristol Cathedral by Bishop Barry Rogerson, a long-standing supporter of MOW. Despite fears that the service might be disrupted by protesters (a team of vergers patrolled the congregation in search of troublemakers), the historic service passed off without incident amid scenes of tearful jubilation. The following day many of the priests celebrated their first Eucharist in their local churches. At St Paul's Church in Clifton, Angela Berners-Wilson presided over a packed congregation that included veterans of the campaign such as Una Kroll, Margaret Webster, and Joyce Bennett. The feelings of those present, as elsewhere, were mixed: delight at what seemed both right and natural, surprise and sadness that it had taken so long to achieve.[94]

The bitterness of opponents of the measure was increased by the narrowness with which it received the necessary two-thirds majority: had only two lay members voted the other way, the measure would have been lost. This, however, was to ignore the fact that notwithstanding the high degree of unanimity needed to bring about any fundamental change within the Church through synodical government, a clear majority of its members, episcopal, clerical, and lay, in votes expressed in deanery, diocesan, and general synods, were in favour of opening the ordained ministry to women. In fact, much of the feeling surrounding the issue is hard to convey from a bare summary of theological debates, since it included hostilities and suspicions that could not readily be admitted in the measured proceedings of Synod. Women deacons often felt slighted and snubbed by their treatment by male colleagues, whom they saw as clinging to status and power.[95] The alleged misogyny and conservatism of Anglo-Catholic priests was also linked to the question of homosexuality. As one writer in the *Sunday Telegraph* put it, 'Every unmarried bishop in the synod either abstained or voted against women priests last November. The opposition to women's ordination has relied on secretive male homosexuals with a fear of women's sexuality.'[96] Feelings of this kind were real enough, even if they did not form part of overt theological discourse.

At this level, part of the reason for the success of the women's ordination movement lay in the flaws in the arguments put forward by its opponents. Most appealed to notions of Scripture and tradition that implied that the Christian revelation had been given in a form whose content and interpretation were above and beyond the flux of history. Yet, as this book has tried to show, the constraints of culture cannot be so easily dismissed, and in this respect the Church's theology might best be described not as a process of objective reasoning, but as one of thinking impure thoughts about women, some of them very impure indeed. Ironically, Evangelicals and Anglo-Catholics who opposed the ordination of women were themselves living proof of the impossibility of a direct appeal to authoritative truth, free from the limitations of human interpretation, since they were in nearly all other contexts sharply divided over the nature of the Church and the authority of Scripture and tradition.

Divisions over hermeneutical first principles were to be of particular importance within the Evangelical camp, where there were clear differences over the significance of the Pauline doctrine of headship, and the force of the Pauline prohibitions on women's speaking in public.[97] In an article that he contributed to *Feminine in the Church* in 1984, George Carey, who was then at Trinity Theological College, Bristol (which under Jim Packer had been a stronghold of Evangelical fundamentalism), argued that St Paul 'lived within the limitations of his own culture and he could not have known the total implications of the Christian concept of humanity'. What was needed, he went on, was 'to maintain a proper balance between the finality of the Christian revelation as contained in Scripture and its openness to new possibilities in Christ'.[98] It was this kind of reasoning – which seemed to assert both the paramount authority of Scripture while allowing for its reinterpretation by later generations – as well as the lead given by an Archbishop with impeccable Evangelical credentials, which did much to weaken the force of biblical fundamentalism and to win over crucial Evangelical votes.[99]

Organized Anglo-Catholic opposition remained firmer, but was never enough on its own to defeat the measure.[100] Since the heady days of the 1930s, the Anglo-Catholic wing of the Church of England had been in decline (for example, in 1983, the celebrations to mark the one hundred and fiftieth anniversary of the beginnings of the Oxford Movement hardly made any impact on the Church), and part of its problem lay in a crisis of identity as to what constituted the Catholic tradition within Anglicanism – particularly in relation to the Roman Catholic Church.[101] The argument that the Church of England lacked the authority to ordain women as priests did not persuade those within the Church who regarded the Reformation as a fundamental and justifiable break with Rome; and the fact that the 1896 papal declaration stating that Anglican orders were null and void remained in force, weakened the persuasiveness of the claim that ordaining women would do significant damage to Anglican–Roman relations.[102]

On the other side, the frequently made assertion that supporters of the ordination of women had capitulated to essentially secular values was more of a debating tactic than an accurate description of their primary motivation. Nor is there much evidence that feminist theology played a decisive part in the formation of their thinking.[103] This charge was made, for example, in a volume of essays published in 1972 entitled *Why Not? Priesthood and the Ministry of Women*, edited by Michael Bruce and G. E. Duffield. The latter claimed that 'feminist thinking is widespread today and has influenced churchmen', and that for opponents of change, 'The crucial question is how we react to secular feminist pressure.'[104]

In the same year, the Anglican Group for the Ordination of Women to the Historic Ministry of the Church held a one-day conference to consider the future, which did not show much sign of being dominated by the kinds of consideration outlined by Duffield. Thus Miss Mollie Batten alluded to the women's liberation movement as one that the Church in general ought to welcome, but not uncritically, since it contained elements 'which taken to extreme we would none of us as Christians wish to support'; moreover, she went on, 'we must not be labelled Women's Lib in the life of the Church, because our aims are really not based on women's rights but on the good of the Church of God and because we think the Holy Spirit is leading the Church of God in relation to the contribution of women in every form of ministry'.[105] The rest of the conference was largely devoted to discussing the difficulties women encountered as a result of the limitations imposed upon their ministry. Thus Una Kroll described the way her work as a deaconess was undermined by having to seek express permission from a family in order to take a funeral, while a member of a religious community outlined the difficulties her order faced in always having to rely on the availability of a male priest to give absolution and to celebrate the Eucharist. Such limitations imposed upon their ministry had long been felt to be frustrating and incomprehensible. In the evidence submitted by the Anglican Group for the Ordination of Women to the Historic Ministry to the Archbishop's Commission in 1963, one deaconess wrote:

> In fulfilling missionary and ministerial functions one seems naturally to be led on to wish to fulfil them in every respect, and to find barriers against doing so purely artificial. For instance, why should one preach, but not celebrate the Holy Communion? Or why should one visit the sick but not give absolution? Theologically, Word and Sacrament should not be separated. [106]

Despite such frustrations, the experience of women's ministry by lay people was often a positive one, which made such restrictions seem unacceptable. As one member of the House of Laity – who had witnessed the ministry of six women in her parish over twenty-two years – told the Synod at York in July 1992, 'It feels right and good to have female clergy in the parish', and she went on to argue that it was valuable to be able to benefit from 'a woman's insight and experience'. Such an argument was all the more powerful since it was based not upon radical notions of identity between the sexes, but upon the more conservative ideal of their complementarity to which, in a different sense, opponents of women's ordination also appealed.

This is not to deny that changing social conditions were an important factor in the process of doctrinal change. This was particularly the case over the question of the significance of Christian symbolism and gender relations. Evangelical arguments about male headship in the order of creation and in the Pauline texts implied what Roger Beckwith called 'the exclusion of the subordinate partner in the human race from the principal offices in the Christian ministry'. [107] The same principle of 'authority and subordination' also applied to marital relationships. Yet however much proponents of this case endeavoured to explain that subordination as a theological principle implied no element of inferiority, and allowed for full reciprocity between men and women, economic and social changes that affected familial and professional relationships robbed such language of the credibility and meaning that it possessed in the past.

This was equally true of Anglo-Catholic appeals to the notion of the priest as an icon of Christ whose maleness was not incidental to the theology of creation and redemption, but integral to it. Those who argued in this way were careful to stress that the attribution of gender to God was not possible since, as the Rev. Harry Smythe admitted, 'all such language is in any case metaphorical and, at the level of philosophical analysis, analogical', but nevertheless, he went on, 'it remains the inspired expression of a distinctive and transcendent truth'. This truth was that at the level of symbolism God was endowed primarily with masculine traits.[108] As the Bishop of London, Graham Leonard, claimed, while also denying that God is masculine, Christian symbolism represents 'the fact that in terms of our relationship to God we are essentially feminine and he is masculine to us', and he went on to argue that 'I believe that Christ was incarnate as male because I believe psychologically, and symbolically and to a large extent biologically, the initiative is seen as male.'[109]

Yet such thinking appealed to ideas about gender roles that no longer had much resonance in contemporary society. In his speech to the General Synod in 1978, Graham Leonard regarded 'such fundamental symbolism as the Fatherhood of God and the Sonship of Christ' as given by God 'to represent eternal truths and are therefore not negotiable', but the social context in which symbolic systems acquire, sustain, and lose their meaning and authority could not be so easily dismissed. As Rowan Williams put it, 'If we want to argue the "women's issue" in symbolic terms, we need to see what we are doing in the society we are in', and went on to ask whether in the late twentieth century, the traditional symbolism had come 'to reinforce patterns of inequality' and to be part of 'a systematic devaluing of human female experience'.[110] The Houses of Synod were not, as traditionalists claimed, dominated by passionate advocates of feminist theology and secular feminism, but by far more cautious and conservative members and representatives, for whom appeals to what were essentially Victorian patterns of gender identity and relationships no longer made much sense.

Conclusion

Despite paying considerable attention to the way in which, since the eighteenth century, the Church of England has contributed to, and been influenced by, such socially constructed ideas about gender, this study has not attempted to give any clear-cut answer to the question of how far religion has helped to liberate women's talents and sense of self-worth, or to constrain and deny them. This is partly because of the limited nature of the evidence I have examined. The Anglican

Church has been socially and intellectually among the most conservative of English denominations, and, as indicated by both eighteenth-
century Quaker and Methodist female preaching, and the ordination
of women in the Free Churches in the twentieth century, no overall
conclusions about the role of religion in women's emancipation can
be drawn from the Anglican case alone.

Even within Anglicanism, the record is far from clear cut, which
points to the second difficulty in making any overall assessment –
namely, the fact that the effects of religion on women's lives have
been ambiguous and contradictory. While by its theology and attitudes the Church of England has often limited the roles open to
women within its life, and thereby wasted their talents and denied
their full humanity, Christianity has also sometimes functioned as a
liberating force; this has empowered women to undertake
philanthropic and missionary work, and to make important contributions to Anglican spirituality and worship. Women have not been
mere passive recipients of patriarchal prescriptions, but active agents
in the history of the Church; and this remains true whether they are
seen as accepting, negotiating, or transcending the limitations that it
has tried to impose upon them.

Assessing the significance of women's ordination to the priesthood
is equally problematical. At the level of ecclesiastical politics, which
often misleadingly goes by the name of ecumenism, the shift away
from Rome is decisive at a time when the English Free churches have
been in numerical decline, the Roman Catholic Church in England
has become the largest churchgoing denomination, and when the conservative stance of the Vatican makes it unlikely that the ordination of
women to the priesthood will occur for some time yet. Not just the
decision, but the manner of making it, has reinforced the essentially
Protestant nature of Anglicanism. However much supporters of the
ordination of women have been angered by the power of its opponents
to deny the wishes of the majority for a generation, and traditionalists
have charged the Church with having no stable and coherent basis for
the formulation of doctrine, the course of the debate has highlighted
the importance of the Anglican appeal to contemporary reason and
experience in interpreting Scripture and tradition, and the implications
of the introduction of synodical government for lay participation in
the formulation of fundamental doctrine – a system far removed from
that of the Roman magisterium. This is not to deny that the decision-
making process within the Catholic Church is less monolithic than the
disciplining of theologians such as Hans Küng and Leonardo Boff

might suggest, nor that government by synod is an imperfect model of democracy.[111]

The likely impact of women priests within the Church of England is harder to judge. The mere fact of ordaining women within other denominations, for example in the Baptist Church, has not automatically led to their widespread acceptance, and the rights of incumbents, including the possibility of alternative episcopal oversight, along with the safeguards offered to dissenting bishops and congregations, will make for long-term pockets of hostility to women priests within the Church of England. It seems likely, however, as opponents have tacitly conceded, that as with women's ministry in the diaconate, the enthusiasm, and the spiritual and pastoral gifts that women can bring to the ordained ministry, will hasten their acceptance by the laity, and that in due course women priests will be ordained to the episcopate even though this falls outside the scope of the current legislation.

Such gifts are sorely needed by the Church of England, and it would be idle to pretend that women's ordination will of itself solve the many pressing problems it faces. While the ordination of over a thousand female deacons and the subsequent influx of women seeking ordination would compensate for any loss of disaffected clerical man-power, this does not of itself go to the heart of the crisis facing a Church that increasingly lacks the financial resources to train and pay its full-time ministry. Only by a greater reliance on a non-stipendiary ministry, and on increased lay financial support, can this problem be overcome, yet this in turn raises fundamental questions about the nature and purpose of the priesthood, which has in the past been seen largely in clerical and hierarchical terms. It might, however, be suggested that women's experience of marginalization and powerlessness within the Church may make them less wedded to outdated models of clericalism, and more committed to a vision of enabling and co-operative forms of ministry that embrace both clergy and laity.

Any discussion of the past experience of women entering the priesthood raises other questions. Contrary to the blanket stereotypes of such women as theologically radical militant feminists promulgated by some opponents of women's ordination, their backgrounds, experience, and theological outlooks have been much more diverse. Women seeking ordination will include the wives of clergymen, members of celibate sisterhoods, and lesbian women; and therefore their responses to the social and theological issues of gender and sexuality, which have been thrown into sharp focus by the debates over ordination, are likely to be far from uniform. One ongoing issue concerns the role

265

and significance of feminist theology within the life of the Church. Feminist theology represents potentially the greatest challenge facing contemporary Christianity, since it combines a fundamental critique of the existing social and ecclesiological order with a thoroughgoing deconstruction of the formation and content of traditional doctrine.[112] In that feminist theology highlights the extent to which all theological language about God has in the past been literally man-made, it raises disturbing questions about how far it can ever be said to be more than that. Yet feminist theologians have already been deeply divided over the implications of this for Christian belief, with thinkers such as Daphne Hampson declaring herself to be a post-Christian; while others, such as Pamela Young, see feminist theology as an essentially preservative methodology that seeks to uncover a message of sexual equality implicit in the gospel.[113] Women who have stayed in the Church as deacons, despite its blatant sexism, are perhaps more likely to reinforce the latter, more conservative, strand of feminist thought.

A second important question that arises when considering the nature of women's experience of the Church concerns the argument over male and female identity and sexual complementarity. As this study has tried to show, women have sometimes been liberated by definitions of their distinctively maternal qualities of care and compassion, which they have then exercised in the public sphere. Not only opponents of women's ordination, but also some of its advocates, have appealed to the idea of women as 'equal but different' in support of their case. Such a position also finds expression within contemporary feminist theology – for example, in the radical separatist writings of Mary Daly. Yet this kind of anthropology is not without serious limitations. Historically, appeals to the notion of polarized sexual identities have more often been used to define and limit women than to emancipate them, and as a consequence they have had emotionally crippling effects on men who, it is increasingly being realized, have also paid a high cost for the power and privileges of patriarchy. The case for women's ordination to the priesthood ought to rest theologically on the unitary nature of humanness proclaimed in the belief that 'in Christ there is neither Greek nor Jew, male nor female', and on an anthropology in which the qualities of intuitive feeling, imagination, altruism, nurturing, compassion, reason, and moral will are the common possession of men and women; but the implications of this vision remain very much an unresolved area for discussion within the churches.[114]

Yet it would be wrong to conclude merely by emphasizing the

areas of debate and uncertainty that may lie ahead. The first ordinations of women to the priesthood on 12 March 1994 in Bristol
Cathedral were not so much a radical break with the past as the culmination of women's increasing involvement in the life of the Church
over many years. At its heart, the movement for women's ordination
to the priesthood has been a call for justice, and for the overcoming
of patriarchal modes of reasoning and forms of social structure that
have warped and diminished the humanity of both women and men,
and have needlessly limited the creativity and energy available for the
Church's work. A great deal has been heard about the pain and anger
of those who have been opposed to this step, and in so far as this
reflects a proper pastoral determination to live with differences within
the Church this has not been wholly undesirable, yet not to welcome
women's ordination because of the hurt felt by its opponents would be
rather like refusing to dismantle apartheid because of the offence that
would be caused to its defenders. However belatedly, the Church of
England has shown the capacity to transcend the power of man-made
structures and prejudices, and has provided a small but significant
example of the way in which in the history of Christianity there are
never endings, but only beginnings.

Notes

1. B. H. Streeter and E. Picton-Turbervill, *Woman and the Church* (London,
   T. Fisher Unwin, 1917). This volume was produced partly in response to the
   controversy over women preaching during the 1916 National Mission of
   Hope and Repentance; despite Streeter's unpromising conclusion on the subject of women's ordination, he was generally in favour of giving them a
   much larger role in the life of the Church, and of their ultimately being
   admitted to the priesthood.

2. In his *The Myth of the Empty Church* (London, SPCK, 1993), Robin Gill
   points out that there was already an over-provision of church accommodation
   in the nineteenth century, and cautions against adopting over-simplified
   monocausal explanations of secularization. Even so, his figures for the
   decline in Anglican confirmation figures (from 190,000 in 1960 to 62,000 in
   1989) and in Easter week communicants (from 7 per cent of the population in
   1960 to 4.1 per cent in 1988) make stark reading (pp. 217-218).

3. Friedrich Schleiermacher's *On Religion: Speeches to its Cultured Despisers*
   was published in 1799.

4. This is the case, for example, with *The Association for the Apostolic Ministry*, which manages to include such unusual bedfellows as the Bishop of

Chichester, Dr Eric Kemp, and from the Evangelical camp, Dr James Packer. As its literature makes clear, members of the Association 'do not all attach the same force to each of the objections raised' and are sensitive to the charge that theirs is an 'unholy alliance'; what they can agree upon, however, is that 'The whole issue looks depressingly like the Church jumping onto another secular bandwagon', and is yet another example of theological liberalism in a 'Church which has so far been unable to act decisively in the Jenkins affair'. See J. Fenwick, *An Evangelical's Difficulties with the Ordination of Women* (London, Association for an Apostolic Ministry, n.d.).

5. For a clear account of these controversies, see K. W. Clements, *Lovers of Discord: Twentieth-Century Theological Controversies in England* (London, SPCK, 1988).

6. Anne Widdicombe used this image during a BBC Radio 4 interview on the day after the Synod's vote. She has since been received into the Roman Catholic Church.

7. *The Ordination of Women to the Priesthood. The Synod Debate 11 November 1992. The Verbatim Record* (London, Church House Publishing, 1993), p. 23.

8. S. Fletcher, *Maude Royden: A Life* (Oxford, Basil Blackwell, 1989), p. 143. There were also links between those campaigning for women's suffrage and those advocating the admission of women to the ministry in the Free Churches. For example, in 1911, Hatty Baker, who was Secretary of the Free Church League for Women's Suffrage, published a book entitled *Women in the Ministry* (London, C. W. Daniel, 1911), in which she argued that both Paul's teaching on celibacy and his acceptance of slavery had been rightly put aside by the Church, while his reference in 1 Corinthians 11.5 to women praying and prophesying with their heads uncovered indicates that women preached in the early Church. In viewing the biblical evidence *in toto*, she regarded Galatians 3.28 – that in Christ there is neither male nor female – as 'a definitive statement', and claimed that it was impossible to think truly about the nature of God without seeing 'womanly–manly attributes' in the Godhead (pp. 26–27, 47).

9. *Church Times*, 24 July 1914, quoted in Fletcher, *Maude Royden*, p. 143.

10. Fletcher, *Maude Royden*, pp. 146–147.

11. Fletcher, *Maude Royden*, pp. 147–148; B. Heeney, *The Women's Movement in the Church of England 1850–1930* (Oxford, Clarendon Press, 1988), pp. 121–122.

12. Fletcher, *Maude Royden*, p. 152.

13. Heeney, *The Women's Movement in the Church of England*, pp. 123–124.

14. *The Ministry of Women: A Report by a Committee Appointed by the Archbishop of Canterbury* (London, SPCK, 1920).

15. *The Ministry of Women*, p. 9.

16. *The Ministry of Women*.

17. *The Lambeth Conferences (1867–1948)* (London, SPCK, 1948), p. 90.

18. *The Lambeth Conferences (1867–1948)*, pp. 47–48.

19. *The Lambeth Conferences (1867–1948)*, pp. 78–79.

20. The year 1930 also saw the creation of the interdenominational Society for the Equal Ministry of Men and Women, of which Maude Royden was the first President, and Charles Raven the best-known Anglican member.

21. Fletcher, *Maude Royden*, p. 252.

22. G. Neville (ed.), *The Diaries of Edward Lee Hicks Bishop of Lincoln 1910–1919* (Lincoln Record Society, Boydell Press, 1993), p. 227.

23. M. Stansgate, *My Exit Visa* (London, Hutchinson, 1992), p. 74. Margaret Stansgate became a founder member of the interdenominational Society for the Ministry of Women in the Church after the disbanding of the League of the Church Militant, but felt increasingly frustrated by the Church's attitude to women's ordination. The final straw came in 1948 when, after she was invited to be a consultant on women's place in the Church at the first meeting of the World Council of Churches in Amsterdam, Archbishop Fisher felt it necessary to write to the Secretary to warn him that her views were not those of the Church. At this point she became a Congregationalist. Her son Tony Benn was able to continue the family's interest in the campaign for women's ordination by speaking in the debate on the legislation in the House of Commons, asking memorably, what kind of man would refuse to receive the sacrament from a woman.

24. *The Ministry of Women: Report of the Archbishop's Commission* (London, Church Assembly Publications Board, 1935).

25. *The Ministry of Women*, p. 29.

26. *Women and the Ministry: Some Considerations on the Report of the Archbishop's Commission on the Ministry of Women Published on Behalf of the Council of the Church Union* (London, Church Literature Association, 1936), pp. 6–7.

27. *Women and the Ministry*, p. 17.

28. *Women and the Ministry*, p. 24.

29. *Women and the Ministry*, p. 24.

30. *Church Times*, 6 December 1935.

31. *Church Times*, 20 December 1935.

32. Quoted in *The Question of Holy Orders: A Memorandum to the Commission Set Up in 1963 by the Archbishops of Canterbury and York*, p. 53. The memorandum was prepared by the Anglican Group for the Ordination of Women to the Historic Ministry of the Church, and was printed for private circulation in September 1963.

33. Heeney, *The Women's Movement in the Church of England*, p. 134.

34. These statements of aims appear on its publications.

35. *Women and Holy Orders: Being the Report of a Commission Appointed by the Archbishops of Canterbury and York* (London, Church Information Office, 1966), pp. 89–90; Fletcher, *Maude Royden*, p. 281. Li Tim Oi was later a victim of the Cultural Revolution, and spent years in prison doing hard labour. She came to London in 1984 to celebrate the fortieth anniversary of her priesting, and was present at the 1988 Lambeth Conference. She was a supporter of the Movement for the Ordination of Women, and was one of the concelebrants following the consecration of Bishop Barbara Harris in the USA in 1989. In May 1991, she received an Honorary Doctorate of Divinity from Trinity College, Toronto, and she died in Canada on 27 February 1992, aged eighty-four. I have taken these biographical details from *Chrysalis* (July 1992), p. 7. For Archbishop Fisher's involvement in these events, see E. Carpenter, *Archbishop Fisher: His Life and Times* (Norwich, Canterbury Press, 1991), pp. 659–666.

36. *The Lambeth Conference 1948: The Encyclical Letter from the Bishops; Together with Resolutions and Reports* (London, SPCK, 1948), pp. 119–120.

37. C. S. Lewis, *God in the Dock* (London, Collins, 1979), pp. 87–94.

38. R. Howard, *Should Women Be Priests?* (Oxford, Basil Blackwell, 1949).

39. Howard, *Should Women Be Priests?*, pp. 17–19.

40. Howard, *Should Women Be Priests?*, pp. 35–37. The assumption that it was a woman's place to remain at home and bring up children was frequently advanced as an objection to women being ordained. For example, in 1933, Vera Kenmure, who had been accepted as a minister at Partick Congregational Church in Glasgow, was forced to resign on the birth of her first child (Fletcher, *Maude Royden*, p. 267).

41. *Theology*, vol. 57 (1954), p. 325.

42. *Theology*, vol. 57 (1954), p. 328. Criticisms of this kind were often said by opponents of the ordination of women to be a product of the feminism and secularism of the 1960s and 1970s. As Bailey's article indicates, they can be found at an earlier date.

43. *Theology*, vol. 57 (1954), pp. 330–334.

44. Mascall was subsequently Professor of Historical Theology at King's College, London, until his retirement in 1973. He remained a prominent opponent of the ordination of women.

45. *Theology*, vol. 57 (1954), p. 428. Mascall repeated this argument in *Women and the Priesthood of the Church* (London, Church Literature Association, 1960).

46. *Theology*, vol. 57 (1954), p. 454.

47. *Theology*, vol. 57 (1954), p. 455.

48. Bailey's best-known work was *Homosexuality and the Western Christian*

Tradition (London, Longmans, 1955).

49.   *Gender and Ministry: A Report Prepared for the Church Assembly by the Central Advisory Council for the Ministry* (London, Church Information Office, 1962), p. 12.

50.   *Church Assembly Report of Proceedings*, vol. 42, no. 1 (1962) (London, CIO, 1962), pp. 681–714.

51.   *Women and Holy Orders*, pp. 8–11.

52.   *Women and Holy Orders*, pp. 25–29.

53.   *Women and Holy Orders*, pp. 110–112. Demant's view was not an eccentricity of his own. A female contributor to the Roman Catholic journal *The Month* declared that the pastoral role of the priest 'asks for a power of abstraction, in the mind as well as in the emotions, which is probably rarely found in women' (I. Gorres, 'Women in Holy Orders?', *The Month*, vol. 34 (1965), pp. 84–93).

54.   *Women and Holy Orders*, pp. 116–119.

55.   M. Furlong, *A Dangerous Delight: Women and Power in the Church* (London, SPCK, 1991), p. 91. Monica Furlong has been one of the leaders of the Movement for the Ordination of Women, and in 1982 became its first female Moderator.

56.   *Church Assembly Report of Proceedings*, vol. 47, no. 3 (1967) (London, CIO, 1967), p. 281.

57.   *Church Times*, 7 July 1967.

58.   *Church Assembly Report of Proceedings*, vol. 47, no. 3 (1967) (London, CIO, 1967), pp. 278–318.

59.   *Women and the Ordained Ministry: Report of an Anglican–Methodist Commission on Women and Holy Orders* (London, SPCK, 1968).

60.   *Women and the Ordained Ministry*, p. 13.

61.   *The Lambeth Conference 1968: Resolutions and Reports* (London, SPCK, 1968), pp. 39–40.

62.   *The Ordination of Women to the Priesthood: A Consultative Document Presented by the Advisory Council for the Church's Ministry* (London, Church Information Office, 1972), pp. 3, 55–56.

63.   On 5 October 1985, Joyce Bennett, then retired and assisting as chaplain to the Chinese congregation at St Martin-in-the-Fields, wrote an article in *The Times* calling on the General Synod to ordain women to the priesthood.

64.   *Daily Telegraph*, 16 November 1971.

65.   *The Ordination of Women to the Priesthood*, p. 57.

66.   Christian Howard played an important part in the campaign for women's ordination, later becoming a member of the Executive of the British Council of Churches and a Vice-Moderator of MOW. For her involvement, see M.

Webster, *A New Strength, A New Song: The Journey to Women's Priesthood* (London, Mowbray, 1994).

67. Webster, *A New Strength*, p. 29.

68. Webster, *A New Strength*, pp. 40–45.

69. *General Synod Report of Proceedings*, vol. 3, no. 4 (1972) (London, CIO, 1972), p. 716.

70. *The Times*, 10 March 1975.

71. *General Synod Report of Proceedings*, vol. 6, no. 2 (1975) (London, CIO, 1975), pp. 542–614.

72. *Church Times*, 11 July 1975.

73. *General Synod Report of Proceedings*, vol. 9, no. 3 (1978) (London, CIO, 1978), pp. 996–1071.

74. Furlong, *A Dangerous Delight*, pp. 100–102; Webster, *A New Strength*, p. 50.

75. M. Perry, *Towards a Whole Ministry* (London, MOW, n.d.).

76. *Aambit*, vol. 1 (November 1987).

77. *Scriptural Authority; Quite a Revelation!* (WAOW, London, n.d.).

78. M. Hood, 'Woman's Unique Bond with God', *The Times*, 18 January 1986.

79. J. Field-Bibb, *Women Towards Priesthood: Ministerial Politics and Feminist Praxis* (Cambridge, CUP, 1991), pp. 149–155.

80. *The Ordination of Women to the Priesthood: Further Report* (London, CIO, 1984), pp. 50–51. The English Congregationalist Church ordained its first minister, Constance Coltman, in 1917; a Baptist congregation first invited a woman to take pastoral charge in 1918, and women 'pastors' were recognized in 1925, but were not allowed to take the title 'minister' until 1957 (E. Kaye, 'A Turning-Point in the Ministry of Women: The Ordination of the First Woman to the Christian Ministry in England in September 1917', in W. J. Sheils and D. Wood (eds), *Women in the Church*, Studies in Church History 27 (Oxford, Basil Blackwell, 1990), pp. 505–512). The Methodist Church Conference of 1973 voted to admit women to the ministry, and seventeen were ordained in 1974 (Field-Bibb, *Women Towards Priesthood*, p. 66).

81. *The Times*, 12 November 1984. Longley gained a well-deserved reputation as an unusually well-informed and balanced religious commentator, though his treatment of the women's ordination issue was a good example of the way in which his judgements were sometimes coloured by a Roman Catholic perspective.

82. Field-Bibb, *Women Towards Priesthood*, pp. 168–171.

83. *The Ordination of Women to the Priesthood: A Report by the House of Bishops* (London, General Synod of the Church of England, 1987).

84. *The Ordination of Women to the Priesthood: A Report*, p. 2.

85. *The Ordination of Women to the Priesthood: A Second Report by the House of Bishops of the General Synod of the Church of England* (London, Church House Publishing, 1988).

86. *The Ordination of Women to the Priesthood: A Second Report*, pp. 98–99.

87. *Church Times*, 17 July 1992.

88. *The Times*, 11 November 1992.

89. *The Ordination of Women to the Priesthood: The Synod Debate 11 November 1992* (London, Church House Publishing, 1992), pp. 19–21. The rights of incumbents in this matter were already enshrined in canon law. The legislation also included a draft measure that made financial provision for those clergy who felt forced to resign as a result of the measure on women's ordination being passed.

90. *The Ordination of Women to the Priesthood: The Synod Debate*, pp. 70–73.

91. *The Ordination of Women to the Priesthood: The Synod Debate*, pp. 73–76.

92. *The Times*, 30 October 1993.

93. *Guardian*, 23 February 1994.

94. This account is based upon my own impressions.

95. See, for example, Elizabeth Canham's experiences of male chauvinism, in her *Pilgrimage to Priesthood* (London, SPCK, 1983).

96. *Sunday Telegraph*, 28 March 1993. The Lesbian and Gay Christian Movement was in fact largely in favour of women's ordination, seeing it as a step in the process of dismantling traditional gender roles from which homosexual people have suffered. The secrecy and insecurity of homosexual clergy was partly the result of the Church's discriminatory teaching, but the fact that the highest concentration of clerical opposition to women's ordination and that of homosexual clergy are both in the diocese of London gives some plausibility to the writer's claim.

97. These differences were evident, for example, in C. Cranston (ed.), *Evangelicals and the Ordination of Women* (Bramcote, Grove Books, 1973). While Joyce Baldwin could see no evidence in the biblical texts for ruling out women's ordination, Jim Packer used the same texts to argue that the biblical doctrine of male headship was not compatible with women's holding ultimate authority in the Church, though it might be possible, he thought, to envisage some form of 'group presbyterate' in which the leader would be male. In his conclusion, Colin Cranston argued that the process of revelation, which was an educative one, needed further thought by evangelicals, since it took place 'within the framework of human knowledge and understanding at the time'.

98. M. Furlong (ed.), *Feminine in the Church* (London, SPCK, 1984), pp. 48, 53–54.

99. It was not, however, the kind of argument to persuade evangelicals such as

Tony Higton. Higton had based his forthright opposition to the acceptability of homosexual practices upon what appeared to him to be the plain meaning of Scripture, and he could not accept that other equally clear scriptural passages could now be put on one side. Although less publicized than the Anglo-Catholic case, the dilemmas facing evangelicals unable to accept the ordination of women by the Church of England are just as acute. For example, a group of evangelical theological college principals in favour of women's ordination and members of the Reform Group opposed to the measure met together, having recognized 'the clear possibility that Evangelicals in the Church of England could split asunder over the issue of the ordination of women, and that some may feel so marginalised that they are forced to find a home elsewhere' (*Church of England Newspaper*, 30 July 1993).

100. This is not to imply that Anglo-Catholic opinion in the parishes was by any means united in its opposition to the change. This is particularly hard to judge within a tradition that has been characterized by a tightly organized clericalism that has not encouraged lay participation in decision-making.

101. For the modern history of Anglo-Catholicism and a discussion of the problems it faces, see W. Pickering, *Anglo-Catholicism: A Study in Religious Ambiguity* (London, Routledge, 1989). Pickering quotes a survey in the *Daily Telegraph* in 1987, which suggested that about 30 per cent of Anglo-Catholic clergy were not opposed to the ordination of women. It remains to be seen whether a group like Affirming Catholicism can succeed in creating an Anglo-Catholic identity capable of coming to terms with social and intellectual change, or whether in the longer term the crisis created by the ordination issue will prove terminal.

102. An exchange of letters between the Archbishop of Canterbury and Pope Paul VI, in which the latter described the ordination of women to the priesthood within the Anglican Communion as the introduction of 'an element of grave difficulty' into the process of dialogue that had resulted in the Agreed Statements of the Anglican/Roman Catholic International Commission on the Eucharist and the Ministry, was made public and became part of the 1975 debate over women's ordination. This correspondence, and the 1984–1986 exchange of letters between Pope John Paul II, Robert Runcie, and Cardinal Jan Willibrands, President of the Vatican Secretariat for Promoting Christian Unity, have been published as *Women Priests: Obstacles to Unity?* (London, Catholic Truth Society, 1986). Also included with these documents was the Declaration *Inter Insigniores*, issued in 1976, which sets out the theological basis for the Roman Catholic Church's opposition to women's ordination.

103. These charges were made most forcefully by the Rev. William Oddie, who claimed that there was a hidden agenda behind the movement for the ordination of women to the priesthood that was inspired by feminist theologians such as Rosemary Ruether, whose work exhibited, in his view, a 'deep hatred and disgust for the Christian tradition'. These claims were made in an article in *The Times*, 15 October 1984, and formed the substance of his book *What Will Happen to God?* (London, SPCK, 1984). Apart from caricaturing Ruether's position, as well as those of other feminist theologians, Oddie

274

obscured the diversity of theological opinion among those, including female deacons, who were in favour of women's ordination.

104. M. Bruce and G. E. Duffield, *Why Not? Priesthood and the Ministry of Women* (Abingdon, Marcham Manor Press, 1972), p. 18.

105. *The Present and the Future - Women's Ministry in the Church of England: Report of a One Day Conference Saturday, 30th September, 1972* (London, Anglican Group for the Ordination of Women to the Priesthood, 1972), pp. 18-19.

106. *The Question of Holy Orders*, pp. 55-56.

107. R. Beckwith, 'The Bearing of Holy Scripture', in P. Moore (ed.), *Man, Woman, and Priesthood* (London, SPCK, 1978), pp. 45-62.

108. H. Smythe, *Sex, Symbol, Sacrament: Some Theological Considerations in the Question of the Ordination of Women to the Priesthood within the Church of England* (London, Association for the Apostolic Ministry, 1989).

109. Quoted in *The Ordination of Women to the Priesthood: Further Report*, p. 84.

110. R. Williams, 'Women and the Ministry: A Case for Theological Seriousness', in Furlong (ed.), *Feminine in the Church*, pp. 11-27.

111. For the weaknesses of the latter, see K. Medhurst and G. Moyser, *Church and Politics in a Secular Age* (Oxford, Clarendon Press, 1988).

112. This has so far not been true, for example, of South American liberation theology, which, however radically it has challenged existing power structures, has shown itself to be markedly conservative in other areas of doctrine.

113. D. Hampson, *Theology and Feminism* (Oxford, Basil Blackwell, 1990), regards patriarchy as ineradicable from the Christian tradition, while P. Young, *Feminist Theology/Christian Theology: In Search of Method* (Minneapolis, Fortress Press, 1990) can still look to the Jesus of the Gospels as central to the development of women's spirituality.

114. This case is argued by R. Ruether in 'Imago Dei, Christian Tradition and Feminist Hermeneutics', in K. Borresen (ed.), *Image of God and Gender Models in Judaeo-Christian Tradition* (Oslo, Solum Forlang, 1991), pp. 258-281. See also the Bishop of Kingston's (Peter Selby) essay, 'They Make Such Good Pastors', in R. Holloway (ed.), *Who Needs Feminism? Men Respond to Sexism in the Church* (London, SPCK, 1991), pp. 125-134. Selby argues that because women have been on the receiving end of sexism they have developed resources of nourishment and healing that men also need, but that 'the emancipation of women . . . in the Church or anywhere else, does not rest on any supposed endowments which women may be alleged to have because they are women'.
    This position also has important implications for women's wider emancipation, since until it is recognized that men bear full and equal responsibility for the care of children, both covert discrimination against

women in the professions, and inadequate levels of publicly funded child-care facilities are likely to continue.

Bibliography

Unpublished primary sources

Josephine Butler Papers, Fawcett Library, London.
Mothers' Union Council Minutes, Mary Sumner House, London.
Pusey House Papers, Pusey House, Oxford.
United Society for the Propagation of the Gospel Archives, Rhodes House, Oxford.

Newspapers and periodicals

Aambit
Chrysalis
India's Women
Mothers in Council
The Christian Lady's Magazine
The Christian Observer
The Church of England Newspaper
The Church Times
Daily Telegraph
The Gentleman's Magazine
The Grain of Mustard Seed
The Guardian

The International Review of Missions
The Month
The Nineteenth Century
Sunday Telegraph
The Times
Theology

Printed primary sources

Anon., *A Servant of the Poor: or, Some Account of the Life and Death of a Parochial Mission Woman by a Lady Manager* (London, SPCK, 1874).

Anon., *Sisterhoods Considered, with Remarks upon the Bishop of Brechin's 'Plea for Sisterhoods'* (London, Rivingtons, 1850).

Ashwell, R. G., *The Life of the Right Reverend Samuel Wilberforce* (3 vols, London, John Murray, 2nd edn, 1881).

Astell, M., *The Christian Religion as Professed by a Daughter of the Church of England* (London, R. Wilkin, 1705).

Awdry, F., *An Elder Sister: A Short Sketch of Anne Mackenzie, and her Brother the Missionary Bishop* (London, Bemrose & Sons, 1878).

Ayres, J. (ed.), *Paupers and Pig Killers. The Diary of William Holland, A Somerset Parson, 1799–1818* (Harmondsworth, Penguin Books, 1986).

Baillie, E., *The Shabby Paradise: The Autobiography of a Decade* (London, Hutchinson, 1958).

Baker, H., *Women in Ministry* (London, C. W. Daniel, 1911).

Beresford, J. (ed.), *The Diary of a Country Parson: The Diary of the Reverend James Woodforde 1758–1781* (5 vols, London, OUP, 1924–1931).

Billington, M., *Woman in India* (London, Chapman & Hall, 1895).

Bird, M., *Persian Women and their Creed* (London, CMS, 1899).

Blunt, J. H., *Directorium Pastorale. Principles and Practice of Pastoral Work in the Church of England* (London, Rivingtons, 1864).

Bond, D. F. (ed.), *The Spectator* (5 vols, Oxford, OUP, 1965).

Booth, W., *Life and Labour of the People of London, Third Series: Religious Influences*, vol. 7 (New York, AMS Press, 1970).

Browne, G. F., *The Recollections of a Bishop* (London, Smith, Elder & Co., 1915).

Bruce, M., and Duffield, G., *Why Not? Priesthood and the Ministry of Women* (Abingdon, Marcham Manor Press, 1972).

Buckland, A. R., *Women in the Mission Field: Pioneers and Martyrs* (London, Ibister & Co., 1895).

Burdett-Coutts, Baroness (ed.), *Woman's Mission: A Series of Congress Papers on the Philanthropic Work of Women by Eminent Writers* (London, Sampson Low, Marston & Co., 1893).

Burne, C. (ed.), *Shropshire Folk-Lore, A Sheaf of Gleanings* (London, Turner & Co., 1883).

Butler, J. (ed.), *Woman's Work and Woman's Culture* (London, Macmillan, 1869).

Butler, J., *Personal Reminiscences of a Great Crusade* (London, Horace Marshall, 1896).

Butler, S., *The Way of All Flesh* (London, Jonathan Cape, 2nd edn, 1913).

Canham, E., *Pilgrimage to Priesthood* (London, SPCK, 1983).

Carter, T., *Objections to Sisterhoods Considered in a Letter to a Parent* (London, Rivingtons, 1853).

Carter, T., *Is it Well to Institute Sisterhoods in the Church of England for the Care of Female Penitents?* (London, Rivingtons, 2nd edn, 1853).

Carter, T., *Are 'Vows of Celibacy in Early Life' inconsistent with the Word of God?* (London, Rivingtons, 1878).

Carus-Wilson, Mrs Ashley, *Irene Petrie Missionary to Kashmir* (London, Hodder & Stoughton, 1900).

Catherine and Craufurd Tait, A Memoir (London, Macmillan, 2nd edn, 1881).

Chant, L., *Chastity in Men and Women: A Woman's Answer to a Woman in Regard to the Equality of the Moral Law* (London, Dyer Brothers, 1885).

Christie, O. F. (ed.), *The Diary of the Rev. William Jones 1777–1821* (London, Brentano's, 1929).

Church Assembly Report of Proceedings.

Conference on Missions Held in 1860 at Liverpool, edited by the Secretaries to the Conference (London, James Nisbet, 1860).

Crane, J. M. (ed.), *The Autobiography of Maria Vernon Graham Havergal* (London, James Nisbet & Co., 1887).

Cranston, C. (ed.), *Evangelicals and the Ordination of Women* (Bramcote, Grove Books, 1973).

Creighton, L., *The Life and Letters of Mandell Creighton* (2 vols, London, Longmans Green, 1906).

Cust, R. N., *Africa Rediviva. Or, The Occupation of Africa by Christian Missionaries of Europe and North America* (London, Elliot Stock, 1891).

Cust, R. N., *An Essay on the Prevailing Methods of Evangelization of the Non-Christian World* (London, Elliot Stock, 1894).

Deacons Now: The Report of a Church of England Working Party Concerned with Women in Ordained Ministry 1990 (London, ACCM, 1990).

Fenwick, Rev. J., *An Evangelical's Difficulties with the Ordination of Women* (London, Association for an Apostolic Ministry, n.d.).

Fifth Annual Report of the Church of England Zenana Missionary Society, 1884–5.

Fisher, R., *On the Borders of Pygmy Land* (London, Marshall Brothers, 1905).

Fisher, R., *Twilight Tales of the Black Baganda* (London, Frank Cass, 2nd edn, 1970).

Fleetwood, W., *The Relative Duties of Parents and Children, Husbands and Wives, Masters and Servants: Considered in Sixteen Practical Discourses* (London, John Hooke, 2nd edn, 1716).

Fordyce, J., *The Character and Conduct of the Female Sex and the Advantages to be Derived by Young Men from the Society for Virtuous Women* (London, T. Cadell, 1776).

Fourth Annual Report of the Church of England Zenana Missionary Society for 1881–2 (London, CMS, 1884).

Furlong, M. (ed.), *Feminine in the Church* (London, SPCK, 1984).

Gaskell, E. C., *The Life of Charlotte Brontë* (Edinburgh, John Grant, 1924).

Gender and Ministry: A Report prepared for the Church Assembly by the Central Advisory Council for the Ministry (London, Church Information Office, 1962).

Bibliography

General Synod Report of Proceedings.

Giberne, A., *A Lady of England. The Life and Letters of Charlotte Mary Tucker* (London, Hodder & Stoughton, 1895).

Gibson, D. (ed.), *A Parson in the Vale of the White Horse: George Woodward's Letters from East Hendred, 1753-1761* (Gloucester, Alan Sutton, 1982).

Gisborne, T., *An Enquiry into the Duties of the Female Sex* (London, T. Cadell & W. Davies, 3rd edn, 1798).

Gollock, M. C., *River, Sand and Sun Being Sketches of the C.M.S. Egypt Mission* (London, CMS, 1906).

Gomme, G., *The Gentleman's Magazine Library: Being a Classified Collection of the Chief Contents of the Gentleman's Magazine from 1731 to 1868. Manners and Customs* (London, Elliot Stock, 1883).

Gomme, G., *The Gentleman's Magazine Library: Being a Classified Collection of the Chief Contents of the Gentleman's Magazine from 1731 to 1868. Popular Superstitions* (Boston, Houghton, Mifflin & Co., 1885).

Goodman, M., *Sisterhoods in the Church of England* (London, Smith, Elder & Co., 1863).

Goulburn, E., *John William Burgon* (2 vols, London, John Murray, 1892).

Gray, E., *Papers and Diaries of a York Family 1764-1839* (London, Sheldon Press, 1927).

Gregory, J., *A Father's Legacy to His Daughter* (Dublin, Thomas Ewing, 1774).

Hawkins, L., *Letters on the Female Mind, Its Powers and Pursuits* (London, Hookham and Carpenter, 1793).

Hill, B. (ed.), *The First English Feminist. Reflections Upon Marriage and Other Writings by Mary Astell* (Aldershot, Gower/Maurice Temple Smith, 1986).

Hodges, A., *Love's Victory. Memoirs of Fanny Woodman 1888-1895* (London, Marshall Brothers, 1899).

Holloway, R. (ed.), *Who Needs Feminism? Men Respond to Sexism in the Church* (London, SPCK, 1991).

Hopkins, E., *The Present Moral Crisis: An Appeal to Women* (London, Dyer Brothers, n.d.).

Horne, G., *The Female Character as it Ought to Appear when Formed* (London, G. Nicholson, 1801).

Howard, R., *Should Women Be Priests?* (Oxford, Basil Blackwell, 1949).

Howson, J., *Deaconesses: Or the Official Help of Women in Parochial Work and in Charitable Institutions* (London, Longmans Green, 1862).

Jones, W. (ed.), *The Works of the Right Reverend George Horne D. D., The Late Bishop of Norwich; To Which Are Prefixed Memoirs Of His Life, Studies, And Writings* (4 vols, London, Rivingtons, 2nd edn, 1818).

Kingsley, C., *Hypatia or New Foes with an Old Face* (London, Macmillan, 1882).

Kingsley, F., *Charles Kingsley: His Letters and Memories of His Life* (2 vols, London, C. Kegan Paul, 7th edn, 1880).

Lackington, J., *Memoirs of the first forty-five years of the life of James Lackington* (London, 2nd edn, 1792).

Lady Llanover (ed.), *The Autobiography and Correspondence of Mary Granville Mrs. Delany* (London, Richard Bentley, 1861).

Lancaster, N., *Methodism Triumphant, or the Decisive Battle between the Old Serpent and the Modern Saint* (London, J. Wilkie, 1767).

Lavington, G., *The Enthusiasm of Methodists and Papists Compar'd* (London, J. & P. Knapton, 1749).

Lewis, C. S., *God in the Dock* (London, Collins, 1979).

Liddon, H. P., *Explanatory Analysis of St Paul's First Epistle to Timothy* (Oxford, privately printed, 1877).

Liddon, H. P., *Christmastide in St Paul's, Sermons Bearing Chiefly on the Birth of Our Lord and the End of the Year* (London, Rivingtons, 1889).

Liddon, H. P., *The Life of Edward Bouverie Pusey* (4 vols, London, Longmans Green, 1894).

Lloyd, E., *Anna Lloyd: A Memoir* (London, Cayme Press, 1928).

Lyttleton, E., 'Woman's Suffrage and the Teaching of St Paul', *Contemporary Review*, vol. 365 (May 1896), pp. 680–691.

Maden, M., *Thelyphthora: Or a Treatise On Female Ruin, In Its Causes, Effects, Consequences, Prevention, and Remedy; Considered on the Basis of the Divine Law* (2 vols, London, J. Dodsley, 1780).

Marriage and the Church's Task: The Report of the General Synod's Marriage Commission (London, CIO, 1978).

Bibliography

Maurice, F. D., *Queen's College, London: Its Objects and Method* (London, Macmillan, 1848).

Maurice, F. D., *Social Morality: Twenty-One Lectures Delivered in the University of Cambridge* (London, Macmillan, 1869).

Mitchell, L. G. (ed.), *The Purefoy Letters* (London, Sidgwick & Jackson, 1973).

Montgomery, H., *'With the Women'. A Sermon Preached in Westminster Abbey on April 22nd 1915 on the occasion of the commencement of the Jubilee Year of Women's Work* (London, SPG, 1915).

Moore, P. (ed.), *Man, Woman, and Priesthood* (London, SPCK, 1978).

More, H., *Works* (8 vols, London, T. Cadell, 1801).

Mudie-Smith, R., *The Religious Life of London* (London, Hodder & Stoughton, 1904).

Neale, J. M., *Ayton Priory; Or, the Restored Monastery* (London, Rivingtons, 1843).

Newman, J. H., *The Church of the Fathers* (London, Rivingtons, 1840).

Oddie, W., *What Will Happen to God?* (London, SPCK, 1984).

O'Rourke, L. E., *The Life and Friendships of Catherine Marsh* (London, Longmans Green, 1917).

Paley, W., *The Principles of Moral and Political Philosophy* (2 vols, London, R. Foulder, 12th edn, 1799).

Parliamentary Papers, 1819, Report from Commissioners: *Charities in England for the Education of the Poor*, vol. x, pp. 382–383.

Pennington, M., *Memoirs of the Life of Mrs Elizabeth Carter* (London, Rivingtons, 1807).

Pennington, M. (ed.), *A Series of Letters between Elizabeth Carter and Miss Catherine Talbot from the Year 1741 to 1770* (4 vols, London, 1809).

Quinn, V., and Prest, J. (eds), *Dear Miss Nightingale: A Selection of Benjamin Jowett's Letters to Florence Nightingale 1860–1893* (Oxford, Clarendon Press, 1987).

'Pilot Letters' Describing the Work of Women Missionaries of the S.P.G. reprinted from the Home Workers' Gazette (London, SPG, 1916).

Report of the Church Congress Held at London in 1899 (London, Bemrose & Sons, 1899).

Report of the Church Congress Held at Portsmouth (London, Bemrose & Sons, 1885).

Report of the Church Congress Held at Shrewsbury (London, Bemrose & Sons, 1896).

Report of the Church Congress Held at Southampton in 1913 (London, George Allen, 1913).

Report of the Proceedings of the Church Congress of 1862 (Oxford, J. & H. Parker, 1862).

Report of the Women's Meeting Held in Connection with the Pan-Anglican Congress of 1908 (London, SPCK, 1908).

Roberts, W., *Memoirs of the Life of Mrs Hannah More* (2 vols, London, Seeley & Burnside, 1836).

Scott, T., *The Holy Bible; Containing the Old Testament and New Testaments According to the Authorized Version; With Explanatory Notes, Practical Observations, and Copious Marginal References* (6 vols, London, James Nisbet & Co., 1866), vol. 6, n.p.

Second Annual Report of the Church of England Zenana Missionary Society for 1881-2 (London, CMS, 1882).

Sharp, J., *A Sermon Preach'd at the Coronation of Queen Anne in the Abbey Church of Westminster April 23rd 1702* (London, Walter Kettliby, 1702).

Shepherd, A. P., *Tucker of Uganda, Artist and Apostle 1849-1914* (London, SCM, 1929).

Shipley, O. (ed.), *The Church and the World: Essays on Questions of the Day* (London, Longmans Green, 1866).

Shipley, O. (ed.), *The Church and the World: Essays on Questions of the Day in 1867* (London, Longmans Green, 1867).

Sister Katherine, *Towards the Land of the Rising Sun, Or, Four Years in Burma* (London, SPCK, 1900).

Smith, J., *Polygamy Indefensible* (London, Alexander Hogg, 1780).

Smythe, H., *Sex, Symbol, Sacrament: Some Theological Considerations in the Question of the Ordination of Women to the Priesthood within the Church of England* (London, Association for the Apostolic Ministry, 1989).

Some Account of the Life and Writings of Mrs Trimmer, with Original Letters and Meditations and Prayers, selected from her Journal (2 vols, London, Rivingtons, 1814).

Spender, D. (ed.), *The Education Papers: Women's Quest for Equality in Britain 1850–1912* (London, Routledge & Kegan Paul, 1987).

Spottiswoode, G. A., *The Official Report of the Missionary Conference of the Anglican Communion on May 28, 29, 30, 31 and June 1, 1894* (London, SPCK, 1894).

Stanhope, G., *A Paraphrase and Comment upon the Epistles and Gospels, Appointed to be Used in the Church of England on all Sundays and Holy-Days throughout the Year* (4 vols, London, 7th edn, 1751).

Stoddart, Anna M., *The Life of Isabella Bird* (London, John Murray, 1906).

Streeter, B. H., and Picton-Turbervill, E., *Woman and the Church* (London, T. Fisher Unwin, 1917).

Talbot, J. C., *Parochial Mission-Women: Their Work and its Fruits* (London, Rivingtons, 1862).

Talbot, J. G., *Memorials of the Hon. Mrs. John Chetwynd Talbot* (London, Spottiswoode & Co., 1876).

The Lambeth Conference 1948: The Encyclical Letter from the Bishops together with Resolutions and Reports (London, SPCK, 1948).

The Lambeth Conference 1968: Resolutions and Reports (London, SPCK, 1968).

The Lambeth Conferences 1867–1948 (London, SPCK, 1948).

The Ministry of Women: A Report by a Committee Appointed by the Archbishop of Canterbury (London, SPCK, 1920).

The Ministry of Women: Report of the Archbishop's Commission (London, Church Assembly Publications Board, 1935).

The Ordination of Women to the Priesthood. The Synod Debate 11 November 1992. The Verbatim Record (London, Church House Publishing, 1993).

The Ordination of Women to the Priesthood: A Consultative Document presented by the Advisory Council for the Church's Ministry (London, Church Information Office, 1972).

The Ordination of Women to the Priesthood: A Report by the House of Bishops (London, General Synod of the Church of England, 1987).

The Ordination of Women to the Priesthood: A Second Report by the

House of Bishops to the General Synod of the Church of England (London, Church House Publishing, 1988).

The Ordination of Women to the Priesthood: Further Report (London, 1984).

The Present and the Future - Women's Ministry in the Church of England: Report of a one day conference Saturday, 30th September, 1972 (London, Anglican Group for the Ordination of Women to the Priesthood, 1972).

The Question of Holy Orders: A Memorandum to the Commission set up in 1963 by the Archbishops of Canterbury and York (London, printed for private circulation, 1963).

The Tatler, ed. D. F. Bond (3 vols, Oxford, Clarendon Press, 1987).

The Works of Mrs. Chapone (4 vols, London, John Murray, 1807).

The Works of the Reverend William Law (9 vols, London, G. Moreton, 1893).

Third Annual Report of the Church of England Zenana Missionary Society for 1882-3 (London, CMS, 1883).

Thirteenth Annual Report of the Church of England Zenana Missionary Society for 1891-2 (London, CMS, 1893).

Trimmer, S., *The Oeconomy of Charity; Or, an Address to Ladies Concerning Sunday Schools* (London, T. Longman, 1787).

Venn, H., *The Complete Duty of Man: Or, a System of Doctrinal and Practical Christianity* (London, Longmans Green, 1841).

Venn, J., *Annals of a Clerical Family* (London, Macmillan & Co., 1904).

Wake, W., *The Principles of the Christian Religion Explained in a Brief Commentary upon the Church Catechism* (London, Richard Sare, 3rd edn, 1708).

Waugh, E., *Brideshead Revisited* (Harmondsworth, Penguin Books, 1962).

Webb, A. B., *Sisterhood Life and Woman's Work in the Mission-Field of the Church* (London, Skeffington & Son, 1883).

Wheler, G., *The Protestant Monastery: Or, Christian Oeconomicks Containing Directions for the Religious Conduct of a Family* (London, 1698).

Williams, T., *Priscilla Lydia Sellon. The Restorer after Three Centuries of the Religious Life in the English Church* (London, SPCK, 2nd edn, 1965).

Women and Holy Orders: Being the Report of a Commission appointed by the Archbishops of Canterbury and York (London, Church Information Office, 1966).

Women and the Ministry: Some Considerations on the Report of the Archbishop's Commission on the Ministry of Women published on behalf of the Council of the Church Union (London, Church Literature Association, 1936).

Women and the Ordained Ministry: Report of an Anglican–Methodist Commission on Women and Holy Orders (London, SPCK, 1968).

Women in Ministry: A Study (London, Central Board of Finance of the Church of England, 1968).

Women in Training: A Report of a Working Party Set Up by Women Staff Members of Theological Colleges and Courses (London, ACCM, 1983).

Women Priests: Obstacles to Unity? (London, Catholic Truth Society, 1986).

Yonge, C., *The Daisy Chain* (London, Virago Press, 1988).

Yonge, C., *Womankind* (London, Walter Smith & Innes, 2nd edn, 1889).

York Journal of Convocation (London, Rivingtons, 1885).

Printed secondary sources

Abbey, C. J., and Overton J. H., *The English Church in the Eighteenth Century* (2 vols, London, Longmans Green, 1878).

Aldridge, A., 'In the Absence of the Minister: Structures of Subordination in the Role of Deaconess in the Church of England', *Sociology*, vol. 21 (1987), pp. 377–392.

Allchin, A., *The Silent Rebellion: Anglican Religious Communities 1845–1900* (London, SCM, 1958).

Amussen, S., *An Ordered Society: Gender and Class in Early Modern England* (Oxford, Basil Blackwell, 1988).

Angerman, A. *et al.* (eds), *Current Issues in Women's History* (London, Routledge, 1989).

Anon., *Ann Wilson Carlile and the Church Army* (London, The Church Army Bookroom, 3rd edn, 1928).

Anon., *A Valiant Victorian: The Life and Times of Mother Emily*

Ayckbowm 1836–1900 (London, Mowbray, 1964).

Anson, P., *The Call of the Cloister: Religious Communities and Kindred Bodies in the Anglican Communion* (London, SPCK, 1955).

Armstrong, A., *The Church of England, the Methodists and Society 1700–1850* (London, University of London Press, 1973).

Armstrong, C. J., *Evelyn Underhill: An Introduction to her Life and Writings* (London, Mowbray, 1975).

Armstrong, N., *Desire and Domestic Fiction. A Political History of the Novel* (Oxford, OUP, 1987).

Baker, J. E., *The Novel and the Oxford Movement* (Princeton, Princeton UP, 1932).

Banks, O., *Faces of Feminism: A Study of Feminism as a Social Movement* (Oxford, Martin Robertson, 1981).

Battiscombe, G., *Charlotte Mary Yonge: The Story of an Uneventful Life* (London, Constable, 1943).

Battiscombe, G., *Reluctant Pioneer: A Life of Elizabeth Wordsworth* (London, Constable, 1978).

Bebbington, D., *Evangelicalism in Modern Britain. A History from the 1730s to the 1980s* (London, Unwin Hyman, 1989).

Bell, E., *Josephine Butler, Flame of Fire* (London, Constable, 1962).

Binfield, C., *Belmont's Portias: Victorian Nonconformists and Middle-Class Education for Girls* (London, Dr Williams Trust, 1981).

Black, J., and Gregory, J. (eds), *Culture, Politics and Society in Britain, 1660–1800* (Manchester, Manchester UP, 1991).

Bland, L., '"Purifying" the Public World: Feminist Vigilantes in Late Victorian England', *Women's History Review*, vol. 1 (1992).

Borresen, K. E. (ed.), *Image of God and Gender Models in Judaeo-Christian Tradition* (Oslo, Solum Forlag, 1991).

Bouchier, D., *The Feminist Challenge: The Movement for Women's Liberation in Britain and the USA* (London, Macmillan, 1983).

Boyd, N., *Josephine Butler, Octavia Hill, Florence Nightingale* (London, Macmillan, 1982).

Braithwaite, R., *The Life and Letters of the Rev. William Pennefather* (London, J. Shaw & Co., 2nd edn, 1878).

Brierley, P., and Langley, D., *UK Christian Handbook 1992/93*

(London, MARC Europe, 1991).

Bristow, E. J., *Vice and Vigilance: Purity Movements in Britain Since 1700* (Dublin, Gill & Macmillan, 1977).

Brittain, V., *The Women at Oxford, A Fragment of History* (London, George Harrap, 1960).

Brown, C., *The Church's Part in Education 1833–1941 with Special Reference to the Work of the National Society* (London, SPCK, 1942).

Brown, E., *Women of Mr Wesley's Methodism* (New York, Edwin Mellen Press, 1983).

Brown, S. (ed.), *Married to the Church?* (London, Triangle/SPCK, 1983).

Bryant, M., *The Unexpected Revolution: A Study in the History of the Education of Women and Girls in the Nineteenth Century* (London, University of London Institute of Education, 1979).

Bullock, F., *Voluntary Religious Societies 1520–1799* (St Leonards-on-Sea, Budd & Gillat, 1963).

Burman, S. (ed.), *Fit Work for Women* (London, Croom Helm, 1979).

Burstyn, J., *Victorian Education and the Ideal of Womanhood* (London, Croom Helm, 1980).

Bushaway, R., *Ceremony and Community in England 1700–1800* (London, Junction Books, 1982).

Byrne, L., *The Hidden Journey: Missionary Heroines in Many Lands* (London, SPCK, 1993).

Cairns, H. A. C., *Prelude to Imperialism: British Reactions to Central African Society 1840–1890* (London, Routledge & Kegan Paul, 1965).

Carroll, B. A. (ed.), *Liberating Women's History. Theoretical and Critical Essays* (Urbana, University of Illinois Press, 1976).

Cerasano, S. P., and Wynne-Davies, M. (eds), *Gloriana's Face: Women Public and Private in the English Renaissance* (Hemel Hempstead, Harvester Wheatsheaf, 1992).

Chadwick, O., *The Victorian Church* (2 vols, London, A. & C. Black, 1971 and 1972).

Chilcote, P., *John Wesley and the Women Preachers of Early Methodism* (Metuchen, New Jersey, Scarecrow Press, 1991).

Chitty, S., *The Beast and the Monk: A Life of Charles Kingsley* (London, Hodder & Stoughton, 1974).

Clark, J. C. D., *English Society 1688–1832: Ideology, Social Structure and Political Practice during the Ancien Regime* (Cambridge, CUP, 1985).

Clark, L., 'Women and John Locke: or, Who Owns the Apples in the Garden of Eden?', in V. Chappell (ed.), *John Locke's Political Philosophy* (New York, Garland Publishing, 1992).

Clements, K. W., *Lovers of Discord: Twentieth-Century Theological Controversies in England* (London, SPCK, 1988).

Cliff, P., *The Rise and Development of the Sunday School Movement in England 1780–1980* (Nuffield, Surrey, National Christian Education Council, 1986).

Cott, N. F., 'Passionlessness: An Interpretation of Victorian Sexual Ideology, 1790–1850', *Signs*, vol. 4 (1978), pp. 219–252.

Davidoff, L., 'The Rationalization of Housework', in D. Leonard Barker and S. Allen (eds), *Dependence and Exploitation in Work and Marriage* (London, Longman, 1976).

Davidoff, L., 'The Family in Britain', in F. M. L. Thompson (ed.), *The Cambridge Social History of Britain 1750–1950*, vol. 2 (Cambridge, CUP, 1990).

Davidoff, L., and Hall, C., *Family Fortunes. Men and Women of the English Middle Class 1780–1850* (London, Hutchinson, 1987).

Davis, R. W., and Helmstadter, R. J. (eds), *Religion and Irreligion in Victorian Society: Essays in Honour of R. K. Webb* (London, Routledge, 1992).

Deacon, A., and Hill, M., 'The Problem of "Surplus Women" in the Nineteenth Century: Secular and Religious Alternatives', *A Sociological Yearbook of Religion*, vol. 5 (1972), pp. 87–102.

Dennison, K., 'Dr Pusey as Confessor and Spiritual Director', in P. Butler (ed.), *Pusey Rediscovered* (London, SPCK, 1983).

Donaldson, M., '"The Cultivation of the Heart and the Moulding of the Will . . ." The Missionary Contribution of the Society for Promoting Female Education in China, India, and the East', in W. J. Sheils and D. Wood (eds), *Women in the Church*, Studies in Church History 27 (Oxford, Basil Blackwell, 1990), pp. 429–442.

Douglas, A., *The Feminization of American Culture* (New York, Avon Books, 1977).

Bibliography

Douglas, M., *Purity and Danger. An Analysis of Concepts of Pollution and Taboo* (London, Routledge and Kegan Paul, 1966).

Dowell, S., and Hurcombe, L., *Dispossessed Daughters of Eve: Faith and Feminism* (London, SPCK, 2nd edn, 1987).

Drain, S. *The Anglican Church in the Nineteenth Century: Hymns Ancient and Modern 1860-1875* (Lampeter, Edwin Mellen Press, 1989).

Duffy, E., 'Primitive Christianity Revived; Religious Renewal in Augustan England', in Derek Baker (ed.), *Renaissance and Renewal in Christian History*, Studies in Church History 14 (Oxford, Basil Blackwell, 1977), pp. 287-300.

Dyhouse, C., 'Miss Buss and Miss Beale: Gender and Authority in the History of Education', in F. Hunt (ed.), *Lessons for Life: The Schooling of Girls and Women, 1850-1950* (Oxford, Basil Blackwell, 1987), pp. 22-38.

Eaves, T. C., and Kimpel, B. D., *Samuel Richardson* (Oxford, Clarendon Press, 1971).

Faber, G., *Oxford Apostles* (Harmondsworth, Penguin Books, 1954).

Field-Bibb, J., *Women Towards Priesthood: Ministerial Politics and Feminist Praxis* (Cambridge, CUP, 1991).

Firth, C. B., *Constance Louisa Maynard* (London, George Allen & Unwin, 1949).

Fischer, G. V., and Farnham, C. (eds), *Journal of Women's History Guide to Periodical Literature* (Bloomington, Indiana UP, 1992).

Fletcher, S., *Maude Royden: A Life* (Oxford, Basil Blackwell, 1989).

Forster, M., *Significant Sisters: The Grassroots of Active Feminism 1839-1939* (London, Secker & Warburg, 1984).

Furlong, M., *A Dangerous Delight: Women and Power in the Church* (London, SPCK, 1991).

Gibson, R., *A Social History of French Catholicism* (London, Routledge, 1989).

Gill, R., *Theology and Social Structure* (London, Mowbray, 1977).

Gill, R., *The Myth of the Empty Church* (London, SPCK, 1993).

Gill, S., 'The Power of Christian Ladyhood: Priscilla Lydia Sellon and the Creation of Anglican Sisterhoods', in S. Mews (ed.), *Modern Religious Rebels: Essays Presented to John Kent* (London, Epworth Press, 1993), pp. 144-165.

Gittings, R., *The Older Hardy* (Harmondsworth, Penguin Books, 1980).

Glock, C., and Hammond, P. (eds), *Beyond the Classics? Essays in the Scientific Study of Religion* (New York, Harper & Row, 1973).

Gollock, Georgina, *The Story of the Church Missionary Society* (London, CMS, 1909).

Gorham, D., 'The "Maiden Tribute of Modern Babylon" Re-examined: Child Prostitution and the Idea of Childhood in Late-Victorian England', *Victorian Studies*, vol. 21 (1977–1980), p. 353–379.

Greene, D., *Evelyn Underhill. Artist of the Infinite Life* (London, Darton, Longman & Todd, 1991).

Greenleaf, W. H., *Order, Empiricism and Politics. Two Traditions of English Political Thought 1500–1700* (Oxford, OUP, 1964).

Grierson, J., *The Deaconess* (London, CIO, 1981).

Grimshaw, P., '"Christian Woman, Pious Wife, Faithful Mother, Devoted Missionary": Conflicts of American Missionary Women in Nineteenth-Century Hawaii', *Feminist Studies*, vol. 9 (1983), pp. 489–521.

Guskin, P., 'The Context of Witchcraft: The Case of Jane Wenham (1712)', *Eighteenth-Century Studies*, vol. 15 (1981–1982), pp. 48–71.

Haight, G. S., *George Eliot* (Oxford, Clarendon Press, 1968).

Hampson, D., *Theology and Feminism* (Oxford, Basil Blackwell, 1990).

Harrison, B., *Separate Spheres: The Opposition to Women's Suffrage in Britain* (London, Croom Helm, 1978).

Hart, A. T., *The Eighteenth Century Country Parson* (Shrewsbury, Wilding & Son, 1955).

Heeney, B., *A Different Kind of Gentleman: Parish Clergy as Professional Men in Early and Mid-Victorian England* (Hamden, Connecticut, Archon Books, 1976).

Heeney, B., 'The Beginnings of Church Feminism: Women and the Councils of the Church of England 1897–1919', *Journal of Ecclesiastical History*, vol. 33 (1982), pp. 89–109.

Heeney, B., 'Women's Struggle for Professional Work and Status in the Church of England, 1900–1930', *Historical Journal*, vol. 26 (1983), pp. 329–347.

Heeney, B., *The Women's Movement in the Church of England 1850–1930* (Oxford, Clarendon Press, 1988).

Hempton, D., and Hill, M., *Evangelical Protestantism in Ulster Society 1740–1890* (London, Routledge, 1992).

Hennell, M., *John Venn and the Clapham Sect* (London, Lutterworth Press, 1958).

Hill, B. (ed.), *Eighteenth-Century Women: An Anthology* (London, George Allen & Unwin, 1984).

Hill, B., 'A Refuge from Men: The Idea of a Protestant Nunnery', *Past and Present*, no. 117 (1987), pp. 107–130.

Hill, G. B. (ed.), *Boswell's Life of Johnson* (6 vols, Oxford, Clarendon Press, 1934).

Hill, M., *The Religious Order* (London, Heinemann, 1973).

Hilliard, D., 'Unenglish and Unmanly: Anglo-Catholicism and Homosexuality', *Victorian Studies*, vol. 25 (1982), pp. 181–210.

Hole, R., *Pulpits, Politics and Public Order in England 1760–1832* (Cambridge, CUP, 1989).

Hollis, P. (ed.), *Pressure from Without in Early Victorian England* (London, Edward Arnold, 1974).

Hopkins, M., *Hannah More and Her Circle* (New York, Longmans Green, 1947).

Horn, P., *Victorian Countrywomen* (Oxford, Basil Blackwell, 1991).

Hunter, L. S., *A Parson's Job* (London, SCM, 1931).

Innes, J., 'Jonathan Clark, Social History and England's "Ancien Regime"', *Past and Present*, no. 115 (1987), pp. 165–200.

Innes, C. L., and Lindfors, B. (eds), *Critical Perspectives on Chinua Achebe* (London, Heinemann, 1978).

Isaacs, T., 'The Anglican Hierarchy and the Reformation of Manners 1688–1738', *Journal of Ecclesiastical History*, vol. 33 (1982), pp. 391–411.

Isherwood, J., 'An Analysis of the Role of Single Women in the Work of the Church Missionary Society, 1804–1904, in West Africa, India and China', University of Manchester MA thesis, 1979.

Jeffreys, S., *The Spinster and Her Enemies: Feminism and Sexuality 1880–1930* (London, Pandora Press, 1985).

Jones, K., *Learning Not to be First: The Life of Christina Rossetti*

(Moreton-in-Marsh, Windrush Press, 1991).

Jones, M. G., *The Charity School Movement* (Cambridge, CUP, 1938).

Jones, V., *Women in the Eighteenth Century: Constructions of Femininity* (London, Routledge, 1990).

Kamm, J., *How Different From Us: A Biography of Miss Buss and Miss Beale* (London, Bodley Head, 1958).

Kamm, J., *Hope Deferred: Girls' Education in English History* (London, Methuen, 1965).

Kaplan, S. (ed.), *Understanding Popular Culture: Europe from the Middle Ages to the Nineteenth Century* (Berlin, Mouton Publishers, 1984).

Kaye, E., *A History of Queen's College, London 1848-1972* (London, Chatto & Windus, 1972).

Kent, J., *The Unacceptable Face: The Modern Church in the Eyes of the Historian* (London, SCM, 1987).

Ker, I., *John Henry Newman* (Oxford, Clarendon Press, 1988).

King, U. (ed.), *Feminist Theology from the Third World: A Reader* (London, SPCK, 1994).

Kleinberg, S. J. (ed.), *Retrieving Women's History: Changing Perceptions of the Role of Women in Politics and Society* (Oxford, Berg, 1988).

Langford, P., *A Polite and Commercial People. England 1727-1783* (Oxford, Clarendon Press, 1989).

Laquer, W., *Religion and Respectability: Sunday Schools and Working Class Culture 1780-1850* (New Haven, Yale UP, 1976).

Laslett, P., *Patriarcha and Other Political Works of Sir Robert Filmer* (Oxford, Basil Blackwell, 1949).

Laslett, P. (ed.), *John Locke. Two Treatises of Government* (Cambridge, CUP, 2nd edn, 1967).

Leech, K. (ed.), *Essays Catholic and Radical* (London, Bowerdean Press, 1983).

LeGates, M., 'The Cult of Womanhood in Eighteenth-Century England', *Eighteenth-Century Studies*, vol. 10 (1976-1977), pp. 21-39.

Leites, E., 'The Duty to Desire: Love, Friendship, and Sexuality in Some Puritan Theories of Marriage', *Journal of Social History*, vol. 15 (1981-1982), pp. 383-408.

Lewis, J., *In the Family Way: Childbearing in the British Aristocracy, 1760-1860* (New Brunswick, New Jersey, Rutgers UP, 1986).

Lyles, A., *Methodism Mocked: The Satiric Reaction to Methodism in the Eighteenth Century* (London, Epworth Press, 1960).

Maclean, I. *The Renaissance Notion of Woman* (Cambridge, CUP, 1980).

MacDonagh, O., *Jane Austen. Real and Imagined Worlds* (New Haven, Yale UP, 1991).

Malcolm, R., *Popular Recreations in English Society 1700-1850* (Cambridge, CUP, 1973).

Malmgreen, G. (ed.), *Religion in the Lives of English Women 1760-1930* (London, Croom Helm, 1986).

Marshall, M., *What I Remember* (Cambridge, CUP, 1947).

Marshall, S. (ed.), *Women in Reformation and Counter-Reformation Europe* (Bloomington, Indiana UP, 1989).

Mather, F. C., 'Georgian Churchmanship Reconsidered: Some Variations in Anglican Public Worship 1714-1830', *Journal of Ecclesiastical History*, vol. 36 (1985), pp. 255-282.

McHugh, P., *Prostitution and Victorian Social Reform* (London, Croom Helm, 1980).

McLeod, H., *Religion and the People of Western Europe 1789-1970* (Oxford, OUP, 1981).

McWilliams-Tullberg, R., *Women at Cambridge: A Men's University - Though of a Mixed Type* (London, Victor Gollancz, 1975).

Medhurst, K., and Moyser, G., *Church and Politics in a Secular Age* (Oxford, Clarendon Press, 1988).

Monaghan, D., 'Mansfield Park and Evangelicalism: A Reassessment', *Nineteenth Century Fiction*, vol. 33 (1978-1979), pp. 215-230.

Myers, S., *The Bluestocking Circle: Women, Friendship, and the Life of the Mind in Eighteenth-Century England* (Oxford, Clarendon Press, 1990).

Newton, J. A., *Search for a Saint: Edward King* (London, Epworth Press, 1977).

Norman, E. R., *Church and Society in England 1770-1970* (Oxford, Clarendon Press, 1976).

Oakley, A., *The Sociology of Housework* (Oxford, Basil Blackwell, 1985).

Obelkevich, J., *Religion and Rural Society: South Lindsey 1825-1875* (Oxford, Clarendon Press, 1976).

Obelkevich, J. *et al.* (eds), *Disciplines of Faith: Studies in Religion, Politics and Patriarchy* (London, Routledge & Kegan Paul, 1987).

Offen, K., 'Defining Feminism: A Comparative Historical Approach', *Signs*, vol. 14 (1988-1989), pp. 119-157.

Otter, J., *Nathaniel Woodard. A Memoir of His Life* (London, Bodley Head, 1925).

Parker, O., *For the Family's Sake: A History of the Mothers' Union 1876-1976* (Folkestone, Bailey & Swinfen, 1975).

Pascoe, C. F., *Two Hundred Years of the S.P.G.: An Historical Account of the Society for the Propagation of the Gospel in Foreign Parts 1701-1901* (London, SPG, 1901).

Peck, E., *The Social Implications of the Oxford Movement* (New York, Scribner's, 1933).

Pemble, J., *The Mediterranean Passion: Victorians and Edwardians in the South* (Oxford, OUP, 1988).

Perkin, H., *The Origins of Modern English Society 1780-1880* (London, Routledge & Kegan Paul, 1969).

Perry, R., *The Celebrated Mary Astell, An Early English Feminist* (Chicago, University of Chicago Press, 1986).

Pickering, W., *Anglo-Catholicism: A Study in Religious Ambiguity* (London, Routledge, 1989).

Preston, T. R., 'Biblical Criticism, Literature and the Eighteenth Century', in I. Rivers (ed.), *Books and their Readers in Eighteenth-Century England* (Leicester, Leicester UP, 1982), pp. 97-126.

Prochaska, F. K., *Women and Philanthropy in Nineteenth-Century England* (Oxford, Clarendon Press, 1980).

Pugh, M., *Women and the Women's Movement in Britain 1914-1959* (London, Macmillan, 1992).

Purvis, J., *Hard Lessons: The Lives and Education of Working-Class Women in Nineteenth-Century England* (Oxford, Polity Press, 1989).

Rack, H., *Reasonable Enthusiast: John Wesley and the Rise of Methodism* (London, Epworth Press, 2nd edn, 1992).

Reed, J. S., '"A Female Movement": The Feminization of Nineteenth-Century Anglo-Catholicism', *Anglican and Episcopal History*, vol. 57 (1988), pp. 199–238.

Reynolds, B., *Dorothy L. Sayers, Her Life and Soul* (London, Hodder & Stoughton, 1993).

Reynolds, M., *The Learned Lady in England 1650–1760* (Boston, Houghton Mifflin, 1920).

Robson, D., 'Some Aspects of Education in Cheshire in the Eighteenth Century', *Chetham Society*, vol. 13, 3rd Series (1966).

Rodgers, B., *Cloak of Charity: Studies in Eighteenth-Century Philanthropy* (London, Methuen, 1949).

Rogers, K. M., *The Troublesome Helpmate: A History of Misogyny in Literature* (Seattle, University of Washington Press, 1966).

Rogers, K. M., *Feminism in Eighteenth-Century England* (Brighton, Harvester Press, 1982).

Rover, C., *Love, Morals and the Feminists* (London, Routledge & Kegan Paul, 1970).

Rowell, G. (ed.), *Tradition Renewed: The Oxford Movement Conference Papers* (London, Darton, Longman & Todd, 1986).

Ruether, R., *Religion and Sexism: Images of Woman in the Jewish and Christian Traditions* (New York, Simon & Schuster, 1974).

Rupp, E. G., *Religion in England 1688–1791* (Oxford, Clarendon Press, 1986).

Russell, A., *The Clerical Profession* (London, SPCK, 1980).

Russell, G., *Arthur Stanton* (London, Longman, 1917).

Said, E., *Orientalism* (Harmondsworth, Penguin Books, 1985).

Schochet, G. J., *Patriarchalism in Political Thought. The Authoritarian Family and Political Speculation and Attitudes Especially in Seventeenth-Century England* (Oxford, OUP, 1975).

Scott, J. W., 'Gender: A Useful Category of Historical Analysis', *American Historical Review*, vol. 91 (1986), pp. 1053–1075.

Scott, J. W., 'Women's History', in P. Burke (ed.), *New Perspectives on Historical Writing* (Cambridge, Polity Press, 1991), pp. 42–66.

Sharpe, E. J., *Faith Meets Faith. Some Christian Attitudes to Hinduism in the Nineteenth and Twentieth Centuries* (London, SCM, 1977).

Sharpe, J. A., *Early Modern England: A Social History 1550-1760* (London, Edward Arnold, 1987).

Sheils, W. J., and Wood, D. (eds), *Women in the Church*, Studies in Church History 27 (Oxford, Basil Blackwell, 1990).

Shiels, R., 'The Feminization of American Congregationalism 1730-1835', *American Quarterly*, vol. 33 (1981), pp. 46-62.

Shiman, L., *Women and Leadership in Nineteenth-Century England* (London, Macmillan, 1992).

Showalter, E., 'Florence Nightingale's Feminist Complaint: Women, Religion, and Suggestions for Thought', *Signs*, vol. 6 (1981), pp. 395-412.

Sissons, C. H. (ed.), *The English Sermon, volume II: 1650-1750* (London, Carcanet Press, 1976).

Sister Joanna, 'The Deaconess Community of St. Andrew', *Journal of Ecclesiastical History*, vol. 12 (1961), pp. 215-230.

Smith, A., *The Established Church and Popular Religion 1750-1850* (London, Longman, 1971).

Smith, B. G., *The Ladies of the Leisure Class: The Bourgeoises of Northern France in the Nineteenth Century* (Princeton, New Jersey, Princeton UP, 1981).

Smith, H. (ed.), *British Feminism in the Twentieth Century* (Aldershot, Edward Elgar, 1990).

Soloway, R. A., *Prelates and People: Ecclesiastical Social Thought in England 1783-1852* (London, Routledge & Kegan Paul, 1969).

Spacks, P. M., 'Evr'y Woman is at Heart a Rake', *Eighteenth-Century Studies*, vol. 8 (1974-1975), pp. 27-46.

Spencer, J., *The Rise of the Woman Novelist From Aphra Benn to Jane Austen* (Oxford, Basil Blackwell, 1986).

Stanley, B., *The Bible and the Flag: Protestant Missions and British Imperialism in the Nineteenth and Twentieth Centuries* (Leicester, IVP, 1990).

Stenton, D. M., *The English Woman in History* (London, George Allen & Unwin, 1957).

Stephen, B., *Emily Davies and Girton College* (London, Constable, 1927).

Stock, E., *The History of the Church Missionary Society: Its Environment, Its Men and Its Work* (4 vols, London, Church Missionary Society, 3 vols, 1899, vol. 4, 1916).

Stone, L., *The Family, Sex and Marriage in England 1500-1800* (London, Weidenfeld & Nicolson, 1977).

Symonds, R., *Far Above Rubies: The Women Uncommemorated by the Church of England* (Leominster, Gracewing, 1993).

Taylor, B., *Eve and the New Jerusalem: Socialism and Feminism in the Nineteenth Century* (London, Virago Press, 1983).

Virgin, P., *The Church in an Age of Negligence: Ecclesiastical Structure and Problems of Church Reform 1700-1840* (Cambridge, James Clarke & Co., 1989).

Thomas, K., *Religion and the Decline of Magic* (London, Weidenfeld & Nicolson, 1971).

Thompson, H. P., *Into All Lands: The History of the Society for the Propagation of the Gospel in Foreign Parts 1701-1950* (London, SPCK, 1951).

Todd, J., *The Sign of Angelica: Women, Writing and Fiction 1660-1800* (London, Virago Press, 1989).

Trumbach, R., *The Rise of the Egalitarian Family: Aristocratic Kinship and Domestic Relations in Eighteenth-Century England* (New York, Academic Press, 1978).

Tulloch, G., *Mill and Sexual Equality* (Hemel Hempstead, Harvester Wheatsheaf, 1989).

Vance, N., *The Sinews of the Spirit: The Ideal of Christian Manliness in Victorian Literature and Religious Thought* (Cambridge, CUP, 1985).

Vicinus, M., *Independent Women: Work and Community for Single Women 1850-1920* (London, Virago Press, 1985).

Walby, S., *Theorizing Patriarchy* (Oxford, Basil Blackwell, 1990).

Walkovitz, J., *Prostitution and Victorian Society: Women, Class and the State* (Cambridge, CUP, 1980).

Waller, P. (ed.), *Politics and Social Change in Modern Britain: Essays Presented to A. F. Thompson* (Brighton, Harvester Press, 1987).

Walsh, J. D., 'The Anglican Evangelicals in the Eighteenth Century', in *Aspects de L'Anglicanisme* (Paris, Presses Universitaires de France, 1974), pp. 87-102.

Warne, A., *Church and Society in Eighteenth-Century Devon* (Newton Abbot, David & Charles, 1969).

Webster, M., *A New Strength, A New Song: The Journey to Women's Priesthood* (London, Mowbray, 1994).

Weeks, J., *Sex, Politics and Society: The Regulation of Sexuality since 1800* (London, Longman, 2nd edn, 1989).

Wickham Legg, J., *English Church Life from the Restoration to the Tractarian Movement* (London, Longmans Green, 1914).

Willey, B., *The Eighteenth-Century Background: Studies on the Idea of Nature in the Thought of the Period* (Harmondsworth, Penguin Books, 1962).

Williams, C. P., 'The Recruitment and Training of Overseas Missionaries in England between 1850 and 1900', University of Bristol M.Litt thesis, 1976.

Wilton, G., 'Mary Sumner's Mothers' Union (1876–1901)', Cheltenham and Gloucester College of Higher Education and Trinity College, Bristol, MA thesis, 1992.

Winnett, A. R., *The Church and Divorce: A Factual Survey* (London, Mowbray, 1968).

Wolfe, J., *The Protestant Crusade in Great Britain 1829–1860* (Oxford, Clarendon Press, 1991).

Women's Studies International Forum, vol. 13 (1990).

Wordsworth, C., *Christian Womanhood and Christian Sovereignty* (London, Rivingtons, 1884).

Young, P., *Feminist Theology/Christian Theology: In Search of Method* (Minneapolis, Fortress Press, 1990).

Zeldin, T., *Conflicts in French Society* (London, George Allen & Unwin, 1970).

Index

Baker, Gilbert 250
Baker, Hatty 268 n.8
Baldwin, Joyce 273 n.97
Ball, Hannah 49
Ball, Mrs 185
Banks, Olive 80
Bannister, Mrs 176, 179
Baptist Missionary Society
174, 200 n.23
Barbauld, Mrs 141
Barmby, Goodwyn 92
Barnett, Samuel 135
Barrington, Shute 24
Bastardy Act (1733) 56
Batten, Mollie 261
Baxter, Kay 247, 248
Beale, Dorothea 122-3
Bebbington, David 79
Beckwith, Roger 262
Bell, Andrew 113
Bell, Gertrude 207
Benn, Tony 269
Bennett, John 15, 17, 46
Bennett, Joyce 250, 259, 271
n.63
Benson, Archbishop 158
Berdyaev, Nicholas 210
Berners-Wilson, Angela 259
Biblewomen's movement, the
146, 154, 167
Billington, Mary 185-6, 195-
6, 204 nn. 97, 98
Bird, Isabella 138, 178, 184,
190
Bird, Mary 195
Bishop, Mrs 184
Blunt, J. H. 132, 135
Blunt, John 85
Bodichon, Madame 123
Body, Canon 164
Boff, Leonardo 264
Booth, Charles 135-6, 159,
162
Booth, Mary 47
Booth, William 84
Booth-Clibborn, Stanley 254
Bosanquet, Mary 61
Boswell, James 7 n.1
Boyd Carpenter, Mrs 132,

175, 192
British Women's Temperance
Association 133
Brontë, Charlotte 115, 127
n.11, 139
Brontë, Patrick 139
Brown, L. W. 251
Browne, Alice 67 n.5
Browne, Bishop 136, 166
Browne, G. F. 126
Bruce, Michael 261
Bryant, Margaret 115
Buckland, Augustus 176-7
Bullock, Louisa 173, 189,
202 n.73
Burdett-Coutts, Baroness 190
Burgon, J. W. 116, 128 n.20
Burke, Edmund 45
Burnet, Gilbert 21
Buss, Frances 122
Butler, Joseph 64
Butler, George 9 n.13, 98, 99
Butler, Josephine 4, 5, 98-9,
100-3, 120, 121, 131-2,
140
Butler, Samuel 97, 108 n.23
Butler, W. J. 159
Butterfield, William 160
Byrd, Louise 138
Byrne, Lavinia 203 n.75

Camden Society, the 147
Campbell, Lord 157
Canham, Elizabeth 273 n.95
Cappe, Mrs 49
Carey, George 234, 259, 260
Carlile, Marie 168
Carlile, Wilson 168
Carlisle, Earl of 24
Carter, Elizabeth 39, 44-5,
64, 68 n.15
Carter, Nicholas 44
Carter, Thomas Thellusson
152, 153, 157, 161-2
Casteras, Susan 155
Catherine of Siena, St 101
Cave, Edward 44
Central Advisory Council for